TALES
FROM THE
OPERA

by

Anthony J. Rudel

SIMON AND
SCHUSTER
New York

Copyright © 1985 by Anthony J. Rudel
All rights reserved
including the right of reproduction
in whole or in part in any form
Published by Simon and Schuster
A division of Simon & Schuster, Inc.
Simon & Schuster Building
Rockefeller Center
1230 Avenue of Americas
New York, New York 10020
SIMON AND SCHUSTER and colophon are registered trademarks of Simon & Schuster, Inc.
Designed by Irving Perkins Associates

Manufactured in the United States of America
Printed and bound by Fairfield Graphics

1 3 5 7 9 10 8 6 4 2

Library of Congress Cataloging in Publication Data
Rudel, Anthony J.
Tales from the opera.

"A Fireside book."
1. Operas—Stories, plots, etc.   I. Title.
MT95.R8 1985   782.1'3   85-11814
ISBN: 0-671-45943-0 (Pbk.)
0-671-61222-0

ACKNOWLEDGMENTS

I would like to thank my entire family for their patience, understanding, and help with this book:

Mom, Dad, Kristy, Joan, Madeleine, Sol, Jeff, Rachel, Jennifer, Christopher, Daniel, and **Emily;**

and special thanks to my editors, **Charles Rue Woods** and **Barbara Wasserman,** for their tireless efforts;

and to **Ivy Fischer Stone** for her support!

To my loving parents: **Dr. Rita Gillis Rudel**
and **Maestro Julius Rudel**
To **Dad,** who conducted the operas
To **Mom,** who always took me with her
and explained what was going on!

CONTENTS

CONTENTS

II.
RELIGION AND THE SUPERNATURAL

III.
HISTORY AND HUMANITY

FOREWORD

THE OPPORTUNITY to spend a career entertaining thousands of people in opera houses all over the world falls to a very few, very lucky people. To be an opera singer is at once a tremendous challenge and a great honor. Performers like myself are in the privileged position of being paid to re-create beautiful music. An opera performance, however, consists not only of the ability to sing the notes, but of the ability to be storytellers, able to portray and to project our characters across the footlights night after night, remembering always that what may be our 100th performance of *La Bohème* may be the first time some member of the audience is seeing Puccini's masterpiece. Yet, in trying to bring opera to life for new and old viewers alike, we are aided by the wonderful assortment of characters that we become for only a few hours each performance. And we have the great thrill of acting out the wonderful stories that fill the opera. But if you can't go onstage and become these characters and live these fabulous stories, then the best way to enter this enchanted world is to read the tales.

PREFACE

OPERA. The word still conjures up images of overweight singers bellowing out strange sounds in foreign languages.

But opera is more than that; much more than that. Opera is filled with wonderful stories that can be enjoyed, told and retold on any number of levels. They are stories about gods, kings, queens, peasants, witches, devils, nuns, revolutionaries, warriors, clowns, poets, lots of lovers, birdmen, barbers, shoemakers, bohemians, smugglers, even musicians! These stories are filled with a wealth of elements which when blended together yield the rich texture of life itself: the sense of joy at the end of *The Marriage of Figaro*; the pathos of *La Bohème* that caused its composer to weep; the "whipped-cream-like" charm that oozes through *Die Fledermaus*; the personalization of history in *Boris Godunov*; the traditions of mythology in *Orfeo*; the mysteries of the supernatural in *Faust*; the real-life cost of religious belief in *Dialogues of the Carmelites*; the twists of fate in *Il Trovatore*; the horror of jealousy in *Pagliacci*; and the splendid pomp of *Aida*.

In this book of fifty tales from the opera, I have tried to tell these dra-

13

matic stories for those people who want to know not so much what the famous arias are as what the characters say and do. After all, if you've never seen *Tosca*, or for that matter even if you have, you want to know what Tosca is thinking and feeling when she sings the "Vissi d'arte," not only what the aria is called. The point too often missed is that operas contain narrative tales comprising all the elements that go into good short stories, novels, or plays. In fact, many operas are based on great works of literature. But in performance the story of the opera is too often overwhelmed by the production.

In fact the seed of this book was actually planted when I first heard an opera explained as a story. The incident occurred when I was about five years old. My mother took me to a Saturday night performance of Verdi's *La Traviata* given by the New York City Opera at the City Center. As was the habit in our family, we slipped into our seats just as the house lights were being dimmed. The orchestra was just finishing their final tuning up. A hush of anticipation came over the audience. Finally the conductor took his place on the podium. Out of the silence came the quiet, sad strains of the first-act prelude. The music of Verdi's opening bars slowly hinted at the tragedy that was about to unfold. Then after a few moments, the music's mood changed, the curtains opened and we were thrust into the middle of a merry party scene, with drinking, dancing, and general frivolity. It all seemed so splendid, I totally forgot that I had no idea what was going on. The beautiful music sped the first act by, and before I knew it the act was over and it was the first intermission. As we stood near our seats, we overheard a woman tell her husband, "That was their engagement party. They're going to be married!" Hearing this charming piece of misinformation, my mother decided that I should know the real story. She spent the rest of the first intermission explaining the act I had just seen and outlining the second act—how Papa Germont would try to end the illicit relationship of his son and his beautiful mistress. While she brought these characters to life a few other members of the audience listened to her story. When the second act began, I could easily follow the basic idea of what the characters were saying.

Suddenly the music made even more sense. Before I knew it, Act II was history. Intermission; and time for the story of Act III.

As my mother described the great party we were about to see, complete with gambling and false accusations, a few more members of the audience listened to her story. Act III whizzed by and now we were at the final intermission and quite a crowd gathered round to hear the end of the story.

PREFACE

"It's a very sad scene," she began, and proceeded to outline the tragic last act where Alfredo and Violetta are finally brought together only to have Violetta's death tear them apart. When she finished describing this tragic last act, a woman in the crowd, visibly moved by this sad tale, said, "Oh! That was beautiful! You must be Eye-Talian!!!"

Well, you don't have to be Italian, German, French, or anything else to be familiar with stories of the opera. Whether you want to know what the opera you are going to hear is really all about, or whether you just want to read a good yarn, you can enjoy these dramatic tales. So, in the hope that they will give you the same pleasure that they have given me, I have attempted here to retell them. To paraphrase Tonio's last lines in the Prologue of *Pagliacci*, "Now pay attention to their unfolding!"

New York City
April 1, 1985

15

LOVE
AND
JEALOUSY

LA TRAVIATA

Opera in Three Acts
by
GIUSEPPE VERDI
Première: Teatro La Fenice, Venice, March 6, 1853

ACT I

DURING the middle of the nineteenth century, the social season in Paris was always alive with intrigue and frivolity. At soirées held in grand houses, the socially prominent mingled amiably with the demimondaine. Perhaps the only sin was to take oneself too seriously.

One of these elegant meeting places is the home of the beautiful courtesan Violetta Valery. As the party is beginning one evening, the Viscount Gaston de Letorières introduces to Violetta a young man of provincial gentry who has come to Paris to further his poetic ambitions. "Alfredo Germont is one of your most fervent admirers," he tells her. "While you were ill recently he visited everyday to ask about your health." She is impressed, and turning to her patron, the rich and powerful Baron Douphol, teases him for not having done as much. The Baron is annoyed and when asked to propose a toast refuses in a fit of pique. Alfredo is then asked to do the honors and rises to the occasion, singing a song to beauty, pleasure, and love, sentiments echoed and applauded by everyone assembled.

Strains of dance music are heard and Violetta suggests to her guests that they gravitate to the ballroom, when suddenly she feels faint and must sit down. She asks her guests to go on without her, promising to join them in a moment. Alfredo, however, remains discreetly behind.

Looking into a mirror, Violetta gasps at how pale she has become, then notices Alfredo.

He counsels her to care for herself more. "If you were mine, I would watch over you all the time!"

She is affected by his concern but laughs at his puppy love.

He persists. "One day a year ago you passed me and I fell in love with you!" She tells him he takes love too seriously for her. She can only offer him friendship. "If you want love, you must find someone else and forget about me!" When Alfredo says in that case he must leave, she flirtatiously gives him a flower, a camelia, instructing him, "Return it when it has wilted, tomorrow!" Again declaring his love for her he rapturously bids her goodbye and rushes out the door just as the other guests return to thank Violetta for a wonderful party. Dawn is beginning to break and they must rest for the next night of parties and pleasures.

Sitting alone after the party, in the generally dishevelled room, Violetta is lost in her thoughts. "How strange," she muses. "I have never fallen in love with any man, yet Alfredo's words have stayed with me. Maybe he's the one man who has the power to move my soul!" Recalling his concern during her illness, she becomes more and more lost in dreams of love. Suddenly she snaps out of her reverie and tells herself that such thoughts are mere folly, that she is just feeling sorry for herself, and that a life of earthly pleasures is all that she desires. Just as she has convinced herself of this she hears Alfredo outside wooing her with words of love. While he relentlessly recounts the joys of being in love, she repeats to herself all of her reasons for remaining free, the more feverishly as *his* words grow more and more appealing to her.

ACT II

SCENE 1

Some months have gone by. Violetta has succumbed to Alfredo's wooing, and they now live blissfully in a lavish house in the countryside near Paris. One day in a room off the garden Alfredo is rapturously musing on the wonderful life they have together, when he is interrupted by the maid, Annina. He asks where she has been, and is surprised to learn that she has been to Paris. In answer to his probing, she hesitantly explains that Violetta sent her to sell her horse and carriage and some of her jewels.

"But why?" Alfredo asks.

"Because living here is very expensive!"

Alfredo is beside himself with guilt and shame for having been so thoughtless, and hurries off to Paris to obtain funds.

Violetta enters the room. She has lost the painted patina of the courtesan, and has become a gracious, dignified young woman. She reads a letter which has just been delivered. It is from her friend Flora, inviting her to a party that very evening. No longer interested in that life, Violetta tosses the invitation on the table as a servant, Giuseppe, comes in to announce the arrival of a gentleman who wishes to see her.

An elderly gentleman enters. "Mademoiselle Valery," he says, "I am Alfredo's father, Giorgio Germont!" She is surprised, but asks him to sit down. Insultingly he accuses her of ruining his son.

"Sir, I am a woman, and in my own house. Please allow me to leave you, more for your sake than for mine."

Germont is impressed with her dignity, despite himself, but accuses her of wanting Alfredo for his fortune. He gestures to the luxury in which they are living. How else could she afford all that?

Violetta tells him that her past ways are over, and shows him the details of her plan to sell everything so she can afford to remain with Alfredo. Germont is touched by this proof of her devotion, but tells her that Alfredo must leave for the sake of his sister, who is engaged to marry but whose fiancé refuses to be united with a family whose son is living in sin.

Violetta refuses to give Alfredo up, telling his father that she has been ill. "To give him up will kill me. Without him I would rather die!"

Unrelenting, Germont continues to demand that she make this sacrifice for the good of Alfredo as well as of his family. Unable to counter his arguments, and realizing the helplessness of their situation, she finally gives in. "Tell your daughter, sir, that I make this sacrifice knowing it will kill me!" Then she asks him to embrace her like a father in order to give her strength. "Wait for him in the garden," she instructs. "You shall have him back, and when I am dead tell him of my suffering so that he won't curse my memory." Germont and Violetta embrace again and bid each other farewell.

He goes out into the garden to wait. Alone, Violetta writes a note to Flora accepting her invitation to the party and asks Annina, whom she has summoned, to deliver it. Weeping, she has begun a second letter, when Alfredo returns and interrupts her. Startled, she tries to conceal the letter she is writing, thereby arousing in him some suspicion and concern. He tells her that he has received a stern letter from his father and surmises that he has visited Violetta and is the cause of her being so obviously upset. Violetta denies it and, fighting back tears, comforts Alfredo, lying to him that his father will see that they love each other and leave them together in peace. On the edge of hysteria she swears eternal love and asks for his, and runs out to "wait in the garden."

She has been gone only a few minutes when a messenger arrives with a letter for Alfredo: "A lady in a carriage gave me this letter to deliver to you." Alfredo thanks him and is surprised to see that it is from Violetta. Nervously he opens it and is thunderstruck when he reads that she is severing their relationship. As he turns to run after her, he is met by his father.

"My son, dry your tears," Germont implores, "and return to your family." In an impassioned plea he begs him to leave this life, to restore the pride and honor that are his due. But the loss of Violetta is all Alfredo can think about and he ignores his father. He wonders if Violetta has gone back to the Baron. The older Germont begs him to forget this woman and to come back to his family. They will heal his wounded heart. Suddenly, Alfredo sees Flora's invitation and knows that he will find Violetta there. In a fit of jealous rage he vows that he will avenge himself and rushes out of the house while his father vainly tries to stop him.

SCENE 2

The splendid party at Flora's is in full swing. The guests are entertained by gypsies, who mingle with them reading palms and telling fortunes. Then some men dressed as matadors simulate a bullfight to everyone's great enjoyment. In one corner a gaming table has attracted a number of the guests. Alfredo enters, and everyone turns to him. "Where is Violetta?" they ask.

He casually answers that he doesn't know, and they compliment him on his carefree attitude. He joins the group at the card table.

Violetta, accompanied by the Baron Douphol, now enters the room and is greeted effusively by Flora. The Baron whispers to Violetta that Alfredo is there and forbids her to speak with him.

Across the room Alfredo is winning handily. "He who is unlucky in love is lucky at cards," he declares loudly enough for Violetta and the Baron to hear.

Although she tries to restrain him, the Baron challenges Alfredo to a game. The guests gather round to watch as the cards are dealt. Deal after deal goes to Alfredo, who wins a large sum of money from the Baron. While they remain polite, the hostility between them makes the air spark. When the game is interrupted by a servant who announces that dinner is served, Alfredo offers the Baron the option to continue, but he refuses saying they shall play again later.

The salon has barely emptied when Violetta, in great agitation, rushes back in, followed closely by Alfredo. She tells him that she is frightened by the tension between him and the Baron and counsels him to leave before someone gets hurt. He agrees to leave but only if she will come with him.

"I can't. I promised I would leave you."

"But who could ask that of you?"

Slowly she says, "One who had the right to ask it."

"The Baron?"

With great effort, Violetta lies. "Yes."

"You love him?"

"Yes," she whispers, "I love him."

Enraged, Alfredo runs to the door and calls to the other guests to come in and bear witness. He announces to the gathering that Violetta has spent large sums of money to pay for his love and then, throwing his winnings at her, he declares, "Now I have paid you what I owe!"

The guests are stunned and reproach Alfredo for his insult.

Suddenly the voice of Germont is heard over the crowd: "You are not my son!" he tells Alfredo. "To insult a woman is beneath contempt." Alfredo is now stricken with remorse, unable to believe that his jealousy has taken him to such extremes. The Baron challenges him to a duel and his father leads him away. Violetta, still in a state of shock, allows Flora to lead her to another room.

ACT III

Some time later, sick and destitute, Violetta sleeps quietly while her faithful Annina dozes in a chair nearby. Awakening slowly, she weakly asks Annina for some water. As Annina opens the shutters, she tells Violetta that she sees the Doctor coming. Violetta is touched by his kindness and, with Annina's assistance, manages to sit up just as the Doctor enters. He examines her and asks how she feels.

"My body is suffering, but my soul is at peace," she replies.

He tells her that she will soon recuperate, and bids her goodbye. On his way out he solemnly whispers to Annina that her mistress has but a few hours to live.

Annina returns to Violetta and reminds her it is carnival time in Paris. Violetta instructs her to take half of the little bit of money they have left and give it to the poor. As soon as Annina is gone, Violetta opens a letter she keeps tucked in her sleeve, and reads again the words she knows by heart. "You kept your promise. The Baron was wounded in the duel, but not seriously. Alfredo has temporarily gone to a foreign country, but I myself have told him of your sacrifice. We shall both come to ask your pardon. Get well, so you may have a better fate. Giorgio Germont." "I wait and wait," she laments, "but they do not come!" Aware of how very ill she is, she turns her thoughts to happy days gone by and prays to God for forgiveness.

From the street the sound of revelers breaks the depressing quiet of the sick room. Annina returns and excitedly tells Violetta that Alfredo is on his way to see her. Violetta suddenly seems vibrantly alive as Alfredo comes in and embraces her, full of apologies for what happened.

"Forgive me and my father," he begs. "I love you and no force on earth can part us now."

She joyously welcomes him back and willingly shares his guilt. They vow to move away from Paris to the country where her health will return. She says she wants to go to church to give thanks for his return, but as she tries to get up her strength fails her and she collapses. Alfredo, seeing how ill she is, curses their cruel destiny. Bravely she tries to get dressed but she is too weak, and while Annina rushes out to get the Doctor, Violetta tells Alfredo, "If your return cannot cure me then I am doomed!" She cries out against her terrible fate, at having to die so young and sinks back exhausted just as Alfredo's father comes in followed by the Doctor.

They rush to Violetta's side and the elder Germont declares, "I embrace you now as a daughter."

"You are too late," she sighs, "but see, Doctor, I die in the arms of the only loved ones I have." Each word fills Germont with remorse.

With what little strength she has left Violetta calls Alfredo to her side and gives him a locket with her portrait. She tells him, "If you should marry some young girl, give her this portrait and tell her it is from someone who prays for you from among the angels!"

Alfredo, in anguish, tells her she must not give up the fight to live. Germont begs for forgiveness.

Suddenly, she says how strange it is, she feels better, strength resurging within her. Rising to her feet, she tells them that the spasm of pain has passed. "I am reborn! Oh, joy!" she cries. And collapses lifeless into Alfredo's arms.

DIE FLEDERMAUS
(The Bat)

Opera in Three Acts
by
JOHANN STRAUSS

Première: Theater an der Wien, Vienna, April 5, 1874

ACT I

DURING THE nineteenth century, in its Belle Epoque, Vienna was a co-quettish, playful, fun-loving city. Frivolity was a way of life, and many Viennese waltzed from one glittering affair to another, expending great energy and talent in entertaining themselves and each other.

One beautiful day Alfred, an opera singer, stands below the balcony of the Eisenstein house serenading the owner's wife. "Return to me, my darling Rosalinde!" sings he. His song wafts through an open window of the house momentarily intriguing the chambermaid, Adele. But she is more interested in her immediate problem. She has just received a letter from her sister inviting her to a splendid ball tonight at the home of the eccentric Prince Orlovsky. "Figure out a way to get the evening off so you can come with me."

"Oh, why," moans Adele, "did fate make me a lowly chambermaid?" She *must* figure out a way to free herself this evening.

Just then Rosalinde von Eisenstein, the lady of the house, calls her. "Yes, Madame," she answers through copious tears.

"What's wrong with you?" Rosalinde inquires.

"Oh, Madame, my poor aunt has been taken ill. I must go visit her. May I have this evening off?"

"Impossible!" Rosalinde replies, adding that this night is particularly bad because her husband, Gabriel von Eisenstein, must go off to prison to serve a five-day term.

"Why does he have to go to jail?"

"Oh, for some silly fight he had in a restaurant."

"My little dove," Alfred resumes singing from the street below, capturing Rosalinde's attention, for she recognizes the voice she once could not resist. Suddenly, he bursts through the open window and demands a kiss.

"You must leave!" she says, but sensing a lack of conviction in her rejection, he bargains. "Only if I can return after your husband is in jail!"

To hurry her ardent suitor out of the house before her husband's imminent return, Rosalinde consents, but without great reluctance.

No sooner has Alfred left than Gabriel von Eisenstein storms in, trailed by his lawyer, Dr. Blind. Eisenstein rages, "This bumbling idiot has managed to get my sentence increased from five days to eight!"

The stuttering Dr. Blind accuses his client of getting the sentence increased himself by singlehandedly offending the judge. "But no hard feelings," he says. "I will defend you again should you ever need me." Despite his wife's efforts to calm him, Eisenstein angrily throws the lawyer out of the house.

The condemned man decides to spend his final free hours having a last meal with his wife, but before they can eat Adele announces the arrival of an old friend, Dr. Falke. Rosalinde asks Falke to cheer up the prisoner-to-be while she sees to some duties around the house.

"I'll do my best," he assures her, and when she has gone, says, "Dear Gabriel, I have just the remedy for your pre-prison blues: don't go! Instead come with me tonight to a spectacular party at the home of the Prince Orlovsky. He's put me in charge of the invitation list, and has instructed me to be certain that there be some witty people in attendance. You are a perfect choice!"

Eisenstein agrees that he is the life of every party. "Remember that costume party," he laughs. "I was a butterfly, and you were a bat. And you got so drunk that on the way home I dropped you out of the carriage and left you sound asleep beneath a tree. When you woke up there was a crowd around you. You were the funniest event of the day."

"And I had to walk all the way home dressed as a bat," Falke adds.

Bubbling happily, Eisenstein says, "I'll never forget it."

"Neither will I," says Falke dryly. "But now I want to discuss this evening's party. There will be loads of beautiful women there, all of whom will succumb to your charming repeater watch. So don't go to prison tonight, go tomorrow!"

Eisenstein argues at first but really cannot resist the temptation and agrees to kiss his wife goodbye and join Falke for the party.

"To keep you incognito," his friend counsels, "I will introduce you as a Frenchman, Marquis Renard!" Unable to contain their delight, the two men dance playfully about the room, until Rosalinde, returning, congratulates the doctor on his ability to cheer her husband up. His mission complete, Dr. Falke takes his leave.

Adele, still feigning despair over her aunt, enters to serve supper. Rosalinde tells her, "I have reconsidered, and decided you may have the evening off." Adele is ecstatic.

Eisenstein re-enters and Rosalinde is astonished to see him dressed in white tie and tails. "Dr. Falke thinks I should look good for prison; the best people are there these days," he explains. "And now I'd better be on my way."

"Why are you in such a hurry to leave, and before dinner? And without even a kiss goodbye?"

He remembers to be sad and all three bemoan the terrible separation they must endure. But beneath their laments, each one is relishing the evening ahead. Their farewells over, Eisenstein and Adele depart and Rosalinde prepares for her rendezvous.

Suddenly Adele returns to give Rosalinde a package that has just been delivered, and lingers inquisitively until Rosalinde orders her to leave. Opening the box, Rosalinde finds a mask and a note: "Come to Prince Orlovsky's tonight. Wear this mask as a disguise and I will introduce you as a Hungarian countess. At the party you will see how your husband is serving his prison sentence. (Signed) Dr. Falke."

"The wretch," she sputters. "When I get through with him, he'll be happy if he's allowed to stay in jail forever." Just then Alfred bursts into the room, and she forgets her anger. She has other problems. To Rosalinde's dismay, Alfred dons her husband's dressing gown and cap and announces, "Now we can be husband and wife." Pouring two glasses of champagne he bids her relax and drink with him, and when she tries to make him leave, he sings to her (which she can't resist).

A commotion outside the apartment confirms her worst fears. Suddenly the door opens to admit a formally dressed gentleman, who, entering in the name of the law, introduces himself as Governor of the Prison, Frank. "Madame, excuse the intrusion, but duty must be done. I have come to arrest your husband."

Alfred, by now sufficiently full of wine to be giddy, invites the Governor to drink with him.

"I am delighted you are taking this matter in such good humor, Herr von Eisenstein."

"But I am not Eisenstein," Alfred says.

Quietly Rosalinde hisses, "Do you want to create a scandal? Say that you are." And to the Governor, "This man is indeed my husband!"

Alfred resigns himself to going to prison in Eisenstein's place and decides to play his role to the hilt. "Well, before I go I must have one last kiss!" And with that he grabs Rosalinde and repeatedly and passionately kisses her goodbye, until Frank's patience wears thin.

"I have to go to a soirée and don't have time to wait. So please delay no longer and come to my beautiful birdcage with me!"

Kissing Rosalinde one more time, Alfred finally goes peacefully, if somewhat drunkenly, off to prison.

ACT II

Prince Orlovsky's lavish villa is ablaze with light and gaiety. The elegantly dressed guests mingle, calling for drinks and food as the servants pass among them. Adele greets her sister, Ida, who is astonished to see her there, and is not too nice about it.

Adele protests, "But you invited me." Ida is totally baffled; "I never sent you an invitation. Someone must be playing a joke on you. Just behave yourself," she cautions.

Adele is offended, after all the trouble she had to get the night off and to surreptitiously borrow one of her lady's gowns.

Escorted by Dr. Falke, Prince Orlovsky enters the main ballroom. He invites his guests to enjoy themselves, but complains to the doctor, "If only you knew how bored I am. I have everything and I have done everything. I hope tonight there will be something to make me laugh."

Falke tells him that the evening's entertainment will be a sort of domestic comedy. "You might call it 'The Revenge of the Bat!' I will explain the plot to you as it unfolds. Allow me now to introduce Ida of the Ballet!"

Ida curtsies and introduces her sister, "the actress Olga." Adele enthuses over the palace and the party. "Everything is so delightful. How are you?"

"I'm bored," says Orlovsky. "But perhaps you ladies would like to gamble some of my money at the tables."

Eagerly they accept his largesse and go off into the game room. A servant announces the arrival of the Marquis Renard (Herr von Eisenstein), and Falke explains to the Prince that this is the hero of the drama. Graciously he introduces the "Marquis" to the Prince, who explains the house rules. "My dear Marquis, in my house the guests all do as they please. My motto is very simple: *Chacun à son gout!*"

"Oh Prince, we lost all your money!" Returning from the game room, Adele shows the empty wallet. She carefully restrains herself when she recognizes Eisenstein, but he insists that this "actress" reminds him of a certain chambermaid. "My dear Marquis, you must be mistaken!" she audaciously counters. "Clearly I am an actress. After all, could a lowly chambermaid be so at home in these surroundings? I am as much an actress as you are a marquis!"

"The Chevalier Chagrin," a servant announces, and in walks Governor Frank in his role for the evening. Orlovsky, fluent in many languages, introduces the "Chevalier" to his countryman the "Marquis Renard." It is obvious that everyone is waiting for them to greet each other in their native tongue.

"L'amour . . .," says Eisenstein tentatively.

"Toujours," says Frank.

They throw their arms around each other. "Vive la France." As everyone begins to laugh, Falke announces that the guest of honor will be arriving momentarily. "She is a beautiful Hungarian countess, and she has an incredibly jealous husband. Therefore, she will wear a mask and she requests that you respect her need to remain incognito."

"Oh you can count on me," says Eisenstein.

In wig and mask, Rosalinde enters and Dr. Falke immediately directs her attention to her husband, surrounded now by several lovely women, and to Adele, her chambermaid, wearing her gown. She is furious, but regains her composure as Eisenstein approaches, and is introduced. Eisenstein, stunned by the mysterious lady's beauty and intriguing Hungarian accent, is trapped. Falke leaves them alone. Eisenstein takes out his beautiful repeater watch and demonstrates it to the "Countess."

"It's lovely," she coos, "I would love to have a watch like that!" As he moves even closer she suddenly snatches it from him. "Thank you for this lovely gift." He is upset and tries to get her to return it, but their negotiations are interrupted by the other guests, who demand proof that the mysterious countess is really Hungarian. Without hesitating, Rosalinde calls on the Prince's orchestra to defend her. "Let them play; the melodies of my homeland will speak for me." She joins them in a Czardas.

Orlovsky bids his guests drink a toast to the king of wines, champagne, and they more than willingly do so. "Chagrin" and the "Marquis Renard" encounter each other in the crowd and drunkenly exchange vows of eternal friendship to the amusement of the Prince, Falke, and Rosalinde, who anticipate the reunion these two will have in jail. Then Falke, as master of ceremonies, compliments the many loving couples who wander arm in arm around the palace, and raises his glass in a toast. Eisenstein tries to persuade Rosalinde to unmask, and when she eludes him, chases after her.

Suddenly the clock chimes six times. Eisenstein and Frank are alarmed; "Get my hat and cloak!" they command. "I'm going to be late!" The servants oblige, and to the amusement of the other guests, who continue dancing, the two "Frenchmen" charge frantically out of the palace into the streets of early morning Vienna.

ACT III

"Quiet!" screams Frosch the jailer as Alfred sings the "Miserere" from *Trovatore*. "There's a law against singing here." But despite the jailer's protests, Alfred, still serving Eisenstein's prison term, belts out the drinking song from *Traviata*. Frosch, unable to bear it any longer, nurses himself with a bottle of spirits.

A tipsy Governor Frank stumbles into the prison, still whistling one of the lilting waltzes. Removing his cloak and gloves with exaggerated care, he picks up the morning paper and tries to read, but is soon sound asleep.

Frosch staggers back into the reception area and wakes Frank. "Jailer Frosch reporting, sir! All is quiet except Eisenstein, who won't stop singing! He keeps asking for a lawyer, so I called for the barrister Blind!"

Frank sleepily acknowledges the report. Suddenly the doorbell rings, and he sends Frosch to open it.

"Governor, these two lovely ladies are looking for a Chevalier Chagrin," says Frosch as he escorts in Adele and Ida.

"What a surprise!" Frank says.

They remind him that he invited them, and now confess to having told a little lie. "You see," Ida explains, "my sister is not an actress. Actually she is a chambermaid at the Eisenstein house. But now she wants to leave her lowly estate there and pursue a stage career. She was hoping you would sponsor her!"

Frank asks if Adele has any talent. This launches her into a bravura display of her theatrical abilities, a performance cheered by Frank, who promises to help. The doorbell rings again and Frosch reports that a "Marquis Renard" has arrived. "Ah, Frosch," says Frank. "Escort these ladies to cell number . . . no, I mean room number 13."

Eisenstein enters and is surprised to see the "Chevalier" in jail. Frank admits that he is not a chevalier at all but actually the warden of the prison. This leads to another confession and the "Marquis" reveals his true identity as Gabriel von Eisenstein. "That's impossible," Frank counters; "I personally arrested Eisenstein last evening at his home, in his robe and cap. I can tell you it was sad having to separate him from his beautiful wife."

Eisenstein is furious and demands to see the prisoner. At this juncture, enter Dr. Blind, the lawyer. Eisenstein turns on him. "What are you doing here, you worm?"

"How dare you? You sent for me."

Eisenstein denies this, but is suddenly struck by a brainstorm. "Give me your wig, beard, and glasses. I am going to disguise myself as you. Then I will be able to meet this other Herr von Eisenstein!" Trying to resist, Blind runs from the room with Eisenstein in hot pursuit.

Rosalinde now arrives at the prison and Frosch leads Alfred in to meet her.

"My angel of mercy, you have come to save me!" As usual, he tries to wax rapturous and operatic, but is interrupted by Eisenstein, who, now disguised as Blind, comes in to meet with his "clients." Through cunning legalisms, he believes, he will get the pair to make a full confession of infidelity.

"Give me the whole truth!" he counsels.

"Well," Rosalinde begins, "it's a very strange case. This man was visiting me last evening. It was, in fact, quite innocent, but could be embarrassing if my husband should find out. (He's hardly innocent himself but I'll settle that score.) In short, this man was arrested in his place." Acting as counsel, Eisenstein tries to keep cool and get her to reveal more details, but his anger keeps getting the better of his charade, and finally, ripping off his disguise, he reveals his true identity. "I'm the one you deceived, for I am Eisenstein!"

"How dare you," is Rosalinde's calm rejoinder, "when I know exactly what time it is and where you were last night? Isn't this your watch?" she asks, dangling the precious repeater before his disbelieving eyes.

As they throw recriminations at each other and Eisenstein threatens to leave Alfred in jail in his place, Frank muddies the situation a little more by bringing Adele and her sister back in. Adele, of course, identifies the Eisensteins, and Rosalinde recognizes her gown, which Adele is still wearing.

But all is saved by the arrival of Dr. Falke, Prince Orlovsky, and all the party guests, who have come, bearing champagne, to see the denouement of Falke's little plot. When Orlovsky realizes that the end of the play is taking place in prison, he actually laughs.

Everyone cries, "Your Highness, you're laughing."

Thus, Falke wins a medal from the Prince, and explains to Eisenstein that he has been the victim of a joke called "The Revenge of the Bat."

Eisenstein begs forgiveness of his wife. "I am truly faithful," he tells her. "It is the champagne that was to blame."

The glasses are filled again and the happy Viennese once again toast the power of the bubbly.

MANON

Opera in Five Acts
by
JULES MASSENET
Première: Opéra-Comique, Paris, January 19, 1884

ACT I

ONE DAY in the year 1721, outside an inn in Amiens, a group of travelers eager for dinner are stamping their feet on the cobblestones and calling to the innkeeper that service is too slow. The party consists of two men, an old wealthy roué, Guillot de Morfontaine, his friend Monsieur de Bretigny, and their traveling companions, three young women, Pousette, Rosette, and Javotte, wearing the somewhat vulgar finery of "actresses." At last the innkeeper comes out, followed by a procession of waiters carrying trays of food, and he quiets his guests with a recital of all the marvelous dishes they are about to enjoy. Mollified, they move off to the dining pavilion.

The courtyard begins to fill with people in anticipation of the arrival of the coach from Arras. In the crowd is a guardsman, Lescaut, with a couple of his fellow officers. He has come to meet Manon, his cousin from the provinces. The coach arrives and amid much noise and confusion, Lescaut finally spies a pretty young girl who he knows must be she.

Manon is not only young and beautiful. She is also naive and charming.

MANON

First she proffers her lips for a kiss, then she prattles away about how
exciting the trip has been, since this is the first time she has ever been away
from home.

Lescaut finds her delightful and tells her to wait while he and his friends
go to get her luggage.

The courtyard has emptied considerably, and Manon strolls about. The
quiet is shattered as Guillot comes back, shouting, "Hey! Innkeeper! Are
we ever going to get some wine?" Catching sight of Manon, he quickly
introduces himself. "Mademoiselle, I am Guillot de Morfontaine and I am
very wealthy. I would pay anything to hear but one loving word from you."

Not knowing how to respond, Manon bursts into laughter.

Guillot's dining partners join him now. The three "actresses" ridicule the
old man, but de Bretigny recognizes that his lecherous old friend has indeed chanced upon a remarkably beautiful woman. Irritably, he calls for
Guillot to return to dinner. Ignoring his companions, Guillot whispers to
Manon that his coach will be arriving shortly. "You can take it, and after-
wards . . ." Before Guillot can finish his proposition, Lescaut returns and
angrily chases the old man away.

With phony respect for the family's honor, Lescaut rebukes his young
cousin for the incident and pompously instructs her on how she should
conduct herself. But when his two companions come back and invite
Lescaut to join them for some gambling, he tells Manon that he must go to
discuss some urgent business. "Don't budge 'til I get back, and don't smile
at strangers," he instructs as he strolls away with his companions.

Manon's intentions are good but the sound of laughter in the dining pavilion reminds her of the fancy gowns Guillot's young women were wearing,
and she cannot help but dream about the joyful, carefree life in which she
herself might wear such clothes. Suddenly, she hears someone approaching
and hurries back to the spot where Lescaut told her to stay.

A young man strolls in. He is completely lost in thought and at first
seems oblivious to his surroundings. But when he notices Manon, he is so
struck by her beauty that he is immediately and irresistibly drawn to her.
Impulsively, he says, "Mademoiselle! Forgive me if I am forward, but I
cannot pass by as if we have never met. Although I know that we have never
seen each other before, I feel as if I have always known you. Please, tell me
who you are."

Impressed by his manner, and touched by his sincerity, Manon tells him,
"I am a poor girl. I don't believe I am wicked, but my family accuses me of

35

enjoying worldly pleasure too much, and so I am being sent to a convent. That is the story of Manon Lescaut!"

The young man is appalled, and tells her that she can instead turn to him, the Chevalier des Grieux. "I will go to any length to keep and protect you," he vows.

Thrilled by the possibility of freedom, she exclaims, "My life and soul belong to you!"

At that moment Guillot's coach arrives. With a devilish impulse, Manon tells des Grieux that the old man has offered to give her a ride, and suggests they pay him back by going off in it together. Hurriedly they decide that they are in love and that they will live together forever in Paris. The sound of laughter in the dining hall momentarily reminds Manon of the glamorous life she also covets, but then she hears Lescaut returning from the barracks, and the irrepressible Guillot coming out of the inn, and she rushes off with des Grieux arm in arm.

Lescaut and Guillot are both dismayed to find that Manon has gone. Rashly, Lescaut accuses the old man of stealing the girl. Of course Guillot denies it and the argument grows heated, drawing a crowd. When the innkeeper informs them that the young girl departed in Guillot's coach, escorted by a young man, everyone laughs—except Lescaut and Guillot, who swear to take revenge.

ACT II

Seated at the table in their simply furnished apartment on the Rue Vivienne in Paris, des Grieux is penning a letter to his father. He writes of the charm, the beauty, and the grace of his love, the sixteen-year-old Manon. He tells Manon that he is afraid the letter will anger his father, but "it is worth the risk because I adore you, and I want to make you my wife."

Manon is overjoyed by this proof of his love and orders her Chevalier to kiss her and post the letter. He is about to leave when he notices a bouquet of flowers in the room. "Where did they come from?" he demands.

Lightly, she explains that the bouquet was thrown to her from the street below the window by an unknown admirer. Suddenly, they hear loud voices and a servant rushes in to tell them that two angry guardsmen outside are demanding admittance.

Manon catches her breath. "It must be Lescaut." The servant whispers to her that the other is the man who sent the flowers, the rich de Bretigny, disguised as a guardsman.

Lescaut enters combatively, swearing to avenge the honor of his family. As he rants on, de Bretigny advises calm, but Lescaut pays no attention.

Des Grieux threatens to thrash Lescaut if he doesn't act more politely, and then explains that he has, in fact, just written to his father for permission to marry Manon. He offers to show the letter. As Lescaut moves him closer to the window, de Bretigny seizes the opportunity to inform Manon that des Grieux's father is planning to have his son abducted this very day in order to get him away from her. He advises her to let des Grieux go, luring her with the advantages his fortune can bring her. "With my fortune and your beauty you shall be a queen." Torn between love and the life of ease and glamour de Bretigny promises, Manon tentatively agrees not to warn des Grieux of the impending abduction.

Lescaut pretends to be delighted that Manon and des Grieux plan to marry. After he and de Bretigny leave, des Grieux tells Manon again how much he loves her and goes out to mail his letter.

Alone, Manon is unhappy at the thought of losing des Grieux, but rationalizes that she is not worthy of him. She wonders if a life with de Bretigny can possibly be as blissful as the days she and des Grieux have spent together. Tearfully, she bids farewell to the innocent life she already knows is past.

Des Grieux returns and notices her tears, but she changes the subject by pointing out that supper is waiting.

Once again he talks about how much he loves her. "Just you and me alone, Manon, makes me so happy." And he tells her of a dream he has had—of a white cottage in the woods with shade, clear streams, and singing birds. "It would have been Paradise, only everything was melancholy because Manon was missing."

Manon cannot bear it. "It was only a dream," she says.

A knock is heard at the door. Des Grieux gets up to answer, saying that he will send the intruder away.

"Don't answer," she begs.

Laughing tenderly at what he considers her capricious fear, he goes off to answer the door. She hears a brief struggle and, shortly after, the clatter of carriage wheels on the cobblestoned street. As it moves away, Manon runs to the window and cries, "My poor Chevalier!"

ACT III

SCENE 1

On the promenade of the Cours-la-Reine in Paris, a large holiday crowd strolls on the walks and wanders among the stands of the open air market. Merchants, nobles, and workers mingle, all enjoying the fine weather and the colorful displays. Vendors shout their wares—shoes, kerchiefs, and caps; hoops, plumes and jewels; and all varieties of food. Everywhere people merrily drink to the health of the King. Friends and strangers greet each other, everyone open to the intoxication of a chance encounter. Pousette, Javotte, and Rosette run out of the public dance hall and join three young men, delighted at having escaped the clutches of their jealous old suitor, Guillot.

In the midst of the crowd, Lescaut has attracted a swarm of vendors, as he flippantly offers to buy everything they have for his newest love, Rosalinde. "Why choose?" he asks. "Why be economical when one knows how to throw the dice at the Hotel Transylvania?"

Guillot de Morfontaine spies Pousette, Javotte, and Rosette in the crowd and approaches them, but as each in turn spurns him the old man grows so enraged that he declares, "Woman is a wicked creature!"

Seeing him in such a state, de Bretigny cannot refrain from mocking Guillot. "Promise me you won't take Manon away."

But the old roué is just as clever and quick and asks de Bretigny about a rumor. "Is it true that you refused Manon's request to have the Opéra perform at your house?" When de Bretigny brusquely confirms the rumor, Guillot hurries off, gleeful because he thinks he has found a way to steal Manon from de Bretigny.

Suddenly a buzz of excitement runs through the crowd as Manon makes her way among the strollers. Looking absolutely stunning, she is escorted by de Bretigny and trailed by a cortege of young noblemen. All the attention delights her and she amuses the crowd with a song, immodestly celebrating a life of carefree love and laughter, and her own beauty. "I am beautiful and I am happy. If I have to die, let it be laughing." The throng is charmed, and having established herself as queen of the Cours-la-Reine, Manon goes off to make a purchase.

Left alone, de Bretigny recognizes a distinguished older gentleman. It is the Count des Grieux and he has come to Paris to see his son, the *former*

Chevalier des Grieux. "My son," the Count explains, "has heard a heavenly summons and is studying for the priesthood. He is studying at Saint-Sulpice and tonight he gives a sermon."

Standing in the crowd nearby, Manon overhears the Count as he tells de Bretigny, "You are the one who caused this change by breaking up his love affair."

De Bretigny points out Manon to the Count, who, like everyone else, is struck by her beauty.

Manon joins them and to get rid of de Bretigny tells him she wants a certain bracelet she herself has been unable to find. Obligingly, he leaves in search of it. Manon apologizes to the Count for having overheard his conversation with de Bretigny, but she explains that this Abbé des Grieux had once been in love with a friend of hers and she would like to know if he has been cured of his infatuation.

The Count replies, "Once my son's broken heart mended, it sealed itself and he has now forgotten his love." Bowing respectfully, he takes his leave.

His cold words infect Manon's mood and thoughts. Could des Grieux so soon have forgotten her?

Nearby, de Bretigny is conversing peevishly with Guillot, who smugly admits that he has just engaged the Opéra's ballet to perform for Manon. Smoldering at Guillot's coup, de Bretigny sees tears in Manon's eyes, and is further troubled. She denies that anything is wrong, and their conversation is interrupted by the shouts of the crowd declaring, "The Opéra is here!!!!"

With great ostentation, Guillot welcomes Manon to this special perform-ance by the Opéra's ballet company, and pulls her over to sit beside him. The crowd is suitably impressed by Guillot's largesse, and everyone settles down to enjoy the spectacular performance.

The dances are performed right in front of Manon, but she, lost in thoughts of des Grieux and haunted by the Count's words, is oblivious to them. Suddenly she calls to her cousin, "Get me my sedan chair. I wish to go to Saint-Sulpice." Lescaut is stunned by this bizarre request, but obliges and calls for her chair. Astounded at her precipitous departure, Guillot asks Manon how she liked his ballets. He is livid when she flippantly says, "I didn't watch any of it."

Scene 2

Inside Saint-Sulpice the reception area is filled with pious women leav-ing the Seminary chapel, and chattering about the wonderful sermon just delivered by the Abbé des Grieux. When they have gone, the church's silence is broken by the Count. "Bravo, my son." He is sarcastic. "Our family can be proud to have produced the new Bossuet. But do you really think it good to commit yourself to heaven forever?"

"Yes," the young man replies. "Since in the world I have found only disgust and bitterness."

The Count counsels him to reconsider, begs him to try life again, to marry a nice girl worthy of the family. But his son is determined to take the vows. Though still deriding him for what he perceives as weakness, the Count tells his son he will nonetheless send him the large sum of money that he inherited from his mother. With a last mocking taunt, he bids him farewell.

Des Grieux is relieved to be alone and prays to God to purify his soul and by so doing cast out of his mind the bitter obsessive memory of Manon. His impassioned prayer is disturbed by the Seminary porter, who informs him that the service is beginning in the chapel.

Manon rushes into Saint-Sulpice and, seeing the porter, asks to speak with the Abbé des Grieux. The porter goes into the chapel to find him. As she waits, Manon is chilled by the silent walls and cold air, and hopes that these surroundings haven't turned des Grieux against her. She prays for forgiveness and for the return of des Grieux's love.

As soon as he sees her, des Grieux orders Manon to go away.

She pleads with him. "I was to blame, but remember how you loved me."

"It was just for a moment. It could not last." But he reveals his true feelings by adding, "Oh, Manon. Unfaithful Manon."

Manon begs for pity and forgiveness and asks him to return to her. "Feel my hands. Isn't this the same sweet caress? Aren't these the eyes that adore you? Isn't this the voice you love? Am I no longer Manon?"

Weakening, des Grieux cries to the Lord for help, but Manon seductively continues to remind him of the charms he loves until he can no longer resist. "Manon, I cannot struggle any more. My life is in your heart, in your eyes. Come. I love you!"

Leaving Saint-Sulpice, they once again run off together arm in arm.

ACT IV

At the gaming tables of the chic gambling house, the Hotel Transylvania, players place their bets and petty arguments break out, punctuated by occasional cries of victory or defeat. Pousette, Javotte, and Rosette are joined by Lescaut, who, jingling a pouch of coins, gleefully recounts the joys of gambling.

There is a great commotion as Manon, escorted by a reluctant Chevalier des Grieux, enters. Guillot de Morfontaine, who has been speaking to Lescaut, tells him how much he hates the man who has won Manon's heart.

For a while, Manon and des Grieux watch the games. Manon tries to persuade des Grieux to gamble what remains of his inheritance in an effort to bring them greater wealth. Des Grieux hates Manon's values—her love of gold and frivolous pleasures—but he is helplessly in love with her. She promises to love him even more if he will only win back a fortune. Lescaut also encourages him to play, predicting that he will have beginner's luck and reminding him that Manon does not like being poor. When Guillot approaches and challenges him to a game, the Chevalier accepts. While Guillot and des Grieux play cards, Manon, Javotte, Poussette, and Rosette laugh and drink champagne, and extol the joys of living for the moment.

The Chevalier wins hand after hand. Manon cheers him on. "You see, I knew you would win," she says.

"I love you," des Grieux tells her.

Abruptly, Guillot stops the game and accuses des Grieux of cheating. Des Grieux is furious. Everyone is stunned and the two men are cautioned to calm down, but declaring that des Grieux and Manon have not heard the end of the incident, Guillot storms out.

"Let us leave," Manon begs des Grieux but he refuses.

"If I leave now, they will all believe I was guilty of cheating."

There is a loud knock at the door and the money and cards are quickly hidden from sight.

The command "Open in the name of the King" is heard. "Take to the roof," Lescaut shouts, and rushes out.

The police burst through the doors, led by Guillot de Morfontaine, who identifies des Grieux and Manon. "He is the thief and she is his accomplice."

Des Grieux is outraged and threatens to throw the old man out the window, but he has not noticed that his father has entered, and now stepping forward, coldly asks, "Will you throw me out too? Your life is a scandal and you are ruining our family name. I have come to take you away from this world." The Count tells the police to arrest his son but whispers to him that he will be freed later.

"What about Manon?" des Grieux asks.

Guillot gloats, "She will be taken where women of her sort are sent."

Des Grieux jumps to defend her but he is held back and Manon is led away by the police.

ACT V

Manon has been sentenced. She is to be deported to the colony of Louisiana. Near the port of Le Havre, des Grieux waits by the side of the road for Lescaut to bring some armed men, so that they can attack the guards who are taking the women to the boat and thus free Manon. But Lescaut arrives alone and disheartened; he tells des Grieux that his friends, seeing the well-armed guards, decided it wasn't worth the risk and ran off.

In the distance can be heard the weary sounds of the approaching convicts. As they draw nearer, des Grieux, in desperation, decides that he and Lescaut alone will attack the guards. But Lescaut is more realistic and bids des Grieux get out of sight.

The convoy stops for a break nearby, and in the brief pause the Sergeant and a guard mention a prisoner who is dying—the one called Manon. Des Grieux is shattered.

Lescaut presents himself to the Sergeant and asks if he may speak with the dying prisoner. The Sergeant refuses until Lescaut, with des Grieux's money, gives him a substantial bribe. The Sergeant then agrees that Lescaut may spend some time with her but must return her by nightfall. He cautions further, "One of my men will keep watch from a distance so don't try to abduct her." The Sergeant then orders a guard to unchain Manon and he leaves with the soldiers and prisoners for a nearby village.

Lescaut tells des Grieux that he will buy Manon's freedom by bribing the remaining soldier with what is left of the money, and des Grieux is ecstatic.

Manon trudges wearily up the road. Des Grieux takes her in his arms and vows that now she will be his forever. "We will escape together."

She is silent a moment, then says, "You are so good. How could I have hurt and deceived you when I loved you so well? I hate myself for having made even a single day of your life unhappy. Forgive me."

"What have I to forgive," says des Grieux, "now that we shall once again be happy together?"

Dreamily Manon remembers their former happiness—the inn, the coach, his letter, and the small table they shared in their first apartment.

He urges her to flee with him while they have the chance, but as the first star of night appears, she collapses, too weak to walk. Des Grieux tries desperately to revive her, using the very same words with which she lured him from Saint-Sulpice—the voice of love, the arms that caress, the eyes of adoration. But it is too late. She dies in his arms whispering, "And that is the story of Manon Lescaut."

COSÌ FAN TUTTE
(Women Are Like That)

Opera in Two Acts
by
WOLFGANG AMADEUS MOZART
Première: Burg Theater, Vienna, January 26, 1790

ARE WOMEN ever truly faithful? In the annals of misogyny, men have probably been arguing the point since we left the Garden of Eden. Some have insisted that fidelity is in no woman's nature. Others, more sanguine, have allowed as how every woman except his own is faithless.

ACT I

SCENE 1

So it could have been any time. But this time is a day in the late 1700s (when there is, by the way, a fad for all things Albanian). Three men sit under the lovely morning sun in a café in Naples, heatedly debating the fidelity of women. The two young officers, Guglielmo and Ferrando, boast to Don Alfonso, an aging cynic, that their fiancées, Fiordiligi and Dorabella, are utterly faithful.

Their arguments fall on amused ears. "Dear sirs, the amazing thing about

44

woman's faithfulness is that everyone says it exists but no one has been able to find it! What proof do you have that your women are not as heartless as all the others? I'll tell you what; let us have a little wager, say a hundred gold pieces. If, within the next twenty-four hours, I give you absolute proof of their infidelity, then I win."

The two soldiers confidently accept the wager, agreeing to keep it secret from the ladies, and to follow Don Alfonso's instructions to the letter throughout the day. All three look forward to victory and in good cheer raise their glasses in a toast to the venerable Goddess of Love.

SCENE 2

In a garden near the bay of Naples, the two sisters, Fiordiligi and Dorabella, stare lovingly at portraits of their fiancés. They compare the pictures, each in turn exulting in her beloved's handsome features and each declaring her eternal love and devotion.

In the midst of all this gushing, Don Alfonso arrives, looking distressed and out of breath. Immediately the women grow concerned, and he slowly increases their alarm with a series of ambiguous statements. "My dear ladies, how I hate to bring you this news. You must be strong. I feel so sorry for you and for them!"

Fiordiligi and Dorabella finally demand to know if their lovers are dead.

"Ladies, your fiancés have been summoned to the front. As soldiers they must obey and leave immediately. They didn't have the heart to tell you themselves, but if you insist, they will come in for a fond farewell." On cue, Guglielmo and Ferrando join the despondent women. Playing their parts to perfection, the two young officers try to comfort their lovers, who are inconsolable.

"Lend me your sword," says Fiordiligi, "so I can end this torture."

Dorabella says, "I do not need a weapon, I shall die of grief."

Their fiancés beg them to wait patiently until they can return. Quietly observing the tender scene, Don Alfonso is thrilled with the performance. They are doing better than he ever expected.

A military march and the arrival of a boat signal the moment of departure. The women, weeping hysterically (much to Don Alfonso's amusement), bid their lovers write every day. To continued cries of "Farewell," Ferrando and Guglielmo go off to fight the wars, leaving behind two very unhappy women and one merry cynic!

"They are gone," he sighs, "but look, from the distant boat your sweethearts still wave to you." The women watch until the boat disappears from sight, and they pray that the winds will blow gently. They leave the garden and Don Alfonso, alone, relishes the plot he has set in motion, completely confident that he will prove the women's faithlessness.

SCENE 3

In a room inside the sisters' house, Despina, their chambermaid, bewails the life of a domestic. She is shrewd, impudent, and realistic. Awaiting the arrival of her mistresses, who are already half an hour late for breakfast, she samples the coffee.

Fiordiligi and Dorabella enter, too distraught for anything as mundane as food. Fiordiligi is still bent on suicide, while Dorabella is convinced that the anguish she feels will eventually destroy her.

Despina can't understand why they are so upset. "The men will return bearing medals. Meanwhile, no woman has ever died of longing. If you can love one man, you can love another. Instead of pining away waiting for their return, why don't you enjoy their absence?" The two women are appalled by the insensitivity of their maid's remarks, but Despina forges ahead anyway. "Treat men the way they treat us. Love only for convenience and vanity!" Contemptuous of their despair, Despina mockingly follows her forlorn mistresses out of the room.

Don Alfonso enters and notes the silent gloom of the house. While he waits for Guglielmo and Ferrando to disguise themselves before rejoining him, he decides his scheme may need a bit of protection against the clever Despina; she might recognize them. Calling her from her room, he proposes, with a gold coin in his hand, that she help him introduce two handsome, wealthy young men to her mistresses to help console them during the absence of their fiancés. Nothing, of course, could delight Despina more, and she accepts the bribe.

Enter Ferrando and Guglielmo, disguised in exotic-looking clothes, turbans and heavy moustaches, appearing vaguely Albanian. She is wildly amused by their appearance, but she doesn't recognize them—which gives them confidence that their disguises will work. The ladies of the house enter and berate Despina for allowing men into the house at such a time. Despina and the disguised lovers drop to their knees begging the women to forgive them, which only leads to further expressions of outrage. The men of course are delighted by such proofs of fidelity.

Don Alfonso comes in again, feigning surprise at all the commotion. Ferrando and Guglielmo greet him as their dear friend, while Dorabella and Fiordiligi continue to decry the presence of men in their house so soon after the sad "departure" of their fiancés. Don Alfonso calmly refers to the men as his "dearest friends," and given this vote of confidence, the "Albanians" brazenly tell the ladies that they have been irresistibly drawn to them by love.

Dorabella does not know what to do, but Fiordiligi orders them to leave the house. She claims, "My love is constant and cannot change. We are proof against temptation, no matter how much you may implore."

Don Alfonso bids the ladies to be kinder to his friends, a sentiment heartily seconded by Guglielmo, who resumes his plea: "How can you refuse us when we promise to make you so happy?"

Unable to listen any longer, Fiordiligi and Dorabella storm out of the room. Alone with Don Alfonso, Ferrando and Guglielmo laugh at the cynic and urge him to pay up on the bet they are sure he has lost.

"You may laugh now," Don Alfonso cautions, "but our time is not up. Until it is, you must maintain your characters and obey me. Now, go to the garden and await my instructions."

Obediently, Ferrando and Guglielmo leave for the garden, still crowing over their beloveds' fidelity.

SCENE 4

Later that day the sisters sit in the garden lamenting the absence of their lovers. Suddenly they are interrupted by the two Albanian suitors, followed by a frenzied Don Alfonso in hot pursuit. "You still have hope!" he cries. "Don't do it! Don't do it!" Despite these pleas, each man drinks down a phial of liquid, calling on the arsenic to deliver him from the cruelty he has suffered! The women watch aghast as the two men thrash wildly about waiting for the poison to do its work and relieve them of their desperate lovesickness.

Finally, they fall to the ground in a dead faint and the sisters, in desperation, call for Despina. When she arrives, Despina tells the women to stroke their heads while she and Don Alfonso go for the doctor. Left alone with the two "dying" men, and seeing them in such "extremis," the women are roused to pity. They tell each other that they will cry if these two poor helpless men should die. The two disguised men worry that their sweethearts are beginning to crack.

Don Alfonso returns with Despina, now disguised as a doctor. "Here are the wretches who have swallowed the poison," he tells her. "Save them if you can!"

Calmly the "doctor," who "has studied with the famed Dr. Mesmer in

Germany," produces a giant magnet and waves it over the two prone bodies, making them writhe. After a few such passes the two "suicides" recover and, acting dazed and confused, use their recent trauma as an excuse to resume their passionate advances. But when they ask for a kiss, the sisters are outraged.

"All that hostility will soon turn to love," Despina and Don Alfonso agree as the suitors and their prey continue their amorous negotiations and protestations.

ACT II

Scene 1

"My dear ladies," Despina counsels later in the day as she is helping them make new toilettes, "one should never resist a possible flirtation and you can do that without arousing anyone's suspicions. We'll just let everyone know that your suitors are coming to this house to see me! Leave it all to me. Just use your feminine wiles to keep your suitors in love with you!" She leaves them, so that the thought may simmer.

Timidly, the sisters discuss the pros and cons of such a strategy. But the more they talk about it, the more attractive becomes the notion of just a little dalliance. Shortly, the only matter remaining to be decided is which suitor belongs to which sister.

"I'll take the handsome dark one," Dorabella declares.

"And I prefer the blond," Fiordiligi asserts.

They both agree that it may be naughty, but at least it will be fun.

Scene 2

Escorted by Despina and Don Alfonso, the sisters visit a garden by the shore. Wafted on the sea breezes come the strains of a love serenade. The singers, of course, are the Albanians, who tentatively approach the women as they finish their song. Suddenly, all four are shy and awkward. With some encouragement from Despina and Don Alfonso, they finally manage a few platitudes about the weather, and then pair off—Ferrando with Fiordiligi and Guglielmo with Dorabella—each with the other's fiancée!

The couples stroll separately through the garden. Guglielmo melodramatically tells Dorabella of his love for her. "I am dying for your love. I am yours. You have to surrender to me. Accept my love!" At first Dorabella refuses his advances but her reluctance melts when he threatens once again to kill himself. She happily agrees to be his love. Guglielmo declares his delight, while inwardly regretting the betrayal of his friend, Ferrando, whose fiancée has just proved herself unfaithful. As she grows more and more enthusiastic and passionate about her suitor, Dorabella exchanges lockets with him.

Meanwhile, the disguised Ferrando has relentlessly wooed Fiordiligi, but with less success. She begs him to stop, declaring that her love for Guglielmo cannot be broken. Feigning utter despair, Ferrando is convinced to give up, and they part.

Soon Guglielmo and Ferrando meet to compare notes. Ferrando reports happily that Fiordiligi has remained constant, but when he asks, "And my Dorabella was no doubt faithful too?" Guglielmo must respond, "A little doubting might be useful," and substantiates Dorabella's infidelity with the locket. Stunned and enraged, Ferrando is about to dash off to tear out Dorabella's heart, but Guglielmo stops him by counseling him not to destroy himself over a heartless woman; he succeeds in reducing Ferrando to a state of passive misery.

Don Alfonso joins them, but when pressed by Guglielmo to pay him his share of the wager, he insists on the right to one more test.

SCENE 3

Dorabella, delighted by her decision to permit some dalliance with her Albanian admirer, shares her excitement with Despina. Fiordiligi comes into the room, angry with Despina and Dorabella for taking such pleasure in these amorous attentions. "May the devil take you, Don Alfonso and the cursed Albanians too. What's worse, I'm in love too, and not only with Guglielmo!"

This news pleases Despina and Dorabella, who encourage her to lose control and to take advantage of the situation. "You'll feel better after you've given in!" They leave her alone to consider their advice.

Fiordiligi is still offended by her sister's attitude and once again decides that she will remain faithful. Don Alfonso, Ferrando, and Guglielmo watch unobserved from behind the door as Fiordiligi calls for Despina. When the maid arrives she orders her to fetch Guglielmo's military clothes. "Disguised as a soldier, I will go join my beloved on the battlefield. Perhaps my sister will follow my example!"

At this moment of heroic resolve, Ferrando enters in his exotic disguise to further his wooing. He begs Fiordiligi to surrender. "If you cannot take pity on me, then take my sword and pierce my heart."

Fiordiligi can resist no longer, much to the chagrin of Guglielmo, and she and her suitor leave arm in arm.

A raging Guglielmo comes out of hiding with Don Alfonso, who, for his part, can scarcely conceal his satisfaction. Ferrando too feels a little better now. Despina comes in, gleefully announcing that the two sisters are now disposed to marry the Albanian suitors. As betrayed lovers, Guglielmo and Ferrando would rather plot revenge to punish the women for their transgressions, but Don Alfonso counsels them to forgive: "Women are capricious creatures, and you should not be upset by this because all women, young and old, beautiful and ugly, behave this way." He gets the betrayed lovers to admit that they still love their Dorabella and Fiordiligi, and the preparations for the wedding proceed.

SCENE 4

Servants and guests greet the brides and their bridegrooms as they enter for the wedding banquet. Still playing their roles to perfection, the men toast their brides as Don Alfonso announces the arrival of the notary. Of course it is Despina, now disguised as a notary, who reads the marriage contract. Dorabella and Fiordiligi sign the document, but before the men can do the same, a drum roll is heard which puts a halt to the proceedings. Don Alfonso looks out and in mock horror announces the return of the soldiers. "My husband!" each of the sisters cries out. The Albanians, simulating terror, dash about looking for a place to hide and manage, in the confusion, to slip out of the room.

"My dear ladies," Don Alfonso comforts, "trust me." Just then Ferrando and Guglielmo, once again in military garb, come in to greet their faithless fiancées. Their joyful arrival is met by silent embarrassment. Don Alfonso, as if to explain, shows them the marriage contracts which the sisters had signed. Guglielmo and Ferrando feign shock and dismay. They are about to depart but are stopped by the sisters, who admit their guilt but put the blame on Don Alfonso and Despina. Don Alfonso, relentless in his exposure of their duplicity, offers proof of their guilt "in the next room." The men go to investigate while the women tremble with fright. A moment later they return haphazardly garbed in some of the Albanians' clothes, and announce, "Ladies, your Albanians stand here before you! And over there," pointing to Despina, "is your doctor and your notary!"

The clever Despina has for once been fooled herself, and the sisters are speechless but recover enough to call these deceptions "heinous." Nonetheless, they beg forgiveness, and Don Alfonso, whose challenge started this wild day, urges them all to laugh about what's past. Reconciled, the couples reunite—Fiordiligi with Guglielmo and Dorabella with Ferrando. Once again they declare their undying love, and then joined by Don Alfonso and Despina all agree that the man who faces adversity with reason and laughter is a lucky man indeed.

AIDA

Opera in Four Acts
by
GIUSEPPE VERDI

Première: Opera House, Cairo, December 24, 1871

IN ANCIENT Egypt the Pharaoh was considered divine and religious ritual
was an integral part of daily life; the gods were continually consulted by a
caste of priests who were intimately involved in the running of the government and the conduct of the wars that the Egyptians so often waged with
their neighbors.

ACT I

SCENE 1

Our story begins in the time of the Nineteenth Dynasty, around 1230
B.C. The Egyptians have been attacked by the Ethiopians, who are advanc-
ing through the Valley of the Nile almost to the outskirts of Thebes. In a
hall of the Pharaoh's palace, Ramfis, chief of the priests, and Radames, a
young warrior and captain of the guards, discuss this perilous situation.
The priest informs Radames, "Holy Isis has named the man who shall be

the supreme commander of our armies. He is young and brave and I must tell our king of the god's decree." Having dropped this hint, Ramfis goes to speak to the Pharaoh.

Radames knows that the High Priest's advice will determine the Pharaoh's decision, and hoping that he will be the one chosen to head the armies, he dreams of returning to Memphis cloaked in the glory of victory, and able to present his laurels to the beautiful Aida, a captured Ethiopian girl who has been made slave to Amneris, the Pharaoh's daughter.

His intoxicating reveries are interrupted by the entrance of Amneris. She senses that he is in love and, in the hope that she is the woman, tries to coax him into an admission. Radames, concerned that she has discovered his secret passion for Aida, protests that it is only the expectation of battle that excites him. At this moment, Aida appears. Radames' talk of war visibly upsets her, and Amneris, intercepting a glance between the lovers, grows suspicious and asks the reason for Aida's tears. Concealing her concern for Radames, Aida says, "I have heard the sounds of war and I fear for my country, for you and for myself." But Amneris suspects that she and her slave love the same man.

Suddenly her father, the Pharaoh, enters, followed by a retinue of ministers, officers, and Ramfis with his priests. A messenger arrives with news of the invasion and tells them that the enemy is led by a relentless warrior, Amonasro, the king. "My father!" Aida whispers to herself, for she has managed to hide this knowledge from the Egyptians.

The Pharaoh announces that Radames has been chosen by Holy Isis to lead the Egyptian counterattack. "Go to the Temple of Vulcan, great warrior. There you will receive the sacred arms. Then go forth to victory!"

Led by Amneris in cries of "Return victorious," the crowd cheers Radames as their chosen leader.

Carried away by the emotion of the moment, and by her love, Aida too joins in, but she is torn. As the cheering assemblage marches out with Radames, she remains behind, tormented by the conflict of love and loyalty. "For whom do I cry and pray?" she thinks. "I love Radames, but he is the enemy of my country." Anguished, she prays to the gods to take pity on her.

SCENE 2

In the Temple of Vulcan at Memphis, incense fills the air, the altar is decorated with sacred symbols, and a mysterious light shines from above. Ramfis leads a group of priests and priestesses in a ritual invoking the spirit of the mighty Phtha, the life-giving spirit of the world. Radames is brought into the temple and led through the rows of massive pillars to the altar. The priests place a silver veil over his head and the priestesses perform a sacred dance. Ramfis tells Radames that he, beloved of the gods, will determine the destiny of Egypt, and they all pray to the gods to guide Egypt through battle. "Protect and defend our sacred soil," intone the priests. The priestesses resume their dance, Radames is given the sacred arms with which to do battle, and they all praise "Great Phtha."

ACT II

SCENE 1

The Egyptian army wins the battle and spirits are high in Amneris' room as her slave girls dress her for the victory celebration. Youthful Moorish slaves dance joyously about waving large feather fans. Seeing Aida enter, Amneris signals the other slaves to leave. Aida is clearly dejected and Amneris, feigning compassion, tells her that her anguish at the Ethiopian defeat will pass. "Fate has been cruel to us also," Amneris says, "for your people killed our leader on the battlefield!"

At this news of Radames' death, Aida's grief overwhelms her. "I shall never stop crying," she declares, thus falling right into Amneris' trap.

"So you love him and you are my rival," Amneris says and admits that Radames lives.

Aida cannot conceal her joy. "Alive, oh praise be the gods!"

Amneris is furious and swears to destroy her. "Slave, fear me!" As the victorious shouts of the exultant populace outside filter into the room, Aida pleads for mercy, but Amneris is unmoved. "If you think you are worthy, you can try fighting for him."

Distraught, Aida again prays to the gods to take pity on her.

SCENE 2

Near the Temple of Ammon the exuberant people of Egypt throng the triumphal gate of the city of Thebes. The Pharaoh and his retinue march in, followed by Amneris and her slaves, including Aida. The Pharaoh takes his place on the throne and Amneris sits at his side. As the trumpeters, troops, sacred vessels, and statues of the gods pass in review before them, the populace and the priests hail the glory of Egypt. Slave girls carrying treasures taken from the defeated enemy dance before the Pharaoh. Finally the victorious Radames, borne aloft by his captains, is carried in, and the crowd again breaks into cheers for the conquering hero and the glory of Egypt.

Descending from his throne, the Pharaoh embraces Radames calling him the savior of the land and bidding him bow before Amneris. She crowns him with the wreath of triumph. "Ask for anything that you want, Radames. Nothing will be refused you today," the Pharaoh tells him. Radames asks that first the Ethiopian prisoners be brought in.

Among them and dressed like the other prisoners is Amonasro, king of Ethiopia. Aida cannot contain herself and blurts out, "What do I see? My father a prisoner?" Amonasro whispers to Aida cautioning her not to betray him as king. Called forward by the Pharaoh, he cunningly explains that he is indeed Aida's father and that he is an officer who has defended his country and has watched his king, Amonasro, die on the field of battle. "Great king, have mercy on these captives." This sentiment is echoed by the slave girls and other prisoners. But the priests, led by Ramfis, tell the Pharaoh that the gods have said these prisoners should be executed and that he should ignore their pleas for mercy.

Radames, moved by the grief that he sees in Aida's eyes, turns to the Pharaoh and tells him that his wish is for the Ethiopian prisoners to be freed.

Ramfis is aghast and protests that the Ethiopians want vengeance and should be executed.

"But with Amonasro, the warrior king dead, they shall no longer be able to fight," Radames counters.

Ramfis asks that at least Aida and her father should remain in Egypt as a token of good faith.

The Pharaoh accepts this counsel and adds, "Radames, you shall have the hand of Amneris, and one day you shall rule over all Egypt." Amneris exults while the people renew their loud cries of victory and joy. The shouts of "Glory to Egypt" grow even louder as the prisoners too praise the merciful victors. Amonasro quietly counsels his daughter to be patient and wait for happier times because their day of vengeance is coming.

ACT III

It is a soft moonlit night on the banks of the Nile. From a temple among the palm trees, hymns to the god Osiris filter through the air. A boat lands near the temple and two figures alight. They are Amneris and Ramfis, come to pray that the union of Amneris and Radames be blessed.

As Amneris and Ramfis disappear into the temple, Aida enters, her face concealed by a veil. She is waiting for Radames and, afraid that this will be their last meeting, she promises herself that she will find oblivion in the waters of the Nile. She is sorry that never again will she see her beloved homeland with its blue skies and calm breezes.

Just then her father appears and reveals that he knows of her love for Radames and how it torments her. Amonasro plays on her rivalry with Amneris, and on her frustration that she, the daughter of a king, is now a slave, and he tries to console her with the conviction that she will one day see their homeland again. "Our countrymen are prepared once more for battle," he tells her. "The only thing I need to know is the route that the enemy will take. I know you are waiting for Radames, and you could find out what we need to know from him." Aida is horrified at the thought of using Radames this way, but it only fans Amonasro's anger. "You are a king's daughter and your refusal will allow the Egyptians to destroy our people yet again; you will remain a slave forever." Aida begs for pity, but Amonasro is relentless and tells her that he sees a specter in the shadows that is her mother who curses her. Aida cannot bear it any longer and succumbs, declaring, "My country, I pay a high price for thee!" Radames is seen approaching and Amonasro, counseling his daughter to be brave, hides behind a palm tree to eavesdrop on their conversation.

Radames speaks lovingly to Aida but she repulses him because of his impending marriage to Amneris. He is dumbfounded and tells Aida again of his love for her. "I have a plan," he explains. "The Ethiopian people have rearmed and are once more ready to fight. I shall again lead the Egyptian forces to victory, whereupon I shall throw myself at the mercy of the Pharaoh and tell him of our love. You shall be my victory wreath." Aida is unconvinced and asks if he does not fear Amneris' wrath. She tells him, "If you truly love me the only escape is to flee together!" He cannot believe his ears. "How can I abandon my homeland?" he argues. Aida persists and as he still resists, she accuses him of not loving her and orders him to leave and marry Amneris. He is too much in love with her and finally he yields to her plan.

She asks him how they can flee without encountering the Egyptian forces.

"My men will march tomorrow against the enemy. Until then it will be clear. The route is the pass of Napata!"

Radames' words are echoed by Amonasro, who steps from behind the palm tree declaring, "Aida's father, the king of Ethiopia, has overheard your plans!"

Radames is stunned and overcome with remorse at having unwittingly betrayed his country. Aida and Amonasro try to convince Radames that he will be better off beyond the banks of the Nile, where he and Aida can enjoy their love and build a throne together. They beg him again and again to come with them, but Radames is rooted to one spot, unable to recover from his tragic error. As they try to drag him away, Amneris emerges from the temple and in a jealous rage denounces Radames as a traitor. Amonasro draws his dagger and tries to attack Amneris, but Radames defends her, allowing Aida and Amonasro to flee. Ramfis orders the guards to chase them, as Radames disarms himself in surrender.

ACT IV

SCENE 1

In a great hall of the king's palace, Amneris stands near the entrance to Radames' cell. Aida has escaped, and while Amneris knows that Radames should, as a traitor, be executed, she realizes how much she still loves him. "I could save him," she thinks, "if only he would love me." She orders the guards to bring Radames to her. She offers him the chance to live. "I shall get you a pardon if only you will renounce your love for Aida."

Radames says that life is not worth living without Aida.

Amneris tells him that Aida is still alive but has disappeared. She asks him again to renounce his love so that he may live, but Radames is determined to die.

Surrounded by guards, Radames descends to the underground cell where he will be tried. Amneris watches as the priests, dressed in long white robes, file into the vault. Horrified by the sight, she is now filled with remorse at having caused almost certain death for the man she loves. Listening to Ramfis utter the accusations, Amneris protests each count by declaring Radames' innocence, but alone in the hall she is powerless to affect the proceedings. Three times Ramfis orders Radames to defend himself, and each time Radames refuses. Finally Ramfis pronounces sentence: "Radames, you shall die as a traitor, buried alive beneath the Temple of Vulcan, the god whom you have offended."

As the priests re-enter the hall, Amneris, stricken with anger and remorse, tries to convince them that they have condemned an innocent man, but their only answer is, "He is a traitor and must die!"

In a last desperate effort, Amneris tells Ramfis that "You are angering the gods and man," but the High Priest is deaf to her entreaties, and the priests file out of the hall, leaving Amneris to call down upon them all the curses of heaven.

SCENE 2

In the Temple of Vulcan, priests chant their endless prayers. Below, in his sealed tomb, Radames muses on his fate and how he shall never again see the light of day nor his Aida, but he hopes that she will at least be able to live happily. Suddenly, in the darkness, he senses a figure standing before him.

"It is I, Aida," she tells him. "I have found my way here because I want to die with you."

Radames cannot bear it and insists she must not. He even tries to move the stone that seals the tomb. But Aida is already weak and soon grows delirious. She sees the angel of death approaching to bring them to heaven where they may share the joys of eternal love.

In the temple above, the priests sing a hymn to the gods. "It is our funeral hymn," she tells Radames, and he sadly resigns himself to their fate. They embrace and bid the earth farewell.

In the temple, Amneris, dressed in mourning clothes, prostrates herself on the stone tomb, and prays for the peace of her beloved and for the forgiveness of Isis, so that heaven may open to him. As the priests intone their prayers to the Great Phtha, Aida sinks dying into Radames' loving arms.

LA BOHÈME

Opera in Four Acts
by
GIACOMO PUCCINI
Première: Teatro Regio, Turin, February 1, 1896

ACT I

IT IS Christmas Eve in nineteenth-century Paris. Marcello, a painter, and Rodolfo, a writer, are trying to work in their freezing garret. They are young and hopeful, and full of spirit, but they have no money and have run out of firewood. Their fingers are so stiff it is almost impossible to write or paint. Marcello curses the bitter cold, likening it to the heart of his former lover Musetta, and grabs a chair. He is about to throw it into the empty stove, but Rodolfo stops him. Marcello then reaches for the canvas that he is working on, but Rodolfo again dissuades him and instead offers the play he has just finished and which he says will burn better. Gleefully they light the pages of "Act I."

Colline, a philosopher, comes in with an armful of books he has been unable to pawn and complains that all of the pawn shops are closed on Christmas Eve. He joins his friends around the stove just as the warmth of "Act I" dies down. Rodolfo generously donates "Act II" and eventually tosses in the rest of his manuscript. The fuel does not last long, but the author is applauded. "Since brevity is the soul of wit," says Colline, "this drama was truly sparkling." Another friend arrives—the musician Schaunard, laden with food, wine, cigars, firewood, and money which he tosses onto the floor. The others are incredulous at this wanton display of wealth, and listen with delight as he tells them how a wealthy Englishman with a dying parrot paid him a liberal sum to play music to the parrot for three days. They savagely attack the food, but Schaunard urges them to save it for another day. Tonight they must go to the Café Momus where everyone in the Latin Quarter celebrates Christmas.

They raise their glasses in a toast, but are interrupted by Benoit, the landlord, who has come to collect the rent. They offer him a chair and a glass of wine, and skillfully coax him to talk about himself, and his nagging wife. When he boasts about an evening recently spent with a charming young girl, the quartet abruptly assumes a higher moral stance and calling him a reprobate with offensive principles, they throw him out of the garret. Once again they have avoided paying the rent!

In high spirits, Marcello, Colline, and Schaunard take off for the Café Momus. Rodolfo says he will follow in a few minutes, as soon as he finishes the article on which he has been working.

Rodolfo no sooner returns to his writing table than he is disturbed by a knock at the door. A timid female voice asks, "Can you help me? My candle has gone out." He opens the door. A pretty young girl is standing there and he asks her to come in. She suddenly begins to cough and tries to explain that she is out of breath from the stairs. Then she faints, dropping her candle and key.

Rodolfo carries her to a chair and sprinkles some water on her face. When she revives, he recovers her candle and lights it for her. She makes her way to the door, thanks him, and bids him good night, but suddenly realizes she can't find her key, which fell from her hand in her swoon, so she stands in the doorway searching through her belongings. The wind blows out her candle again. Rodolfo surreptitiously blows out his candle, leaving them both in the dark. They search for her key, which Rodolfo finds but quickly hides. In the dark, their hands touch. The girl is startled, but he holds on, saying, "They are so cold. Let me warm them in mine." Sitting his lovely neighbor down again, he waxes intimate and romantic. "I'm a poet," he declares, "I write and I live on dreams and visions. But your eyes are more beautiful than any of my fantasies. Who are you?"

Simply she tells him about herself: "They call me Mimi, I don't know why because my name is Lucia." She makes her living by embroidering flowers on linens and silks, but she prefers the scent of real roses.

They charm each other with their young hopes and longings, until the moment is shattered by the impatient cries of Rodolfo's friends from the courtyard below. He tells them to go away and he will join them later. But when he tries to kiss Mimi, she pushes him away gently, reminding him that his friends are waiting. "However," she says, "I will go with you to the Café Momus." Lightheartedly, they declare they love each other and walk out into the cold night together.

ACT II

The Café Momus is situated at the corner of one of several streets that intersect to form a typical Parisian square. The square serves as eye and magnet of the neighborhood, allowing those within the square to watch the life in the converging streets, while inexorably drawing into its orbit the denizen on his daily errands, the casual passerby, the curious, the expectant, and the idle. On this Christmas Eve, the square is filled with students, working girls, servants, police, children and their parents, vendors hawking fruits and sweets, toys and trifles, and shoppers strolling in and out of the stores. On the way to the restaurant, Schaunard buys a book, and Marcello tries to pick up a girl. Rodolfo and Mimi enter the square. He spends what little money he has on a bonnet for her, and they join his friends at one of the outdoor tables of the Café Momus. Schaunard's windfall has made them feel richer than they are and they order a sumptuous dinner.

Suddenly Marcello almost chokes on his food. "Bring me a dose of arsenic," he says, for he has seen Musetta approaching with her aged admirer, Alcindoro. He turns his back on her, but with a dramatic flourish, she sits at the next table and tries to get his attention. In a loud voice she boldly touts her own attractions while Alcindoro mutters uncomfortably, trying desperately to quiet her down. But Musetta continues her outrageous behavior, and succeeds in making herself the center of attention for everyone except Marcello. She realizes that she must get rid of the old man. Suddenly, she screams in pain, complaining that her foot hurts. Alcindoro tries to calm her and removes her shoe, but nothing will placate her until he agrees to buy her another pair. He leaves for the shoe store and Musetta and Marcello fall into each other's arms.

The waiter presents the Bohemians with a bill, which even with their pooled funds they are unable to pay. Musetta instructs the waiter to add the amount to her bill, which will be paid when the old gentleman returns. As a procession of soldiers marches through the square, Marcello and Colline carry the one-shoed Musetta, and the happy celebrants follow the military guard down one of the streets.

As they disappear, Alcindoro returns with Musetta's shoes only to find the two bills waiting to be paid. He falls stunned into a chair.

ACT III

It's a cold, dark February dawn. The streets are snow-covered. At a city gate on the outskirts of Paris, near the Rue d'Orléans, the sleepy guards stay warm around a brazier. The street sweepers, waiting outside, stamp their feet and blow on their hands and call to the guards to open the gates and let them pass. Peasant women enter with them, bringing milk to town. The early morning quiet is shattered now and then by happy voices from inside a tavern that sits at the edge of the square. Over its sign hangs one of Marcello's paintings. Mimi asks a servant girl who is about to enter the tavern if she would please ask Marcello, the painter, to come outside for a moment. The woman agrees and soon Marcello comes out.

He and Musetta are working at the tavern, he painting, she singing, in exchange for room and board. He invites Mimi to come inside where it is warmer.

"Is Rodolfo there?"

"Yes."

"Then I cannot go in."

Marcello is surprised. "What has happened?"

"Oh Marcello, please help me. Rodolfo is constantly jealous. He becomes suspicious of the slightest thing and flies into rages."

Marcello agrees that is no good and, boasting a little, advises that they be more like himself and Musetta, who take their love lightly. Otherwise they should part. He agrees to intervene, however, and tells Mimi to go home. Mimi begins to cough violently and moves off, but lingers behind a tree as Rodolfo emerges from the tavern.

Rodolfo tells Marcello he can no longer live with Mimi. Although he still loves her, she is a bitch, constantly flirting, particularly with any silly, titled dandy who comes along.

"Rodolfo," Marcello says, "I don't think you are quite sincere."

Rodolfo breaks down. "You're right. What really tortures me is that I will lose her because she is so ill. And I know I should not keep her with me because the garret is so cold; her cough gets worse every day."

Mimi has heard it all. She begins to sob, and to cough so loudly that she can no longer remain hidden. Running over to her, Rodolfo takes her in his arms.

Musetta's brazen laugh shatters the air, and Marcello rushes into the tavern to find out who she is flirting with now. Left alone, Mimi tells Rodolfo that she realizes she must leave, but they cannot really bring themselves to part as they reminisce to each other about what they will be missing. "If you wish," Mimi says, "you may keep my little bonnet as a memento." Their tenderness is in sharp contrast to the loud bickering of Marcello and Musetta, who have come out of the tavern to continue their fight.

As Musetta and Marcello exchange insults, Rodolfo and Mimi resolve finally to remain together until the flowers of spring begin to bloom. Arm in arm, they walk down the snow-covered street, hoping that spring will never come.

ACT IV

It is spring, and in the garret Marcello is standing at his easel, Rodolfo sitting at his writing table, both distracted and unable to work. Rodolfo tells Marcello that he saw Musetta riding in an elegant carriage, and that he told her he could not hear her heart, it was buried so deeply in velvet. Between gritted teeth, Marcello says he appreciates the *bon mot,* and tells Rodolfo about his encounter with Mimi, who was also dressed magnificently and riding with her new and prosperous lover. Plunged into thoughts about their lost loves, they finally give up pretending to work and decide it is time for dinner, just as Schaunard and Colline come in, carrying four rolls and a herring. The four friends gather round the table and break the gloom of poverty by pretending that the paltry meal is an exotic feast of salmon, oysters, and parrot. Soon their spirits rise until they are dancing giddily as if at a ball. Colline and Schaunard stage a mock duel and the others cheer them on.

This boisterous horseplay comes to a sudden stop as Musetta bursts into the room, crying, "It's Mimi. She came with me and she's so ill she can't make it up the stairs."

Rodolfo rushes out and helps Mimi into the garret. Putting her on the bed, they try to make her as comfortable as possible. Musetta brings her some water, and Rodolfo sits with her, begging her to rest.

Musetta says, "I heard that she had left the Viscount, so I went to look for her. I found her very ill, barely able to walk. All she wanted was to see Rodolfo."

Mimi, revived a little, greets the others and tells Marcello what a good person Musetta is. She complains about the cold, and Rodolfo tries to warm her hands. Musetta takes off her earrings and tells Marcello to sell them so they can get a doctor and some medicine. On second thought, she decides to go with him so that she can buy a muff for Mimi's hands. They leave and Colline folds his beloved cloak into a small bundle, bidding it farewell. He will sell it. Schaunard, knowing Rodolfo and Mimi would like to be alone, goes out with him.

As soon as the door is closed Mimi opens her eyes and calls to Rodolfo. "I pretended to be asleep so they would leave us alone. There is so much I want to say to you, you the love of my life." Rodolfo shows her the bonnet he bought her for the night they met. "I have saved it for your return." This starts a flood of memories and they reminisce about their first meeting in the garret, until another coughing fit makes Mimi faint. Rodolfo's cry brings Schaunard back in. Mimi recovers and Rodolfo pleads with her to rest. She drifts off again.

Musetta and Marcello return with a muff and some medicine, and the news that the doctor will come soon. Their voices wake Mimi, who thanks Musetta for the warm muff. Seeing tears in Rodolfo's eyes, Mimi tells him not to cry. "I'll be all right; my hands are so warm now." She lies back and her eyes close.

Off to one side of the garret, Musetta warms the medicine over an open flame all the while praying to the Madonna to save Mimi. Rodolfo asks Musetta for assurance that there is hope for Mimi and Musetta tries to reassure him. He busies himself covering the window in order to protect Mimi from the light.

Schaunard approaches the bed. Shaken, he turns, goes to Marcello and whispers, "She has died!" Just then Colline comes back and gives Musetta some money. "How is she?" he asks Rodolfo.

Rodolfo says, "She seems more tranquil now," but seeing the terrified expression on Marcello's and Schaunard's faces, he panics and demands to know what is going on.

"Courage!" Marcello says.

Rodolfo runs to the bed and, overwhelmed by despair, cradles her lifeless body, crying, "Mimi! Mimi!"

CARMEN

Opera in Four Acts
by
GEORGES BIZET
Première: Opéra-Comique, Paris, March 3, 1875

ACT I

ONE SUNNY afternoon in Spain early in the nineteenth century, strollers, vendors, and dragoons mingle in a square flanked by a cigarette factory and the dragoons' barracks. In the crowd is a shy young girl named Micaela who is looking for Don José, a young peasant from her village who has become a soldier. The soldiers know him and tell Micaela that he will be on duty in a little while. Meanwhile they invite her to flirt, but she refuses politely and, saying she will return soon, leaves the square.

A bugle call marks the changing of the guard and the dragoons fall into line, the rigid precision of the ceremony mimicked and mocked by a group of ragged street children. One of the departing soldiers sees Don José among the replacements and tells him of the lovely girl who was looking for him. The military formalities over, one group marches out and the others enter the guardhouse. Don José and his lieutenant, Zuniga, remain outside with the strollers.

A bell signals the beginning of the noonday break at the cigarette factory, attracting men of all ages to the square where they can mix with the women who work at the factory. Mostly, they are waiting to see the gypsy Carmen. Heralded by a burst of excitement and a path that is cleared through the crowd, she makes her way to the center of the men, taunts them and, dancing to the rhythm of an habanera, sings a song about the perils of love. The only man not absolutely mesmerized by her is Don José, so she slowly makes her way to him and, with a provocative look, throws him a flower. Before he can react, a bell calls the women—including Carmen—back to the factory.

Don José is angered at Carmen's effrontery, yet carefully hides the flower in his uniform when he sees Micaela returning to the square. He is delighted to see her and eager for news from his mother and their village. Tenderly, she tells him that his mother misses him and dreams of him often. Shyly, Micaela says, "She asked me to give you a kiss for her," and kisses him. Don José is moved and implores Micaela to tell his mother that he loves her dearly and that she should be proud of him. Satisfied that all is well, Micaela bids him farewell and promises to visit again.

Don José stays in the square thinking of his mother, but thoughts of Carmen, "that sorceress," keep intruding. He takes out the flower and is about to toss it away when the somnolent calm of the afternoon is shattered by shrieks from the factory. Women rush out screaming that there is a fight inside. Zuniga tries desperately to calm the crowd which quickly fills the square, and finally orders José to take two men with him into the factory to investigate. Within moments they emerge, dragging a defiant Carmen, and reporting that she started the fight. Zuniga confronts Carmen, but his questioning is greeted with an insolent "Tralala." Irritated, but strongly attracted to the gypsy, Zuniga decides that she will have to learn her lesson in prison, and orders Don José to tie her hands while he goes into the guardhouse to write the orders. Don José does as he is told, but Carmen proceeds to sing seductively of the pleasures that await him, and of "the sorceress" whose flower has put him under her magical spell. Despite himself, Don José cannot resist her and agrees to let her escape in exchange for the promise of her love. He loosens the rope that binds her hands just as Zuniga returns with the orders for him to take her to prison. As he begins to lead her away, she whispers to him: "I'll push you. Pretend to fall, and leave the rest to me." Don José follows closely behind Carmen, so that she can free her hands. Suddenly, she pushes him to the ground and disappears through the laughing crowd.

Don José goes to prison in her place.

ACT II

In Lillas Pastia's tavern on the outskirts of Seville, two gypsy girls dance to the music of guitars, watched by a motley crowd of officers, soldiers, and gypsy smugglers. The tables are littered with glasses and the air is filled with smoke. Carmen is there and moves around, singing to the music. Frasquita and Mercedes, two of her friends, join her for the choruses, and as the music reaches a frenzied climax, the three friends join in the dance. Once again Carmen mingles with the cheering crowd and ignores Zuniga, who keeps trying to speak to her. Finally he catches her attention by telling her that Don José has completed serving *her* sentence, and has just been released.

Cheers and shouts from outside interrupt the conversation, and the tavern is suddenly flooded with exuberant revelers accompanying the victorious toreador Escamillo. Playing his hero role to the hilt, Escamillo thrills the crowd with a vivid description of combat in the arena—the fears, the tension, the bulls. The crowd toasts him yet again, promising him that love certainly awaits a victorious bullfighter. His eyes light upon Carmen, and he goes to her. "What is your name, my beauty?" he asks. "For in my next moment of danger I want to say it."

His bravado and recklessness appeal to her but she is still yearning for José, and tells him not to fall in love with her.

During this exchange the officers have prepared to leave, and when Escamillo moves away from Carmen, Zuniga says to her, "Since you're not coming with us now, I will come back later to see you."

"And you'll be sorry," she retorts.

The crowd leaves, emptying the tavern.

Carmen, Frasquita, and Mercedes remain behind together with their friends, the smugglers Dancairo and Remendado. The men ask the three women to help them in a bit of business because, as they humbly explain, "Smuggling, cheating, thieving and duping always work better when there are beautiful women along!"

Frasquita and Mercedes are eager to leave with the men, but Carmen insists she will stay behind to wait for the man she loves. The others are all stunned by this news and the deaf ear she turns to their entreaties. They are trying to convince her that he will not show up, when Don José is heard in the distance singing the song of the Dragoon of Alcala. Carmen, vindicated and delighted, tries to rush the others out, but before they leave they urge her to get her handsome dragoon to join their smuggling operation. She promises to try, and Don José enters.

Carmen asks Don José if he regrets the two months he spent in prison in her place. "For you," he says lovingly, "I would willingly be there still." Carmen ignites his jealousy by telling him that his superiors have just been there to see her dance, then calms him by saying she will dance for him alone. Humming and playing the castanets to accompany herself, she dances seductively. He cannot take his eyes off of her—until he hears a distant military bugle sounding retreat.

He explains to Carmen that he must return to quarters for roll call, but she is in no mood to listen and flies into a rage, deriding and mocking him for his blind obedience. Furiously she tells him to get out and go to his precious roll call. Trying desperately to convince her of his love, he removes from his pocket the flower he has cherished since she threw it at him on their first meeting. "This magical flower stayed with me in my prison cell," he tells her; "its fragrance made me drunk." He tells her of the time he spent dreaming of his beloved Carmen, ending his impassioned declaration with the simple words, "Carmen, I love you!"

Seizing the opportunity, Carmen tells him that if he really loved her, he would come with her to the mountains to lead a free gypsy life. Her alluring description of how they will live almost seduces him and he is about to agree when he realizes the shame of what he would be doing. Pulling away from her, he refuses to desert his regiment and face dishonor.

"Then I love you no longer," she screams. "Farewell forever!"

Resigned to this outcome, Don José rushes to the door. But before he can leave there is a loud knock, and Zuniga struts into the tavern. Seeing Don José, he tells Carmen that she is foolish to choose a mere soldier when she could have an officer. Then he brusquely orders his underling to leave. Don José refuses, and draws his sword, threatening Zuniga. Carmen shouts for help. Dancairo and Remendado, accompanied by a band of gypsies, rush in with drawn pistols, halting Zuniga in his tracks. Carmen ridicules the officer as the smugglers lead him away, then turns to Don José, asking, "Are you one of us?"

Realizing that his insubordination leaves him no alternative, Don José announces: "I have to be!"

Overjoyed, Carmen welcomes him to a life of liberty, while the other gypsies and smugglers warmly receive him into their ranks, describing the mountains and wide open land they will cross together.

ACT III

It is a dark night on the barren, desolate ledge of a mountain pass. A few smugglers can be seen already preparing camp; slowly the others arrive, carrying bundles—the fruits of their latest foray. They assemble in groups, gathering about small fires for warmth; some wrap themselves in cloaks and lie down to sleep, while others speak softly together. Don José sits off to one side, alone, staring into space. Carmen comes to him and asks what he is thinking about.

"My mother," he says, "who thinks I am an honest man."

Annoyed by his answer, she suggests that he leave the band of gypsies and return to his mother.

Don José, still totally enamored of Carmen, angrily tells her never again to suggest that he leave her.

She turns her back on his sulking figure and walks over to the fire where Frasquita and Mercedes are reading their fortunes in the cards. Carmen watches as her friends see processions of lovers and precious jewels in their futures. To try her own luck she grabs a deck and slowly turns up the cards. But while Frasquita and Mercedes see love and wealth, she sees only death. She shuffles the cards and tries again and again. But each time Carmen's cards foretell only death.

Shaking away gloom, Carmen turns to Dancairo and Remendado, who have come over to the three friends to tell them that the trail looks clear. The smugglers quietly break camp and gather up their bundles. Don José is posted with a rifle on a high rock to serve as watch while his comrades file out through the narrow mountain pass.

Unseen and led by a guide, Micaela enters the smugglers' camp. Left alone, she spies Don José in the distance looking intently in the opposite direction. She begins to make her way toward him, but the sudden loud crack of gunfire frightens her and she hides behind some rocks.

Just as Micaela disappears, Escamillo walks into the camp holding his hat in his hand and looking at a hole in it. He approaches Don José saying, "If you'd shot just a little bit lower, I'd be dead."

José recognizes the famous bullfighter and welcomes him, but asks why he has risked his life to come into the mountains.

Escamillo answers: "I came to see the woman I love, a gypsy named Carmen!"

Don José, furious at what he has heard, draws his knife and challenges the bullfighter to a duel. Escamillo accepts the challenge and the two lock in combat, but moments into the struggle the toreador snaps his knife on a rock. Don José, his dagger at Escamillo's throat, is about to finish him off, when the smugglers, alarmed by the shot and the noise, rush back into the camp. Carmen throws herself between the two men, holding Don José away from the bullfighter. Regaining his composure, Escamillo thanks Carmen for saving his life, and with his usual bravado invites them all to the bullfights in Seville. Gazing at Carmen he adds, "Anyone who loves me will be there." As Escamillo turns to leave, Dancairo and Remendado have to restrain Don José from going after him.

The gypsies are once again about to depart when Remendado notices someone moving in the shadows, trying to hide between the rocks. Moving quickly, he grabs Micaela and brings her into the open. "Why are you here?" Don José demands. "I have come to bring you back to your poor weeping mother, who is calling for her son." Carmen ridicules Don José, taunting him and urging him to leave. He accuses her of wanting to run after Escamillo, and overwhelmed with jealousy, Don José at first refuses to go with Micaela. But when the girl tells him his mother is dying and wants to see him once more, he realizes that he must go.

Just as Don José and Micaela are about to leave, Escamillo is heard singing the Toreador Song in the distance. Carmen is drawn irresistibly in the direction of his voice, but José blocks her path, and darkly warns her that they will meet again. He and Micaela finally begin the long climb down one side of the mountain while the smugglers, with Carmen, head down the other side of the pass to complete their night's work.

ACT IV

A large excited crowd mills around outside the arena in Seville. It is the day of the bullfights. Under a bright sun vendors, soldiers, peasants, aristocrats, beautiful women, all in their best clothes, mingle near the gates, waiting for the bullfighters' procession to enter the square. Zuniga and a fellow officer accompany Frasquita and Mercedes down the street toward the stadium. The streets are jammed, and shouts of glee herald the quadrille (a procession of toreadors) as it approaches. The chulos, banderilleros, and picadors lead the procession, all brilliantly garbed in resplendent outfits. Cheers and shouts of "Bravo" reach a crescendo when Escamillo marches in, Carmen beside him, magnificently dressed and glowing with pride. Escamillo draws Carmen aside and tells her that she will soon have reason to be very proud of him. She tells him how totally in love with him she is and he strides confidently into the arena, followed closely by the mayor and the rest of the crowd.

Carmen remains outside, and Frasquita and Mercedes warn her, "Don't stay out here. Don José was seen today; look over there!" Carmen sees him lurking nearby, but tells her friends not to worry because she is not afraid of him. Frasquita and Mercedes caution her to be careful, and then go into the arena.

As soon as she is alone, a distraught Don José approaches meekly, humbly. He begs her to renew their love: "There is still time for us," he pleads. Carmen tells him that what he asks is impossible because she no longer loves him.

Don José keeps pleading, offering to do anything, be anything, if she will only love him, but Carmen is unmoved and contemptuous. Suddenly from inside the arena, cheers for Escamillo resound. As Carmen, exhilarated, moves to enter the arena, Don José desperately grabs her. "You're not going to Escamillo!" he shouts.

"I love him!" Carmen screams.

As the stadium crowd again cheers for Escamillo, Don José realizes that he has lost Carmen and threatens to kill her. Her answer is: "Stab me then, or let me go! This ring you once gave me—take it!" and she removes a ring from her finger and flings it at him.

Don José, crazed, rushes at her, knife in hand, and stabs her. As she slumps to the ground, the cheers for Escamillo again resound, in contrast to the hushed silence of the few passersby who gather around as Don José throws himself beside Carmen's lifeless body sobbing, "Arrest me! I killed her! I killed my adored Carmen!"

DER ROSENKAVALIER

Opera in Three Acts
by
RICHARD STRAUSS

Première: Konigliches Opernhaus, Dresden, January 26, 1911

IN THE 1840s, during the reign of Maria Theresa, the life of the aristocracy was, as in most courts of the time, riddled with intrigue and frivolity and adorned by an opulence of dress, its elegant manners ordered by rigid, snobbish notions of hierarchy. The further back one's noble lineage could be traced, the higher one's status in the social firmament. For the newly rising class of wealthy bourgeoisie, the only way to enter the upper ranks of the nobility was through marriage.

ACT I

One day in the elaborate and beautifully appointed bedroom of the Feldmarschallin von Werdenberg, the early morning sun streams in upon the bed where she is enjoying her young lover Octavian, while her husband is out hunting. Playfully, they exchange words of love, oblivious to the world around them. A young black page comes in carrying a tray with breakfast.

Octavian discreetly disappears for a moment while the child places the tray on a table and quietly withdraws.

When Octavian comes out of hiding, the Marschallin lightly chides him for having left his sword in view. They begin to breakfast happily, tenderly touching each other. Suddenly her mood changes as she recalls that during the night she dreamt her husband returned early from hunting. Octavian is outraged that she could dream of her husband while in his arms and she tries to placate him with assurances that she is not responsible for her dreams. But then, does she actually hear noises in the courtyard or is she just imagining them? They soon realize that the noises are all too real. Octavian grabs his clothes and sword trying frantically to find an escape route. Desperate, he disappears into the Marschallin's dressing room. She now hears the voice more clearly, and laughingly assures him that it is not her husband the Feldmarschal at all but an unexpected visit by a cousin, the vulgar Baron Ochs, who, a moment later, barges into her room despite the servants' efforts to restrain him. Octavian reappears disguised in the clothes of a chambermaid.

Ochs, literally throwing his weight around, shoves the servants out of his way and obsequiously greets the Marschallin, all the while casting covetous glances at the disguised Octavian. After the usual opening pleasantries the overbearing Baron states the purpose of his visit. He has chosen a bride. She is Fraulein Faninal, the pretty young daughter of Herr von Faninal, a wealthy burgher who has just been raised to nobility by Her Majesty.

Calling him "Mariandel," the Marschallin orders the disguised Octavian out of the room. But all the while he talks about his bride-to-be, the Baron refuses to let Mariandel go and, in whispered asides, tries to set up an assignation.

The Marschallin is highly amused and has a difficult time restraining her laughter.

At last Baron Ochs comes to the point. "I have come to you, dearest cousin, to ask your advice; as you know, I must send a representative to Fraulein Faninal to present the silver rose as a pledge of love. I ask Your Grace to recommend a cavalier to make the presentation. I will also need the help of your notary to advise on the marriage contract."

The Marschallin agrees to consider his requests, all the while trying to get rid of him. The majordomo, responding to her call, announces that a crowd is waiting in the antechamber to meet with her during her morning audience. While she prepares to receive the supplicants, vendors, and staff, Ochs shamelessly continues his pursuit of the "chambermaid," Mariandel, and asks whether she has ever had a tête-à-tête with a cavalier. The Marschallin mockingly accuses the Baron of lecherous behavior not befitting a betrothed man. His defense is an account of his many conquests with his own servants, and he concludes by asking if he may have the pretty chambermaid to serve in his new household.

This request gives the Marschallin an idea and she orders the "chambermaid" to fetch a particular locket. Knowing that the locket contains his portrait, Octavian quietly cautions her but she is adamant. "Here is the man who will present the rose for you!" she tells Ochs. "He's my cousin, Count Octavian, younger brother of Marquis Rofrano!"

Ochs stares at the portrait and seeing the resemblance between the Count and "Mariandel" comes to the conclusion that the maid is probably an illegitimate offspring now in the family's employ. "I too have an illegitimate son whom I employ as my valet!" he boasts.

By now the Marschallin has heard enough and orders her "chambermaid" to leave and the levée to commence.

The room fills. Retainers and various petitioners clamor for the Marschallin's attention: three orphans, a milliner, an animal seller, an Italian singer with a flutist, the notary, the chef, and two Italian intriguers, Valzacchi and Annina. The orphans beg for alms while the animal seller extols the merits of his exotic animals, and Valzacchi tries and fails to interest her in scandalous gossip. During all of this the hairdresser is trying his best to finish her coiffure, while the Italian singer and his flutist prepare to perform. At last the singer launches into a melancholy Italian love song. Three of the Baron's oafish servants, among them his son, Leopold, come into the room carrying the case with the rose. As the concert proceeds, Ochs begins to discuss his impending betrothal with the notary. The Baron has very unorthodox monetary plans, which the notary tries to set straight, explaining that it is the groom who gives the bride a gift, not the other way round. Undaunted, the Baron continues to enumerate his demands, and when the notary tries to explain once again that what he wants is not permitted by law, Ochs explodes, effectively stopping the Italian singer in mid-verse. The Marschallin looks into a hand mirror and disconsolately tells her hairdresser that today he has made an old woman of her. Then she orders the majordomo to remove the whole crowd.

While the footmen are ushering people out, Valzacchi and Annina slink over to the Baron and offer him their services. "We know everything about everyone," they say. But when Ochs asks about the Marschallin's chambermaid, Mariandel, they are momentarily dumbfounded; pretending to know who he means, they offer to find out everything about her. Ochs gives the Marschallin the case containing the silver rose.

"I will be certain that Count Octavian delivers it for you," she says graciously, "but now, my cousin, you must leave me, for I must go to church!"

The Count makes his obeisance and leaves, taking the notary with him and trailed by his footmen, Valzacchi and Annina.

The Marschallin is alone and her mood has now turned melancholy. Sighing, she laments the ways of the world and particularly how this wicked, wretched cousin will get a pretty young girl right out of the cloister and all her money as well. Gazing at herself in the mirror, she regrets her own lost youth.

Octavian returns, dressed in his own clothes and riding boots. "You are unhappy," he notes, and playfully tries to tease her out of her gloom, reminding her that her husband is still away. He grows passionate, but she is not in an amorous mood.

Gently, she warns him not to be like other men, causing him to become only more possessive. She moves away from him again. "All things pass, Octavian. Sooner or later our love will fade too!" These words upset her young lover and tears well up in his eyes. "Time," she tells him, "is all around us, and when we grow older it becomes more and more oppressive. Often I get up in the middle of the night and stop all the clocks. Today or tomorrow you will leave me for another woman. To make it easier for both of us, we must treat our love lightly."

Octavian does not want to believe her and desperately tries to assure her she is wrong.

She cuts him short. "I must go to church now. Later you can ride alongside my carriage. Now you must leave."

"As you command," says Octavian, and he departs abruptly.

Realizing that she has not even kissed him goodbye, she grows agitated and calls to her footmen to get the Count to return for a final word. But the footmen report that they are too late, for the Count has already galloped away. The Marschallin rings again for her small black page. "Take this case containing the silver rose to Count Octavian. He will know what to do." When the servant has left, the Marschallin looks sadly into her mirror.

ACT II

Two days later, the lavish palace of the *nouveau riche* Faninal is abuzz with excitement as everyone awaits the arrival of the cavalier bearing the silver rose from Baron Ochs. Herr von Faninal must leave the house, as custom demands that he be absent when his daughter receives the rose. He still lingers, however, to tell Sophie once again what a great, solemn, and holy day it is. Finally, as his majordomo hurries him away, Faninal declares to his daughter, "When I return, I will bring your future husband!"

Sophie's duenna, Marianne, looks out the window and gives the girl, who is having difficulty composing herself, a running account of the cavalier's approach. Soon excited shouts of "Rofrano! Rofrano!" can be heard from the street below. "He is getting out of the coach!" Marianne reports. "He's dressed all in silver and looks like an angel!"

To calm herself, Sophie tries to pray, but she is too excited.

Soon the doors of the hall swing open to admit Octavian, followed by his retinue of footmen and servants. Sophie goes into a deep curtsy as the splendidly clad cavalier strides toward her and puts the silver rose into her hand. For a moment, the two young people stare steadily at each other, speechless. Then Octavian remembers what he is supposed to say. "I have the honor of presenting the rose of love on behalf of my cousin to you, most highborn bride!"

Graciously, she accepts this symbol of betrothal, noting that its scent is as beautiful as a live rose, and then gives it to Marianne to put in its case. Octavian's servants leave. The footmen place three chairs in the center of the room for Octavian, Sophie, and Marianne, who take their places rather stiffly.

"I know you well, my cousin," Sophie begins. "Each night I read of Austria's nobility so that I will know my future relatives. I know you are seventeen and your full name is Octavian Maria Erenreich Bonaventura Fernand Hyacinth but your friends call you Quinquin!" Stunned by her beauty and amused by her guileless innocence, Octavian urges her to talk on. In her ingenuousness Sophie tells him that no other gentleman has pleased her as much as he.

They are interrupted by the arrival of Faninal leading the intended groom, Baron Ochs, and his ragtag retinue into the hall. The Baron looks at his bride-to-be as if she were some object for sale, complimenting her on her dainty wrist but noting that she is still a bit thin. Octavian watches this boorish lecher with mounting anger. Greeting his rose-bearer, the Baron comments snidely about the resemblance to his illegitimate sister, the chambermaid Mariandel!

Refreshments are served. Ochs's behavior grows ever cruder. He tries to embrace Sophie and makes her sit on his lap. The young girl protests, repelled by his actions. "We are still strangers, sir," she says.

Octavian slowly seethes and mutters his wish to attack the Baron with his sword, while poor Sophie tries valiantly to evade Ochs's clutches. Ochs only finds her resistance appealing. Oblivious to the feelings of Sophie, Herr von Faninal and Marianne express their delight at this nobleman, so simple, so unaffected, so terribly funny!

The notary and his clerk arrive bearing a sheaf of legal papers. "My son-in-law," says Faninal, "there is some business we should attend to if you please!"

The Baron agrees with alacrity and, as he makes his way to the door, leeringly tells Octavian that if he wishes, he may make eyes at Sophie. "It would be useful if you would 'loosen' her up for me!" he says. He then instructs the awed Faninal to be sure he stays the prescribed three paces behind him as they leave the room.

"You're not going to marry that oaf, are you?" Octavian asks.

"Never!" Sophie responds.

The Majordomo bursts in to report that members of the Baron's retinue are drunk and attacking the female servants. In response to his cries, Marianne rushes out to help, leaving Sophie and Octavian alone.

"I will help you," Octavian offers, "but for the sake of both of us, you must remain steadfast!" Within minutes they have confessed their love for each other and are kissing.

They are so enraptured that they fail to notice as Valzacchi and Annina enter the room, grab them and hold them fast. The Italian schemers call for the Baron to come see his fiancée in the arms of another man. Quickly Ochs charges in. Terrified, Sophie clings to Octavian.

The Baron does not seem all that much put out. "What do you have to say about this, my dear?" he asks.

Gallantly, Octavian steps forward to declare, "Sir, there has been a change in plans! The young lady does not care for you and will not marry you!"

The Baron mocks the very young cavalier and refuses to take him seriously. But Octavian persists and finally in frustration challenges the Baron to a duel. Undaunted the Baron says it would be inconvenient at that moment, since the notary is waiting for the marriage contract to be signed. Octavian persists with his insults and challenges, and the Baron continues to sidestep them, only drawing his sword when the tempestuous and frus-

77

trated youth rushes at him. Octavian's sword scratches the Baron's arm, whereupon the Baron screams for help. His band of riffraff clumsily try to attack Octavian, who deftly fends them off. Faninal's servants rush in from all sides to aid the wounded Baron.

In the midst of all this commotion Herr von Faninal returns and is presented with a spiteful version of the events by Annina and Valzacchi. Beside himself with shame and remorse that this could happen in his palace, he rushes to the Baron's side, ordering his servants to fetch a doctor. He tells Octavian that better behavior was expected of him but the youth denies responsibility, offering to explain later what occurred. To complete her father's misery, Sophie tells him that she no longer considers the Baron her intended. Faninal is beside himself, and shouts at his daughter that she will marry the Baron. But she is adamant in her refusal, threatening to answer no to the priest. Finally, Marianne gently pushes her from the room.

The injured Baron is lying on a couch surrounded by footmen, the doctor, the Italians, and the maids. Faninal embraces the Baron (which causes him to howl with pain) and then grovels before him begging forgiveness for the injuries. But Ochs is not to be placated; he curses Octavian and vows vengeance, cries echoed by his ragged retinue. A servant comes in with wine and Ochs drains it greedily; he is getting bored. He orders the doctor to leave and has another glass of wine.

Stealing quietly up to his bed, Annina delivers a letter that says, "Sir: I'm free tomorrow evening. I'm Mariandel, the shy chambermaid of Her Highness. I hope you've not forgotten me. I am waiting for an answer!" The Baron's spirits now lift again, and he orders the messenger to return after dinner for his written reply. Annina holds out her hand with the reminder that the messenger's reward should not be forgotten, but the Baron ignores her. She leaves in a barely restrained fit of anger. Draining yet another glass of wine, the Baron, his happy mood restored, hums his favorite waltzes.

ACT III

The next evening, in a private room at the seedy inn Ochs has selected for his assignation with Mariandel, Valzacchi, unsavory as ever, is busy putting the final touches on Annina's disguise as a widow. Soon they are joined by Octavian, who is again dressed as Mariandel. The cavalier throws a purse of money to the Italians, who kiss his hand effusively. They are joined by a number of strange-looking men whom Valzacchi plants in various hiding places behind sliding wall panels, at windows, in a floor trap door, and in the fireplace. To test the effect, Valzacchi claps his hands and like jacks-in-the-box their ghostly faces pop into the room. A clock strikes and Octavian hurries out. Then, a waiter comes in and lights the candles. The preparations are complete.

Baron Ochs, his arm in a sling, enters escorting "Mariandel." The Baron's stinginess asserts itself once more as he extinguishes most of the candles and dismisses the waiters and the innkeeper, explaining that his personal valet will do all the serving. Finally, with all the servants gone, Ochs grabs "Mariandel," telling her how much he wants her, and while "she" tries to elude him he shamelessly chases her around the room. Suddenly, looking closely at Mariandel's face, and again struck by her resemblance to Octavian, he is reminded of his injury and clutches at his wounded arm. To comfort himself, he removes his wig. He greedily eats his soup and tries to ply "Mariandel" with wine. Finally, he tries to embrace her. A trap door opens and one of the strange faces appears and quickly disappears. He is shaken. Was it real? Or does he have a fevered brain? "Mariandel" distracts him with a maudlin melancholy that makes her seem like an unresisting target. He begins to loosen her bodice. Again, those ghostly faces, to which "Mariandel" appears to be oblivious, pop out at him. Terrified by the apparitions, he rings for help. In charges Annina in her widow's disguise, followed by a troop of children who begin a chant of "Papa! Papa!" while she denounces the befuddled Baron as her long lost husband.

When Valzacchi, the landlord, and some waiters rush in, the Baron appeals to them for help, but Annina's accusations gain more sympathy. Ochs can bear no more and, despite Valzacchi's warnings, he opens the window and calls for the police. Meanwhile Octavian dispatches Valzacchi to bring Faninal, while Leopold steals away with the bright idea of fetching the Marschallin to protect the Baron.

"Nobody move!" orders the Commissioner of Police as he enters the fray. Peremptorily, he asks who Ochs is. Valzacchi says maybe he is the Baron Leicherau, and then again maybe he isn't, which of course makes Ochs choke with rage.

The Commissioner turns to Octavian, still disguised as Mariandel. "Who are you and what are you doing here?" he asks.

Ochs, seeing a possibly embarrassing situation, hastens to give a respectable explanation. "She is my fiancée, the daughter of Faninal, and we were dining together!"

Herr von Faninal, forcing his way through the crowd at the door, hears his name and says, "Here I am."

"Then this," the Commissioner says, pointing to Mariandel, "must be your daughter."

Faninal is outraged that this lower-class creature could be called his daughter. He asks that Sophie be summoned from the carriage.

Annina and the children continue to chant their accusations that the Baron is husband and father while he searches frantically for his wig.

Faninal pours out his grief to Sophie, who, of course, is delighted by the scandal which has put an end to the betrothal. But it has all been too much for Faninal; he collapses and has to be carried to another room.

Ochs tries to leave but the Commissioner stops him and clears the room of everyone except Annina, the children, "Mariandel," and of course, the Baron, who in an effort to get "Mariandel" to corroborate his story to the Commissioner tries to bribe her with the promise of marriage. "Mariandel" now whispers something to the Commissioner and he escorts her to a curtained alcove behind which she disappears. The Baron is almost apoplectic as he watches while "her" clothes fly over the curtain piece by piece. He would rush over, but the constables hold him back.

All comes to a sudden halt when the innkeeper enters to announce the arrival of "Her Most Noble Highness, the Feldmarschallin!" and everyone snaps to attention.

The Baron, of course, claims that his noble cousin has come to his aid, and, his composure restored and not wishing any further complications from Sophie or her father, tries to block the door from Faninal's chamber. He is so preoccupied with this that he does not notice Octavian, now in his own clothes, emerging from behind the curtain.

Despite Ochs's efforts to keep the door to Faninal's room closed, it soon bursts open and two of the servants clear the way for Sophie, who tells the Baron she and her father will have nothing further to do with him, and haughtily goes back through the door.

The Baron tries to follow her but is barred by the footmen. "All right," he shouts through the door, "I'll forgive you that impertinence."

"To save *any* dignity," the Marschallin counsels him, "you should leave!" and turning to the Commissioner she tells him, "The whole thing was nothing more than a charade!" Satisfied with her explanation, the police withdraw. Sophie, having just re-entered the room, is crushed; was the *whole* thing a charade?

With the Commissioner gone, the thick-skinned Ochs again pursues his quest for Sophie but the Marschallin asks Octavian to "persuade" him otherwise. Ochs is amazed to see him here but the Marschallin coolly says, "Certainly you know the Count Rofrano." The Baron begins to put the pieces together. Slyly, he says, "I don't know what to think."

The Marschallin tells him, "In such a case it best befits a gentleman to refrain from thinking." The Baron does not take the hint. He offers to forget the whole thing if his cousin will intercede for him with Faninal.

She says, "Don't you know when enough is enough? It's all over now!" Before the Baron can react, the innkeeper, followed by waiters, maids, and musicians, storms in, demanding that the beleaguered Ochs pay his bill. With his "valet," he forces his way through the crowd, out of the room and into the night with the horde close behind him.

Sophie, Octavian, and the Marschallin are alone. "Octavian, go to the young lady and do as your heart bids you!" says the Marschallin.

The cavalier obeys. Sophie is tense and upset, worried about the impression she and the evening's events have made on the great lady, and anxious about her father. She says she must go to him. Octavian restrains her, declaring his love, and Sophie, sensing something she does not really understand, tells him to go to the Marschallin instead.

"Today or tomorrow he will leave me for another woman." The Marschallin repeats the words she so prophetically uttered a few days before.

Octavian stands between the two women, torn, unable to decide which way to turn.

The Marschallin decides for him. She asks Sophie if she loves Octavian, and the girl's embarrassment is answer enough. "I think Octavian knows how to help your pale cheeks, and I will ask your father to ride home with me in my carriage; that should make him feel better." The two young lovers are rather awed by her generosity, and she leaves the room with a quiet sigh. She had not expected that her promise to let Octavian go would be called upon so soon. "He will be as happy as any man," she concludes. "So be it!"

Octavian and Sophie, gripped by passion, fall into each other's arms swearing eternal devotion. Soon the Marschallin returns escorted by a beaming, contented, and much recovered Faninal, who comments, "That's how young people are." "Yes! Yes!" the Marschallin agrees. Arm in arm they leave the inn. Softly and happily Sophie and Octavian repeat their vows of love and follow the others.

The room is dark and empty, until the Marschallin's little black page enters, candle in hand, and appears to be searching for something. He finds it, a handkerchief, picks it up and silently tiptoes out of the room.

TURANDOT

Opera in Three Acts
by
GIACOMO PUCCINI
Première: La Scala, Milan, April 25, 1926

ACT I

OUTSIDE THE Imperial Palace in Ancient Peking, a large crowd gathers. At the top of the steps high above them a Mandarin official reads a proclamation: "People of Peking! According to decree, our Princess Turandot will marry only a man of royal blood who can solve her riddles. Any who try and fail must be beheaded. Today the Prince of Persia has failed the test and so he will be executed at moonrise!"

The news excites the bloodthirst of the unruly throng, and growing impatient for the execution, they surge forward, only to be pushed back by the guards.

A young girl, Liu, cries out for help. Her poor old master, the blind, exiled Tartar king, Timur, has been thrown to the ground. A young man in the crowd rushes to her aid and, upon helping the old man up, cries out happily, "Father! I have found you!" Timur too is overjoyed to find his son alive, but Calaf cautions him to be quiet, for they are hunted and always in danger. Timur then introduces Liu, the loving, kind young slave who has

83

made it possible for him to survive. Calaf wonders at her courage and self-sacrifice.

"I saved him because once when we were in the palace you smiled at me," she tells Calaf.

As the moon rises, the condemned Prince of Persia is ceremoniously led into the square. Although calling for his death but a few moments before, the crowd is moved by the Prince's handsome face and pale, hopeless demeanor, and they call to the Princess to be merciful. Calaf too calls for mercy, appalled that anyone could be so cruel. The words die on his lips as Turandot appears on the palace balcony, a dazzling vision of beauty and imperious splendor. As the crowd falls prostrate before her, she heedlessly signals that the execution is to proceed and disappears again behind the palace walls. She has sealed Calaf's fate as well, for he is smitten. In silent ecstasy, he stares after her.

"My son, what are you doing?" Timur worriedly asks when he realizes what has happened to his son.

Deaf to the pleas of Liu and Timur and to the horrifying last cry of the Prince of Persia as he is executed, Calaf declares his determination to woo the Princess. He runs to strike the gong that announces each new quest for Turandot, but before he can reach it three of the Emperor's ministers, Ping, Pang, and Pong, stop him. "Go away!" they warn. "This is a place of butchery. Go away, we have buried enough of our own men, we don't need foreigners to lose their lives for this Princess!"

Calaf is obdurate and demands that he be allowed to pass so that he may hit the gong. As they argue, three of the Princess's ladies in waiting appear on the balcony and order the ministers to stop the commotion, for it is the hour of their lady's repose.

Calaf is only further inflamed by thoughts of this icy Princess. Ping, Pang, and Pong, united with Liu and Timur, again plead with him to give up the fatal quest, and their arguments are joined by ghostly voices from the wall where sit the grisly heads of the failed suitors. Calaf, lost in visions of Turandot, brushes off all their arguments. Not even the sight of the executioner adding the head of the Prince of Persia to the ghastly array upon the wall deters him.

Liu, unable to bear it, passionately begs Calaf to reconsider for her sake: "Think of how far I have walked always with you in my heart. If you are executed your father and I shall die in exile! Have mercy!"

Calaf is compassionate, but unyielding. "Don't cry, Liu. You must guide my father in his exile. This I ask of you!"

The ministers try to hold him back. Calaf breaks free. "Not even divine force can stop me," he cries. The crowd returns, urging him on so they may have still another victim, and Calaf, sensing glory, flings himself at the gong and hits it three times while he intones the magical name, "Turandot! Turandot! Turandot!"

ACT II

In a pavilion of the Imperial Palace, the ministers Ping, Pang, and Pong meet, Pong to prepare the wedding and Pang the funeral. Ruefully, they lament what has become of their beloved China since Turandot has played her game of riddles. "In this year alone, thirteen men have tried to solve her riddles and thirteen have died. We have become Ministers of Execution!" Longingly, they dream of returning to their beautiful peaceful homes far from this palace where madmen continue to come only to be executed by Turandot.

Outside, the noisy crowd demands that the proceedings commence so that they may see another trial and another execution. Invoking the gods for help, Ping, Pang, and Pong pray that they may celebrate a wedding that will restore peace to China. But the noise of the crowd, the drums and trumpets heralding the ceremony of riddles bring them back to sad reality. Reluctantly, they leave to witness the proceedings.

In the courtyard the crowd watches as the wise men, carrying the sealed scrolls with the answers to the riddles, mount the palace stairs and take their places. Seated on his throne above all the others, the venerable old Emperor presides. In an ancient quavering voice he tells of the terrible power of his scepter that now drips with blood. Three times he warns Calaf to withdraw and save his life, and three times Calaf refuses. He is willing to gamble his life and insists to be put to the test. Finally resigned to this suitor's determination, the Emperor orders the ceremony to proceed.

Turandot comes forward to tell a tale that explains her bloodthirsty stance. "Thousands of years ago, my ancestor the Princess Lou-Ling ruled in this very place. It was a time of war and the Empire was conquered and Lou-Ling was captured." She looks coldly at Calaf. "It was a man like you who ravaged her and killed her. And to revenge her, I have sworn that no man shall ever possess me. Do not tempt fate, stranger. There are three riddles, and only one death!"

Undeterred, Calaf retorts, "There are three riddles and one life."

Turandot poses the first riddle. "There is an iridescent phantom that flies through darkest night above the black, infinite masses; everyone calls to it. At sunrise it vanishes but is reborn in every heart. Each night it is reborn, and each day it dies!"

Gleefully Calaf cries out, "Turandot, it is hope!"

The wise men unfurl their scrolls and confirm that the first answer is correct. The crowd murmurs in surprise.

Dryly, Turandot says, "Yes, hope that always deludes!" She presents the second riddle. "It burns like a flame, but it is not a flame. If you lose faith or die it grows cold, but think of conquering and it excites. It glows like the setting sun!"

As Calaf hesitates, the Emperor, Timur, Liu, and the people all encourage him and finally he answers, "Princess! It is blood!"

When the wise men confirm this answer Turandot grows angry and quickly poses the third and final riddle: "There is ice that sets you aflame but grows still colder from the heat of your heart. If it wishes to free you, it will enslave you. If it accepts you as slave, it will make you king. Come, stranger, I see you blanching with fear. You are lost. What is the ice that sets you afire?"

Calaf looks at her and his momentary desolation turns to triumphant joy. Proudly he answers, "You cannot escape me . . . for in victory . . . you are mine, and my fire will melt you. The answer is . . . 'Turandot.'"

His third answer is confirmed and the people cheer wildly.

Turandot begs her father, the Emperor, not to give her to this stranger, but he rejects her plea. The stranger won her hand fairly and his oath is sacred. She turns to Calaf and demands to know how he can take her when she is so unwilling.

"I solved three riddles to win you," Calaf tells her. "I will give you but one. You do not know my name. Discover what it is before sunrise and I shall be willing to die!"

Turandot agrees. And as the crowd hails his generosity, the Emperor hopes that by dawn he can call this stranger his son.

ACT III

It is night. Throughout the city, the heralds spread Turandot's royal decree: find the name of the stranger or die. Their voices echo and re-echo the

order. The identity of the stranger must be found. No one in Peking shall
sleep this night.

Calaf roams the streets, confident that he can keep his secret, but waiting
impatiently for the night's stars to disappear and for the sun to rise so he
can claim the Princess.

The ministers Ping, Pang, and Pong approach him accusingly. Because
of him death threatens every door. "What do you want?" they demand. "If it
is love, take these!" Beautiful women surround Calaf, dancing seductively.
While the ministers extol their charms, Calaf pushes them away.

The ministers ask, "Then you want riches?" and produce baskets of gold
and jewels.

Again, Calaf refuses.

A crowd has gathered, and led by the ministers, they beg the stranger to
flee so the cruel Turandot will not take revenge on them.

"All I want is Turandot," Calaf cries.

There is a ripple of excitement in the crowd as some soldiers drag in
Timur and Liu, shouting, "Now we shall find out the name."

Calaf rushes forward. "They know nothing."

But Ping remembers that he saw them with the Prince and sends for
Turandot. Turandot arrives and orders Timur to reveal the name, but Liu
intercedes. "I am the only one who knows his name."

Calaf rushes to protect her but is seized and held by the soldiers.

Ping orders Liu to speak but she refuses. He orders the soldiers to twist
her arms. Although she screams with pain, she says nothing. When she can
no longer bear it, she collapses.

Turandot is coldly curious and orders a halt to the torture. "What makes
you so brave?" she asks.

"Love!" Liu replies. "Though my silence gives him *your* love, my suffering is joy, because I am able to give him this gift." Turandot's temporary
wonder quenched, she orders the torture resumed, and, obediently, Ping
calls for Pu-Tin-Pao, the executioner.

Liu can no longer trust herself to remain silent and she turns to Turandot.
"Listen to me." Everyone waits expectantly. "You too will love the Prince,
and I will die before dawn so that *he* may win!" With these words, Liu grabs
a dagger from one of the soldiers and plunges it into her own heart. Then
she staggers toward Calaf and falls dead at his feet. Turandot covers her
face with a veil while Timur kneels beside Liu's lifeless body begging her to
rise. Some people lift the corpse and carry it away. Even the cynical Ping,

Pang, and Pong are moved, and the people pray to Liu to forgive them as they follow the procession.

The Prince and Turandot are left alone, and stare at each other across a distance. "Princess of death and ice," he calls, "remove your veil and look at the blood you have shed!" Impulsively he rushes toward her and rips the veil from her face.

"How dare you! I am the daughter of heaven." She draws back, confused and frightened, but still threatening. "No man will ever possess me or repeat the crime visited on my ancestor."

"Your coldness is a lie."

"Do not touch me. It is a sacrilege."

"But your kiss gives me eternity." He takes her in his arms and kisses her passionately.

Her iron bearing dissolves. "I am lost," she whispers. "You have won."

Ecstatically, Calaf murmurs of her warmth and his love.

She weeps, sweetly resigned. "My glory is ended." Quietly she tells him that when she first saw him she was afraid, for in his eyes she saw signs of a hero. "I hated you but loved you also. I was torn by two equal fears—to defeat you or be defeated by you. Stranger, you have won. Do not seek greater victory, but go with your secret."

But Calaf, confident of her love, is willing to die if she wishes. He tells her, "My name is Calaf and I am the son of Timur!"

Recognizing these hated Tartar names, Turandot draws herself up, once again haughty and ferocious. "Your name . . . Now I know your name." As the rays of dawn begin to appear, the trumpets signal the hour of trial, and Turandot bids Calaf come with her before the people of Peking.

"You have won," he says.

Outside the Imperial Palace a large crowd praises the Emperor. Turandot mounts the stairs and her voice rings out. "Father, I have learned the stranger's name." She turns to look down at Calaf and her voice turns sweet. "His name is . . . Love." Calaf rushes up the staircase and he and Turandot embrace as the crowd rejoices.

CAVALLERIA RUSTICANA

Opera in One Act
by
PIETRO MASCAGNI
Première: Teatro Costanzi, Rome, May 17, 1890

"OH, LOLA, with the fair skin and cherry lips, how happy the man who can kiss you. I would not enter heaven itself if you were not there." The sounds of this romantic serenade float at dawn through the streets of a Sicilian village. It is Easter Sunday and slowly the empty town square fills with villagers on their way to church. On one side of the square is the wineshop and dwelling of Mamma Lucia, mother of the ardent serenader, Turiddu. She comes out of the house on her way to church but is intercepted by Santuzza, a troubled young woman, who wants to know where Turiddu is. Mamma Lucia does not want to answer the girl but Santuzza pleads so importunately that Mamma Lucia finally tells her that Turiddu went to another village, Francofonte, in order to bring back some wine. Santuzza tells her that is impossible, for he was seen in the village during the night. This agitates Mamma Lucia, who knows Turiddu has not been home, and she invites Santuzza into her house to discuss it further. But the younger woman unhappily reminds Mamma Lucia that she has been excommunicated, and in the custom of the village may not enter the houses of the faithful.

Their conversation is interrupted by a boisterous crowd that makes its way into the square following Alfio, the carter. He is a cheerful man who tells of the joys of his life and his love. "To crack the whip and hear the horses stamp, let it rain or snow, I don't care. Lola, my faithful wife, waits for me. It's Easter and I am home." Turning to Mamma Lucia, he asks, "Do you have some of that old wine?" When she says that her son Turiddu has gone to get some more, Alfio is surprised. "Just this morning I saw him near my house."

"Really?" says Mamma Lucia.

Santuzza quickly hushes her and Alfio announces that he must go get ready for church.

As he leaves, a group of people comes out of the church and in unison with the others in the square sings the praises of the Lord. In spite of having been excommunicated, Santuzza joins in the prayer. When it is over the crowd disperses, but Santuzza and Mamma Lucia remain behind.

"Why did you hush me?" Mamma Lucia demands.

Santuzza reminds her that before Turiddu left to be a soldier he had pledged his love to Lola, only to find her married to Alfio when he returned. "To ease the pain he turned to me," she continues, "but now Lola has stolen Turiddu back. She has betrayed Alfio and I am deprived of both love and honor."

Mamma Lucia is shocked and while Santuzza is still pleading with her to speak to Turiddu, she goes into the church to pray.

Turiddu arrives and is not too pleased to see Santuzza, who says they must talk. "Where were you last night?" she asks.

"In Francofonte!"

"That's a lie. Alfio saw you near his house."

"Are you trying to get me killed?" he demands.

They argue fiercely; he accuses her of spying on him, of not leaving him alone. Santuzza becomes defensive, begging him to forget about Lola and return to her.

Their fight is interrupted when Lola, beautifully clothed, enters the square. Seeing Turiddu she flirts with him, angering Santuzza even further. The women exchange a few cutting remarks. Turiddu is confused and torn. Obviously, he wants to go to church with Lola, but allows Santuzza to detain him. Lola shrugs and goes into the church. Santuzza resumes her relentless pleading, begging Turiddu not to abandon her. He is now furious with her and finally throws her to the ground as he rushes into the church.

She swears, "Betrayer, may you have a cursed Easter!"

As Santuzza picks herself up from the ground, Alfio returns to the square. "The Mass is almost over," she informs him. "But I have some news for you. While you were out working hard to earn money, your Lola was betraying you with another man—with Turiddu!"

Enraged, Alfio swears that if Santuzza is lying he will kill her, but when she convinces him that the story is true, he vows to take revenge before the day is over. As they leave the square, he declares, "Now my love has turned to hatred!"

Her anger spent, Santuzza is appalled at what she has done.

A solemn Easter calm has come over the square. The Mass has ended; the celebrants make their way out of the church. Mamma Lucia goes into her house while Lola and Turiddu linger in the square with some of the villagers. Turiddu invites the crowd to drink some wine. The glasses are passed around and while the villagers drink merrily, Lola and Turiddu surreptitiously flirt. Alfio appears and Turiddu offers him a glass of wine, but he contemptuously refuses.

"Your wine would turn to poison in my stomach."

In response to this challenge Turiddu vehemently spills his own wine. Tension fills the air and sensing trouble the villagers leave, taking Lola with them.

After a few terse remarks, the two men lock in a taut embrace and in the Sicilian tradition Turiddu accepts the challenge by biting Alfio's right ear.

"We understand each other well," Alfio says.

Turiddu, knowing his guilt, declares, "I would let you kill me, only that would leave Santuzza alone. Therefore I will have to kill you with my knife!"

Alfio coolly tells Turiddu that he will wait for him beyond the garden.

Turiddu calls his mother, who comes out of the house; he tells her that the wine was strong and that he must get some fresh air. "Before I go, Mamma, bless me as you did when I left to be a soldier, and promise that if I don't return you will become a mother to Santuzza, for I vowed to marry her." Mamma Lucia, confused and frightened, asks what he means. He dismisses his dramatic outburst, blaming it all on the wine. Kissing his mother again and again, he bids her farewell and runs off to face Alfio. Desperately, she starts to follow him but runs into Santuzza.

Santuzza throws her arms around Lucia. "Oh, Mamma, Mamma."

There is the ominous murmur of a crowd in the distance. Suddenly a woman's voice is heard in the square, her shouts piercing the quiet air of this Sicilian Easter with the words they have been dreading they would hear. "Turiddu's been killed! Turiddu's been killed!"

PAGLIACCI

Opera in a Prologue and Two Acts
by
RUGGIERO LEONCAVALLO
Première: Teatro dal Verme, Milan, May 21, 1892

PROLOGUE

A TRADITIONAL FORM of popular theater in Italy, the Commedia dell'Arte began in the sixteenth century when itinerant bands of actors traveled from village to town to castle, performing plays for the audiences that would collect at each place. The plots and the characters were always the same, but the actors improvised the dialogue, which would vary according to the nature of the audience, and possibly the mood of the actors. An actor might devote his life to perfecting his interpretation of one stock character, trying through this portrayal to illuminate the foibles of society and the contradictions of the human soul. The audience both savored the familiarity of these time-honored comedies and waited eagerly for any surprises a new performance might bring.

ACT I

Into the Calabrian village of Montalto one warm evening in 1860 comes a troupe of traveling actors. The villagers gather around excitedly as the brightly painted carts pull into the crossroad at the entrance to the village. Riding on the carts, or walking beside them, are Nedda, the prima donna; Canio, her husband, the head of the troupe; Beppe, another character actor; and Tonio, a hunchback.

As the villagers cheer, Canio calls for attention and asks them all to come to the evening's performance: "It will be a great show. Pagliaccio will get his revenge, Taddeo will tremble, and lots of intrigue will thicken the plot, but you must be here at eleven tonight."

Tonio tries to help Nedda down from the cart, but with a box on the ear, Canio knocks him away and takes her down himself.

"He will regret this," Tonio mutters to himself.

Some of the villagers linger and invite the players to join them for a drink in town. Canio and Beppe accept, but Tonio declines, saying he will stay to groom the donkey.

Laughingly, one of the villagers suggests that Tonio is remaining behind to woo Nedda. "My friends," Canio replies with unexpected vehemence, "on the stage I would treat such an event with humor. However, in real life the ending would not be so happy, for I love my wife." He kisses Nedda and leaves with the other villagers for the tavern.

Left alone, Nedda shudders at the fierce look in her husband's eyes, and hopes he does not suspect her secret passion. But she pushes away her fears and begins to enjoy the warmth of the midsummer sun. Watching a flock of birds high in the sky, she yearns for the freedom which they symbolize, and dreams of living in the beautiful and unknown land toward which she imagines they are flying.

Tonio, seeing her alone, pours out his heart to her. "I may be deformed, but I feel a passion burning inside every time you pass by. I love you, Nedda!" Mockingly, she laughs at him and threatens to tell Canio, but Tonio persists, demanding a kiss. Seeing he is about to seize her, she grabs a whip, and strikes him. He limps away, promising she will pay dearly for this.

A voice calls "Nedda." It is Silvio, her handsome young lover. She reproves him for taking such a risk, but he is unafraid. "I saw Canio and Beppe going to the tavern, so I knew the coast was clear."

Still shaken, Nedda tells him of her encounter with Tonio. "We must be careful of him. He loves me and should be feared."

Silvio, very much in love with Nedda, pleads with her to elope with him. "You have told me that you hate this wandering life, so leave it and flee with me instead!"

Thrilled by his words, she nonetheless begs him to stop. "Do not tempt me! Destiny is against us, but I shall always love you."

Silvio reminds her of the rapturous hours of their love, a love he can never forget. How can she? Finally, she yields to the promise of bliss and agrees to go away with him. Oblivious to everything, they passionately embrace.

Without being seen, Tonio has witnessed the entire exchange. He goes off to get Canio, and returns with him just as Silvio and Nedda, having agreed to meet at midnight, are about to part. Canio hears her say, "Tonight and forever," and he lunges toward them. Silvio jumps over a wall and Nedda tries to bar Canio's way. As Canio gives chase, Nedda prays for Silvio's safety and Tonio laughs.

She turns on him. "Well done, Tonio. You disgust me!"

Having lost his prey Canio returns raging, and demands to know the name of Nedda's lover. Drawing a knife, he threatens to cut her throat, but she courageously refuses to reveal the name. In a fury he moves to attack her, but is halted by Beppe, who cries out, "Stop! The church service is over and people are coming to see the play." To Nedda he says, "You'll have to explain later. Now go to your dressing room and prepare for the show."

Tonio counsels Canio to be calm: "Her lover will return. He may even come to see tonight's play. Then you can find out who he is." Beppe tells Canio it is time to get into costume and orders Tonio to bang the drum to call the audience.

Canio is overcome by Nedda's betrayal and can barely get himself together to dress for the play. Brokenly, he asks himself, "How am I to perform when my life is falling apart? But I must force myself to put on my costume and makeup. I am not a man! I am a clown and that is what people pay to see. I must laugh at my own tears. Laugh, Pagliaccio, laugh! Laugh at the sorrow that has ripped your heart!" Sobbing, he goes backstage to dress.

ACT II

As Tonio beats the drum, and Beppe sets out the benches, and Nedda passes the plate, the villagers congregate, jostling each other for the best seats. As the curtain rises, the audience is prepared to see Nedda as Columbine, Beppe as Harlequin, Canio as Pagliaccio, and Tonio as Taddeo, all standard roles of the Commedia dell'Arte.

Pacing nervously, Columbine informs the audience that her husband, Pagliaccio, won't be home until later and she wonders where that idiot Taddeo might be. From offstage Harlequin can be heard calling to his "beloved Columbine," bidding her open the window so they may be together. Taddeo enters and gives Columbine the chicken he has bought for her and declares his love, but she does not even bother to respond. Harlequin leaps onstage, stops Taddeo's adoring declaration, and kicks him out the door. Harlequin and Columbine happily settle down for an illicit romantic dinner, exchanging amorous banter.

Taddeo charges back in, reporting that Pagliaccio has returned early and is in a rage. Frightened, Harlequin leaps out the window, much to the delight of the audience, who applaud the lively action. To his departing form, Nedda calls softly, "Tonight and forever."

Hearing the same words she used earlier, Canio can almost not go on, but forcing himself to play Pagliaccio, he questions Columbine: "Why are there two place settings if you were alone?"

"Taddeo was here."

Canio's rage surges again. "Tell me the name of your lover. I have the right to know. Tell me!"

"Pagliaccio! Pagliaccio!" she lightly admonishes him, trying to bring him back to character.

"I am not Pagliaccio. I am not a clown, and I want vengeance!" he cries.

The audience is thrilled by the seeming reality of the act. Silvio is among them and on seeing what is happening onstage, he tries to get closer but has trouble getting through the crowd.

As the audience cheers, Canio rages, calling Nedda "a heartless woman." Desperately, Nedda tries to stay in character and responds to his fury with a song and dance to the almost audible relief of the audience. But this only further enrages Canio, who draws his knife. "Tell me his name! His name!"

Silvio, realizing the drama has come to life, draws his own dagger and rushes to the stage, but he is too late. Canio has brutally stabbed Nedda, bellowing, "You'll tell me his name with your dying breath." Horrified, the audience shouts at him to stop. Nedda gasps for Silvio to help her. But as Silvio jumps onto the stage, Canio turns and mortally wounds him.

As women cry and men rush to subdue him, Canio lets the knife fall, numbly turns to the audience and whispers, "The comedy is over."

MADAMA BUTTERFLY

Opera in Three Acts
by
GIACOMO PUCCINI
Première: La Scala, Milan, February 17, 1904

TOWARD THE end of the nineteenth century, following the "opening of
Japan" by Commodore Perry, ships of the American navy often came to call
at Japanese ports, putting in for periods of time which, while not prolonged,
allowed at least some of the men to pursue the sailor's tradition of "a girl in
every port." To an American sensibility, the Japanese way of life, with its
miniature gardens and ceremonial habits, seemed exotic and charming and
probably not quite real. It was all too easy to misunderstand the emotions
behind the courtesy and the giggles, and to treat the people as toys.

ACT I

On a hill overlooking the harbor of Nagasaki where his boat is anchored,
a young naval officer, Lieutenant Benjamin Franklin Pinkerton, inspects
the Japanese house he has just leased. He is briefly amused by the sliding
walls which open or enclose the rooms according to one's shifting needs and

desires. With him is the rental agent, Goro, who is also a marriage broker, and who has leased not only the house to the young naval officer, but also a bride—both for a period of 999 years, with the privilege of annulment at any time.

While Pinkerton waits for his bride to arrive for the wedding ceremony, the American consul, Sharpless, arrives. Goro brings them some refreshments and the two men toast, "America forever." As he enthuses to Sharpless about the beauty of the young geisha girl by whom he has been captivated, Pinkerton waxes merry about the offhand conditions of his marrying her. He says, "In this country, it seems both houses and agreements are elastic."

Sharpless warns him that the girl's feelings may not be as casual as his, but Pinkerton does not consider this seriously. Instead, he offers a final toast, "To the day I marry a real American wife."

The bird-like chatter of young girls heralds the arrival of the bridal party. As they come into view over the crest of the hill, Cio-Cio-San (Butterfly), the young bride, points to Pinkerton and tells her friends to kneel before him. Pinkerton greets the young girl kindly but with some condescension. Sharpless questions her to find out more about her. He learns that she is just fifteen years old, and that she comes from a respectable family, but since her father's death she has had to support herself and her mother by working as a geisha. The friendly interview is interrupted by Goro, who brings in Cio-Cio-San's relatives to meet the American bridegroom, a ceremony that Pinkerton treats with mock seriousness.

As everyone watches, Cio-Cio-San begins to unpack her belongings, emptying the voluminous, billowing sleeves of her kimono. To Pinkerton's amazement, handkerchiefs, a pipe, a sash, a mirror, a fan, and even a jar of rouge appear. When he asks her about a long sheath that she removes with particular solemnity, she tells him evasively that it is "sacred and private," but Goro whispers that it is the knife with which her father committed hara-kiri on order of the Emperor. As testimony to her love for him, Butterfly then tells Pinkerton she intends to embrace his God, despite the objections of her uncle who is a priest.

Goro quickly quiets the assembled crowd, for the Commissioner has arrived to perform the brief, formal ceremony. When it is over Cio-Cio-San's friends all exclaim, "Madam Butterfly!" She proudly corrects them: "Madam Pinkerton!"

Sharpless and the Commissioner take their leave as the guests toast the marriage. Suddenly the celebration is interrupted by the terrifying appearance of Cio-Cio-San's uncle, the Bonze, who storms in cursing her, and announces to the shocked family that Cio-Cio-San has visited the Christian mission and renounced her ancient faith. Urged on by his maledictions, her relatives disown her, and Pinkerton orders the entire angry family off his premises.

Butterfly's eyes are filled with tears, but her husband comforts her with loving words until she is happy again. In the peace of the moment Pinkerton becomes aware of some mumbling from another part of the house, and Butterfly explains that it is only Suzuki, her maid, saying her prayers. Soon Suzuki comes in to dress the bride in her white night dress, while Pinkerton, more than ever enamored of her loveliness and delicate compliance, eagerly waits. Suzuki bids them good night. Pinkerton slowly approaches his beautiful wife. Under the beautiful, calm, starlit sky, he courts her with tender loving words until she admits that she is his. Passionately he tells her that he loves her, and they vow to stay together forever.

ACT II

Three years have passed. Not long after their marriage Pinkerton left with his ship, leaving Cio-Cio-San in the caring hands of Suzuki. Now their money is almost gone, and Butterfly weeps often.

Suzuki prays quietly for the gods to make Butterfly happy again. Butterfly scoffs, calling the Japanese gods lazy. "My husband's God will answer our prayers more quickly." She chides Suzuki for not believing that Pinkerton will return, and to allay her fears says bravely, "One fine day there will be a thread of white smoke at the edge of the sea and a ship will carry Pinkerton back to me."

She dismisses Suzuki just as Goro and Sharpless arrive in the garden. While Goro waits outside, the American consul enters the house. Butterfly is delighted to see him and offers him a pipe, which he refuses. His mood is grim. Hesitantly he tells Butterfly that he has received a letter from Pinkerton. She is overjoyed.

"Tell me," she says, "do the robins nest less frequently in your country than they do here?"

He is startled, and she explains, "Because my husband promised to return to me when the robins nested again."

Sharpless is embarrassed. "I'm afraid I'm not really up on ornithology," he says, and tries to go back to the letter, but is interrupted by Goro, excitedly arriving with Yamadori, a wealthy man who wishes to marry Butterfly. Cuttingly, she rejects the offer, leaving no hope that she will change her mind. Escorted by Goro, Yamadori leaves angered and disappointed.

Sharpless now sits down determined to read Butterfly the letter. But she keeps interrupting him, happily interpreting each sentence as an assurance of Pinkerton's return, and Sharpless cannot bring himself to continue. He puts down the letter and asks her what she would do if Pinkerton should never return.

Her answer is simple and direct: "I could entertain people with my singing, or, better, I could die!"

Very touched, but not knowing what else to do, Sharpless suggests that she marry Yamadori. Infuriated she calls Suzuki to show the consul out, but as he turns to leave, Butterfly asks simply, "Has he forgotten me?" Abruptly she leaves the room, returning with a little boy, and asks, "Can he forget this too?" She begs the astonished consul to tell Pinkerton that a wonderful son awaits him.

Sharpless comments on his pretty blond curls and asks the boy what his name is.

Butterfly answers for him. "Today my name is Trouble, but when you tell my father and he comes back my name shall be Joy."

Deeply moved and shaken, Sharpless promises to tell Pinkerton.

Shouting and insulting him, Suzuki drags Goro into the house. She tells Butterfly that this vicious viper has been saying terrible things about her and her child. While Suzuki protectively carries the boy out of the room, Butterfly drives Goro from her house.

Suddenly, a distant cannon shot is heard, and both women run to the terrace. Peering through a telescope Butterfly spells out the name of the ship. It is Pinkerton's—the *Abraham Lincoln.* Her faith and fidelity have been vindicated! Exultantly, she orders Suzuki to fill the house with flowers from the garden and prepares herself for the long awaited reunion, all the while happily ridiculing those who said that Pinkerton would never return. Suzuki brings in the child and helps her mistress into the gown she wore on her wedding day. As the sun sets, Butterfly pierces three holes in the shoji screen so that each of them can watch for Pinkerton's appearance. Night comes. The boy falls asleep and then Suzuki. Alone, standing erect and motionless, Butterfly keeps the vigil.

ACT III

It is early morning. The gray light of dawn and the distant sounds of the harbor filter into the room. Suzuki awakes to find Butterfly still standing at her watch post, and still certain that Pinkerton will come. Gently, Suzuki urges her to get some rest, and Butterfly accedes, retiring to a bedroom with her sleeping son.

Suzuki prays once again for her mistress, when there is a knock on the door. Standing there are Sharpless and Pinkerton. Before Suzuki can cry out with joy, they motion to her to be silent. She notices a woman standing in the garden and fearfully asks who it can be. Pinkerton is agitated and answers somewhat ambiguously until finally it is Sharpless who must tell Suzuki that the woman is Pinkerton's new American wife.

Desolated for the sake of her mistress, Suzuki is told that Pinkerton and his wife want to adopt Butterfly's child. Sharpless asks for her help in convincing the mother, while Pinkerton wanders around the room, more and more overwhelmed by memories of the sweet spring love he shared with Butterfly, and by remorse as he realizes that what he has done will break her heart. No longer able to bear it, he asks Sharpless to speak for him, and leaves.

Suziki promises Mrs. Kate Pinkerton that she will advise her mistress to give up the child. Certain that Pinkerton has come, Butterfly rushes into the room, but her joy turns to suspicion when all she finds is Sharpless, a strange American woman, and Suzuki in tears. With mounting fear, she asks if Pinkerton is alive. Suzuki nods.

"But he won't return?"

Reluctantly, Suzuki admits that this is so.

"And this woman?" But she hardly needs an answer. She has guessed the truth—that Kate is married to Pinkerton and that they have come to take away her child.

Magnanimously, she agrees to give up her son, but only on condition that Pinkerton come himself to take him away.

Kate and Sharpless leave, and Butterfly tells Suzuki to play with the boy.

Left alone, Butterfly lights a candle and removes her father's dagger from its cabinet, slowly reading the inscription on the blade: "Let him die with honor who cannot live with honor." As she is about to put the knife into her

101

throat, Suzuki pushes her son into the room and he comes running to her. She smothers him with kisses, then tells him to have a good life beyond the sea. Gently, she ties a scarf around his eyes. Picking up the dagger once again, she plunges it into herself. As Pinkerton rushes into the house, calling her name, Butterfly falls dead. Sharpless comes in and quickly sweeps the child into his arms, while Pinkerton sinks to his knees beside Butterfly's lifeless body. Both men sob, one with grief, the other with shame.

EUGENE ONEGIN

Opera in Three Acts
by
PETER ILYICH TCHAIKOVSKY

Première: Imperial College of Music, Moscow, March 29, 1879

ACT I

Scene 1

SET AMONG the meadows and forests of the Russian countryside in the early nineteenth century is the modest estate of the Larin family. It is early evening of a late summer day. The foliage and flowers are lush and the air is soft.

Over an open fire in the garden the widowed mother, Madame Larina, is making jam with the help of the old family Nurse, Filippyevna. Through the open French doors of the house can be heard her two young daughters, Olga and Tatyana, singing a song about love. Hearing the tune reminds Larina of her own youth and the love she lost.

The Nurse of course has heard it all before. "Your parents made you wed against your heart."

Larina sighs, but not unhappily. "Yes, but my husband was always kind and devoted and habit is very consoling. I have had my house and my family, and I have been content."

A group of peasants, celebrating the conclusion of a successful harvest, enter the garden, singing, and do a joyful folk dance. Attracted by the celebration, Tatyana and Olga come out of the house. Although sisters, they are very different; Tatyana is moved to daydreams by the peasant songs, while Olga wants to join in. "We are so dissimilar, dear sister," Olga says. "I cannot be melancholy, always daydreaming, always sighing. I want to play and be happy. They call me a child, but I hope life will always be like this!"

When the peasants have left, Madame Larina notices that Tatyana seems pale and asks if she is feeling all right.

"No need to worry, Mama," she replies. "I am upset now because I am reading the most heart-rending story about two lovers." Her mother counsels her not to get so involved.

Olga interrupts. "Mama, take your apron off. Lenski is coming."

The Nurse comes in to announce Lenski's arrival, and adds that he has brought a friend—Mr. Onegin. The shy Tatyana panics and is about to run away but is restrained by her mother, who orders the Nurse to show the two gentlemen into the garden.

Lenski, who is engaged to Olga, introduces his friend. Onegin has the superior and condescending air of a man who expects to be bored, but his manners are impeccable. The women greet him warmly. Larina invites them to come into the house.

Lenski says, "It is so lovely in the garden. Let us stay awhile."

Larina excuses herself to go in and get dinner ready. The four young people stand awkwardly, the girls on one side of the garden and the men on the other. Lenski and Onegin discuss the girls and Lenski identifies Tatyana as the one who is melancholy and quiet.

At that very moment Tatyana, watching Onegin, thinks, "This is the man I have dreamed of for so long!" She cannot help herself. She is in love.

Onegin, in his jaded way, expresses his surprise at Lenski's choice of women. "Had I been a poet like you, I would have picked the other."

"My dear friend," Lenski counters, "while we may be the best of friends our views are as similar as fire and ice!" He can wait no longer and goes to Olga. "How I have missed you. It has been so long since yesterday," he declares as he walks her around the garden.

Onegin is left little choice but to talk to Tatyana. He immediately expresses his disdain for the country by asking how she keeps from being bored here.

"I dream a lot. And I read a great deal."

Lenski and Olga stroll about the garden as they continue their ardent declarations of love, until called to dinner by Larina and the Nurse.

The Nurse goes off to look for the others and hears Onegin tell Tatyana, "I have inherited my late uncle's estate. He was a highly principled but very boring man—especially near his death, when I sat there day after day. I must say, I miss the city."

They go into the house followed by the Nurse, who is worried about her melancholic Tatyana. "She's so shy," she muses, "always looking down with drooping eyes. Or, perhaps she is attracted to this strange young gentleman."

SCENE 2

Tatyana, dressed in a nightgown, prepares for bed with her Nurse's help. But she is not tired and bids Filippyevna sit beside her and cheer her up with stories from her past. The Nurse begins to tell the story of her own marriage but soon realizes that Tatyana is not paying attention. "My dear child, are you not well?"

"No, I am not ill. I am in love!" Emotionally, Tatyana throws her arms around her Nurse. "But leave me now. I'll go to sleep soon. Just give me a pen and some paper."

Shaking her head, the Nurse does as Tatyana requests and wishes her good night.

Tatyana sits at her desk, lost in thought. Suddenly gripped by determination she starts to write, stops, reads what she has written, and then rips it up for fear it isn't right. Finally she begins again. "I write to you who have the power to cause me great pain. But if you have any pity at all you will not ignore me. I didn't want to let you know, but now I have decided I must tell you all. Had you never come to our house I would never have felt this incredible torment. Clearly it is the will of the fates that I must be yours. I have waited all my life for God to send you to me, and when I saw you arrive I said 'This is he!' I am yours forever as I always have been. I await your answer. With your answer you can restore my hope or break my heart. I end." She seals the letter, too frightened to read it over. Going to the window, she opens the curtains and bright morning sun shines into the room; she has spent the whole night writing.

The Nurse comes in to rouse her and is surprised to find her awake.

Tatyana says, "Nyanya, you must do me a favor and send your grandson to deliver this letter to the one I love. It goes to Eugene Onegin but no one must know."

Torn between delight and confusion, the Nurse finally grasps the situation and carries away the fateful letter.

Scene 3

In another part of the Larin garden, in a dense copse of acacia and lilac bushes bordered by ill-kept flower beds, servant girls busily pick berries growing wild amongst the overgrown shrubbery. Suddenly, Tatyana rushes through and, visibly agitated, collapses onto a bench. "He is here! My God, he has come to speak with me. He must have received my letter. What will he say!"

She sees Onegin approaching and jumps up, but cannot look him in the eye. Her head droops.

He addresses her like a calm and patient father. "I have read your letter, don't deny you wrote it. Your feelings are touching and I like your candor. I will be just as honest. If I had the desire to confine myself to a domestic condition, you probably would be the woman I would choose. But I know myself. Soon after marriage I would grow tired of you." For Tatyana, the coldness of his words and the detachment in his voice are devastating. Onegin continues: "I love you as I would love a sister. I do not want to be unkind. Take my advice. Young women often change their dreams. From this misfortune you will gain experience, but you must learn to use more self-control." He offers Tatyana his arm. She gives him one imploring look, then lets him escort her out of the garden.

ACT II

Scene 1

Some months have passed. It is winter now and to celebrate Tatyana's Name Day there is a party in progress at the Larin house. The reception room is ablaze with light as the guests congregate in small groups. Much to the delight of the girls, Captain Zaretski, a friend of Lenski, has brought a military band to provide dance music.

Among the young couples dancing are Tatyana and Onegin. The older women sitting along the wall openly gossip about them. They say that it is about time for Tatyana to marry, but that Onegin will prove an unfaithful husband. He overhears some of the unflattering chatter and is infuriated. "It is Lenski's fault for having brought me here. I will get even with him!" he vows. Just then Lenski and Olga pass by and Onegin deftly grabs her and sweeps her onto the dance floor before either of them can protest.

Lenski grows jealous as he watches them dance and when the music stops he rushes over to Olga. "How could you do it? I asked you to dance but instead you danced with Onegin! And you were flirting with him, blushing and smiling and dancing close together!" Olga is annoyed by his jealousy, refuses to take him seriously, and when Onegin approaches she decides to dance the cotillion with him instead of with Lenski.

At this moment, the whisper of a new arrival delays the dance. It is the Frenchman Triquet and the guests gather around him as he reads a couplet written in tribute to Tatyana on her Name Day. When they have applauded the pretty poem, the dancers take their places for the cotillion. Unfortunately, the charming interlude has not cooled Lenski's anger and he continues to smolder as Olga and Onegin dance. It is so obvious that after one turn Onegin confronts his friend. "Why are you sulking?"

At first Lenski sarcastically denies that he is upset, but he cannot maintain his calm and grows rapidly more angry. "Clearly Tatyana is not enough for you. You are such a loyal friend that now you must turn Olga against me. You are mean and vile and insulting, sir. You are no friend of mine. I hate you Onegin!" His voice rises, attracting the attention of all the guests.

Embarrassed, Onegin tries to calm Lenski, assuring him that he is mistaken. But Lenski's rage can no longer be quelled and with all the guests listening, he demands satisfaction.

Tatyana and Olga are stunned.

Onegin does not want to fight but things have gone too far and in order to protect his honor he must accept the challenge. "You are insane," Onegin declares, "but I will have to teach you a lesson."

Rushing toward him, Lenski retorts, "Perhaps. But you are a scoundrel."

The guests restrain Lenski, and Onegin leaves.

Olga says, "Please, Vladimir."

Lenski merely bids her goodbye and hurries away. Distraught, Olga tries to follow him, but the shock overwhelms her and she faints.

SCENE 2

It is dawn, near a water mill. The winter sun has barely risen and its pale light only defines the long gray shadows on the snow. Lenski and Zaretski wait for Onegin and his second to arrive for the duel. Bored, Zaretski walks toward the mill.

Alone, deep in thought, and sensing his destiny, Lenski muses, "Where has my life gone?" He thinks of Olga and how he loves her. "Oh, Olga. I am forever yours. The world may forget me, but perhaps you will shed some tears upon my grave!"

Zaretski returns announcing the arrival of Onegin and his second, his servant, Guillot, who carries the pistols. While the two seconds talk quietly, establishing the rules for the duel, Onegin and Lenski stand apart, not looking at each other. Each man is filled with thoughts of how pointless this duel really is, how it could be avoided with a simple apology. But neither is willing to be the first to back down, and when the seconds announce that all is ready, Onegin and Lenski take their weapons and move to their places. Zaretski calls the orders and the adversaries march inexorably toward each other, slowly taking aim.

A shot rings out and Lenski falls to the ground.

Zaretski examines him and to Onegin's horror pronounces him "Dead!"

ACT III

SCENE 1

Four years later, Onegin finds himself at a gala ball in a fashionable St. Petersburg mansion. The ball is just beginning and as he watches, the elegantly dressed guests dance the traditional introductory Polonaise. Onegin is bored. "The same faces," he thinks, "the same formalities, the same gossip . . . never a new thought." Unable to bear his country home after the duel with Lenski, he has been traveling abroad, trying to distract himself, but in vain. He is still haunted by grief and remorse. So he has returned to Russia, and the scene before him only serves to emphasize how tiresome his life has become. He, who had hoped to accomplish something useful, has done nothing in life but kill his best friend.

There is an excited buzz of interest as word of a new arrival travels the room. Looking up, Onegin gazes in disbelief as Tatyana descends the stairs on the arm of the elderly Prince Gremin. Dressed magnificently, she has the serenity and dignity of an empress, and she has become extraordinarily beautiful. He does not know, as he observes Tatyana graciously greet the guests who have surrounded her, that she is concealing an inner turmoil the sight of Onegin has caused.

When Prince Gremin approaches him, Onegin asks, "Who is that beautiful woman?"

The Prince replies, "You have been away a long time. That is my wife." He has been married to Tatyana for about two years. "She has made life wonderful for this old gray-haired warrior. She makes me feel young again. And she is so kind, so pure, so devoid of malaise, so unlike all the silly,

gossiping ladies of the court. I adore her. Come, let me present you to her."
Ignoring the fact that Tatyana and Onegin know each other, Prince Gremin
formally introduces them. They casually exchange pleasantries, acknowledging that they once met long ago in the country. Then turning to her
husband she says that she has grown tired and, escorted by the Prince,
gracefully leaves the room.

Onegin cannot believe that this is the same Tatyana he knew in the
country, the romantic little girl whose confession of love hardly stirred his
interest. "She has changed so. She is so calm, so composed, so regal."
Suddenly he realizes that what fills him is far greater and deeper than
surprise. He is consumed with the desire to see her, to be with her, to hold
her in his arms. For the first time in many years, he wants something with
all of his being, and in astonishment he tells himself, "I have fallen in
love."

Scene 2

Elegantly clothed in a morning dress, Tatyana paces about the drawing
room of the Gremin mansion. She is visibly upset. For weeks Onegin has
been sending her letters and gazing at her passionately whenever they
chance to meet. "Oh, why did he have to return and reawaken my love?"
she weeps.

Appearing at the door Onegin hurries to Tatyana to comfort her. "You
must forgive me for that time long ago when I rejected you!"

But she is unable to forget. "I still shudder to think of the look in your
eyes that day. Onegin, why am I suddenly so attractive to you? Could it be
that now my position in society and my wealth make me more appealing?"

Onegin denies her accusations, hurt by any thought that he is being
devious. "All I want is to hold you in my arms. My life depends upon you. I
would die to prove how much I love you."

She is moved to tears and together they ponder what might have been.
"It's impossible," she concludes. "I am married and you must leave!" Devastated, he begs to stay with her. "I cannot part from you. I want only to feel
the bliss of your existence."

Although she keeps telling him to leave, it is evident that she is torn with
emotion. Finally, she confesses. "I cannot lie. I still love you!"

They embrace passionately, and Onegin murmurs, "You are once again
my old Tatyana."

Realizing what has happened, Tatyana pulls away. "What is gone cannot
return. I must remain true to my husband."

In a desperate effort to change her mind, Onegin relentlessly begs her not to reject him. "God has sent me to you and we were meant to be together. You must leave this life, this lie, and come with me."

He tries to lead her away but she resists. "Enough! It cannot be! I gave my word and will not leave my husband. Onegin, farewell!" As he continues to plead his love, she quickly leaves the room.

Onegin cries out in pain. He finally realizes that all hope is gone. He has lost Tatyana. He leaves the Gremin house—a lonely man.

IL TROVATORE

Opera in Four Acts
by
GIUSEPPE VERDI
Première: Teatro Apollo, Rome, January 19, 1853

GYPSIES HAVE always been objects of suspicion, and in the Middle Ages they were often thought to possess the magical powers of witches. And perceived as witches, they sometimes suffered the terrible fate of being burned at the stake.

ACT I

Scene 1

One night during the fifteenth century in the Spanish province of Aragon, outside the palace apartments of the Count di Luna, his captain, Ferrando, is trying to keep the guards and servants awake while his master is out wooing the woman he loves. When they ask to hear again what really happened to the Count's brother, Ferrando recounts the gruesome tale of an event he witnessed many years before.

"When our Count was but a child, he had a baby brother. Every night the nurse slept beside the baby's cradle. One morning she awoke to find an old gypsy leaning over the cradle and staring at the baby with bloodshot eyes. The nurse screamed for the servants to throw out the old hag, who claimed she wanted only to cast the child's horoscope. But soon he developed a fever, and his color drained, and we were certain that he had been bewitched. So the gypsy was caught and burned at the stake. We never thought that her daughter would seek revenge. She stole the Count's baby brother and all we ever found were some bones burnt in the ashes of the witch. Strangely enough, the old Count continued to believe that this second son was still alive, and as he neared his own death he made our master vow to continue the search for the boy. But it has been in vain. Nor has the gypsy's daughter ever been found. Someday I hope to find her. If I ever see her again, I will know her."

"So you can help her to join her mother in Hell?" a soldier asks.

"In Hell? I do not know. It is said that the witch's spirit still wanders here on earth and that she has been seen in the form of an owl screeching from the rooftops."

The soldiers shudder, and curse the evil witch. The midnight gong sounds ominously and a drum roll marks the changing of the guard. The soldiers and retainers run to man their posts.

SCENE 2

Thick clouds obscure the moon as Leonora and her confidante Inez stroll through the gardens of the palace. Inez wishes to go in, but Leonora lingers as if in search of someone, and she confides that she has fallen in love with a strange knight who appeared at a tournament dressed all in black and won every joust. "I crowned him. But when the civil war began he disappeared. Then one hushed and tranquil night I heard a sweet, melancholy air sung by a troubadour whose heavenly verses were addressed to me. The troubadour was he!"

Inez has evil premonitions and counsels Leonora to forget him.

Leonora says simply, "I cannot."

As the women mount the stairs to the palace, the Count di Luna enters the garden. Seeing the flame of light still flickering in Leonora's window he is about to climb the stairs but stops suddenly when he hears the strains of an unseen lute. He curses the troubadour whose love song is obviously intended for the object of his own passion. Suddenly Leonora appears and the Count withdraws into the shadows.

Spying his figure in the dark, Leonora hurries toward him. "You are late tonight, but now I have you," she says. The still hidden troubadour cries, "Faithless woman!"

The moon moves from behind the clouds, revealing both men, and Leonora realizes she has addressed the wrong one. She throws herself at the troubadour's feet, protesting her undying love for him. The Count, consumed with jealousy, confronts the troubadour, demanding to know his identity.

He is Manrico, a supporter of the Prince of Biscay, with whom Aragon is at war. Despite Leonora's entreaties the rivals vow to kill each other and, drawing swords, rush off into the night to duel. Leonora faints.

ACT II

Dawn is about to break over the gypsy camp in the Biscay Mountains. Near a great bonfire, Manrico, recovering from wounds he sustained in battle with the forces of the Count di Luna, lies wrapped in his cloak, staring intently at his sword. As the sky lightens the gypsies set to work forging their metals over the hot fire and pounding the anvils. Nearby, Manrico's mother, Azucena, memories raised by the roaring fire, relives once again the day her mother was burned at the stake. Her voice is harrowing, echoing her emotion. "I hear the crackling fire engulf its victim. I hear her screams." The gypsies gather round. Azucena turns to Manrico. "Her last words were: 'Avenge me!'"

Their work completed, the gypsies pack up their tools and make their way down the slope. But Manrico, haunted by Azucena's story, asks his mother to explain it.

Still spellbound by the horror, she continues. "When the old Count di Luna accused my mother of witchcraft and burned her at the stake, I followed nearby with you, a baby, in my arms. They would not let her see me as they threw her on the pyre, but I heard her dying words—she cried, 'Avenge me!' Trying to follow her wishes I stole the Count's younger son and brought him to the fire. He screamed piteously, but over it all I heard her cry 'Avenge me!' and I threw the child into the fire. Soon he was consumed by the flames and I turned, only to see that very same child coming toward me. In my haste it was my own son I had burned!" Exhausted, Azucena falls back.

Manrico, stunned by the tale, is momentarily silent.

"Am I not then your son?" he asks at last.

Azucena shakes herself free of her trance. "What did I say? Of course I am your mother. Did I not search for you among the dead and bring you back here to heal your wounds? Why," she asks, "did you not kill the Count, when you had overcome him in your duel?"

Manrico says, "I don't know. I was about to strike the fatal blow when I suddenly heard a voice from heaven say 'Don't kill him!' and I was unable to move my hand."

"Next time, my son," she urges, "plunge your dagger into his heart. I must have revenge!"

A messenger arrives and delivers a letter to Manrico which reads, "We have captured Castellor, and by order of the Prince you are to take command. Come quickly for Leonora believes you are dead and has decided to enter a convent!" Manrico is overwhelmed by this last piece of news and orders the messenger to get him a horse so he may leave immediately. Azucena tells him to wait until his wounds have fully healed, but the fear of losing Leonora overrides all other considerations and, ignoring his mother's entreaties, he dashes off.

SCENE 2

At a convent near Castellor, Count di Luna, accompanied by Ferrando and some of his men, sneaks into the cloister under cover of night. The Count, who believes that his rival is dead, has assembled his men so they can abduct Leonora before she takes the sacred vows. The tolling of the convent bells announces the beginning of the service. The Count's men hide among the trees, while the Count waits anxiously for his beloved to appear. Inside the church the nuns begin to sing, and he withdraws from view.

Soon Leonora enters, accompanied by her ladies-in-waiting. Inez's eyes are filled with tears.

Leonora tries to console her. "Dry your eyes, my dear friend. There is no hope or joy for me until the day I rejoin my beloved in heaven. Now lead me to the altar!"

Hearing these words, the Count comes out of his hiding place and stops her. "For you the only altar shall be a wedding altar." But as he moves toward her, Manrico suddenly appears and steps between them.

Leonora starts back, but her disbelief is quickly overwhelmed by her happiness. "I cannot believe what my eyes see. Are you a vision? My heart cannot hold my joy!"

Equally startled, the Count asks how the man he left for dead can have returned.

"It is true that your men wounded me," Manrico tells them, "but God saved me!"

While the Count's followers, convinced that Manrico enjoys supernatural protection, hang back, Manrico's faithful lieutenant, Ruiz, charges in with a band of soldiers. Whatever the odds, the Count cannot bear to lose Leonora and, brandishing his sword, he attacks the troubadour. But Ruiz and his men encircle the Count and disarm him. Almost maniacal with fury, the Count must watch, captive and helpless, as Manrico takes the still bewildered Leonora away with him.

ACT III

SCENE 1

On a field near the Castellor fortress in which Manrico is safe with his beloved Leonora, the Count di Luna and his soldiers have set up camp. Ferrando tells them that their leader plans to attack the fortress at dawn, and the soldiers rejoice excitedly in anticipation of the victory that awaits them.

The Count emerges from his tent, still tormented by the vision of Manrico with Leonora. His thoughts are disrupted by a sudden commotion. The soldiers have captured a gypsy woman and they drag Azucena into the Count's presence. Questioning her, he discovers that she is from Biscay and that she is wandering in search of her only son. "Do you remember when the Count's son was stolen from the castle some twenty years ago?" di Luna asks. He notices that she looks frightened. "I am his brother. Do you know anything about him?"

"No," she says, but she cannot hide her face. "Let me go. I must look for my son."

Ferrando has been staring at her and now he accuses her of being the witch who burned the child. Despite her denials the Count orders her bonds tightened. In pain, she cries out for Manrico to help her, and the Count realizes that fate has delivered his rival's mother into his hands. Grimly, he savors the opportunity to avenge his brother and himself as well.

Azucena curses her captors, predicting that God will punish them.

Ferrando and the soldiers tell her she will be burnt at the stake.

SCENE 2

Inside the besieged fortress, Manrico and Leonora are about to be married, but their joy is tempered by the threat of attack. Manrico tries to cheer Leonora, promising that their forces will prevail, and comforts her with tender words of eternal love.

As they are about to enter the chapel, Ruiz rushes in and blurts out, "They have captured the gypsy and are preparing a fire for her execution!"

Trembling with rage, Manrico tells Leonora that he is the gypsy's son, and orders Ruiz to assemble their forces. To Leonora he tries to explain that he was, after all, a son before he was a lover, so he must try to save his mother. "Even your grief cannot keep me here."

Feeling helplessly buffeted by life, Leonora is left alone.

ACT IV

SCENE 1

On an ominously dark night, Ruiz brings Leonora to the ramparts of Count di Luna's palace where inside the tower a defeated Manrico lies imprisoned, along with Azucena. Leonora sends Ruiz away. She feels protected because the ring she wears contains poison. If all else fails, she can end her life. Somehow she hopes to save her beloved Manrico, but her spirit is chilled by the mournful prayers for the souls of those soon to be executed emanating from within the prison. Then she hears Manrico's sweet voice, now sad with lament for his approaching end, and bidding her farewell. "I pay with my life for our love. Beloved Leonora, do not forget me!"

Hearing the Count approach, Leonora withdraws into the shadows.

The Count gives his men instructions for the dawn executions. "Behead Manrico and burn his mother!" As the men enter the tower, he muses, "I may have abused my powers, but it is my love for Leonora that has driven me to this. Oh, cruel lady, where are you?"

She steps out of the shadows. "Before you! I have come to beg for mercy for Manrico!"

The Count is cold and vengeful. He tells her he would happily torture her for the pain she has made him suffer.

Leonora grows desperate and throwing herself at his feet offers herself in exchange for Manrico's freedom. She swears she will be his.

The Count calls for a guard. While he whispers the orders, Leonora swallows the poison in her ring. "Manrico will live!" the Count tells her and he ecstatically anticipates his unexpected bliss. "Remember, you've sworn."

"My word is sacred," Leonora declares, and each feeling triumphant, they enter the tower.

SCENE 2

Within their gloomy prison cell, Manrico tries to comfort Azucena, who tosses restlessly in dread of the frightful execution that awaits her. "It was on a day like this that they dragged my mother to the stake!" she tells him. He begs her to sleep so she may banish these thoughts, and gradually he calms her, until taking comfort in memories of his songs and of their peaceful home, she falls asleep.

Suddenly the cell door opens and Leonora rushes in to tell Manrico he is free and must leave. But she admits she must remain and he will not leave without her. "What price have you paid for this?" he asks.

She does not answer, and immediately guessing the price, he berates her for being unfaithful. Beginning to lose strength she sinks to the ground telling him he is blind and unfair, and begs him to flee. He curses her and tells her to leave. She is too weak and he rushes to her side, suddenly realizing that she is dying—dying so he may be free. Manrico is beside himself with grief as Leonora lies in his arms. The Count and his retainers enter the cell; recognizing that he has been cheated, the Count helplessly watches as Leonora with her final breath bids Manrico farewell.

Enraged, the Count orders Manrico be taken to his execution. As he is dragged away Manrico shouts a last farewell to his mother.

Azucena awakens and cries "Wait! You must not do this. Listen to me." The Count will not listen. He pulls the old woman to the window, as the axe falls. "It's over! He's dead!" he gloats.

Azucena tells him, "You have just murdered your own brother!" Holding up her arms to heaven, she wails, "Mother, you have been avenged!"

As the horror of it all bears in upon him, the Count whispers, "And I live on!"

LA FANCIULLA DEL WEST
(The Girl of the Golden West)

Opera in Three Acts
by
GIACOMO PUCCINI
Première: Metropolitan Opera, New York, December 10, 1910

ACT I

IN THE primitive, untamed air of the California gold rush, miners' camps were ragtag and polyglot groups of men who would gather in the evenings to drink and gamble away their boredom and often the fruits of their daily labor, and to pool their loneliness in the hope of making it ache a little less.

In one such camp, the social center is the Polka Bar, run by Minnie, a young Californian who has inherited the business from her father. She knows the miners well. She is pretty, and one of the few women around, and they adore her.

As they straggle into the bar one night, ordering whiskey and cigars, joining the poker tables, and drifting in and out of conversations, one of the men, Sonora, pulls aside Nick the bartender and asks, "Has Minnie decided she loves me?"

Nick assures him she has.

"Cigars all around," shouts the jubilant man.

Then another miner asks Nick, "Has Minnie given you any hints about me?" When Nick tells him that *he* is the lucky one, he orders up a round of whiskey for the house. Shrewd businessman that he is, Nick knows full well that Minnie favors neither of them, but that this is a good way to keep business booming.

From outside, a plaintive ballad floats into the room, and soon a traveling minstrel with a guitar arrives, singing poignantly about the people they have all left behind. Others join in, but the melancholy strain upsets Tim Larkens so much he bursts into tears. "I can't bear it any more!" he cries. "I'm homesick. I want to see my mother!"

Knowing how he feels, the others try to comfort him. Sonora passes a hat, collecting five bucks from each, then pours the contents into Larkens's hands so he can afford to go home.

After Larkens leaves, the mood turns suddenly ugly when one of the card players, Sid, is accused of cheating. "Lynch him! String him up!" the others shout. But the sheriff, Jack Rance, intercedes.

"Calm down!" he orders. "There's no need to hang him. I know a worse punishment." He pins the two of spades onto the front of Sid's shirt. "Now everyone will know he's a cheater. If he ever tries to remove it, then hang him!"

Blubbering and wearing his card, Sid disappears into the night.

The Wells Fargo representative, Mr. Ashby, comes into the bar and Rance introduces him to the miners. "He's been chasing the Mexican bandit, Ramerrez, and his gang."

There is another round of drinks on the house, this time a gift from Minnie. As all the men toast her, Rance announces that she will soon be Mrs. Rance. This boast angers Sonora and leads to an argument so heated that only the entrance of Minnie herself can restore peace.

"I won't give you your lesson unless you are good!" she threatens as if they were children.

They plead with her not to be so harsh. As she makes her way around the room, greeting the customers, the men offer her small gifts—flowers, a ribbon, a silk handkerchief. Sonora gives her a bag of gold in settlement of his account.

"That money would be safer at the Wells Fargo bank!" Ashby cautions.

He and Rance quietly resume their conversation, while the miners gather round Minnie for the day's Bible lesson, but before she can get very far into the Psalms of David, the Postman arrives. Distributing the mail to the excited miners, he warns of a rough-looking bandit he passed on the road. His words go mostly unheeded by these men engrossed in news from home.

Nick comes in, chuckling, "There's a stranger outside who wants a whiskey and water. I think he's from San Francisco because he doesn't know that here we drink our whiskey straight."

"Bring him in," Minnie says. "We'll curl his hair for him."

As Nick goes out again Rance sidles up to Minnie and lecherously offers her a thousand dollars for a single kiss. When she laughs at him, he offers to marry her. "Just say the word and I'll get rid of my wife!"

Minnie rejects him harshly and tries to tell him what real love means. She knows because even though her family was poor and had to struggle to survive, she could see how much in love her parents were, and this is what she is waiting for. Rance dismisses this as romantic nonsense.

At that moment Nick returns with the stranger, who throws down his saddle in a way that announces he will brook no nonsense. Minnie gives a start of recognition, but quickly catches herself. "Nick, our guest will take his whiskey as he likes it." Rance frowns and rudely asks if he didn't mean to go elsewhere. The stranger introduces himself. His name is Johnson and he has dismounted only for a brief rest and possibly to play a round of cards. He draws Minnie aside and whispers discreetly, "Do you remember me? We met on the road to Monterey."

Minnie whispers back, "I remember you said you would never forget me. I have thought about you often."

Rance comes up to them and knocks Johnson's glass off the counter. As sheriff, he demands to know the nature of the stranger's business. Contemptuously Johnson reaches for his pistol. Rance calls to the miners, who quickly and threateningly surround him. But Minnie quells the incipient violence by declaring that she knows Johnson and can vouch for him. This is all it takes for the miners to accept him, and Johnson waltzes Minnie into the adjoining room.

While they are gone, Ashby, with a few miners, hauls a bandit into the bar. His name is Castro and they suspect he is a colleague of Ramerrez. "Hang him!" they demand.

Noticing Johnson's saddle gear on the floor, Castro mumbles to himself, "They have captured my leader!" Castro tells them that he is a fugitive from the gang and from his boss. "I will lead you to his hideout. I hate him!" His captors are trying to decide whether to trust him, when Castro glimpses Johnson in the dance hall and realizes that his leader has not been taken, but instead is safe in the camp of the enemy.

The music ends and Johnson comes back in. Seeing Castro, he busies himself with his saddle gear. Under his breath Castro whispers, "I let them catch me in order to lead them on a wild goose chase. Our men will follow me into the woods. When we whistle, you whistle back if all is well. Then we can rob this camp."

As the others leave in search of Ramerrez, Johnson remains behind with Minnie. While she straightens up the bar, he tells her, "It is so strange to find you here where any man can steal a drink or the money, or even a kiss from you!"

"Oh I can defend myself. In fact," she confides, "I've still to give my first kiss."

He looks at her admiringly. "You are better than all of this."

She demurs. She is so ordinary, and has had so little education. She loves the way he speaks.

Johnson says, "Your heart reveals what you do not say. You made me feel such peace and joy as we danced."

Just as Minnie begins to reveal her feelings, Nick returns to report that there is another Mexican bandit lurking around outside. A whistle pierces the air. Johnson recognizes the signal but does not respond. Concerned, Minnie tells him that there is a fortune in gold in the barrel. "The miners put their money there. Usually they take turns sleeping here to guard it. Tonight they are out chasing that bandit. But they have worked so hard for it, anyone who wants to steal this money will have to kill me first."

"No one will dare attack you!" Johnson impulsively assures her. "I must go now, but I'd like to say goodbye to you later. May I come to your cabin tonight?"

She agrees, but as he packs his gear she shyly tells him not to expect much. "I'm worth so little," she cries.

"Ah, but I find you good-natured, pure of soul, and you have the face of an angel!" Picking up his saddle, he goes to the door and regards her a moment before summoning up the resolution to leave.

Stunned by the loving words of this kind, gentle man, Minnie stands transfixed. "The face of an angel," she murmurs wonderingly.

ACT II

A snowstorm is brewing, and as the cold winds howl outside Minnie's small cabin on the mountain, Minnie comes in and, taking off her boots, orders her Indian maid to prepare dinner for two. Nervously she changes her clothes. Wanting to look elegant, she puts on a pair of silk shoes and gloves. She hasn't worn them in so long they are tight. She adds a little perfume, then worries that she's overdoing it. "Am I too dressy?" she asks Wowkle.

"Hello!" Johnson calls as he comes in. "You look so pretty!"

He moves toward her to kiss her, but she pushes him away, saying, "You're a bit too fast."

He apologizes, then asks why she lives this strange lonely existence.

"It's exciting," she exults. There are the wild mountains and the great outdoors where she rides her horse. In the winter she finds peace and comfort in teaching the Bible to the miners. She loves to read, especially love stories, and to her love is forever and not for just an hour.

"Ah, but there are some women," Johnson asserts, "with whom just one hour of love would be enough to die for." He tries again to embrace her, and again she rebukes him. "Your lips reject me," he challenges her, "but your heart wants me!"

Struggling with herself, Minnie looks for something to do. Slowly, she takes off her gloves and puts them away. Then abruptly, she orders Wowkle to leave. With the maid gone, Johnson reaches for her and overcome with love, Minnie throws herself into his arms. They kiss passionately, and he tells her how he has loved her from the first, but suddenly, and with great resolution, Johnson announces, "It's no use. I'm going! God keep you Minnie!"

She tries to convince him to stay, suggesting he wait until morning when the snow covered path will be cleared. As he pulls on his coat, pistol shots break the night's silence. Minnie is now more determined than ever to convince Johnson to stay. "Perhaps it's a bandit, even Ramerrez!" she warns.

Johnson succumbs. He throws off his coat, and turning to her with a fierce intensity swears, "I'll never give you up now. I want to be with you forever."

Lovingly she prepares the bed for him, generously offering to sleep on the rug near the fire. As they settle down for the night, the cold winds and sleet continue their ominous harmony.

Soon there is a knock at the door and Nick calls, "Minnie, Ramerrez has been seen!"

Minnie orders Johnson to hide and unbolts the door, admitting Nick along with Rance, Ashby, and Sonora. Sonora blurts, "Thank God you're safe."

Rance spitefully explains, "That Johnson you danced with this evening was none other than Ramerrez."

Minnie is incredulous.

Ashby tells her that Johnson was at the Polka Bar earlier to rob it.

"But he didn't," Rance says. "We know he's Ramerrez because his lover, Nina Mickeltorena, has identified him! She gave us a picture."

Minnie looks at the photograph, then shrugs indifferently, "Charming company he keeps! You'd better go now boys."

Nick offers to stay, but she refuses.

As soon as they are gone, Minnie shouts, "Liar! Come out! You came to rob!"

Johnson denies it and tries to defend himself.

"I *am* Ramerrez, and I was reared on stolen money, but I never knew my father was a bandit until six months ago when he died and left my mother and me with no money. Then my fate seemed sealed. I was to be a thief. But when I met you I dared to dream that I could take you away with me so you would never know of my shame. That's all, I'm done!"

"I could forgive you for being a thief. What I can't forgive is that I gave my first kiss to a man I thought was mine alone. Get out!"

Unarmed, Johnson leaves, and Minnie bursts into tears.

Moments later she hears a shot, rushes to the door, and drags the badly wounded man back into the house. He tries to refuse her help, but she pushes him up the ladder into the crawl space to hide. "You must not die," she begs. "Later we'll go away together." Painfully he climbs up and out of sight just as there is a knock at the door.

Minnie opens it and Rance storms in, demanding Ramerrez. She feigns ignorance but Rance is sure he has wounded Johnson, and he can be nowhere else. Brandishing his pistol, he searches the room swearing to find and kill the culprit. Mockingly, Minnie taunts Rance, "You'd better go on looking."

Rance turns on her. "Just tell me you don't love him."

"You're mad!"

"I'm mad for you." He grabs and kisses her, but she wrenches free.

"Get out, you swine."

Rance backs off, sneering, "I'll never let him have you." As he stands there, a drop of blood falls from above them onto his hand. He stares at it. Another drop of blood falls and the sheriff realizes he has trapped the bandit. Minnie tries to hold him back, but Rance forces his way to the ladder and finally, unable to prevent his capture, she helps the wounded man down. Fainting, he slumps into a chair.

Desperately, Minnie offers Rance a gamble. "I will play you a game of poker. If you win you get us both, this man and me. But if I win, you must give me your word, Jack, that this man is mine!"

Rance accepts the terms. Minnie goes to the cupboard to get the cards, and behind it she surreptitiously tucks some into her stocking. Returning to the table, she deals the first hand, which Rance wins. She wins the second hand and deals the third and decisive hand. As they peruse their cards she suddenly looks ill. "Jack, I feel faint. Quick, get me something to drink!" He runs to the cupboard and while he does so she reaches for the cards hidden in her stocking and substitutes them for those in her hand.

As he brings her the drink, he says, "You feel faint because you know you are going to lose." Triumphantly he lays out his hand: "Three kings."

"The game is mine," Minnie shouts, producing three aces and a pair.

Rance picks up his coat and hat. "Good night," he bids her coldly.

Locking the door behind him, Minnie throws her arms around the motionless Johnson. "He's mine," she sobs in triumph.

ACT III

A week has passed. It is dawn in the California forest. At the edge of a clearing in the dense woods, horses are tied up for safekeeping while nearby their masters sleep or chat quietly. Nick and Jack Rance talk. Nick wishes fervently they had never seen Johnson, and Rance is frustrated and angry at not being able to catch him. "What can Minnie possibly see in that dog to take him in like that!"

The sound of shouting in the distance wakes Ashby, who immediately assumes that the bandit has been spotted. Organizing the miners into search parties, he commands them to bring their quarry in alive. Rance and Nick remain behind. Gesturing toward Minnie's cabin, Rance gloats, "Now, Minnie, you shall cry and I shall laugh." But he is morose as he sits on a tree stump or paces up and down.

Reports come in as miners scurry in and out. "He's surrounded!" Then: "He's on horseback trying to get away! The Wells Fargo men are chasing him." Finally, Sonora rides into the camp and announces, "The damned Spaniard has been caught. They're bringing him here!"

Rance mumbles smugly, "I didn't help, but it's over now, Minnie! Your fascinating vagabond will look like a pendant swinging from the rope in the wind."

Nick looks unhappy and suddenly hurries off.

Ashby rides in with his bound prisoner. "Sheriff, I turn this man over to you. Let your people pass judgment."

Enjoying his moment of victory, Rance mocks and taunts the prisoner.

"Let's get it over with fast!" Johnson says contemptuously.

"It will only take a couple of minutes to get rid of you. Eh, boys?"

The miners respond with cries of "String him up!" One by one they enumerate the murders that his band is alleged to have committed.

Johnson tries to deny them. "I've been a thief, but I've never killed anyone."

But the mob doesn't believe him. "Hang him!" they yell, and push him toward the waiting noose.

Above their shouts, Johnson tries to tell them that it isn't death he fears; he wishes only to speak of the woman he loves. His words are greeted with angry catcalls until Sonora intercedes, crying, "He has a right to be heard!"

The prisoner pleads into the sudden silence. "Don't let Minnie know how I died. Let her believe that I am far away and free. Protect Minnie, the one beautiful thing in my life, the Minnie who loved me so well!"

The jealous Rance hits Johnson in the face. "You pig! Do you have more to say?"

"No. Get on with the hanging," Johnson answers.

Rance selects an appropriate limb of a tree and Sonora attaches the rope. Courageously the bandit marches toward the gallows, mounts the stone, puts his head through the noose, and awaits his end. The miners train their pistols on him. But they pause as the furious gallop of a horse rapidly approaches. Someone shouts, "It's Minnie."

Rance tries to hurry the execution, but no one heeds him, as Minnie rides ino their midst, dismounts, and rushes to her lover.

"Justice requires that we kill him!" Rance yells.

"You wouldn't dare!" Minnie responds.

Rance orders his men to drag her out of the way, but she pulls out her pistol to keep them at bay. The crowd mills about in some confusion and some miners move in on Minnie, but she threatens to kill herself if they come any closer. The kindly Sonora intervenes. "Leave her alone! Let her be!" he orders.

Calm is momentarily restored and Minnie, trembling and white, but angry, appeals to the miners, reminding them of all the times she shared their troubles, nursing them when they were sick, and teaching them to read and write. "Now all I ask is that you let me have this man for myself. You cannot kill him because the robber he was died a week ago in my cabin."

There is silence, broken only when Sonora pleadingly tells his friends, "We must. We owe Minnie so much!"

The others are more reluctant to release the bandit. Determined, Minnie continues to beg them, reminding each in turn what she has done for him. "Look, I throw down my pistol. I am your friend!"

Sonora persuades some of the miners to relent. Others hesitate because they fear they will become a laughingstock if they release a criminal. But one by one, as they remember the debt they owe their Minnie, they realize they cannot refuse her.

Sonora removes the noose, unties Johnson's hands, and turns to Minnie saying, "Yours are words from God and your love is great. On behalf of all of us I give him to you!" He cannot keep from weeping, and others in the crowd can be heard sobbing softly.

Minnie and Johnson mount their horses and bid goodbye to the "sweet land of California" which they will never see again.

Sadly, the miners wave to their Minnie as she and her beloved bandit ride off into the distance.

LUCIA DI LAMMERMOOR

Opera in Three Acts
by
GAETANO DONIZETTI
Première: Teatro San Carlo, Naples, September 26, 1835

ACT I

SCENE 1

IN SEVENTEENTH-CENTURY Scotland, religious rebellion and political strife periodically swept the country and spawned bitter feuds between noble houses.

During the reign of William and Mary, toward the end of the century, the Ashtons and the Ravenswoods have become mortal enemies. Indeed, Lord Henry Ashton of Lammermoor has succeeded in taking title to the Ravenswood estates, leaving Edward Ravenswood, the last of his line, in possession of only the crumbling family castle. But Ashton is actually in desperate straits, both politically and economically, and he hopes to save himself and his fortune by marrying his sister Lucy to the powerful Lord Arthur Bucklaw.

While Ashton's Captain of the Guard, Norman, and his men are out scouring the woods in search of a stranger who has been seen trespassing, Ashton complains to his chaplain, Raymond, that Lucy has refused to marry Bucklaw.

"The girl is grieving," says Raymond. "How can she think of marriage when she is still mourning for your mother?"

But the Captain, returning from the search, contradicts the cleric. He tells them that one day while Lucy was walking near her mother's grave, a wild bull charged at her. "Suddenly a shot rang out and the bull lay dead. Lucy was saved and I think she has fallen in love with the man who saved her. And he, I believe, is none other than your enemy, Edward of Ravenswood!"

Ashton says, "I'd rather she were dead."

Norman's guards return, reporting that they spotted a man on horseback, and that it was indeed Edward.

Enraged, and swearing vengeance, Henry rejects Raymond's attempts to intercede.

SCENE 2

With her companion Alice, Lucy strolls through the castle's gardens to a secluded glade. She has been urgently summoned here by Edward and she is nervous that her brother may discover them. A fountain at one end of the clearing particularly unnerves her and she explains, "This fountain makes me tremble. It was right here that a Ravenswood, crazed with jealousy, killed the girl who loved him. She fell into this fountain and she still haunts it. One dark night her ghost appeared, beckoning to me. Then she vanished and the water which had been crystal suddenly ran red with blood!"

Only too certain that she understands the hidden meaning of this horrible story, Alice counsels Lucy to abandon her love for Edward. But the dire warnings do not shake Lucy. She is never so happy as when they are together and she cannot give him up.

"He is coming," Alice exclaims; "I will stand watch."

Edward is apologetic for having insisted on this dangerous and hurried meeting. "But I had to see you before I left. I sail for France tomorrow. From those shores I hope I will be better able to negotiate Scotland's future!" Edward continues, "But before I leave I want to meet your brother peaceably and ask for your hand in marriage!"

"Ah, no," she begs, "that is not possible yet."

"So he still wants my blood." Edward is bitter. "You know, Lucy, that I cast aside my pledge of revenge for your sake even though your evil brother killed my father and stole what was rightfully mine. Now I must renew my vow of vengeance!"

She tries to appease him: "Do not say such things. Give up vengeance and let only love move you!"

Calmed by her tender words, Edward says, "Then let us pledge our hearts as bride and groom before God. This unbreakable divine vow unites our paths forever. I am your husband."

Exchanging rings they swear eternal love and devotion. Tenderly, they bid each other farewell, she imploring him to write occasionally, he reminding her they are eternally bound.

ACT II

SCENE 1

Many months later Lord Henry Ashton nervously awaits Lucy in his chamber. To Norman he frets, "Lord Arthur Bucklaw will be here soon. What if she still refuses to marry him?"

"Don't worry," the henchman counters; "Edward has been gone a long time and we have successfully intercepted all of his letters. And here is a forged letter from Edward in which he says that he has found another lover. That will put an end to her love for him!"

Hearing his sister approach, Henry takes the forged letter from Norman, and orders him to meet Bucklaw and escort him to the castle.

Lucy enters reluctantly, looking distraught, pale and somewhat shaky. Henry tries to cheer her up. "I thought it would make you happy to see the castle ablaze with light in preparation for your wedding."

"I look this way because of the misery you have subjected me to!" is her pained rejoinder.

In an effort to sweep the past out of the way, he tells her he has forgotten his anger and that now she must forget her former love and accept the noble husband he has selected for her. But she tells him it is impossible since she is already bound to another man.

Handing her the forged letter, Henry says, "Read this. It will make apparent how unfaithful is the man to whom you have pledged your faith."

She is crushed by what she reads. Henry says how fortunate to have found out in time that Edward is a villain. But she wants only to die.

Sounds of merriment rouse her from her shock.

Henry says, "Your bridegroom has arrived."

"I cannot marry him."

129

"Listen," Henry implores. "Our party has fallen on evil days. Without this marriage our family will be ruined. Only Arthur can rescue us."

"But what of me?"

"You must save me. If you refuse I will be executed, and my ghost will haunt you." He leaves to greet his guest.

"Oh, God, please let me die," Lucy whispers.

Raymond comes in to tell her that the letter he sent to Edward in France has received no reply. "I'm afraid all is lost. My advice is to give in to your brother. Your vows with Edward were not blessed and are therefore neither valid nor sacred. If you do not accept Bucklaw only evil will befall the family!" Relentlessly, he begs her to make this sacrifice, until finally, too weak to continue arguing, she yields. He is so relieved, he likens her agreement to the clouds disappearing. She asks only that he guide her through a life of torment.

SCENE 2

In the great hall of the castle, knights, ladies, pages, soldiers and friends of the Ashtons joyfully welcome Arthur Bucklaw. The bridegroom greets Henry and asks for Lucy, adding that he has heard that Edward was seeking her hand. Henry dispels his fears just as Lucy enters. When her brother introduces her intended bridegroom she pulls back. Her obvious dislike of Arthur when he makes his vows of tender love only makes Henry want to hasten the signing of the marriage contract. Arthur gladly obliges. Lucy, guided by Alice and Raymond, gripped by hopelessness, urged on by her brother, slowly and reluctantly signs the contract, declaring quietly, "This is my death warrant!"

Suddenly a commotion erupts near the door. "Who is it?" people cry.

As he bursts through the crowd, Edward announces himself. "I am here."

Lucy faints and is lifted to a nearby chair by Alice. Sword in hand, pistol in belt, Edward confronts Henry, but both are quickly restrained by their concern for Lucy, who seems closer to death than to life. Recovering, Lucy regrets only that death has not come to relieve her torment.

Edward tells her he loves her still, and she is horrified to learn of her brother's deceit. Henry and Arthur, drawing swords, try to force Edward out. But he is willing to fight both of them. "I may die, but I will draw your blood in the process!"

Raymond intervenes and, invoking the name of God, orders the combatants to cast aside their swords.

They obey, but Henry demands to know why Edward has come, and he declares simply that he has come for Lucy, who has sworn to be his.

"Forget her vow of love," Raymond counsels, "for she is bound to another." He shows Edward the signed marriage contract.

Shocked by the document before his eyes, Edward curses Lucy, returns her ring, and demands the return of his. "You have betrayed me! I curse the moment we met and now I will leave this hated house!"

Angrily he adds, "May the Lord cast you down!"

Appalled by his rage, the guests order him to leave.

Boldly baring his chest, Edward offers himself as a sacrifice. "Run your swords through me and leave my corpse on the threshold so that she may walk over it on the way to the altar!"

Lucy prays to God to hear her and to save Edward. Exhausted and emotionally spent, she collapses, while Edward storms out.

ACT III

SCENE 1

A wild storm rages outside the tower of Wolf's Crag, a monumental ruin on the grounds of the Ravenswood estate. Edward believes he is safely hidden inside, and is surprised when Henry enters. He can't believe his enemy's brazenness. "This house is filled with the spirits of those you have killed!" he reminds Henry.

Henry taunts him: "Lucy has been married and now enjoys the bridal chamber."

Face to face, their enmity flares.

"I have come to challenge you so I may seek vengeance for what you have done!" Henry declares.

"And I swore by the ashes of my father to kill you!" Edward counters. As the storm swirls and crashes around the tower, they agree to settle their differences with a duel at dawn among the tombstones of their ancestors in the Ravenswood graveyard.

SCENE 2

Back in the great hall of the castle the wedding festivities are in full swing; the celebrants dance joyfully about through brilliantly lit rooms. Suddenly Raymond appears. He is in a state of extreme shock and calls the rejoicing to a halt. Overwhelmed by the horror of what he has seen, he recounts how he heard a strange cry from the bridal chamber, as of a man near death, and rushed into the room to find Arthur dead in a pool of blood and Lucy holding the sword that killed him. "She was demented, and she looked at me with a little smile and asked me where her husband was. Oh, my God, here she comes!"

Lucy appears, clad in a white nightdress, her hair loose, her eyes bright with a strange gleam. Clearly, she does not know where she is. As she talks her mood shifts from calm to anguish to rapture. "Here we sit by the fountain in the garden. But there is a specter that sits between us, keeping us apart. Oh, Edward, let us go to the altar where we are to be married. Don't you hear the heavenly music playing for our wedding? The priest is ready to perform the ceremony. At last we can be together. I will be yours forever!"

Henry bursts in and, informed of the murder, rushes to Lucy, who, locked in her mad world, mistakes her brother for Edward and apologizes to him for agreeing to marry Arthur. "I was sacrificed by my brother. But I have always been in love with you. I swear it, Edward." Henry pulls away from her, appalled and now filled with remorse at the sight of her insanity. Continuing to call to Edward, she collapses.

Henry prays, "May God protect the poor girl!" as Alice and her ladies carry Lucy away.

Unable to control himself any longer, Raymond accuses Norman of being at the root of the calamity and orders him out of the house.

SCENE 3

Alone in the Ravenswood graveyard, Edward walks among the tombstones of his ancestors. He longs for sunrise. Faced with the prospect of a life without Lucy, he has resolved to end it. He will impale himself on Henry's sword. Waiting impatiently for sunrise and his duel, he thinks, "It is a night of joy for her and the fortunate man she married. I will find my refuge in the grave that awaits me!"

His solitude is broken by a group of people from the castle, who are weeping and lamenting. They tell Edward that Lucy is bereft of reason and near death. Before he can quite absorb this news, the tolling of the bell is heard.

Moving to go, Edward declares, "I must see her one more time."

Raymond approaches and tells him that it is too late. Lucy is already dead.

Calmly, Edward addresses the spirit of his beloved Lucy. "You, beautiful creature, are now in heaven, and with you will go your true love. The grudges of mortals, which kept us separated here on earth, yield only agony. But God may unite us in heaven! I will join you!" Drawing his dagger, he ignores Raymond's cries and stabs himself. "I wish to die!" he declares. "May God unite us in heaven!"

While Raymond prays to God to forgive Edward, and the people who have gathered cry out against the horror of what they have witnessed, Edward sinks to the ground and dies among the tombstones.

OTELLO

Opera in Four Acts
by
GIUSEPPE VERDI
Première: La Scala, Milan, February 5, 1887

ACT I

VENICE, IN the fifteenth century, was a militant and aggressive city-state that had spread its rule through much of the Mediterranean. Among its colonies was the island of Cyprus.

One night, in the main port of the island, citizens and soldiers wait for the arrival of their governor—the Moor, Otello, a general in the Venetian army—who has been fighting the Turks. The ship is approaching land in the midst of a violent storm, and the people watch anxiously as winds and a turbulent sea toss it about. At times the ship seems to disappear and they cry that it is lost until they see it rise again above a wave, silhouetted by lightning.

Underneath the fears and prayers that issue from the waiting crowd, two voices gloat over the impending doom of the ship. One is Roderigo, a Venetian nobleman, who is in love with the woman Otello has recently married, the beautiful Desdemona. The other is Iago, Otello's ensign, and a man in whom Otello has great trust. But Iago is furious because Otello has promoted to Captain a young and handsome lieutenant, Cassio, instead of himself, and he wishes neither of them well.

At last the ship pulls into the harbor. A cry of "He is saved" goes up and most of the people rush to the landing to help secure the boat. As Otello comes off the ship, he exultantly announces the defeat of the Turkish fleet and is hailed as a hero.

While Otello enters his palace, and the crowd noisily rejoices, Iago pulls Roderigo aside: "Though I feign loyalty, I hate the Moor as much as you do. If I were he, I would not wish to have Iago around! If you understand me! Roderigo, I have schemes that will make Desdemona yours!"

They join Cassio and some of the other soldiers who are celebrating the victory. Iago plies Cassio with wine. Knowing his own weakness, Cassio tries to refuse.

"But we must drink a toast," Iago declares, "to the wedding of Otello and Desdemona!"

Cassio cannot refuse this and praises Desdemona's beauty with a glass of wine. Once started, he continues to drink and to toast Otello's wife. Noting that Cassio is becoming tipsy, Iago fiendishly urges him to drink more and more, until he begins to stumble about out of control. Iago also encourages Roderigo to pick a fight by hinting that Cassio wishes to seduce Desdemona. But before Roderigo can react, Montano, the former governor of Cyprus, arrives to tell Cassio he is needed on the ramparts. Iago whispers to Montano that the Captain is drunk like this every night. Montano says he will report this to Otello and Roderigo laughingly makes an insulting remark. Cassio, totally out of control, challenges him to a duel, but Montano steps in, calling Cassio "Drunkard" and Cassio turns his sword on him instead. While they duel, Roderigo encourages the crowd to gather and shout, until drawn by the noise, Otello arrives. His presence stops the fighting and he demands to know what's going on.

"Forgive me!" Cassio begs, but his plea falls on deaf ears for Otello is horrified when he sees that Montano has been wounded. He strips Cassio of his rank, just as Desdemona, awakened by the tumult, arrives.

"Iago, restore peace to the city," Otello orders. "Everybody else return to your homes. I will stay here until the ramparts are empty." Iago proceeds with the soldiers to clear the street, leaving Otello alone with Desdemona.

They embrace and he tells her how their love calms his heart after the horrors of war.

"My great warrior," she says. "Do you remember how I fell in love with

135

you as you told me of your adventures, and the dangers and hardships you had suffered? As you described to me the parched deserts of your native land, I looked into your dark face and saw the beauty of your spirit. I loved you for all you had survived!"

"And I loved you for your compassion!" he responds.

The night has cleared and the moon and stars shine overhead. They fervently embrace, praying that heaven will rid them of grief and protect their love. "Another kiss!" Otello says, overwhelmed by his emotion. "One more kiss." He takes her tenderly into his arms. Holding each other, they return slowly to the castle.

ACT II

In a great hall of the palace opening onto the garden, Iago counsels Cassio, who is still distraught over his public embarrassment and fall from grace. "My advice," Iago counsels, "is to ask Desdemona to intercede with Otello on your behalf. He lives for her alone. Go and talk to her as she strolls through the garden. Go now!" Watching Cassio go out to the garden, Iago thinks, "You are but my puppet, impelled by my evil genius," and in a moment of profound self-loathing reflects bitterly, "just as I am impelled by my one and only God, a monstrous God who created me in his own image." His own bleak credo: "Man is nothing more than a plaything of wicked fate. Noble words are but figments of delusion. Only death is certain!" As Cassio talks with Desdemona in the garden, Iago invokes his demon to bring Otello to the scene.

His wish is granted. Otello arrives and asks, "Wasn't that Cassio I saw strolling with my wife?" Iago pretends not to know, but the evasiveness of his answers makes Otello suspicious. As Iago's calculated comments shift between feigned reluctance and sly innuendo, Otello moves from uneasiness to jealousy.

"Beware of jealousy," counsels Iago, but then, playing the good friend, says, "You are too trusting. I have no specific proof, my lord, but watch Desdemona carefully!"

In the garden, Cypriot women and children, bearing flowers and other gifts, surround Desdemona, obviously adoring of her goodness and sweetness. Moved by this Otello thinks, "If she is guilty, the Lord himself has deceived me."

When the island people have left the garden, Desdemona and Emilia, her lady-in-waiting and Iago's wife, enter the palace. Seeing Otello, Desdemona rushes toward him and pleads forgiveness "for a man who displeased you and who suffers now. His name is Cassio!"

Otello is deeply troubled by her intercession and refuses to listen. "My forehead is burning!" he tells her.

She offers to cool his brow with her handkerchief but in a rage he grabs it from her and tosses it to the ground. Emilia retrieves it.

Trying to calm her husband, Desdemona asks him what vexes him, while unheard by the others, Iago demands that his wife give him the handkerchief; Emilia tries to resist but he snatches it away from her. Desdemona pleads with Otello to forgive whatever pain she may unknowingly have caused him, but consumed by his mistrust, he tells her he wishes to be left alone. As Desdemona leaves, Iago quietly warns Emilia to say nothing.

Drowning in the whirlpool of his doubts about Desdemona, Otello tells Iago that her infidelity signals the end of all his glory, and dramatically says goodbye to all his fame, his brave deeds, the companions and accoutrements of his battles. Suddenly, he turns on Iago. "It is you who have made me suspicious. Now give me proof."

Iago is prepared. He whispers to Otello, "My lord, one night as I lay beside Cassio he spoke in his sleep. It was only a dream but his words betrayed his heart. 'Sweetest Desdemona,' he said, 'we must hide our love from the Moor to whom fate has cruelly given you!' Then his dream ended, my lord!" Iago strengthens his story by describing in great detail a handkerchief he has seen in Cassio's hands.

Otello recognizes the description and says, "It was the first gift I gave to Desdemona."

"My lord," says Iago, "that handkerchief was in Cassio's hand just yesterday!"

This is more than Otello can bear and now totally convinced of Desdemona's guilt, he raises his hand to the heavens and swears, "My anger shall blaze as I take my revenge."

ACT III

In the great hall of the palace Iago instructs Otello to wait for him. "I will fetch Cassio and bring him here. With you in hiding I will make him give proof of his love for Desdemona. Remember the handkerchief!"

Iago leaves and Otello turns to greet his wife.

"I must speak to you again of Cassio," she begins.

Otello interrupts. "My headache has returned. Take your handkerchief and bind my forehead."

As she obediently produces her handkerchief, he demands that she use the one he gave her. This makes her nervous as she is not sure where it is. Otello says, "Woe unto you if it is lost. It contains a magic charm and its loss spells damnation. Now go fetch it!"

Desdemona says he is just trying to frighten her, to turn her thoughts from Cassio's just cause.

With each word of supplication Otello's fury mounts until he explodes and, seizing her, accuses her of being a "vile trollop!" When Desdemona swears it is not true, his anger suddenly turns to sarcasm. Taking her by her "very lovely hand" he escorts her to the door, and asks to be forgiven. "How could I have thought Otello's wife a strumpet!" With a vicious twist of her arm he pushes her out of the room.

Alone and dejected he protests his fate. "God! You could have made me poor or taken away my triumphs. But why did you rob me of my peaceful soul and kill so sunlit a love?" Rage engulfs him again and he rants, "I shall have her confession and then Desdemona will die!"

Iago returns and tells Otello to hide behind a pillar to listen while he talks to Cassio. While Otello eavesdrops, Cassio enters the hall. "I thought Desdemona would be here," Cassio begins.

Otello's pain is unbearable as he hears his wife's name on Cassio's lips.

Deftly, Iago steers the conversation to Bianca, a woman with whom Cassio has had an affair. Iago does this so cleverly that Otello only hears Cassio's lecherous comments and laughter, which he assumes relate to Desdemona. When Cassio shows Iago an embroidered handkerchief that he found in his lodging, Otello does not hear him say that he does not know how it got there. Iago takes the handkerchief and holds it in such a way that Otello cannot help but see and recognize it. Behind the pillar the Moor moans, "All is over! My heart has frozen!"

With vicious delight, Iago pushes Cassio to talk flippantly about the handkerchief as the devastated Otello slumps against his hiding post.

A burst of cannon and a trumpet fanfare sounds. Cassio and Iago bid each other farewell. Iago approaches the crazed Moor.

"She is condemned!" Otello cries out. "Get me some poison to kill her!"

Iago advises against this, counseling instead that he strangle her in the bed where she has sinned. "I will take care of Cassio!" he promises.

"Good Iago, you are so just, you shall be my Captain!"

Iago thanks him and warns that the ambassadors have arrived to meet him. He goes off to get Desdemona, so she can appear with her husband, while Otello prepares himself to meet the delegation from Venice.

The ambassadors, together with Lodovico, Roderigo, and other members of the Venetian court, enter hailing Otello "the Lion of Saint Mark!" Iago, Desdemona, and Emilia follow close behind. Desdemona is downcast. As Otello reads the message from the Doge of Venice, Lodovico asks the whereabouts of Cassio and Iago tells him that he has fallen out of favor with Otello. Whereupon Desdemona expresses the hope that soon all will be forgiven. Otello turns on her and raising his hand to strike her orders her to hold her tongue. Lodovico stops him, disbelieving his own eyes.

"Bring Cassio here," Otello orders, and mutters to Iago to watch how Desdemona reacts to his appearance.

Lodovico asks Iago what has happened to the great warrior to make him behave in such atrocious fashion to his wife. Iago sidesteps the question while managing to insinuate that the heroic Moor has always had feet of clay.

Otello tells Desdemona that she will leave for Venice with him in the morning and when he sees that she is weeping assumes these are tears of regret at leaving Cassio. He then announces to everyone that the Doge has ordered him back to Venice and in his absence Cassio is to rule Cyprus. He continues to direct harsh, biting comments to Desdemona and when Lodovico pleads with Otello to treat his wife more gently, Otello loses all control and flings her to the ground.

The crowd is stunned. While they whisper to each other of the shock and confusion Otello has produced, Iago urges Otello to strike quickly and offers to dispatch Cassio himself. Then he approaches Roderigo and by cunningly convincing him that a dead Cassio will prevent the Moor from leaving and taking Desdemona away, he induces Roderigo to take on the task of fighting Cassio. Otello now turns on the crowd and orders everyone to leave while Iago coolly notes to Lodovico that the Moor has lost his senses. Lodovico coaxes Desdemona out of the hall with everyone else. Only Iago remains with Otello.

Seeing in his mind the accursed handkerchief as the symbol of Desdemona's betrayal, Otello reels deliriously until he collapses in a convulsion.

Outside the palace the Cypriots are shouting, "Hurrah for Otello! Long live the Lion of Venice!"

Iago, triumphant, points to the inert crumpled figure and sneers, "Here is your lion!"

ACT IV

In her bedroom, Desdemona prepares to retire. Lit by a lamp above the prayer bench, the room has an air of foreboding. Troubled, Desdemona asks Emilia to put her wedding sheets upon the bed. "I feel very low tonight, Emilia. I remember when I was a child, my mother's maid had a lover who deserted her. There was a song she sang." As Emilia helps her with her hair, Desdemona sings it, the melancholy refrain echoing her somber mood. She embraces Emilia and bids her an emotional farewell. Alone, Desdemona kneels before a portrait of the Madonna and prays. Then she goes to bed.

Otello comes in through a secret door. He approaches the bed and stops to gaze at Desdemona's sleeping form. He kisses her several times, almost tenderly, and she wakes. "Have you said your prayers tonight?" he asks. "If there is a sin for which you have not atoned, pray now. Though I kill you, I would not condemn your soul!"

"You wish to kill me?" Disbelieving and desperate, she protests that her only crime is that she loves Otello.

"It is Cassio you love," he angrily tells her.

She denies it. "Ask him," she says.

"Cassio is dead now!" he replies.

She weeps bitterly, begging Otello to let her live, if only to say one more prayer.

"Too late, too late," he says, and putting his hands around her throat, he strangles her.

Suddenly there is a loud knocking at the door and Emilia calls to Otello to let her in. "Cassio has killed Roderigo!" she cries.

From the bed there comes a faint moan. "I die but I am innocent."

"She is a liar and I have killed her," Otello says.

Emilia, horrified, shrieks at him, "You are a murderer."

Otello defends himself. "She betrayed me with Cassio. Ask Iago!"

"And you believed him!" Emilia shouts for help. "Otello has killed Desdemona!"

Lodovico, Cassio, and Iago rush in.

"Iago," Emilia asks, "did you believe Desdemona unfaithful?"

"Yes," he replies.

Otello says, "She gave my handkerchief to Cassio."

Emilia cannot bear this. Despite Iago's attempt to silence her, she confesses, "Iago took the handkerchief from me and placed it in Cassio's quarters!"

"So that is how it came to me," Cassio mutters.

Montano, now entering the room, reports that Roderigo with his dying breath has revealed Iago's evil scheme. Otello whirls on Iago, who flees from the room.

Beside himself with grief, Otello tries to pick up his sword, but Lodovico takes it from him. Slowly he moves to the bed where the dead Desdemona lies and gazes at her, lamenting the loss of his beautiful and beloved angel born under crossed stars. Without a word he pulls a dagger from his doublet, and while Cassio, Lodovico, and Montano helplessly watch, he stabs himself.

"I kissed you ere I killed you. Now I'm dying. . . ." He puts his lips to hers. "One more kiss . . ."

DON PASQUALE

Opera in Three Acts
by
GAETANO DONIZETTI
Première: Théâtre Italien, Paris, January 3, 1843

ACT I

SCENE 1

A RICH, ELDERLY bachelor, Don Pasquale, has decided to disinherit his nephew Ernesto because he does not approve of the woman Ernesto loves—a young widow named Norina. In fact, Don Pasquale has decided he will get married himself in order to have a family he can leave his fortune to, and he is waiting impatiently for his friend, the good Doctor Malatesta, to arrive, Malatesta having promised to help him find a bride. He is also rather looking forward to the shock this news will give his nephew.

The Doctor arrives and announces that he has found the perfect bride for Don Pasquale. "Let me describe her: She is pretty as an angel, fresh as a plucked flower; with a glance that could melt any heart. She is innocent and of incomparable modesty. A kind, gentle soul clearly sent here by the heavens!"

The delighted old bachelor asks her name.

"Malatesta," says the Doctor, "for she is my sister! She has just come out of the convent, and I will bring her to meet you this evening."

For Don Pasquale this means waiting too long and he pleads with the

Doctor to arrange the meeting sooner, virtually throwing him out of the house in his hurry to see this angel.

The confirmed old bachelor can hardly wait to be married. Consumed by fantasies of his impending blissful marriage, he even tries to envision the children they will have. His dreams are interrupted by the arrival of his nephew. Don Pasquale decides to give Ernesto one last chance. "You have come in time. I am not going to lecture you, I only want to speak to you for a moment. Two months ago I offered you a very generous inheritance if you would marry a certain very beautiful, noble, and rich young woman. However, if you refused, I warned I would disinherit you and get married myself. Well, my offer still stands."

Ernesto tells his uncle that marriage to another would be impossible since he is in love with Norina.

"All right then, you're on your own now, and I am going to get married!"

Ernesto thinks his uncle must be joking, but soon realizes that the old man is deadly serious. He counsels his uncle to seek the advice of the wise Doctor Malatesta.

"I already have," Pasquale counters, "and he thinks it is a terrific idea. In fact, just between you and me, my intended bride is his sister!"

This is more than Ernesto can bear. That his friend Malatesta should double-cross him is almost impossible to believe. Crushed, he contemplates the poverty and loneliness that lie before him. In one fell swoop he has lost not only his inheritance, but his best friend and the possibility of ever marrying the woman he loves. His rather voluble desolation only fuels Don Pasquale's gloating joy.

Scene 2

In another part of town, the charming Norina is reading a romantic story about a knight captivated by a lady's glance. "Ah yes," she knowingly muses, "I too know how to make men fall at my feet with one smoldering glance." As she itemizes her feminine wiles, her thoughts stray to Doctor Malatesta, who has promised to deceive Don Pasquale, and she wonders what scheme he has devised. While she waits for Malatesta to arrive, a servant brings her a letter from Ernesto. She opens it and her cheerfulness turns to consternation just as the Doctor enters. Handing him the letter she announces, "I want nothing more to do with you."

Doctor Malatesta is stunned, but quickly comprehends the problem as he reads the letter, in which Ernesto speaks of "death in my heart" and how that "two-faced scoundrel, Doctor Malatesta, has double-crossed me by getting Don Pasquale to marry his sister. I will be disinherited," Ernesto's letter concludes. "And because I love you I must leave Rome and go far away. I will depart this very day! Farewell, my love!"

The good Doctor assures Norina that he will fill Ernesto in on the plot to deceive Don Pasquale, which he now outlines. "You see," he explains, "the Don knows I have a sister who has been in a convent, but he has never met her. I will introduce you as her and then I will call in my cousin Carlotto, who, disguised as a notary, will pretend to marry you both. The rest is up to you, Norina; you must drive Pasquale crazy. When he is at our mercy things will work out for you and Ernesto." Norina likes this scheme and Malatesta sets to teaching her how to act the part of his simple shy sister. She is an apt pupil and before long gives a highly believable performance. Giddily, Norina and Doctor Malatesta anticipate the fun they will have tricking old Don Pasquale.

ACT II

Poor Ernesto! Alone in Don Pasquale's house, he still believes he has been abandoned by his friend, disinherited by his uncle and separated from his Norina. He bemoans his future and is determined to end his sad days in another part of the world. "As long as my beloved Norina is happy, then I will be content," he gallantly but sadly concludes as he leaves the room.

Don Pasquale, dressed in his finest clothes, awaits his future. He warns the servants that after they have admitted Doctor Malatesta and the other guest, they are not to allow anyone else into the house. Preening himself for the impending meeting, he admires his physical condition. "Well preserved and active, not bad for a man almost seventy years old."

Doctor Malatesta arrives with Norina, who is hidden behind a veil. While she feigns fear and hesitation, he coaxes her to come into the room. "You mustn't be afraid, I will stay here with you!" Malatesta assures her and tells Don Pasquale that her shy demeanor is only natural for a girl who has just left the convent. Norina continues to play her part, all the while relishing the vengeance she will take on the man who has disinherited her beloved Ernesto. As Malatesta officially introduces his "sister" Sofronia to Don Pasquale, she claims she is "terrified" by the sight of a man. Her brother must assure her that Pasquale is friendly, chivalrous, and honorable. Obediently, she curtsies before the Don. He is delighted by what he can see but is a bit discouraged by the veil. Malatesta tells him she thinks it improper to expose her face to a strange man and advises the Don to talk to her a bit, advice the Don accepts. Each question he asks reveals anew what a shy, sheltered, and demure young woman she is, and she impresses him with accounts of her ability to sew, embroider, knit, and cook. Don Pasquale is thrilled by his bride-to-be while Doctor Malatesta quietly enjoys Norina's performance.

Malatesta now orders "Sofronia" to remove her veil. When Don Pasquale sees her face he is overcome.

"Before I die, dear Doctor, I must know if your beautiful sister will be my bride!"

Obligingly, Malatesta asks her if she will have Don Pasquale.

Demurely, with eyes cast down she whispers, "Yes!"

Pasquale cannot believe his good fortune. "Let's get a notary."

"No need to call for one," Malatesta tells him. "I brought one along just in case," and without more ado brings in his cousin, who has been waiting in the hall. Using rather offhand legal gobbledygook, he dictates the wedding vows while the notary makes a great show of recording every word.

Don Pasquale adds: "Now put down that the aforementioned, in his lifetime, will give half of everything he owns to his darling little wife; she shall be considered mistress of the house, and be given everything that goes along with that position."

Malatesta and Norina (Sofronia) thank Don Pasquale for his generosity and the contract signing proceeds. But just as Norina is about to sign, Ernesto charges into the room, much to the dismay of Malatesta, who hasn't yet informed him of the plan. Forcing his way past the servants Ernesto, in great anger, tells his uncle that he has come to say farewell.

"Your timing is excellent, nephew," says Pasquale. "We need a witness for our wedding ceremony. Come meet my lovely bride." When he sees Norina, Ernesto begins to froth and sputter, which prevents him from immediately saying something to ruin the scheme.

Malatesta rushes between them. "Ernesto," he hisses, "if you don't calm down you will lose Norina. *She* is Sofronia, my sister!" By dint of more mutters and whispers he gets the reluctant Ernesto to act as a witness.

The contract signed, Don Pasquale is ecstatic and turns to his wife for a matrimonial kiss.

"Not so fast!" she warns. "You have to ask for permission to do that!"

Meekly, Pasquale asks permission, which is refused. Don Pasquale is not amused and angrily orders his nephew out of the house.

"What rude behavior," Norina counters. "I say that he will stay!"

Pasquale is beside himself and calls on Doctor Malatesta for help. But, alas, Malatesta now has no advice to offer. In an instant, Don Pasquale's demure bride-to-be has been transformed into a shrewish wife, and her arrogance escalates by the minute. Much to Don Pasquale's outrage she proclaims that it is unbecoming for such a decrepit old man to be seen with so young a woman, and so she will take Ernesto as escort for her walks. When Don Pasquale tells her he won't allow it she replies that she is the boss. Ernesto and Malatesta observe the battle with detached amusement. Growing ever more despotic, Norina threatens the Don with physical punishment if he fails to obey her. Dazed and disillusioned, he retreats.

Norina now rings a bell for the servants and when only three arrive, she decides their household will need more. Over her husband's renewed protests she doubles the head steward's wages and orders him to "find some new servants, young ones we can be proud of. I also want two carriages and horses by tomorrow. Then I want to redecorate the house."

Pasquale is virtually apoplectic by now and demands to know who will foot the bill for all this. "You will, you blockhead!" says Norina.

Enraged, Don Pasquale turns to Malatesta who, in sham despair, tries to calm him down. "You're overwrought, perhaps you should go to bed. Sleep will make you feel better."

"I've been tricked into this hellish marriage," Pasquale rants, "and I won't have it!"

While Malatesta tries to quell his outbursts, Norina and Ernesto whisper happily to each other. When he finds a moment, Malatesta warns them not to let the old man see them flirting, but he has to return quickly to the "former" bachelor, whose fury flows unabated.

ACT III

SCENE 1

Later that evening, as the servants scurry about with boxes of the expensive goods ordered by Norina, Don Pasquale peruses the volume of bills that have mounted during the last few hours. "If this keeps up," he moans, "I will be taken off to the poorhouse." Just then Norina, elegantly attired, comes through the room on her way out of the house. "Where are you going?" he asks.

"I'm going to the theater to enjoy myself!"

"On our wedding night? Without me? I forbid it!"

"Oh be quiet and go to bed."

Enraged, he tries to bar the door and calls her a "tart," in response to which she slaps him across the face. This utterly demoralizes him and he feels there is nothing left but to die.

"I'm leaving now," Norina states with finality. "We'll talk in the morning."

"If you leave," he warns, "you will find the door bolted shut when you return."

Norina, deciding that she has to change tactics, gently coaxes him to be calm and lovingly advises him to wait until morning when she herself will rouse him. But her words fall on the deaf ears of a man whose only thought is to end this atrocious marriage. Norina bids him good night, and on her way out drops a piece of paper. Don Pasquale picks it up and reads, "Dearest Sofronia, I will be outside the garden between nine and ten this evening. I will wait for you to let me in through the secret door. You will know I am there by the strains of my serenade. Don't fail me. Your devoted suitor!" Don Pasquale is beside himself and orders a servant to get Doctor Malatesta immediately. He then goes to his room for some much needed rest.

Doctor Malatesta arrives with Ernesto and together they make the final plans. "You go down to the garden," Malatesta instructs, "while I remain here to play my part. Whatever you do, don't let Don Pasquale recognize you." Ernesto agrees and, donning his cloak, goes into the garden.

Malatesta surmises that Pasquale's urgent summons indicates he has read the planted letter and so knows about the assignation.

Pasquale comes in to greet Malatesta looking wan and miserable. "My dear Doctor, you see before you a walking ghost. To think I have been brought to this low estate just by trying to keep Ernesto from marrying his Norina. I would have let him have a thousand Norinas had I known that marrying Sofronia would cause me such grief. She has spent half my yearly income on bows and bonnets. Then she decided to go to the theater without me. When I ordered her to stay at home she slapped me across the face. But all that's not even the worst of it! Here, read this," and he hands over the letter.

Feigning great surprise, Malatesta declares he cannot believe that his sister, the charming convent girl, is capable of such heinous actions.

"But it is true," Pasquale assures him. "In fact I have called you here to

147

witness the revenge I have planned. We shall go down to the garden, catch Sofronia and her lover 'in flagrante,' and haul them before a magistrate."

Malatesta suggests a few changes. "We do not want a scandal. Let us surprise them at exactly the right moment. Faced with the threat of legal action, they will have to end the affair right there. This will save you and my sister any public gossip."

Don Pasquale is not happy with this because it leaves him still stuck with the woman.

"I've got it!" Malatesta says, feigning inspiration. "We will surprise them. With her faithlessness proven you can kick her out of your house."

"Bravo," says Pasquale.

"Just leave it to me," says the Doctor.

Together, they go into the garden, Pasquale relishing the revenge that lies ahead, Malatesta chuckling over the way the old man is falling right into his trap.

SCENE 2

In the garden Ernesto can be heard singing his serenade. Norina lets him in through the secret door. As once again they promise each other eternal love, Don Pasquale and Doctor Malatesta steathily make their way through the bushes and sneak up on the couple. Norina shouts for help while Ernesto slips away and sneaks back into the house. Norina (Sofronia) calmly insists to her husband that she was alone.

Pasquale calls her a brazen liar and orders her to leave his house.

"But this is my house too," she insists.

Malatesta takes over. "For your own good, my child, you should leave. Tomorrow, this house will be occupied by another woman, Ernesto's new wife, Norina!"

"Sofronia" throws a tantrum. "*That* woman! I would rather leave this house forever!"

Malatesta tells Pasquale, "Well, there seems to be no other way. To get rid of your wife you will have to allow Ernesto to marry Norina."

Pasquale eagerly agrees.

Malatesta calls Ernesto from the house. "My dear boy, your uncle has decided to let you wed Norina and he will give you a generous annual allowance."

Ernesto is overjoyed and profusely thanks his uncle, who orders him to fetch his bride-to-be so he can marry her right away.

"We don't have to go far," says Malatesta. He points to Norina. "She is right here."

Pasquale says, "But that is my wife Sofronia."

Sofronia, Malatesta explains, is still in the convent, and the marriage was a charade—his way of stopping Don Pasquale from making a terrible mistake.

Don Pasquale is flabbergasted—and relieved. "You heartless rascal," he says, "how can I ever thank you?"

Ernesto, Norina, and Doctor Malatesta ask him to forgive them.

Overjoyed to have his old bachelorhood back, and realizing he is too old for the ladies, Don Pasquale embraces Ernesto and Norina and bestows his blessing on their marriage.

TRISTAN UND ISOLDE

Opera in Three Acts
by
RICHARD WAGNER
Première: Hoftheater, Munich, June 10, 1865

ACT I

ON A medieval ship crossing the sea between Ireland and Cornwall, the heroic knight Tristan sails homeward, bringing with him the beautiful Irish princess Isolde, who has been taken against her will to be married to Tristan's uncle, King Marke of Cornwall. The proposed marriage is one born of political expediency and has been arranged in the hope that it will at last bring peace to the two nations.

The strife between Ireland and Cornwall has brought much grief to both sides. Isolde's fiancé, the noble Morold, was slain in battle by Tristan, who in a gruesome gesture sent Morold's head back to Isolde. Badly wounded himself, however, and having learned that the Irish princess was highly skilled in magic cures, Tristan disguised himself and sailed to Ireland to put himself in her care. Drawn to him by his plight, Isolde tended him until one day she discovered that a splinter of steel in the severed head of her dead lover fit exactly into a nick in her patient's sword. Thus recognizing Tristan's true identity, she raised the sword to strike and avenge the death of Morold. Just then Tristan, in his weak and piteous state, gazed into her eyes and she could not bring herself to kill him. Instead, she nursed him back to health.

When Tristan recovered he pledged undying gratitude and loyalty to Isolde. But now he stands at the helm of the ship bringing her to a loveless marriage.

Throughout the voyage Tristan has ignored his prisoner and the entire situation has enraged Isolde. "I held his life in my hands and yet I spared him. And now he has rebuked his oath and holds me prisoner. If only I had the magic powers to make these calm seas grow wild and destroy this ship!"

Her lady-in-waiting, Brangaena, tries to calm Isolde and opens the flap of the tent to let in more air. Through the opening Isolde can see Tristan and his faithful aide, Kurwenal. Brangaena is awed by the sight of the hero, but Isolde says, "Your hero cannot even look me in the eye. Fetch him to me so that he may pay proper homage."

Brangaena delivers the message to Tristan, but he refuses to come to Isolde, citing his duty to guide their ship to Cornwall. As Brangaena presses Tristan to give a more satisfactory response, Kurwenal breaks in to boast of his lord's triumphs, especially the slaying of Lord Morold. Tristan rebukes him, and Brangaena, dismayed, returns to her mistress.

Enraged by Tristan's refusal and Kurwenal's derision, Isolde curses Tristan and invokes vengeance. "Let us both die," she cries.

Isolde instructs Brangaena to bring her the chest of magic potions, which contains a balm for healing wounds, an antidote for evil poisons, a love potion, and a death potion. Cries of "Land ho!" issue from the deck. Kurwenal enters and orders the women to prepare for landing. "Tristan requests that you hurry!"

"Tell your lord," Isolde retorts, "that I shall not walk ashore with him until he atones for his guilt." Kurwenal leaves to deliver her message.

Isolde now orders Brangaena to prepare the death potion and bids her farewell, for she plans to share the deadly goblet with Tristan. Brangaena is horrified, and when Kurwenal announces Tristan's arrival she moves out of sight to prepare the drink.

Tristan enters. "What do you wish, my lady?"

Isolde is obviously agitated by the sight of the hero. She accuses him of guilt in the death of Morold. "I cured you only so that some other man could take your life. But now the nations are at peace and the task of vengeance is mine."

Tristan gallantly offers her his sword so she may strike him dead.

She refuses. "Your uncle would be displeased if I were to slay his finest servant, the man who has brought me to him as a peace hostage. Instead," she offers, "let us atone by drinking to reconciliation."

As the sounds and shouts of arrival grow more frequent and boisterous, Brangaena hands the goblet to Isolde, who passes it to Tristan. He suspects it is lethal but drinks anyway, not unwilling to end his own anguish. Before he can drain it fully Isolde snatches the goblet, declaring, "Half is mine! Traitor, here is to you!"

She tosses the empty goblet away. Filled with terror, they gaze into each other's eyes. Suddenly they are seized with an inexplicable, uncontrollable longing. Overcome with helpless passion, they call each other by name and sink into each other's arms.

"Hail, King Marke!" the sailors on deck shout. Tristan and Isolde are stunned and confused, unable to resist the yearning that fills them, oblivious to the commotion, as the shouts of "Hail, King Marke!" continue. Brangaena tries desperately to pull them apart and Kurwenal's announcement of the approach of the King falls on deaf ears.

Tristan stares dazedly at the shore.

Isolde asks, "Brangaena, what draught did you prepare that I am still alive?"

"The love potion," she responds.

With a cry of "Tristan!" Isolde clutches him and faints. Brangaena rushes to her side as the trumpets herald King Marke's arrival.

ACT II

On a lovely midsummer night, sometime after her marriage to King Marke, Isolde stands on the steps leading from the gardens to her apartments in the castle. The King and his courtiers have gone on a hunt, and she is waiting impatiently for the sounds of the horns to disappear in the distance. Waiting with her, Brangaena warns that the sounds are still too near for it to be safe for Tristan to come.

"I hear nothing," Isolde says angrily. "You are just trying to keep us apart."

"I am afraid," Brangaena tells her. "I am sure that the knight Melot suspects you. He may pose as Tristan's great friend, but he is trying to trap you. I fear that you and Tristan are the true prey of this nocturnal hunt."

Isolde scoffs at Brangaena's suspicions and orders her to extinguish the flame of the lamp so that Tristan will know that all is safe. Brangaena begs her mistress to let the flame burn, but Isolde defiantly declares, "Love says it shall be dark as night. Climb to the tower, Brangaena, and keep a careful watch!" As Brangaena slowly mounts the stairs, Isolde extinguishes the lamp and waits eagerly for Tristan to arrive.

Tristan rushes into her embrace. Their joy is so intense they can hardly believe they are actually in each other's arms. "Is it I? Is it you? Is it a dream?" they ask each other, and reassure themselves that they are together and truly blessed in the love that melds them into one rapturous being. If only they did not have to be clandestine. They curse the light of day which keeps them apart, and praise the darkness of the night which consecrates their passion.

As they pray for the night to enclose them forever, and free them from the earth, they sink into a bed of flowers, consumed by the waves of ecstasy that flow from one to the other. They are oblivious to the world and the passage of time.

From the tower above, Brangaena warns them that the night is ending.

"No more waking," Tristan says. "Let us rather die."

In tones of wonder at the power of their love, they voice their belief that not even death can part them. Too absorbed in each other to heed Brangaena's warning cries, they continue to celebrate their love and to extol the eternal night of death from which they will never have to awaken. They are unable to part.

Brangaena shrieks another warning and the faithful Kurwenal rushes in, shouting, "Tristan! Save yourself!"

It is too late. Led by King Marke and Melot, courtiers in hunting dress surround them.

"Now you must believe me!" Melot declares victoriously. "There before you are the lovers; your faithful Tristan with your wife!"

Trembling with shock and anger, Marke asks Tristan, "How could you do this, you, my truest friend?"

Tristan looks at Marke blankly, still so deeply submerged in the night world of his love that the figure of his King seems but a shadow.

The King's mood changes from outrage to deep sadness as he mourns the loss of a faithful servant and his wife.

As Tristan listens, he begins to regard Marke with sorrow and sympathy. But all he can say is, "I cannot answer the questions that you ask!" Then turning to Isolde, Tristan asks if she will follow him to the land where the sun does not shine, "to the land where I was born in that wondrous world of night?"

Isolde says his home shall be hers, and Tristan kisses her gently on the forehead.

Infuriated, Melot draws his sword to attack Tristan, who responds by raising his sword, but allows it to fall as Melot strikes. Tristan collapses into Kurwenal's arms. Isolde rushes to him while King Marke restrains Melot from killing the wounded Tristan.

ACT III

Kurwenal has brought the dying Tristan to his ancestral home in Brittany, a long deserted castle on a rocky and barren estate. Stretched on a pallet, beneath a tree in the desolate garden that overlooks a mournful coast, Tristan lies unconscious. Kurwenal hovers over him, anxiously checking for signs of life, and hoping that Isolde will arrive in time to save him with her magic powers. A shepherd playing a melancholy melody on his shawm can be heard approaching. Soon he appears and asks Kurwenal how their lord is faring. Kurwenal shakes his head and instructs the youth to keep careful watch, and should he sight a sail, to play a joyful tune. As the shepherd leaves, he once again plays his melancholy air, waking Tristan.

Weak and disoriented, Tristan asks where he is.

Overjoyed to see him alive, Kurwenal responds, "Why, in your native land, my lord, your family home of Kareol, where you shall recover from your wounds."

Tristan shakes his head. "I have already been to the realm of night where there is absolute oblivion. Only my incredible yearning to see Isolde again has brought me back to this world of light where *she* still lives. But I know that the gates of death stand open, waiting for me! Oh, Isolde when will you extinguish the flame and grant me eternal darkness?"

Kurwenal tries to turn Tristan's thoughts to living and tells him he has sent word to Cornwall, and if Isolde still lives she will come to cure him.

"Isolde lives. She called me from the night." Almost delirious, Tristan insists he can see the mast of the ship that brings her to him. "Kurwenal! Don't you see it?" he demands.

But the shepherd's shawm still plays the melancholy tune.

It plunges Tristan into a dark mood. "That sad melody has been with me throughout my life. It played for my birth, born as I was to a dead father, and a dying mother. And its strains of yearning and dying haunt me still."

He curses the potion that he hoped would bring death and instead brought this insatiable longing that torments him.

The emotion has worn him out and Tristan falls unconscious again. Trying to revive him, Kurwenal reflects bitterly on the love that has brought this once glorious knight so low.

Tristan revives and once again tells the doubting Kurwenal that he can see the ship carrying Isolde. Kurwenal believes he is raving and tries to restrain Tristan, but suddenly the shepherd plays a joyful tune and Kurwenal rushes to the watchtower from which he can see the ship as it nears the shore. As he reports its every move, Tristan's spirit bounds from joy to despair—when it momentarily disappears behind a reef—and once again to exaltation when Kurwenal announces that Isolde has landed on the beach. Tristan orders him, "Go to the shore and help my lady here!" Delighted, Kurwenal leaves to execute the order.

Overwhelmed by the surge of bliss that courses through his body, and in a state of near-delirium, Tristan tosses on his couch. Suddenly, he rips the bandages from his wounds declaring, "When I fought Morold I bled; now I bleed again so Isolde may heal my wounds!" As Isolde runs in, he staggers toward her with blood flowing and, weakened beyond help, tells her that the light has finally been extinguished. With his dying breath he murmurs, "Isolde!"

Isolde tries to revive him, unable to believe that he is dead. Repeatedly, she pleads with him to wake so they may be together even if just for an hour. She calls him an obstinate man and begs him not to die without her. Finally, utterly frenzied, she believes that he is breathing. "Ah, my beloved; he wakes," she cries, and faints upon his lifeless body.

Kurwenal, having witnessed Isolde's wild behavior in a state of speechless horror, now hears the shepherd shout that he has sighted another ship. A helmsman rushes in with the news that King Marke and his men have attacked. "We are overpowered!" he cries. But Kurwenal decides he will fight to the end. Brangaena now calls to him to allow King Marke to enter. "You too are a traitor," he shouts back, and turning to confront Melot, who has just rushed in, Kurwenal attacks him with savage glee, inflicting a mortal wound.

From outside the walls King Marke calls Kurwenal a "madman" and orders him to cease fighting. But the brave Kurwenal, as if seeking death for himself, rushes out to attack Marke and his men. As the fighting rages on, Brangaena makes her way to the motionless Isolde, and is relieved to find her lady still alive. Kurwenal staggers back, mortally wounded.

King Marke enters. "Where is Tristan?" he asks.

"Where I lie," says Kurwenal, as he falls dying alongside Tristan's corpse. Taking the dead man's hand in his own, Kurwenal gasps, "Tristan! Your faithful servant comes with you!"

Marke is overwhelmed with grief. "They are all dead," he sobs. Pathetically, he begs Tristan to awaken. "My hero knight, my faithful, faithless friend, must you even on this day betray me?"

Isolde has regained consciousness and Brangaena tells her that the King now knows the secret of the substituted potions.

Devastated by the fact that his arrival has only swelled the number of deaths, King Marke says that he came only to forgive his bride and faithful knight and to marry them.

Isolde is oblivious to his words. Slowly, as if drawn magnetically, she turns to Tristan's lifeless form. In mounting rhapsodic rapture she describes how she sees her Tristan, his smile, his open eyes, how he glows like the brightest stars, his breast filled with courage. "Tell me, friends, am I the only one who hears the glorious sounds that come from within him and which pierce me and envelop me and ring ever clearer around me?" Her excitement swells until buoyed on the waves that seem to emanate from her beloved Tristan, she is transported to another world. "The ultimate ecstasy!" she cries, and with these final words, she sinks onto Tristan's body, dead.

IL TABARRO
(The Cloak)

Opera in One Act
by
GIACOMO PUCCINI

Première: Metropolitan Opera, New York, December 14, 1918

ON A barge moored on the banks of the Seine one summer afternoon in Paris around the turn of the century, three stevedores wearily unload heavy sacks of cement onto a horsedrawn cart that stands on the wharf. Nearby, the worn stone facades of tenements in one of Paris's old neighborhoods glow jewel-like in the setting sun. Down the river, the towers of Notre Dame loom against the sky.

At the helm of the barge, the boat's owner, Michele, stares moodily at the sunset, holding his unlit pipe in his mouth. His young wife, Giorgetta, teases him for seeming so far away and absent-minded, and suggests they reward the laborers with some wine.

"You are very thoughtful," he says and moves to kiss her.

Coolly, she turns her cheek to his lips. Without a word, Michele goes down into the hold.

One of the stevedores, Luigi, returns from the wharf, complaining of the heat, and he is echoed by the other two, Tinca and Talpa, as they haul more loads up to the dock. Their spirits lift as Giorgetta appears carrying the wine. They gulp thirstily and she gaily refills their glasses.

Luigi calls to an organ-grinder who is passing by on the bank and asks him to play. As he obliges with a waltz Tinca asks Giorgetta to dance with him. He is awkward, however, and steps on her feet. This gives Luigi an excuse to cut in and she abandons herself to his strong arms. As Michele comes out of the hold, Talpa warns the dancers. They pull apart and the stevedores go back to work.

"Are we moving on or staying until next week?" Giorgetta asks. Michele is undecided about what to do or who among the crew will be asked to remain, for there is not enough work for all of them.

Their discussion is punctuated by the sounds of the Seine and its surroundings: a tugboat whistle, the horns of automobiles, and the hawking of a song seller.

"What a beautiful September sunset," Giorgetta exclaims, "but the end of summer always makes me sad. Look, over there is the ragpicker, Frugola, come to get Talpa no doubt."

Michele does not respond. Instead he says, "Do I treat you so badly?"

She tells him that his silences are worse than beatings and asks what is bothering him.

"Nothing!" he replies as he busies himself about the barge.

The song seller sings a beautiful song about Mimi, the poor little seamstress who has been made famous by Puccini's *La Bohème*. Frugola the ragpicker comes on board to take her husband, Talpa, home. Her sacks are stuffed with the discarded treasures she has salvaged during the day, and she offers Giorgetta a pretty comb, which Giorgetta accepts. Talpa and the others, their work finished, come out of the hold. Tinca is in a hurry to leave. Frugola sarcastically suggests he wants to go off to get drunk.

"Yes, of course," he says. "To get drunk and to forget. What else is there for such as us?"

Bitterly, Luigi agrees. "What is the point of our existence? We toil, we sweat, we live in dirt. Every pleasure turns to pain, even love itself. Why think or dream? It's better to forget."

Tinca says, "Drinking is the only answer," and leaves.

Frugola and Talpa begin to talk of their dreams. They want only a small home in the country with their cat.

"That's not what I want," Giorgetta says. She loves the city, loves the feel of the hard cement sidewalk beneath her feet and, particularly, the suburb of Paris from which both she and Luigi come. He joins her in extolling the beauties of life in Belleville, its bustle, its crowds, its excitement and its people always around sharing, arguing, loving.

Talpa and Frugola leave, but Luigi remains behind, eager for this chance to be alone with Giorgetta. Unable to contain himself any longer, he tells her that his passion for her is unbearable. While she tries to calm him and warns repeatedly that Michele will be back in a moment, her own passion is ignited. They fall into each other's arms and kiss, each still reminding the other of the danger of the situation. They pull apart as Michele comes up from the hold and Luigi, hastily collecting himself, tells his employer that he has waited to say that he would remain with the ship only until they get to Rouen. There he will stay to find work. Michele tells him he is foolish for there is less work in Rouen than in Paris, and with a shrug, he goes into the cabin.

"Why did you ask to leave?" Giorgetta demands the moment Michele has left.

"Because I cannot bear the torment of sharing you with him!"

"I know," she says; "I feel so trapped. Only in your arms do I feel free."

They dream of being free, alone together in some far distant place, and despite the danger of their actual situation decide to meet later that night.

"I'll give the usual signal," she instructs. "When I strike the match, that means all is well."

Luigi slips away onto the shore.

Night has fallen. Michele comes out of the cabin, carrying a lamp. They discuss the stevedores, and Michele says that Tinca drinks to keep from strangling his unfaithful wife. Nervously, Giorgetta says she doesn't wish to gossip.

Suddenly, Michele says, "Why do you no longer love me?"

"You are wrong, Michele," Giorgetta says coldly. "You are kind and devoted. It's time to go to bed."

He does not let her go. Instead, he talks about past years when they were happy together in the cabin. "You would gently rock the baby's cradle. We had wonderful nights when I would wrap you in my cloak, protected in my arms. We were blissfully happy until the baby died."

She can't bear any more and begs him to be quiet, but he goes on reminiscing and begging her to love him again.

She says, "We're older now. We've both changed." This painful conversation has unnerved her; pleading sleepiness, she bids him good night and goes into the cabin.

"Whore!" he mutters.

Taps sounds from a nearby barracks, and two lovers stroll by arm in arm. Michele sinks into morbid thoughts, convinced that Giorgetta has a lover but unable to determine who it is. Talpa is too old; Tinca is always drunk, and just a few moments ago, Luigi asked to leave his employ. If only he could find her lover, he would kill him. To calm himself, Michele takes out his pipe and strikes a match to light it.

Luigi, waiting on the embankment, mistakes this for Giorgetta's signal, and jumps onto the barge. Michele, hidden in the shadows, recognizes him and, pouncing on Luigi, locks him in a stranglehold. "Now I've got you! Admit that you love her! Confess that she is your mistress!"

Luigi, struggling desperately at first, denies the accusations and tries to pull a knife. But Michele makes him drop it. Weakening, Luigi admits that he loves Giorgetta. Ordering Luigi to repeat the confession over and over, Michele slowly squeezes the life out of him.

"Michele," Giorgetta calls from the cabin; "Michele." Quickly, Michele covers Luigi's corpse with the great cloak he is wearing.

Giorgetta comes out of the cabin, anxiously looks around, but sees nothing. She is remorseful. "I was unfriendly before," she admits. "Can I sit with you?"

"Under my cloak, perhaps?" he lovingly asks.

"Yes, near you," she answers. "Once upon a time you told me that under his cloak every man has hidden either a joy or a sorrow!"

"Or a crime!" Michele adds. "Come look beneath my cloak."

As she approaches he opens the cloak and allows Luigi's lifeless body to fall to the ground. Horrified, Giorgetta shrieks and in a violent rage Michele throws her down beside the body of her dead lover.

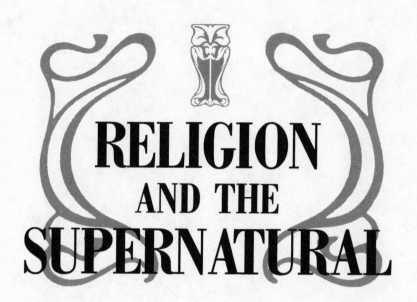

RELIGION
AND THE
SUPERNATURAL

FAUST

Opera in Five Acts
by
CHARLES GOUNOD
Première: Théâtre Lyrique, Paris, March 19, 1859

ACT I

IT IS night. The sixteenth-century study is cluttered with musty parchment rolls, dusty volumes of philosophy and magic, and the beakers, scales, and other tools of alchemy. Amidst the clutter, the aged philosopher and scientist Faust reads by the light of one flickering candle. It is an old book, one he has pored over too many times before in his lifelong quest for the secrets of the universe. Now he does it out of habit, but he no longer really hopes that he will succeed. He is weary of life and disillusioned by all human striving, and as dawn begins to break, he feels he cannot face another hopeless day. He closes the book and, picking up a flask of poison, pours himself a drink that will bring him the death for which he yearns.

As he raises the goblet, he hears people going by outside his window, singing praises to the beauty of the morning and to the God who has created the lovely sky and earth. Their voices enrage him.

"God! What has God done for me? I curse life and all its illusions—love, glory, and fame. Satan, I call on you instead. Come to me now!"

"Here I am!" Standing before the startled Faust is a sinister but attrac-

163

tive-looking man wearing a gentleman's cloak, a sword at his side, and a feather in his cap.

Half afraid, half disbelieving, Faust says, "Go away."

But the mysterious and charming visitor persists. He offers Faust anything he may want—gold, power, or glory.

"All I want is to be young, to be able to feel again, to love and to desire."

"You shall," promises Mephistopheles.

"What is the price?"

"Almost nothing. Here on earth I shall be your humble servant, but in Hell you shall be mine!"

As Faust hesitates, the devil conjures up the apparition of an enchanting young girl sitting at her spinning wheel. Utterly captivated, Faust signs the contract.

Mephistopheles hands him a cup from the table. "Drink this, it is life itself." Faust greedily drains the goblet. His wrinkles and his seedy clothes fall away and he is transformed into a handsomely dressed young man.

"Now let us find the rapture that you seek," Mephistopheles cries, and in mutual bondage they rush off.

ACT II

At a marketplace near the city gates, students, soldiers and townspeople celebrate the Kermesse by reveling in the seemingly limitless wine and beer served at the inn. The students repeatedly toast the wine and each other, while the soldiers boast of their prowess at conquering castles and women. They are about to leave for still another war.

Valentin, a young soldier, comes into the square clutching a holy medal given him by his sister to protect him against death during battle. Joined by two students, Wagner and Siebel, Valentin tells them that he is concerned about leaving his beloved sister, Marguerite, alone. Secretly in love, Siebel offers to watch over her. Valentin thanks him, but addresses a prayer to God as well to protect Marguerite.

In an effort to change the solemn mood, Wagner offers a toast and, mounting a stool, begins a comic story about a rat. But before he can finish, Mephistopheles jumps into the crowd and offers to entertain them with the song of the Golden Calf. The song cynically details the evil men do for the sake of riches, but Mephistopheles is so charming that the students are irresistibly caught up in the lilting melody, and enthusiastically echo the final line, "And Satan leads the ball!"

His demonic song ended, Mephistopheles continues to entertain the crowd by reading palms and telling fortunes. To Wagner he predicts death in war and he warns Siebel never to give flowers to Marguerite for they shall wither.

Valentin is quick to take offense. "Who told you my sister's name?"

Maliciously, Mephistopheles turns on him. "Someone I know will kill you!" and grabbing a glass of wine, mockingly drinks to Valentin's health. "This wine is terrible," he complains, and throws it away. He strikes the barrel, which magically begins to flow with choice wine, and Mephistopheles raises his glass in a toast, "To Marguerite!"

Valentin is furious and draws his sword. Mephistopheles quickly draws a circle around himself and as Valentin thrusts across it, his sword breaks. The crowd is shocked into frightened silence. This is the devil's sign.

"Since you broke my sword," Valentin declares, "it has become a cross which will defend us!" Pointing the crossed handles of their swords at him, Valentin and his fellow soldiers advance on Mephistopheles, who backs away, muttering, "We shall meet again."

Faust now joins Mephistopheles, and asks if the girl in his vision was real. Mephistopheles promises that she will come to the square. And indeed, Faust soon spies her as she makes her way through the crowd; so does Siebel. It is Marguerite. Mephistopheles stands in Siebel's way so that Faust may address Marguerite.

Faust asks if he may walk with her.

"I have no need; I know the way!" she tells him and hurriedly leaves the square.

Faust gazes after her more in love than ever, but complains to Mephistopheles that she has rejected him.

"My good Doctor," Mephistopheles laughs, "I see you need my help in matters of love!" Leaving the revels of the square, they follow Marguerite.

ACT III

Siebel hesitantly enters the fragrant garden that surrounds Marguerite's modest cottage. Flowers of all colors bloom in profusion. He decides that a bouquet is the way to tell her of his love, but each time he picks a blossom it withers in his hand, just as Mephistopheles predicted.

Siebel sees a small holy fountain attached to the wall of the house, and by dipping his hands in the water, he breaks the spell. "So much for you, Satan," he scoffs. As he proceeds to pick some flowers, Faust and Mephistopheles enter the garden and hide behind some bushes. Siebel leaves his bouquet near the holy font so that Marguerite will find it when she prays.

Deciding that Faust's suit for Marguerite will be aided by a more costly gift, Mephistopheles goes off to find one. Faust, alone, ponders the long lost rapture of love that now obsesses him and which he hopes Marguerite will return. Her pure and lovely presence permeates the air, and despite the lack of ostentation in the surroundings, Faust senses a boundless wealth of spirit. His love, he feels, is an angel from heaven. His thoughts are interrupted by Mephistopheles, who returns bearing a casket of beautiful jewels. He puts the jewels next to the bouquet of flowers and leads Faust to a concealed place in the garden, as Marguerite returns.

Marguerite sits down at her spinning wheel, singing to herself as she spins, but thoughts of the handsome stranger who approached her in the square keep intruding. She puts the spinning wheel away and is about to go into the house when she notices the bouquet of flowers. She knows Siebel has left it and thinks fondly, "Poor faithful lad." And then she sees the jewel case. She thinks there must be some mistake, but the key is there, so trembling and hesitant, she opens it. She is sure she must be dreaming because never before has she seen such beautiful things. The case is equipped with a mirror and the temptation is too great. She tries on the jewels—earrings, bracelet, pearls. Like a child dressing up for the first time she is thrilled by the way she looks. She fantasizes about being a queen and laughingly keeps asking herself if indeed it is Marguerite that she sees. It must be a princess or a queen. "How I wish," she thinks, "that fine lord I met could see me now!"

As she stands there totally bedecked, her neighbor, Martha Schwerlein, comes into the garden and exclaims at how beautiful she looks, adding wistfully, "My husband never sent me a gift like that!"

Faust and Mephistopheles come out of hiding, and Mephistopheles asks for Madame Schwerlein. When she identifies herself, he tells her that he has unfortunate news for her; her husband has been killed, leaving nothing more than his blessings. While Mephistopheles consoles the not too distraught Martha by convincing her that she must take revenge on her inconsiderate husband by immediately finding another, Faust and Marguerite try not to betray the joy they feel because they are finally meeting.

Martha fixes her eye on Mephistopheles and strolls about the garden with him. Faust offers his arm to the much more timid Marguerite.

Martha, after learning that her dapper escort has no home, tries to persuade him to settle down.

As Marguerite tells Faust of her lonely life, he falls more and more in love with her, convinced that she is an angel.

Mephistopheles grows tired of Martha's persistence and keeps trying to get rid of her so he can help Faust in the conquest of Marguerite. Finally, he hides.

Faust asks Marguerite if he may stay.

"You must go," she says and slips away, but he pursues her.

Martha searches for her elusive escort but cannot find him.

From somewhere in the shadows, Mephistopheles calls on the darkness of night to help seduce Marguerite's innocent heart.

Allowing Faust to hold her hand, Marguerite tells him once again that it is late and he must leave. He begs for a little more time, and relenting, she picks up a flower, plucks its petals one by one playing "He loves me, he loves me not!" She is happy when the last petal says, "He loves me!"

"Believe it," Faust declares. "My love is eternal."

Irresistibly drawn, they embrace and she tells him that she adores him. Then, frightened at herself, she orders him to leave. He protests but to no avail, and bidding him adieu she goes into the house.

Utterly enraptured, Faust turns to leave, but is stopped by Mephistopheles, who advises him not to be so hasty. "Perhaps she will confide something to the stars that you do not know! Look, she is opening her window."

Marguerite, clearly under the spell of love, declares, "He loves me! How sweet life is, and glorious the night! Why must I wait until tomorrow to see him again. Come to me, my love."

Hearing these words, Faust rushes to her window. As Marguerite falls into Faust's arms, Mephistopheles vanishes into the dark through which echoes his cynical, triumphant laughter.

ACT IV

Scene 1

Months have gone by and Faust has deserted Marguerite. She has come to church to pray for forgiveness, but her prayers are continually interrupted by the voice of Mephistopheles ordering her not to pray and calling on the demons of Hell to aid him. Tormented by the voices she hears, she begs God to be merciful in what she believes to be her hour of retribution. But the voice of Mephistopheles relentlessly reminds her of the days when she was pure and held God in her heart. "Now Hell wants you!" he insists. Terrified by the fear of damnation, she keeps trying to pray, but the hideous hidden voices stop her each time. She faints as the voice of Mephistopheles proclaims, "Marguerite, you are condemned to Hell!"

SCENE 2

On the street outside Marguerite's house a crowd has gathered to welcome home the victorious army. Valentin sees Siebel and asks for his sister. Siebel temporizes and tells him that Marguerite has gone to church. "No doubt to pray for me," says Valentin.

As the soldiers disband, Valentin invites Siebel to the house for a drink. Siebel counsels him not to go in but won't explain why. He just asks that Valentin be merciful and runs off down the street, as Valentin, now truly alarmed, rushes into the house.

Faust and a reluctant Mephistopheles arrive. Faust now regrets the unhappiness he has brought Marguerite, but shame makes him hesitant to enter the house. Mephistopheles is impatient. He would rather be at the Witches' Sabbath. "But since you still want her," he taunts, "you will need my voice," and begins an insulting serenade to Marguerite.

An enraged Valentin stumbles out of the house and with his sword smashes Mephistopheles' guitar. He demands to know, "Which of you is responsible for the shame that has been brought upon my sister?" Reluctantly, Faust draws his sword. Valentin angrily tears the protective medal Marguerite gave him from around his neck and, cursing it, throws it to the ground.

With Mephistopheles' help, Faust mortally wounds Valentin. As the soldier falls to the ground Mephistopheles draws Faust away before they can be caught.

Attracted to the scene by the commotion, townspeople comfort Valentin. Marguerite rushes out of the house.

"Go away," her brother tells her. "It is your lover's sword that has killed me." Despite Siebel's pleas that he be merciful, Valentin curses his sister with his dying breath. The crowd prays that the Lord will welcome his soul and forgive the sinner, while Marguerite helplessly looks on.

ACT V

SCENE 1

It is Walpurgis Night in the dark haunted Harz Mountains, and the souls of the dead gather, their ghostly shadows drifting through flaming trees and burning fields of grass. Mephistopheles leads a terrified Faust into the heart of this blood-curdling scene, and with a wave of his hand transforms it into a brilliant feast, attended by the most beautiful ladies of the past: Cleopatra, Aspasia, Thais, and Helen of Troy. Bidding Faust drink, Mephistopheles promises that the nectar will heal his wounded heart. Intoxicated by the voluptuous orgy enveloping him, Faust forgets his remorse until suddenly he sees a vision of Marguerite, who looks as if she is dying. Throwing down his goblet, he demands that Mephistopheles take him to her. "I must be with her!" he declares.

SCENE 2

Marguerite, driven to madness and condemned for the murder of her illegitimate child, lies asleep in her prison cell. She is to be executed at daybreak. Mephistopheles counsels Faust, "You must convince her to come with you. Do not delay. Here are the keys. I shall keep watch outside!"

Faust is overwhelmed by the sight of Marguerite imprisoned like a common criminal. Calling her name, he wakes her. She recognizes him and realizes that he has come to set her free, but she does not move. He implores her to follow him out of the cell, but lost in her wandering mind, she begins to re-live their first meeting. Anxiously, he tries to hurry her, to no avail. He is growing more and more desperate when Mephistopheles calls out, "Hurry, or you are lost."

At the sound of that voice, Marguerite becomes frantic and orders Faust to drive the devil from this holy place. Once again Mephistopheles calls that time is running out and Faust begs Marguerite to flee with them. But she has recognized the devil and in terror she breaks into prayer. Imploring God to forgive her, she is deaf to Faust's pleas. Finally, he shouts her name, and she turns to him as if seeing him for the first time. "Why do you look at me so menacingly?" she demands. "Why are your hands red with blood? You horrify me!" she screams and falls dead.

Mephistopheles intones, "Judged!"

But Marguerite's soul is borne to heaven as an angelic choir announces that she has been saved and that Christ is again risen.

Mephistopheles flees with his distraught Doctor Faust.

THE MAGIC FLUTE

Opera in Two Acts
by
WOLFGANG AMADEUS MOZART
Première: Theater auf der Wieden, Vienna, September 30, 1791

ACT I

IN THE magic realm of the Queen of the Night, a handsome young prince named Tamino flees desperately from a vicious serpent. Crying for help, he faints from exhaustion and terror. But before he can be harmed, three Ladies-in-Waiting to the Queen materialize from out of the mountains, and fall upon the serpent with their spears.

The Ladies stand around the unconscious youth and admire his beauty. Each wishes to remain with him while the others report to the Queen. It is an impasse resolved to no one's satisfaction when they all agree to leave. As mysteriously as they came, they disappear.

Tamino regains consciousness, amazed to find himself unharmed and the serpent dead at his feet. "Am I really here?" he asks himself. "Who saved me?" He hears a panpipe in the distance, and hides. A strange little man appears. He is dressed in bird feathers, and carries a large birdcage on his back, and proudly announces himself to the world-at-large as Papageno, birdcatcher to the Queen of the Night. He is a simple, happy and practical man who wishes only for a full belly and a pretty girl with whom to share his life.

Thinking this may have been his savior, Tamino comes out of hiding. The fainthearted Papageno is ready to flee at the sight of a stranger, but when questioned by Tamino he boasts he killed the snake with his bare hands (after first ascertaining that it is indeed dead).

The three Ladies reappear, chide Papageno for lying, and padlock his mouth to keep him from uttering any more falsehoods. They tell Tamino that it was they who saved him, and that their ruler, the great Queen of the Night, has sent him a portrait of her daughter. "If you are moved by her beauty," they tell him, "happiness, honor, and fame shall be yours." Bidding Tamino and Papageno farewell they disappear again, but Tamino does not notice their exit for he can look at nothing but the portrait. He has fallen in love.

Soon the three Ladies return to inform Tamino that his reaction has been noted. There is a tremendous roar of thunder, mountains separate, and against the starry heavens, the Queen of the Night appears. "Do not fear," she tells Tamino. "I am the one in need of consolation because my daughter, Pamina, has been taken from me by that evil fiend, Sarastro. Set her free, Tamino," she commands, "and then she shall be yours." There is another crash of thunder and the Queen disappears as the mountains close.

The three Ladies remove the lock from Papageno's lips and order him to help Tamino free Pamina from Sarastro's citadel. Papageno's terror is hardly lessened by a gift of magic bells. To Tamino they give the beautiful magic flute. "These instruments will keep you safe," they explain, "and three spirits, fair, gentle, and wise, will serve as your guides." Bidding the Ladies farewell, Tamino and a reluctant Papageno set off on their journey to Sarastro's palace.

In Sarastro's palace, Pamina is watched over by the wicked Moor Monastatos, who orders his slaves to leave so that he may force his attention on his beautiful sleeping prisoner. At this moment, Papageno, stumbling about outside, peers through the window and, seeing the lovely girl, comes inside to investigate. He and Monastatos come face to face and start back, terrified—Papageno by the other's blackness, and Monastatos by Papageno's feathered finery. Each decides that the other *must* be the devil, and they flee in opposite directions. Soon, however, Papageno returns, having decided that since there are black birds in the world, why not black people? In bumbling fashion, he carefully checks the portrait against the features of the awakening beauty before he is convinced that she is Pamina. He then informs her that he and a handsome prince who has fallen in love with her have been sent by her mother to set her free. Pamina is overjoyed to hear all this and leaves the room with Papageno to try to find Tamino and make their way to freedom.

In another part of Sarastro's stronghold three young spirits lead Tamino into a secret grove in which there are three doors: one leading to the Temple of Reason, the second to the Temple of Nature, and the third to the Temple of Wisdom. As Tamino approaches the first door, a cry of "Go back!" warns him off. At the second door he is greeted by the same injunction. Then, from the Temple of Wisdom an old priest emerges and asks him what he seeks.

"Love and virtue," he replies, "and vengeance against Sarastro."

"Ah, do not jump to conclusions," the priest counsels; "it is not as you think. Be patient and all will become clear to you in time." The priest will say no more, and leaves.

Tamino begins to despair. Is Pamina still alive? Magical unseen voices answer him that she is. In exultation Tamino plays his magic flute, whose beautiful sound proves able to enchant even the wildest beasts—a lion and a zebra come out of the woods and sit peaceably together to listen to the prince. His impromptu concert is interrupted by the distant sound of Papageno's pipes and Tamino, hopeful that his companion has found Pamina, rushes off to try to find them.

He has no sooner left than Papageno and Pamina run into the clearing. Papageno sounds his pipe again and they are about to follow the answering call from Tamino's flute when they are suddenly blocked by Monastatos, who orders his slaves to bring chains and ropes. But Papageno reaches for his magic bells and as they spin their beautiful tune, Monastatos and his slaves are bewitched and peacefully dance off.

Before Pamina and Papageno can go in search of Tamino, they are trapped by Sarastro's retinue, which crowds into the grove, singing his praises and heralding his approach.

"Now there is no escape," Pamina says; "he always knows all." Submissively, she kneels before Sarastro confessing that she has tried to escape from his domain in order to get away from the lecherous Monastatos.

Sarastro is understanding, but explains that he cannot free her because her mother is wicked and her young heart needs the guidance of a man.

Monastatos drags in another captive, Prince Tamino. As soon as Tamino and Pamina see each other they rush into each other's arms, but Monastatos roughly separates them, and reports the attempted escape. Instead of a reward, however, he is sentenced to a whipping as punishment for his advances to Pamina. Sarastro then declares that Tamino and Papageno will be initiated into the temple if they can prove their manhood by passing the traditional trials. Two priests come forward to lead Tamino and Papageno to the temple, while Sarastro leaves with Pamina.

ACT II

In a forest of palm trees, Sarastro has assembled his priests, all members of the order of Isis and Osiris, to discuss the fate of Tamino, who waits at the gate of the temple for their decisions. "He wishes to rid himself of the veil of night so he may enter the realm of eternal light. Do you deem him worthy?" The priests indicate their approval. Sarastro then adds that the gods have designated Pamina to be Tamino's wife, which is why he has taken her from the side of her proud and power-hungry mother. Two priests are assigned to act as guides to Tamino and Papageno. As they leave, Sarastro prays to Isis and Osiris to grant the spirit of wisdom to the two novices so that they may safely pass the tests.

It is night and a storm is raging, as the two priests lead Tamino and Papageno, blindfolded, into the courtyard of the temple. They remove the blinds and leave them alone. The storm puts Papagneo in immediate need of comforting and Tamino tells him to be a man.

"I wish I were a girl."

The priests return with torches and ask the two if they are ready to risk their lives in order to pass the tests. Tamino is eager and ready, but Papageno is dubious, saying that all he really wants is to find a pretty wife. The priest warns Papageno that he will never find a wife unless he endures the trials. As Papageno still hesitates, the priest assures him that his bride has already been chosen—a young and lovely Papagena. As the priests again leave, they caution their charges to remain silent under all circumstances, and to beware the evils of women.

Papageno has no sooner complained about the lonely dark than the three Ladies-in-Waiting pop up to warn them that if they betray the Queen of the Night, certain death awaits them. Papageno begins to discuss the matter only to be reminded by Tamino of his vow of silence, to which Tamino

remains steadfast, breaking it only to scold Papageno every time he irre-
pressibly begins to chatter. Suddenly, unseen voices, accompanied by
thunder and lightning, terrify Papageno and frighten the three Ladies away.

Calm is restored by the priests, who return to congratulate Tamino on his
silence and to chastise Papageno for talking. But both men have survived
the first test, and the priests lead them on to other trials.

In another part of the palace Pamina sleeps while the evil Monastatos
eyes her longingly. "Ah! To steal one kiss!" he muses, creeping closer and
closer to her. He is about to kiss her when there is a loud clap of thunder
and the Queen of the Night appears, chasing Monastatos away. Pamina
wakes, is overjoyed to see her mother, and expects that together they will
escape. But the Queen has lost her powers and is unable to help her daughter. She gives Pamina a dagger and orders her to kill Sarastro in the hope of
thereby recapturing her own power. Pamina is horrified at the thought of
murder, but before she can protest, the Queen, crying out for vengeance,
disappears.

Monastatos has overheard it all. He takes the dagger and threatens Pamina with betrayal of the plan unless she submits to his desires. At dagger
point Pamina says she would prefer death.

"Then die!" roars Monastatos.

Sarastro arrives and holds him back. The now penitent Moor grovels at
Sarastro's feet but is banished forever.

Pamina begs for mercy for her mother; Sarastro assures her that he knows
all, that anyone who is worthy to be called a man does not take revenge.
They leave together, arm in arm.

For Tamino and Papageno the ordeals continue. The priests leave them
alone outside the temple, instructing them to keep their lips sealed and wait
for the sound of a horn. Of course, Papageno immediately tries to engage
Tamino in conversation, but the prince ignores him. Papageno complains
first of boredom, then of thirst. A withered old hag wanders in with a pitcher
of water. Sitting down to chat with Papageno, she tells him that she is
eighteen years old and that she has a boyfriend named "Papageno."
Stunned, Papageno asks her name, but before she can answer, thunder
claps and she disappears. Petrified, Papageno promises not to say another
word.

The three spirits appear bearing food and drink, and returning the magic instruments. In parting they inform Tamino that his goal is near, and they admonish Papageno to be still.

While Papageno gorges himself on the food, Tamino plays his magic flute. Drawn by the music, Pamina runs in joyously. Tamino won't speak to her. He only sighs and motions her away and for once Papageno too remains mute, his mouth full of food. Pamina takes Tamino's coldness to mean that he no longer loves her, and utterly dejected, she leaves.

The distant horn sounds and Tamino starts out, but returns to drag along a reluctant Papageno. Chasing the sound of the horn, they again find themselves surrounded by the priests. Sarastro commends Tamino on how he has so far conducted himself, but now he must face the most dangerous trials. Pamina is brought in to say farewell and she is once again distressed by his reserve. They are each led away in separate directions.

As they all depart, Papageno, who has wandered off by himself, returns to find the place dark and empty. He feels that he has been deserted and berates himself for having agreed to come on this crazy mission. He is joined by a priest who informs him that he has failed the tests and will never join the ranks of the initiated.

To Papageno this is not necessarily bad news. He says, "All I want right now is a good glass of wine." Magically it appears. Papageno is delighted. Now he has but one more wish: a pretty wife. He plays his magic bells; the old hag hobbles in.

"Here I am," she announces.

Papageno is not eager to make this old crone his wife, but she warns him that if he refuses he will be trapped here forever. This seems a worse fate so he swears that he will be true to her forever. Her rags and wrinkles fall away and she is magically transformed into a young girl, dressed in feathers like himself.

"Pa-Pa-Papagena!" As he reaches to embrace her a priest appears and sends her away, because he is not yet worthy. Papageno is furious and swears that the earth will have to swallow him up before he will leave his beloved. Immediately, there is a rumble, the earth beneath Papageno begins to open, and becoming utterly tractable, he follows the priest.

In a small garden, the three spirits watch unobserved as Pamina rushes in, clutching the dagger in her hand. She is delirious with grief, believing her mother has cursed her and that Tamino no longer loves her. As she is about to kill herself, the spirits come out of hiding and stop her. They assure her that Tamino does love her, and that the gods are watching over them.

Amidst the rocky peaks of mountains, the twilight barely penetrates the gloomy caverns that Tamino must brave in order to finish his tests. In one of the caves he must pass through fire. For the trial by water he must enter a cavern concealed by a cataract tumbling from the cliff above.

Tamino approaches the caves fearlessly, but stops when he hears Pamina's voice calling for him to wait. He is told that he may break his silence now, and the couple joyfully embrace.

Pamina insists on joining Tamino for these last two trials, and tells him to play his magic flute to protect them on their treacherous journey. "I shall not leave your side," she says, "for love guides me!" With Pamina's hand on Tamino's shoulder, they enter the cave of fire and walk calmly through the flames as the beautiful melody of the flute carries them through. Emerging unscathed, they embrace, hopeful that the flute's magic power will once more protect them in the final trial. Again, she places her hand on his shoulder and they bravely walk through the waterfall while Tamino plays his magic flute. They emerge, their triumph marked by a chorus of victory from the hidden priests.

Papageno searches everywhere for his Papagena, but his efforts go unrewarded. Fed up, he decides to hang himself from a tree. He'll give the world just one more chance. He'll count to three. Very slowly he counts: "One . . . Two . . . . Two and a quarter . . . . . Two and a half . . . . . . Two and three quarters . . . . THREE!!!!"

Brokenhearted at the world's betrayal, he puts the rope around his neck. The three spirits appear in the nick of time and remind him that we live but once. They then suggest he try playing his magic bells. Papageno strikes his forehead. "What a nincompoop I am not to have thought of it myself." As he plays the bells, the spirits bring in Papagena and the two charming bird people gaily plot their troth. Their greatest joy, they agree, will be all the little Papagenos and Papagenas they will have. Hand in hand, they gleefully run off.

High in the barren, rocky mountains, the Queen of the Night plans an attack on Sarastro's temple. With her are not only her three Ladies-in-waiting, but also Monastatos, who has joined forces with her on the promise of Pamina's hand in marriage.

As they plot, the thunder and lightning grows ever more menacing, there is the sound of rushing waters, and the earth beneath rumbles ominously. Suddenly, the heavens erupt, the earth opens up, and all of them are swallowed up, cast screaming into eternal night.

The gloom disappears and the sun's rays shine on the brilliant colors of the Temple of the Sun. Sarastro, presiding at the altar before all the priests, welcomes Pamina and Tamino into the fold. Praising courage and virtue, the assembly celebrates the triumph of light over darkness and the everlasting power of Beauty and Wisdom.

LES CONTES D'HOFFMANN
(The Tales of Hoffmann)

Opera in Three Acts with Prologue and Epilogue
by
JACQUES OFFENBACH
Première: Opéra-Comique, Paris, February 10, 1881

ERNST THEODOR Amadeus Hoffmann was a writer of some importance in the German Romantic movement of the early nineteenth century. He wrote a number of macabre fantasies, a story form particularly popular with the Romantics. Adapting three of these tales, as well as the evidence that Hoffmann was susceptible not only to love, but also to drink, Offenbach's *Tales of Hoffmann* makes the writer a hero in his own fiction.

PROLOGUE

The story begins early one evening at Luther's tavern in the city of Nuremberg. The popular beer-cellar is still empty, its only customer an elderly man, Councilor Lindorf. As a messenger arrives, Lindorf intercepts him. "Are you carrying a letter from the Milanese Diva, Stella, who is singing next door at the opera?"
"Yes!"

Unscrupulously Lindorf bribes the messenger to give him the billet doux. The note is for Hoffmann, and says, "I love you. If I have caused you pain please forgive me. Enclosed is the key to my room!" Though jealous, Lindorf is confident that he can outwit his competitor. "I may be old, but I am lively!" he cheerily concludes. Settling himself comfortably at a side table, he waits for the crowd to arrive.

Soon Luther comes blustering in, ordering about his assistants. "Faster, faster," he barks, "get the glasses! Light the lamps!" Moments later the room is flooded with boisterous students dropping in for a drink during the intermission of *Don Giovanni*. Noisily they demand beer and wine while Luther and the waiters scurry about trying to fill their requests. One of the students, Nathaniel, arises from his seat and leads a series of toasts to the beautiful diva Stella. "Where is Hoffmann?" another student asks. Banging their steins on the table, all the students start calling for Hoffmann.

"And here he is," says Luther.

The poet Hoffmann and his friend Nicklausse come through the door, calling for drinks. Hoffmann appears angry and disheveled, and when questioned about his foul humor he broodingly alludes to dark dreams and depressing memories, but finally declares, "Life is too short. Let us drink, sing, and laugh!"

The students demand that Hoffmann entertain them with something amusing and cheerful, something like the legend of Kleinsach. Without further ado Hoffmann begins the tale of the dwarf at the court of Eisenach who has a lump instead of a stomach, whose legs go "click-clack" and head "crick-crack." The students are delighted with the fanciful tale, but midway through it, Hoffmann veers off into a rambling tale about a beautiful woman he may once have courted. Nathaniel urges him back from his trance, reminding him that he was telling the tale of Kleinsach. "Ah, yes, better Kleinsach," Hoffmann says, and finishes the tale of the dwarf to the cheers of the students.

Hoffmann gulps some beer and sputters, "This beer is detestable! Bring on the punch! Let's get drunk," sentiments echoed by the students and applauded by Luther.

"I'll bet that Hoffmann is in love!" Nathaniel taunts him.

"Never," says Hoffmann.

The heretofore silent Lindorf says, "What a brazen liar."

"Who's that?" asks Hoffmann.

As he grows more and more tipsy, Hoffmann engages the councilor in an exchange of insults, with the older man getting the better of the verbal duel.

Finally Nathaniel intercedes. "There's no reason to be embarrassed about falling in love. We have all ruined ourselves for women," is his conciliatory remark.

Hoffmann sneers at all other women. Only his mistress, Stella, is worth loving, because she is three women in one. In her soul she combines all the loves of his past—the artist, the young maiden, and the courtesan. "Perhaps you would like to hear the stories of my three loves?"

"Yes!" the students answer eagerly. Ignoring Luther's announcement that the opera next door is about to resume, they settle down to listen.

"The name of the first," Hoffmann begins, "was Olympia!"

ACT I

In his bizarrely furnished home, the scientist Spalanzani is waiting for the guests he has invited to a grand party. The first to arrive is Hoffmann, professing an interest in science so that he can meet Mr. Spalanzani's beautiful daughter, Olympia. Though he has glimpsed her but once through a window, he has fallen in love with her. The doctor greets him warmly and counsels him to forget about music and poetry. "Physics is the only subject worthy of study," and says that he will introduce Hoffmann to his daughter. Taking his inept servant, Cochenile, with him, Spalanzani leaves the room.

Hoffmann peeks through a door to see Olympia sleeping and, more in love than ever, rhapsodizes about the ecstatic future they will have.

Hoffmann's good friend Nicklausse arrives. "I knew you'd be here, admiring Olympia. How can you be in love with someone you've seen just once?"

Hoffmann pays no attention to his friend and continues to gaze at Olympia.

While he is thus entranced, a bizarre-looking man sneaks into the room. "Ah, he is staring at our Olympia! How wonderful!" he declares. He rouses Hoffmann from his vigil. "I am Coppelius, a friend of Mr. Spalanzani. I have barometers, hygrometers, thermometers, but what I have that will interest you most are these special eyeglasses which can see the true colors of a woman's heart! Here, try them!"

Hoffmann puts on the glasses and, returning to stare at Olympia, is staggered by the vision before him. She is more beautiful than ever. So entranced is he that Nicklausse has to pay Coppelius three ducats to prevent him from reclaiming his marvelous glasses.

Returning, Spalanzani is perturbed to see Coppelius. "What do you want?" he demands.

"You are going to make lots of money on our Olympia and I want half of the profits! You may be her 'father' but I made her eyes!" Spalanzani offers Coppelius an additional 500 ducats in exchange for signing over his rights. "Here is the money drawn on the good house of Elias the Jew!"

Coppelius is skeptical but accepts the deal. "I have an idea: marry off our Olympia!" he advises, pointing to the smitten Hoffmann. And with these sardonic words, he gleefully departs with the note for the money.

"Monsieur," Cochenile announces, "the company has arrived!"

The guests make their way into the room, complimenting the host and his house. They tell him they have come to meet his ravishing daughter. "In a moment you will have your wish," Spalanzani says as he and Cochenile leave to fetch Olympia.

Nicklausse smugly tells Hoffmann: "Finally we will see this marvel!"

"Quiet," says Hoffmann, "they're coming."

As Spalanzani leads Olympia in, the guests lavish praise and compliments. Even Nicklausse finds her lovely. The proud father thanks his guests and announces that his daughter will sing an aria for them. Hoffmann is beside himself with joy. Nicklausse is fed up with his romantic passion.

As Spalanzani accompanies her on the harp, Olympia sings a song about the birds in the sky. She has a beautiful voice, but twice she seems to die out. Both times Cochenile places a hand on her back and after a brief "whirring" sound, she revives. When the song is over, the guests all marvel at her vocal prowess, while poor Hoffmann is more deeply in love than ever.

The guests now file slowly into the dining room for supper, leaving Hoffmann and Olympia behind. "We are alone at last, and there is so much I want to tell you," Hoffmann says. "Just to look at you intoxicates me." Impulsively he touches Olympia's shoulder.

"Yes! Yes!" she says.

Encouraged by her positive response he pours out his heart and grasps her hand. Suddenly she grows agitated and walks rapidly around, finally disappearing into her room.

Hoffmann is about to pursue her but Nicklausse returns and intercepts him, injecting a note of caution. "They are saying that Olympia is not alive, and may never have been!" Hoffmann is incredulous. "But she loves me!" he says, and leaves, closely followed by Nicklausse.

An enraged Coppelius bursts into the empty room. "I've been robbed!

That Jew Elias is bankrupt. But I shall wait my chance and take revenge. I will kill someone!" he declares, and with this ominous declaration he slips into Olympia's room.

Led by Spalanzani, the guests reassemble to the strains of a waltz. The good host fetches his daughter. Hoffmann asks her to dance. Her father touches her shoulder.

"Yes, yes," she says, and waltzes away with Hoffmann. The crowd marvels at her dancing, but after a while they realize that she is out of control, spinning poor Hoffmann around faster and faster. Nicklausse tries unsuccessfully to stop them. Finally, Spalanzani steps in. As Olympia comes to an abrupt halt, Hoffmann reels and falls to the ground, dazed, his magical glasses shattered. Spalanzani tries to calm her down, but she is no longer obedient to his wishes. He leads her, as one does a disobedient child, toward her room, where he leaves her. Suddenly Cochenile cries out a warning, but it's too late, for now Olympia is in the clutches of Coppelius. Shouting that Spalanzani is a thief, Coppelius violently rips Olympia apart, tossing the mechanisms all about.

As the guests erupt into loud laughter, Hoffmann sinks into a chair, shocked, and unbelieving. "She was a mechanical doll!"

ACT II

Night in Venice, the soft glide of gondolas through the canals, the muffled sound of light laughter and voices whispering of love. A city of magic and mystery, Venice lends itself to sudden and intense passions.

At her palace on the Grand Canal, the beautiful courtesan Giulietta is holding a party. The guests wander between the rooms or lean over the balconies. Some sit on the richly textured pillows that are scattered around in Oriental fashion. Lovers meet and assignations are made. Among the guests are Hoffmann and his faithful friend Nicklausse.

Clearly enjoying the party, Hoffmann drinks a toast to the passing pleasures of love and wine, sentiments echoed by the revelers. Pitichinaccio and Schlemil, two of Giulietta's admirers, trade insults, but she, the cunning hostess, calms them by suggesting they all go into the gaming room. She leads the way and her guests obligingly follow. Before joining them, Nicklausse warns Hoffmann against falling in love again.

Hoffman scoffs, "With a courtesan like Giulietta? I only want her body, not her love."

"The devil is sly!" Nicklausse warns, as they follow the others into the gaming room.

The magician Dapertutto has overheard, and he declares that he will make Hoffmann, like Schlemil, succumb to Giulietta's seductive charms. Holding a sparkling diamond, he invokes her presence and she appears, drawn by the diamond's glow. He gives her the jewel. "My dear angel," he begins, "through your seductive wiles you have given me Schlemil's shadow and now I desire Hoffmann's reflection. Do you think you can do it?"

"Of course."

"He will not be easy. He wants your love, but does not want to give his heart."

"I will make him my plaything."

Giulietta waits until Hoffmann emerges from the gaming room. He explains that he has lost everything and therefore is leaving.

Closing in on her prey, Giulietta desperately cries out that he is without pity. Hoffmann is smitten, and tells her that he loves her. "Leave tonight," she cautions him, "for Schlemil is very jealous and will kill you. Beginning tomorrow I shall be yours. For now, you must give me but one thing." Taking a mirror in hand she shows him his reflection. "I want your reflection, your soul, your life, so that I may keep them in my heart."

This sounds like madness to Hoffmann, but overwhelmed by the passion he feels as they talk of the ecstasy they will have, he tells her she may have whatever she wants.

Suddenly Schlemil walks in. "I knew I would find you together!" Giulietta whispers to Hoffmann that Schlemil has the key to her room, which only strengthens Hoffmann's resolve to stay. Dapertutto tells Hoffmann that he looks pale, and to prove it gives him a mirror.

Hoffmann glances at it and is terror-stricken. "My reflection is gone!"

Nicklausse says, "Let's go or you'll lose your soul."

But Hoffmann is in love again. "I can't leave yet," he says.

Schlemil asks him what he is waiting for.

"For you to give me a certain key."

"The only way you can take this key is with my life!" Schlemil retorts.

"Then I will take them both!" Hoffmann responds.

"*En garde!*" Schlemil shouts, drawing his sword.

"You have no sword," Dapertutto observes. "Borrow mine!" Hoffmann gladly accepts.

The duel is savage and Hoffmann mortally wounds Schlemil. Taking the key from the dying man, Hoffmann runs to unlock Giulietta's room and to claim her love.

Coolly picking up his sword, Dapertutto re-sheathes it and waits in the night's shadows.

Having found Giulietta's room empty, Hoffmann runs back distraught, just in time to see the enchantress gliding away in a gondola, with her Pitichinaccio. Seeing Hoffmann, she laughs mockingly.

"Wretch!" Hoffmann shouts after her.

Nicklausse pulls him away before the police arrive.

ACT III

In the dusk light of a gloomily furnished drawing room, lovely young Antonia Crespel sits at the clavier accompanying herself in a song. She is melancholy, for her father has recently moved them to Munich so as to separate her from Hoffmann.

Crespel comes into the room and chastises his daughter. "You promised never to sing again. In your singing I hear the beautiful voice of your dead mother. No more, I implore you!" Obediently she agrees, but it makes her even more despondent and she goes to her room.

While Crespel worries about his daughter's involvement with Hoffmann, his servant Frantz enters. Crespel orders him not to allow anyone into the house while he is out. But poor Frantz is so hard of hearing that he misunderstands all of Crespel's instructions, causing his master to storm angrily out of the house.

Unable to understand his master's anger, Frantz tries to cheer himself up by singing and dancing, with results more comic than esthetic. He has just fallen into a chair when Hoffmann appears at the door. "I have found the place at last!" he declares. "Frantz," he shouts, "get Antonia so that I may see her!"

With his usual good-natured incompetence, Frantz says, "What a joy for Monsieur Crespel," and goes to find her.

Waiting for his beloved, Hoffmann sits at the clavier and begins a love song, but is soon interrupted by Antonia rushing in. They embrace, swearing eternal devotion. "Tomorrow we shall marry," they pledge. Lovingly she leads him to the clavier and while he plays they sing together. He notes her abnormally high color, and suddenly she gasps as if exhausted, but she

185

hastily denies any difficulty. "I hear my father!" she says, and quickly runs to her room. Instead of following her or departing, Hoffmann decides that there is a mystery he must uncover and hides behind the curtains just as Crespel returns.

"I was sure Hoffmann was here! May he go to the devil!"

Frantz enters and announces that Doctor Miracle has arrived. "Lock the door," Crespel shouts. "Don't let him in! He will kill my daughter as he killed my wife!" But it is too late.

Doctor Miracle enters, heralded by his menacing laugh. "I have come to cure Antonia of the disease she inherited from her mother!" He points to Antonia's door, and both Hoffmann and Crespel freeze in terror as the door to the room opens by itself and by some remote control the Doctor directs an invisible Antonia to a chair. "Sit down! How old are you? Only twenty; the springtime of life. Let me count your pulse. Sing, Antonia, sing!" Suddenly Antonia's voice rings out clearly and the door swings closed.

Miracle turns to the distraught father. "You see. The singing makes her feverish. If you want my help I have some bottles of medicine I keep in reserve!" He clangs the phials together, as accompaniment to his wild chant. Crespel has had all he can bear and he chases the evil Doctor out of the house.

Stunned by what he has seen, Hoffmann comes out of hiding. "What a sacrifice! Never to sing again!" When Antonia enters, somewhat pale and dazed, he tries to reassure her. "Antonia, forget about great success and a singing career. Marry me."

"Here is my hand," she promises.

"Tomorrow I will return," he says, and kissing her hand takes his leave.

Alone, she contemplates life without singing and is tormented by Doctor Miracle, whose voice keeps interrupting her thoughts. "How can you make such a sacrifice?" he taunts. "Can you give up the cheers of the crowds for the cries of sniveling children?"

"I will be loved and safe with Hoffmann," she counters.

"Hoffmann loves you only for your beauty and soon he shall sacrifice you to his infidelities," comes the mocking voice.

Torn by her doubts, Antonia calls to the portrait of her mother to save her from this demonic torment. Suddenly the portrait comes to life and her mother calls out, "Antonia! Antonia! This is your mother!" Goaded by Miracle, Antonia sings with her mother. While the evil Doctor wildly accompanies her on a violin, Antonia sings herself into a frenzy until at last she collapses on the floor.

Miracle disappears and Antonia's mother is once again but a portrait. Crespel rushes in but he is too late. With her dying breath, Antonia tells him that her mother is calling to her and wants her to sing. Crespel begs her not to die and when Hoffmann and Nicklausse enter, the desperate father turns on Hoffmann with a knife, accusing him of having killed his daughter. Nicklausse restrains Crespel while the panic-stricken Hoffmann asks him to call a doctor. As if in answer to the call, the evil genius Doctor Miracle materializes once again and coolly pronounces her dead.

In despair, Hoffmann cries out, "Antonia!"

EPILOGUE

In Luther's tavern, there is rapt silence. "Well, there you have the stories of my loves!" Hoffmann says.

Luther comes in to announce that Stella's performance has been a triumph. But Hoffmann is so drunk that he barely reacts. In his stead, Nicklausse jumps up to lead a round of toasts to the lovely Stella. Growing jealous, Hoffmann takes offense at his faithful friend and throws his glass to the ground. Nicklausse, his feelings hurt, storms out of the tavern. The staggering Hoffmann orders another round of drinks, and the students vow to refill their glasses until the break of day.

When the beautiful Stella comes in looking for Hoffmann, one of the students points to her lover lying in a stupor on the floor. Stella leaves escorted by the urbane Councilor Lindorf, and poor Hoffmann has lost his love yet again.

NORMA

Opera in Two Acts
by
VINCENZO BELLINI
Première: La Scala, Milan, December 26, 1831

ACT I

Scene 1

THE MILITARY power of the great Roman Empire has spread far and wide, occupying many lands, most often against the will of the people. In Gaul, on the western shores of Europe, the Druid priests and soldiers who formerly ruled the country can barely contain the smoldering resentment they feel toward the occupying forces.

Assembled one evening in a sacred grove of the forest, they listen to their high priest, Oroveso. Addressing them from the stone altar that stands at the foot of a great oak dedicated to their god, Irminsul, he tells them that when the new moon rises, his daughter Norma, high priestess in the Temple of Virgins, whom they all worship as a seeress, will come to cut the mistletoe and tell them what the gods want them to do. The Druids pray that the gods will tell her to rise up against the Romans. They shout, "May our hatred be expressed and this peace be shattered. May we rise against our enemy and the crash of thunder reverberate throughout the city of the Caesars!" On this bellicose note, they file out of the sacred forest, to wait for the new moon. What the Druids do not know is that Norma has been secretly in love with the Roman proconsul, Pollione, for many years and, violating her vow of chastity, has borne two children by him.

Pollione, taking a walk through the forest with his centurion Flavio, confides that he has fallen in love with another Druid priestess, Adalgisa. He feels conscience-stricken, but is helpless in the grip of this new passion.

Flavio is shocked. "Don't you fear the wrath of Norma?"

Pollione nods grimly. "Indeed, yes. I had a dream about it. We were in Rome at the altar of Venus, Adalgisa and I. She was all in white as we were about to be married. I felt utterly blissful. Suddenly, a great shadow like a Druid cloak fell between us and I could no longer see my beloved. There was lightning and the sound of children weeping and a terrible voice cried, 'In this way does Norma repay her faithful lover!'"

Suddenly the great Druid gong peels, followed by trumpet calls.

"We had better leave," Flavio warns. "The moon has risen and the Druids are returning to perform their rituals."

In a fit of anger, Pollione declares that his love for Adalgisa is stronger than their barbarian gods and he will destroy the Druids' religion, but as the solemn procession of Druid priests, priestesses, and people approaches, he allows Flavio to lead him away.

Garbed in her religious vestments, her long hair unbound, Norma raises the golden sickle aloft as she stands on the altar stone. She tells her people that the time for war against the Romans has not yet come. "I have read in the secret books of heaven that one day great Rome will perish of its own decadence. All we need do is wait. Peace is what we will have now!" Using her sickle, she cuts the sacred mistletoe and the Druids kneel and pray. Norma calls the ceremony to an end and, to assuage their frustration, assures her people that when the gods call for Roman blood to flow, her voice will thunder. Excited by her promise, the Druids vow that no Roman shall escape their vengeance and that the proconsul, Pollione, will be the first to fall. Norma has been troubled by Pollione's recent coldness and she thinks now that she has the power to punish him. But she knows she could not bear to. As the Druids march out calling for the gods to hasten the downfall of Rome, Norma prays silently that Pollione will return to her and renew their love.

Adalgisa returns to the now empty grove and, prostrating herself on the altar of Irminsul, implores the gods to give her the strength to resist Pollione's love. She is still praying when Pollione joins her. She pleads with him to leave her, but he will not listen.

"You must pray to the god of love," he tells her. "If you go back to your temple and forget about our love, you might as well offer me as a sacrifice to your god, because I cannot live without you." Adalgisa tries to make him understand how painful it is to break her sacred vows. Undaunted, Pollione presses on. "I must return to Rome and there I can offer you a purer heaven and better gods."

Adalgisa is stricken. "You are leaving . . . ?"

"Tomorrow."

She is breathless with the pain of this news, but says she can never go with him, and keeps begging him to leave her be.

Tenderly, he continues to woo her. "Adalgisa, how can you forsake me? Come to Rome with me; to Rome where there is love, and joy, and life. Let me love you as your husband."

His words, his eyes, her own love finally overwhelm Adalgisa. She struggles to resist but her protests grow weaker until at last, praying to heaven to forgive her, she promises to defy her gods and leave with him.

SCENE 2

Inside a secret dwelling in the forest, Norma tends to her two sons. To Clotilde, their nurse, she confides her mixed emotions. "I love them so much and yet sometimes it tortures me to see them. And what will we do if Pollione goes back to Rome? I cannot believe that he would leave us, yet . . ." Hearing someone approaching, Norma orders Clotilde to take the boys and keep them out of sight.

Adalgisa stands timidly at the door and Norma bids her enter. "You are trembling. What is bothering you?"

Nervously, Adalgisa confesses to the high priestess. "I am in love. Please don't be angry. I tried to fight it, but now I have sworn to betray our altar and flee from our land. I tried to pray, but my lips were stopped by the look of his ardent, pleading eyes."

As Adalgisa relates how she fell ever more deeply in love, Norma thinks, "This is just as it was with me; this man's words of love even sound the same!" Sympathetically, she assures Adalgisa that nothing binds her to the temple forever. "You are forgiven and I free you from your sacred vows of chastity. Wed your beloved and live happily."

Adalgisa is ecstatic.

Norma says, "But tell me, who is the young man?"

"He is a Roman!" Adalgisa responds. "And there he is." Norma turns and is stunned to see Pollione standing at the door.

Her anger is beyond control. Raging, she calls Pollione an evil villain and warns him to fear for his sons. When he does not answer, she seizes Adalgisa's arm. "This man has deceived you. Better to have died than to have known this man!"

While Adalgisa trembles in fright and confusion, Pollione pleads with Norma, "Spare this innocent maiden."

Suddenly Adalgisa understands the situation and turns on Pollione, ordering him to leave her.

Passionately he pleads, "But I am your lover. You are my destiny."

"All right, then. Go with her!" Norma points imperiously to the door. "You are unworthy. Forget me, forget your sons, forget your promises, and your honor. But, remember, you will never escape my contempt and my vengeance will follow you both."

Pollione is wretched, but unyielding. "Though your curse may bring me eternal anguish, this love is greater than you or I."

Adalgisa tries to tell Norma that she will give him up, but Norma continues to spew curses upon Pollione.

Suddenly the Druids call for Norma to return to the sacred altar for "Irminsul has roared!" Threatening him with death, Norma motions Pollione to leave. He angrily complies, but swears that he will fell her god first.

ACT II

Scene 1

Dagger in hand, Norma approaches the bed on which her sons are sleeping, but she cannot bring herself to strike. "How can I take this vengeance on their father when they are my children too! Clotilde," she calls, "bring Adalgisa to me!" The nurse obeys and soon Adalgisa arrives. "I have decided to rid myself of this sick existence, but I cannot take these children with me. I entrust them to you. You must take them to their father at the Roman camp. I hope that he will be less cruel to you. But promise me never to desert my children or let them become slaves."

Adalgisa tells Norma she will never go with Pollione. "You must keep your children. I will go to the camp and tell Pollione of your torment and sorrow. It will reawaken the love he once had for you and again you will live in his heart. You must relent and allow me to do this for you; if not for you, then for your sons!"

Norma objects, "But it is you he loves."

"He must regret it, and I want only to restore your rights. If I cannot convince him, then together we shall shun men forever."

Touched by the sweetness of this selfless woman, Norma embraces Adalgisa and together they swear eternal friendship. They will help each other against the cruelties of the world!

SCENE 2

In the forest the Druid warriors have assembled once again hoping to wage war against the Romans. Oroveso steps forward and forlornly tells them that war is still not the will of the gods. "The Roman general who replaces Pollione is even more fierce, but Norma does not yet wish to revolt. I too would like to fight, but we must hide our scorn until the time is right." Reluctantly, the warriors agree.

Norma has come to the sacred grove to wait for news that Adalgisa has convinced Pollione to return to her. She is already looking forward to the joys of renewed love. But this hope is crushed when Clotilde comes with the news that Adalgisa's efforts have failed. Norma suspects treachery, but Clotilde reports that Adalgisa has returned to the temple begging to renew her vows, while Pollione swears to abduct her from the altar, if necessary.

This is more than Norma can bear. "He has gone too far! To stop him I will make the Romans bleed!" She runs to the altar and strikes the sacred shield of Irminsul three times.

From all directions the Druids, the priestesses, and the soldiers come running. "What is the decree?" they ask.

"War!" she announces. "We will exterminate our enemy." Excited by her call to battle, the warriors respond with a savage chant calling for the total destruction of the Romans.

A sudden commotion is heard and Clotilde rushes forward to report that a Roman has been captured in the temple of the virgins. As the prisoner is dragged to the grove, there are cries of "Pollione!"

Norma thinks, "Now I shall be avenged," and takes a dagger from Oroveso, but stops, once again overwhelmed by pity. As the others urge her on, she explains, "I must question the infidel. Leave us alone."

The Druids gone, Norma confronts Pollione. "You are in my power and I alone can save you. On your gods and your sons you must vow never to see Adalgisa again. I too will never see you again. This you must promise!"

"I would rather die."

"You should know then that I almost plunged this dagger into your sons. I didn't, but another time I might."

192

Pollione is aghast and pleads with her to kill him instead. But Norma is merciless and promises that not only he, but *all* the Romans will be killed, "and Adalgisa will be punished. She will die on the pyre!"

Pollione begs her to take his life instead. "Let that innocent woman live. It is I who should be punished. Give me the dagger so I can kill myself!"

"At last you plead." Norma gloats at his misery, at his being as unhappy as she.

Desperately, he tries to snatch the dagger from her, and she quickly calls the Druids back to the grove.

When they are all assembled she tells them that she will reveal the guilty priestess who has broken her vows. "Prepare the pyre for her sacrifice."

"Speak. Who is she?" they cry out.

Quietly Pollione pleads with her. "Do not say it."

Norma motions them all to silence and, pointing to herself, utters the fateful words. "I am the guilty priestess!"

Everyone is stunned and disbelieving. Oroveso and the Druids beg her to say it is not true, that she is raving. Pollione, overwhelmed by her sublime gesture and his own remorse, feels that his love for her has been reborn. "Forgive me," he begs her. "Let us die together."

To prove that she is indeed guilty, Norma tells her people, "I am the mother of two sons." Then turning to her father, she begs him to guard her sons. "They are innocent. Take pity on them."

Overcome with grief, Oroveso weeps bitterly.

"Your tears forgive me my sins," Norma tells him. She hands her crown to the Druids and turns toward the pyre.

Pollione takes her hand. "Your death is mine. More holy, our eternal love begins."

Together they mount the pyre. As the flames begin to engulf them, Norma turns once more and cries out to her father, "Farewell."

DIALOGUES OF THE CARMELITES

Opera in Three Acts
by
FRANCIS POULENC
Première: La Scala, Milan, January 26, 1957

ACT I

SCENE 1

ONE DAY in April of 1789, as the French Revolution is beginning to rumble, the Marquis de la Force naps in a chair in the sumptuous elegance of his library. Suddenly the large door swings open and the Marquis' son, the Chevalier de la Force, bursts in, and agitatedly demands, "Where is Blanche?"

The Marquis is annoyed. "Where are your manners?" Then he wants to know why the Chevalier is looking for his sister.

"Roger de Damas just told me—he was traveling by coach but had to turn back because a wild mob of angry peasants stopped him. He saw Blanche's coach surrounded at a road near Bucy!"

The Marquis shudders now, remembering the traumatic event that marked Blanche's birth. He tells his son, "There is no sight like a crowd out of control. At the wedding of the Dauphin some fireworks exploded and caught fire and the crowd panicked. We tried to move out of the way, but our carriage was surrounded by the frenzied mob. Fortunately, the soldiers arrived just in time to save us, but later that night in this very house, your mother died after giving birth to Blanche!" With an effort, he resumes his accustomed calm. "The horses and coachman are trustworthy. She will be all right."

"Of course," the Chevalier agrees; "I am only concerned because she is so morbid I do not know what effect it will have upon her."

"Blanche," his father responds, "is only a sensitive girl who needs to marry. Soon she will return and all your fears will vanish, as will hers."

Just then the door quietly opens, and to their great relief it is Blanche. "I was so frightened," she barely whispers, "with only the glass window of the carriage between the crowd and me!" She tries to make light of it now, but almost faints, and claiming the long church service she attended tired her, she proposes to go to her room. Knowing her fear of the dark, her brother cautions her to take a candle. Mysteriously, she declares that each night for her is like the night of Christ's Agony, leaving her father and brother baffled and anxious.

Suddenly a terrified shriek shatters the mood and a servant rushes in to explain that he had been lighting some candles. "My shadow on the wall must have scared Mademoiselle Blanche."

Blanche returns, visibly shaken by the incident but full of resolve. "Father, everything bears a sign from God. If you will permit I want to become a nun!"

The Marquis de la Force is clearly opposed. "You must not hate the world so much that you renounce it."

"I do not hate it, but I cannot live in it." She throws herself at his feet pleading with him. "Let me find something to end the terror that fills my unhappy life! If I renounce everything for Him, God may restore me to honor and grace!"

SCENE 2

Several weeks later in the parlor of the Carmelite Convent at Compiègne, the Mother Superior, Madame de Croissy, questions Blanche. Old and ill, Madame de Croissy is partially hidden from the novice by a screen that separates them. "The harsh rules of our order don't frighten you, do they?"

"They bring me here!" Blanche replies with certainty. "I am looking for a life of heroism!"

The Mother Superior is not impressed. "Our illusions are the most dangerous of our desires. The purpose of our order is prayer. Here God tests not strength but weakness."

Blanche is undeterred. "This is my only refuge."

"The order will not protect you. But I am ill and near my end so I may pity you." She adds: "Difficult tests lie before you." The Mother Superior then asks if Blanche has chosen the name she will bear as a Carmelite.

"I would like to be called Sister Blanche of the Agony of Christ!"

SCENE 3

One day Blanche and another young nun, Sister Constance de Saint Denis, are in the workroom unloading the meager provisions that have been donated to the convent. While they work, Constance chatters gaily.

Blanche is critical. "How can you be so happy while the Reverend Mother . . ."

Constance gently notes that she would gladly give her own life if it would save the Reverend Mother. Blanche challenges her. "Don't you have any fear of death?"

"Life is so wonderful and cheerful," Constance declares, "I believe that death must be the same."

As they turn to their ironing chores, Constance suddenly tells Blanche, "I was sure the very first time I saw you that my wish would be granted."

"What wish?"

Constance hesitates a moment, then blurts out, "I knew that God would not allow me to grow old and that you and I would someday die together!" Unnerved by this heedless talk of death, Blanche accuses Constance of pride and demands she stop.

SCENE 4

In the convent infirmary, the Mother Superior lies dying. Attending her is Mother Marie of the Incarnation, the next most senior nun in the convent and a woman of strong judgment and character.

"Where is Sister Blanche?" the Mother Superior asks. "Of all the sisters I have brought into this convent, she is the one who concerns me most. As my last deed, Mother Marie, I entrust you with the care of Blanche de la Force! She needs the strictness and vision you possess."

A soft knock announces Blanche's arrival. Silently, Mother Marie leaves as Blanche kneels beside the Mother Superior's bed. "I wanted to have a long talk with you," the Mother Superior tells her, "but my talk with Sister Marie has left me too weary. Of all the nuns you are dearest to me. Child, you must never change. Retain your simplicity and remain sweet and soft for God. Now rise and bid me goodbye one last time. I bless you."

Sobbing, Blanche leaves the room.

Mother Marie returns with the Doctor and Sister Anne of the Cross. The Mother Superior is suffering and she begs the Doctor for more medication to kill the pain, but he refuses.

"You must give me something so I can properly say goodbye to the sisters."

Mother Marie advises her not to worry herself any longer about the convent. "Your concern now need only be with God."

In a strange burst of rebellion, Madame de Croissy answers, "Sick as I am, let Him concern Himself with me."

Shocked, Mother Marie decides the dying woman is delirious, and orders that the windows be shut so that her irresponsible words will not scandalize the sisters. Sitting up suddenly in bed, the Mother Superior calls to Mother Marie. "I just had a terrible vision: our chapel was empty and destroyed, the altar broken apart. There was straw and blood spewed over everything. God has forsaken us!" Exhausted, she collapses.

Blanche comes through the door again, walking almost in a daze, and following Mother Marie's instructions kneels beside the Mother Superior's bed.

Gasping for breath, the Mother Superior calls, "Blanche . . . Beg pardon . . . death . . . fear . . . fear of death!" She expires, falling back on the bed.

Blanche tries to speak but cannot, her words lost in her sobs.

A bell tolls.

ACT II

SCENE 1

The Mother Superior lies in state in the dimly lit chapel. Constance and Blanche stand watch, reciting Latin prayers over the body. When the clock strikes the hour Constance rises to fetch the next watch. Alone, Blanche tries to pray, while staring at the corpse. Suddenly gripped by fear, she walks to the door where she is stopped by Mother Marie.

"Where are you going?" the nun asks.

Haltingly, Blanche explains that her hour is over and Constance has left to get their replacements. "I thought it would be all right to walk to the door."

Mother Marie guesses the truth and tenderly suggests, "It was the cool of the night air that made you tremble more than the fright. I myself will take you back to your cell. Tomorrow you will ask God's forgiveness for leaving a task unfinished." Gently, she leads Blanche away.

In preparation for the funeral, Blanche and Constance carry in a large cross made of flowers. Afraid that it may be too large for the grave, they decide to use some of the flowers in a bouquet for the new Mother Superior. Constance hopes that Mother Marie will be appointed. Blanche is caustic. "You always believe that God will do what you wish."

"Why not? Chance is perhaps only the logic of God." She ponders a moment. "But in the death of the Mother Superior the Lord made an error. Why did she die so horribly? I believe her death belonged to someone else. It was much too hard. Someone else will get her death and find it surprisingly easy."

This talk fills Blanche with indefinable dread. "The death of someone else? What do you mean?"

Constance shrugs. "We die one for the other, or maybe instead of each other. Who knows?"

SCENE 2

In the Chapter Room of the convent, with its high vaulted ceilings and a beautiful crucifix, the traditional ceremony of obedience is just concluding. One by one the nuns kiss the hand of the new Mother Superior, Madame Lidoine, then take their places on the hard benches placed along the wall. Blanche and Constance are last and when they have taken their places, the new Mother Superior addresses the assembled sisters. "My dear daughters," she begins, "gone are the calm, happy days we have known in the past when we might forget there is no guarantee against pain and grief. What destiny we face, I do not know. All heaven gives us is our own good will, endless patience, and tenderness—virtues well suited to humble women such as ourselves. We must not try to be martyrs. Prayer is our duty; martyrdom is a reward. Mother Marie, will you say a few appropriate words to end my perhaps too simple speech?"

Mother Marie advises the nuns to follow these noble precepts with their tongues as well as their hearts, and signals them to kneel in prayer.

SCENE 3

The sudden loud ringing of the convent doorbell attracts the Mother Superior and Mother Marie. Constance has already gone to look and reports that a man on horseback is at the gate.

Mother Marie goes to investigate, returning soon with news that the man is Monsieur de la Force, wishing to see his sister Blanche before he goes abroad. Given the extremities of the time, the Mother Superior allows the convent rules to be broken. "Call Blanche de la Force. And Mother Marie, I want you to be present at the meeting!"

Under the watchful eye of Mother Marie, Blanche and her brother meet in the parlor. He finds her reception of him cold, and tries desperately to get through to her in a vain effort to convince her that due to the spread of the Revolution the convent is no longer safe, and she should return to her father. She assures him that she has found happiness as a Carmelite nun. He notices the tremendous change in her, which she attributes to the loss of the fears that had previously haunted her.

"Then you are no longer afraid?" he asks.

"Nothing can hurt me here," she answers.

Convinced she will not be persuaded to leave, he bids her goodbye.

She entreats him not to leave in anger. "I am no longer a little child. Now I am a daughter of Carmel. Accept me as a companion in battle; each of our chosen ways has its risks and dangers." But as the Chevalier de la Force leaves, Blanche swoons and clutches the screen for support. Mother Marie quickly assists her, counseling her to calm herself.

"They still treat me like a child," Blanche laments. "Was it a lie to hide my weakness? Perhaps I was too proud. I shall be punished."

"You must transcend your pride," Mother Marie advises. "Be courageous."

SCENE 4

In the convent's sacristy, surrounded by the nuns, the Chaplain puts the religious ornaments into a cupboard. The revolutionaries have forbidden religious services and with great sadness he tells them, "This was my last Mass. Let us sing." The nuns kneel as the Chaplain leads them in prayer.

Fearful, Blanche asks the Chaplain, "What will you do?"

"I will go into hiding. But have no fear, my child. I will stay near and I will visit as often as possible." Blessing her, he leaves.

"Is there no one left who will come to the aid of our priests?" Constance cries out.

The Mother Superior says serenely, "When there are no priests, an abundance of martyrs will restore the balance of grace."

With sudden passion, Mother Marie suggests that the Carmelite nuns sacrifice themselves, but the Mother Superior firmly corrects her. "Such a decision is not for us to make."

A bell rings violently and the Chaplain returns to tell them that he has almost been trapped between the angry mob and the soldiers. They can hear the noise of the crowd outside drawing closer. Suddenly there is a pounding at the doors. Shouts of "Open, open up!" are heard. The nuns huddle in a corner until the Chaplain can escape through a side exit. Then Mother Marie orders Constance to unbolt the doors.

While two guards restrain the crowd, four commissioners enter to read an order. "The legislative assembly has decided on this date, August 17, 1792, that as of October 1 any houses now occupied by religious orders will be vacated and sold at the discretion of the proper authorities." The nuns are to be expelled.

Maintaining her calm, Mother Marie asks only if the sisters may obtain civilian clothes to wear, since they are forbidden to wear their habits.

"Ah, you can't wait to throw off your silly clothes."

With great dignity, she replies, "We shall always be devoted servants regardless of our uniform."

"The people have no need for servants."

"But they do indeed need martyrs."

"To die during a revolution is pointless!" he counters.

"To live when life is meaningless is as worthless as the Revolution's money!" she retorts.

Eventually, the commissioners leave, and Mother Marie bolts the doors behind them. Blanche, who has been hiding behind the other nuns, sinks weakly onto a low stool. Mother Jeanne tells them all that the Reverend Mother is coming to say farewell before she leaves for Paris. Noticing Sister Blanche as she sits stupefied and alone, Jeanne is filled with pity and removes the Little King of Glory from the cupboard. She hands it to Blanche, saying softly, "Each Christmas Eve we carry this Little King into each cell. I hope it will give you hope and courage."

Blanche takes the statue in her arms adoringly. "So little and so frail," she says. Suddenly, shouts from the crowd outside startle her and she drops the statue to the ground where it shatters. Terrified that this is an omen, Blanche cries out, "The Little King is dead. We have nothing left . . . only the Lamb of God."

ACT III

SCENE 1

The chapel has been devastated and in its remains, Mother Marie has assembled the nuns. The Mother Superior is absent, but the Chaplain, dressed now in tattered mufti, has come to see them. Mother Marie proposes that to save their sacred order they all take a vow of martyrdom. The nuns look unhappy, but no one objects. She suggests they take a secret vote to be certain that the sentiment is unanimous. "If even one is against, we will not do it."

One by one the nuns pass behind the altar to cast their vote with the Chaplain. Blanche looks so weary and bleak, they are sure she will not assent. Constance watches her with concern. And indeed, the Chaplain reports that there is one dissenting vote. The nuns nod knowingly, but suddenly Sister Constance confesses. "It was my vote, as the Chaplain knows. Now I have changed my mind and ask you to permit me to join you in this vow."

The Chaplain agrees to her request, and donning his vestments, he bids the sisters approach him two by two with the youngest in front. Sister Blanche and Constance kneel side by side and take the vow first as the other nuns mill about. Suddenly, in the midst of the confusion, Blanche springs to her feet and flees.

The convent has been closed; the Carmelites, dressed in civilian clothes and carrying their few possessions in bundles, are confronted by officers of the Republic, who warn them that they shall be watched very carefully. "You may not live in communities, nor deal with enemies of the state, nor with priests who are against us. One by one you will come before the court to be given your card, a card assuring you of all the blessings of liberty under the guidance of the law."

When the officers are gone, the Mother Superior instructs one of the nuns to warn the priest to cancel the Mass they had planned to hold this very morning. "It is far too dangerous."

Mother Marie accedes, reluctantly. "How can we reconcile this kind of caution with our vow?" she mutters.

The Mother Superior replies, "Your vows are individual. But I have to answer to God for all of you!"

SCENE 2

The once elegant home of the Marquis de la Force has, like its owner, fallen victim to the violence of the Revolution. Requisitioned by the revolutionaries, the house is a shadow of its former self; once sumptuous furnishings have been destroyed and the majestic fireplace in the library holds a plain earthen pot. Blanche, once the princess of this household, now works in it as a servant so as to escape the blade of the guillotine.

Wretchedly clothed, she is tending the pot when the door of the library opens. She is startled to see Mother Marie, dressed as a civilian. She tells Blanche she has come to take her back to her sisters. Blanche refuses. Even though she is a mere servant in what once was her home, she feels safe here. "They would never think to look for me here. Oh, my stew is burning! What will they do to me?" She rushes to the pot on the fire and, crying hysterically, tries to rescue the stew. Mother Marie helps her but Blanche only grows more hysterical. "Why won't they leave me alone? I was born in fear and I live in fear. Only my father could keep me from declaring my fear, but he is dead. Last week they guillotined him." She chokes up. "Yesterday, they struck me!"

"My daughter," Mother Marie counsels, "to be hated is not a misfortune, only to hate oneself." Then after a pause she adds, "Sister Blanche of the Agony of Christ."

Hearing this name, Blanche seems to gain strength. She stands straight.

"Here is an address," Mother Marie adds. "You will be safe with Mademoiselle Rose Ducor." The visit is suddenly ended as the harsh voice of a woman in another room orders Blanche to do an errand. Blanche hurries away and Mother Marie also leaves.

SCENE 3

The Carmelite nuns have been arrested and await their fate in a prison cell. They are all there but Blanche and Mother Marie, who has somehow eluded the police.

At daybreak, the Mother Superior tries to cheer them: "We have survived our first night in prison. That is the hardest. By tomorrow we will have grown accustomed to our circumstances." She then assures them that even though they took the vow of martyrdom in her absence, she will share their fate, no matter what it be.

Constance asks what has become of Sister Blanche, but the Mother Superior doesn't know. "She will return," Constance decides; "I had a dream that she would."

The others greet this with derisive laughter, laughter which is abruptly ended when the cell door swings open admitting the jailer. Casually he reads the declaration of the Tribunal: "Having gathered together to plot against the Revolution, all the Carmelite nuns of Compiègne are declared

rebels. The Tribunal has therefore decided that they are to be executed!"
He rolls up the fatal document and leaves.

The nuns bow their heads. Softly the Mother Superior tries to find words
of comfort. She had hoped to save them but, "This is God's will. All that's
left now is to die. Bless God who ordained this punishment. We will die
together as a final celebration of our order. For the last time I give you my
blessings!"

On a street near the Bastille the Chaplain meets Mother Marie. "They
have all been condemned to death," he tells her.

She says she must go—to die with her sisters. "I too took the vow!"

The Chaplain argues that she is responsible only to God, and it seems to
be His will to save her.

"They will look for me. I will be dishonored."

"Think only of His gaze," the Chaplain says gently.

SCENE 4

In the notorious Place de la Revolution, a jeering crowd assembles to
watch the day's executions. The Carmelite nuns descend from the tumbrels
and are herded together at the foot of the scaffold. Their Chaplain, dressed
as a civilian, and wearing a Liberty cap, mingles with the crowd and fur-
tively mumbles the absolution as the first sisters climb the steps of the
scaffold. Quickly he disappears.

Above the din of the crowd rise the voices of the Carmelite nuns as they
sing the Salve Regina in unison. Led by the Mother Superior, they bravely
march one by one up the steps to the deadly axe. With each horrifying drop
of the blade, the voices are diminished by one. Soon only the lonely voice of
Sister Constance can be heard. As she climbs the stairs, still singing, she is
suddenly gripped by fear and turns as if to flee. As she does so, she sees
Blanche making her way through the crowd. With a radiant face, still singing, Constance calmly resumes her march to the guillotine.

As Constance's voice is cut off, Blanche de la Force picks up the hymn
and, stepping out of the crowd, mounts the scaffold. As the crowd watches
in stunned silence, she dauntlessly goes to her execution, singing the final
verses of the Veni Creator Spiritus: "Deo Patri sit gloria. Et Filio qui a
mortuis. Surrexit ac Paraclitio. In saeculorum . . ." Before she can finish, a
last crash of the guillotine silences her voice and her fears forever.

THE FLYING DUTCHMAN

Opera in Three Acts
by
RICHARD WAGNER
Première: Hofoper, Dresden, January 2, 1843

ACT I

A VIOLENT STORM rages off the coast of Norway. Through the gloom and the rain and the huge waves, a sailing vessel, all its timbers creaking, pulls into a bay, and casts anchor close to shore. As the grateful crew secures the ropes and lowers the sails, their captain, Daland, goes ashore in order to determine their position. "Sandwyke," he decides, "the storm has driven us seven miles beyond our home port." Telling the steersman to keep watch, Daland takes the rest of the crew belowdecks to rest.

The storm has abated. Taking a seat at the helm, the steersman tries to keep himself awake by singing a song about a beautiful maiden and how the fair south winds will bring them together. Soon he is dozing. A couple of times he wakes to the crack of a particularly heavy wave, but eventually exhaustion overcomes him and he falls into a deep sleep.

A ship with blood red sails silently looms up and moors next to the Norwegian vessel. Without a sound, neither of speech nor of noise, the crew furls the sails, while their captain steps ashore, bemoaning the fate to which he has been condemned—a deathless wandering of the seas. No storm, no pirate, no peril that he courts can hurt his ship or take his life. His ship's hold is laden with the treasure he has amassed and for which he has no use. Now, seven years have passed and he may once again come ashore to seek the one thing he craves—the eternal fidelity that will free him from the curse. But he has tried too many times before to believe that this time he will succeed. "No," he cries, "I have but one hope—the Day of Judgment. Come oblivion! Only nothingness can end my pain." From within his ship, haunting voices eerily echo his plea.

Daland has awakened and comes on deck. The steersman, still half asleep, reports, "All's well."

Daland scolds him for keeping such poor watch, pointing to the ship which now floats next to theirs. Startled, the steersman calls to the silent and seemingly empty ship. There is no answer. Then Daland sights the captain and asks his name and country.

There is a silence. At last, the answer comes. "I am a Dutchman. Would you refuse my ship anchorage in this storm?"

Daland welcomes the Dutch captain and recounts how the winds have blown his ship beyond his home port.

"I cannot tell you how many years I have been roving the seas, and how many lands I have seen. Only my homeland I cannot reach." The Dutchman suddenly makes a strange request: "Allow me to stay at your house for a while, and I will give you some of the treasure with which my ship is laden." As if by magic, two of the Dutchman's crew silently bring forth a chest filled with jewels. Daland cannot believe his eyes. "This is but a small part of my wealth. I will give you all my riches if you give me a home with your family." He then asks another unexpected question. "Do you have a daughter?"

Daland replies, "She is *my* gem."

The Dutchman offers to marry her and the Norwegian captain, filled with greed, is beside himself with joy. Each has what the other wants, and they strike a bargain, agreeing to exchange Daland's faithful daughter for the Dutchman's riches. "When the first winds blow we shall sail to her and if you like her she shall be yours."

The Dutchman muses, "Will she be my angel? Dare I indulge in hope? At least, I'll give myself to hope of hope."

While Daland praises the storm for having brought him such good fortune, the steersman suddenly calls out, "A fair south wind is blowing."

As Daland's men begin to raise the sail, the Dutchman tells him to go ahead, while his own crew rests. "My ship is faster, and we will overtake you."

Joyfully blessing the winds which will take them to their lovers, the Norwegians set sail for home.

ACT II

In Daland's house, some young women of the village are busy spinning thread under the direction of Mary, the housekeeper. Only Daland's daughter, Senta, has stopped working. Her hands lie idle as she gazes once again at a portrait that hangs on the wall. The picture has always fascinated her and today she somehow cannot take her eyes away from it. A strangely pale, dark-haired man, dressed in black, stares back at her. She has been told he is the legendary Flying Dutchman.

Mary notices her strange behavior and admonishes her to work or she will receive no gift from her sweetheart. But Senta pays no attention. She is obsessed with the portrait, and the other girls tease her for being in love. To change the subject, Senta asks Mary to sing the ballad of the Flying Dutchman. When Mary refuses, Senta reproaches her. "But it was you who first told it to me. I will tell it to the others so perhaps they will feel for him as I do." The girls agree to listen and Senta relates this amazing legend:

There is a ship at sea with black masts and blood red sails which travels endlessly and aimlessly without rest. "The captain of the ship is that spectral man"—she points to the picture—"and he is condemned to this fate because he once swore to round a cape during a storm, 'in spite of hell.' Satan heard him and condemned him to sail the seas until he found a wife who would be eternally faithful. Now, once every seven years he is allowed to go ashore to search for this elusive woman. Every seven years he woos, but none has ever proved true and he has always had to return to the sea."

Moved by the tale, the girls wonder where such a woman might be found. Suddenly Senta springs from her chair. "May God's angel bring you to me! I will save you!"

Erik, a young hunter who has long been in love with Senta, walks in at this moment and overhears her final words. He is desperately hurt, the girls think she has lost her mind, and Mary says she will destroy the portrait as soon as Daland returns and gives permission.

"He's on his way here now," Erik tells them. "I saw the ship approaching!" The girls are overjoyed to hear they will soon see their sailors again.

Mary reminds them that there is food to be prepared, and herds them all out of the room. Senta, too, tries to leave, but Erik detains her.

"Senta, I am but a poor hunter, but I offer you a true heart. I want to marry you, but I am afraid your father is interested only in wealth. If he refuses, will you speak for me?"

Senta is evasive and says she must go to the harbor to greet her father, but Erik does not let her. "I fear you love that man in the painting more than you love me."

Senta defends herself. "How can I not feel compassion for him?"

"And what of my pain? Doesn't that affect you?"

"How can you compare your own distress to what that poor man must feel?"

"I fear for you, Senta." Erik tells her of a dream he has had. "I saw a foreign ship come into harbor. In it were two men, one your father, the other"—he points to the portrait—"he! You ran to him and threw yourself at his feet. When he raised you up, you clung to him and kissed him passionately. Then I saw the two of you sail away!"

As if she has seen the vision herself, Senta is transported, and declares, "I am his!"

Erik cannot bear it. He realizes that he has lost her and rushes out of the room.

Alone, Senta prays again that the poor seaman may find his salvation. As the door swings open she turns her gaze from the portrait to where her father and the Dutchman are standing. Spellbound, oblivious to her own father, Senta stares fixedly at the stranger. Daland, shaken by his daughter's strange welcome, goes to her and asks, "Where is my greeting?" Taking her father's hand, Senta asks him to introduce the stranger.

Daland explains. "He is a seaman like myself, far from his home and weary of travel. He will pay well to lodge with us." When Senta dreamily nods her approval, he presses on, asking her to consent to marry this very wealthy man. Daland realizes that his words are going unheeded because Senta and the Dutchman are staring, entranced, at each other. Content that the two are attracted, he diplomatically takes his leave, informing the Dutchman that "She is as faithful as she is fair!"

Senta and the Dutchman continue to gaze at each other, he wondering if he has at last found the angel to heal his soul, she yearning to provide the balm she so clearly sees he needs. At last they emerge from the depths of their mutual contemplation.

"Do you concur with your father's wish for us to marry? Could you be eternally mine? Will I finally find my long sought rest?" The Dutchman's questions tumble forth and Senta quickly assures him that she would never disobey her father. She wants only to comfort him, and swears to be eternally faithful. Both are ecstatic because they have found each other.

Daland comes back to say that his men can no longer wait for the feast. "Senta," he asks, "will you consent? Can we make this meal a double celebration?"

Without hesitation she declares, "Here is my hand! My love will be constant until death!"

ACT III

In the harbor, the Norwegian and Dutch vessels lie moored side by side. The night is clear and lights gleam on board the Norwegian ship where the sailors are eating and drinking and making merry with some young women from the town. But beneath their gaiety, they are made uneasy by the ghostly quiet of the Dutch vessel. They call out to the Dutch sailors and invite them to join in the fun, but their cries are greeted by stony silence. The women offer food to the Dutch crew, but again there is no response. Emboldened by drink, the sailors mock the reputed speed of the Flying Dutchman, and as their tension mounts, they grow more boisterous.

Suddenly, there is a sign of movement on board the Dutch ship; an eerie blue light comes from within and a howling wind rips through the rigging. The sea, elsewhere calm, laps violently around the Dutch ship, while the shadowy crew emerges, singing of how when their captain is unlucky in love, it's once more back to sea. They chant, "Storm winds may howl, but our sails won't rip because they've been blessed by Satan!"

The Norwegian sailors try bravely to continue their revels, but they are soon driven mute by fear and rush belowdecks to the mocking laughter of the Dutchman's crew. Moments later, darkness and silence again envelop the two ships.

Senta comes rushing toward the harbor. She is followed closely by Erik, who cannot accept what has happened. He tries desperately to talk her out of her decision to marry this man she hardly knows.

"It is my duty," she replies.

"How can that be, when you pledged your love to me?"

She is provoked. "When did I pledge you my love?"

"Oh, Senta. How can you forget that day we watched your father sail away? He entrusted you to my protection. Did not the pressure of your hand assure me your love was true?"

The Dutchman, coming toward them, has overheard Erik's last words. He is devastated. If Senta has been untrue to Erik, how can she be true to him? "Senta," he says, "goodbye."

"No," she says. "You must not leave. I will not let you flee from here!"

But the Dutch captain gives a shrill blast on his whistle ordering his crew to hoist sails. "I doubt that you can keep your promise of fidelity," he tells Senta, and assures her she will not be condemned because she did not swear eternal love before God. "The fate for those who break their oath," he warns, "is eternal damnation. I do not want to destroy you." Moving toward his ship he shouts, "Farewell, salvation."

Senta tries to hold him. "I know who you are, and I know your fate. I can save you!"

Erik, still trying to wrest Senta away, calls for help. Daland, Mary, and the sailors arrive just as the Dutchman, pointing to the blood red sails, declares, "This is the ship which all devout men fear and I am the Flying Dutchman!" He jumps aboard and, to the spectral chant of his crew, immediately heads out to sea.

Daland, Erik, and Mary try to restrain Senta, but she breaks free, rushes to the edge of the cliff, and cries out, "Here I stand. Faithful unto death!" With these words she throws herself into the water.

Miraculously, the fleeing ship sinks into the calm sea and its red sails disappear. The Dutchman has been freed from his curse by Senta's love.

The glow of the sun brightens the sky as the lovers' souls, embracing, ascend to heaven and eternal rest.

HANSEL AND GRETEL

Opera in Three Acts
by
ENGELBERT HUMPERDINCK
Première: Hoftheater, Weimar, December 23, 1893

ACT I

ONCE UPON a time, deep in a forest of the Harz Mountains of Germany, stood a small hut, the poor home of Peter, the broommaker, who lived there with his wife and their two children, Hansel and Gretel.

One day, the broommaker and his wife go to town to sell their wares, leaving Hansel and Gretel to stay at home and do the chores. In the sparsely furnished room, Hansel sits on the floor, tying twigs into brooms, while Gretel knits a stocking and sings a nursery song to divert them from their hunger. For weeks they have eaten nothing but dry bread.

Hansel sighs, "How I'd like a good meal with hot rolls and cake."

Gretel advises him to stop complaining and confides that the jug on the table is filled with milk. "When Mother comes home she'll cook something good. Maybe a pudding!" Hansel jumps up to inspect the pitcher but Gretel soberly warns him to get back to work. "If it isn't done when Mother comes home you'll be punished!"

But Hansel has lost interest in work. "I'd rather dance."

Gretel jumps up. "Let me show you how." Clumsily he imitates her, and soon the two children are dancing together, twirling more and more until laughing hysterically, they tumble to the floor.

At this very moment the door swings open and their mother stands there, empty-handed. She has sold nothing and her worries make her quick to anger. "What is going on here? You haven't even finished your chores while your poor father and I have been out working all day. You lazy, naughty children, I will give you a good thrashing!" Grabbing a stick, she chases the children around the table. As she tries to hit them, she knocks the precious jug of milk onto the floor and it shatters. Totally distraught, she cries, "What will we eat now?"

Hansel dips his hand into the pool of milk and licks his fingers, giggling nervously. This makes his mother even more furious, and she orders them out of the house. "Go into the woods and find some wild strawberries for our dinner. Don't you dare come home until this basket is full!" The two children take the basket and run out the door.

The weary woman sinks into a chair. "My poor starving children," she moans. Resting her head on her arms, she falls asleep at the table.

Soon, the father arrives home, singing happily to himself and carrying a full basket on his back. Giving his wife a kiss, he noisily rouses her from her slumber. It is clear that he has been drinking, and she demands to know why he is celebrating when there is no food in the house. Ignoring her foul humor, he happily unloads his basket. "Here is food aplenty." He gaily waltzes his wife around the room, and regales her with an account of the many brooms he has sold this day. Joyfully, they toast all broommakers!

Suddenly, he stops. "Where are the children?"

Hesitantly, she tells him what happened. "When the jug broke I sent them into the woods to look for berries!"

This news horrifies Peter. "Into the woods! But that is where the wicked Nibble witch lives. She lures innocent children to her house and then shoves them into her hot oven. When they turn into gingerbread she eats them! Dear God, our children are in danger."

The mother is now thoroughly alarmed and the two parents dash out of their house into the woods in search of Hansel and Gretel.

ACT II

Deep in the woods, Gretel sits beneath a tree weaving a garland of roses while nearby Hansel fills the basket with wild strawberries. Pleased with himself, he brings it to Gretel. She pops a strawberry into her mouth. He takes another. They begin to fight playfully over the basket and Hansel wins. Greedily he swallows every last strawberry.

Gretel is shocked. "Mother will be very angry if we return empty-handed. We had better look for more!"

But darkness has crept up on them and they are unable to see the berry bushes in the gathering gloom. Nor can they return home, for Hansel realizes he has lost the way. He tries to act brave, but Gretel is frightened by every stump and every noise, even the echo of their own voices. A mist rises and turns the trees into a forest of ogres. Suddenly, a kind-looking little old man materializes through the fog, carrying a lantern and a heavy knapsack. He tells the children, "I am the sandman, and I have come to give you some rest. Now sleep, dear children, and the angels will give you sweet dreams." He throws sand in their eyes and vanishes. The children begin to yawn and, no longer frightened, kneel to say their prayers. They lie down on the ground and are soon fast asleep. A bright light breaks through the darkness and fourteen angels appear to stand guard through the night.

ACT III

Dawn breaks over the forest. The Dew Fairy appears through the still shrouded woods and sprinkles dew drops on the sleeping children, but disappears before they wake. Soon Gretel begins to stir. She rubs her eyes, then tickles Hansel, who jumps up, shouting, "I feel like new." Comparing notes on how soundly they slept, the children are amazed to discover that they had identical dreams about the angels.

As the morning mist dissolves, a large house made of gingerbread and hedged with a fence of gingerbread men is revealed. Hansel and Gretel are amazed and enchanted by this delicious sight and draw toward it. No one appears to be inside and Hansel wants to go in, but Gretel cautions him not to. Hansel confidently asserts that the angels must have brought about this marvel. With this happy idea, the children tiptoe to the house and Hansel bravely breaks a piece off and eats it.

Suddenly, a voice from within calls, "Who's nibbling at my house?" This startles the children, but they decide it was only the wind and continue to eat away at the gingerbread. They have never tasted anything so delicious. Again the voice from the house calls out, but the children ignore it. They are so busily occupied with their munching that they don't notice when the witch comes out of the house and creeps stealthily behind them. Quickly she throws a rope around Hansel, trapping him. Trying to be friendly, the witch tells them that she adores little children and promises them delicious cakes and sweets if they will only let her fatten them up. But all the while she cackles to herself, and her face is so ugly that the children do not trust her.

Hansel manages to struggle out of the witch's grasp and takes Gretel's hand. Together they start to run, but the witch waves her wand and casts a spell which freezes the children in their tracks. Then uttering some more of her hocus-pocus magic, she leads Hansel into a cage and locks the door behind him. Leaving Gretel still frozen in place, the hag disappears into the house.

Momentarily alone, Hansel whispers to Gretel to watch carefully and do what the witch bids. "Now hush. She's coming back."

The witch brings sweets, which she pushes into the cage for Hansel. Then she turns to Gretel and says, "Hocus pocus elderbush. Magic spell is broken, whoosh." Gretel can move again and the witch orders her to go into the house to set the table.

While Hansel pretends to be asleep, the witch admires her prisoner, imagining what a tasty meal he will make once he is properly baked. She checks the roaring oven and, content that all is in order for her grim feast, she celebrates by gleefully riding about on her broomstick, as all witches do! Her ride over, she returns to the job of fattening up Hansel to make him a more tasty dish, feeding him raisins through the bars of the cage.

While she is thus preoccupied, Gretel takes the wand and mutters, "Hocus pocus elderbush. Magic spell is broken, whoosh," to break the spell on Hansel.

The witch turns to Gretel, whom she intends to eat first, and instructs her to check the pastries in the oven. Hansel warns his sister to be careful and slips out of the cage.

Gretel pretends she does not know what to do. "I'm such a goose. Why don't you show me how to do it."

Impatient with Gretel's incompetence, the witch says, "It's lots of fun. Here's how it's done." She opens the oven door and looks in.

Swiftly Hansel and Gretel push her into the oven and slam the door behind her.

They've done it! Joyfully, Hansel and Gretel dance around singing, "The witch is dead. We're safe. We're free." Hansel rushes into the house and throws nuts, candies, and other wonderful sweets from the window into

Gretel's apron. The oven, which has been puffing, suddenly explodes, and the gingerbread men on the fence miraculously turn into little children. But they cannot move until Hansel waves the wand over them, breaking the spell. Freed from the witch's curse, they run about happily, thanking Hansel and Gretel for saving their lives.

In the distance the broommaker can be heard calling for his lost Hansel and Gretel. As he enters the clearing, he cries out, "Hurray! They are here!" Hansel and Gretel run into their parents' arms.

Meanwhile, some of the children sift through the remains of the oven and pull out a large gingerbread, baked in the shape of the witch. Everyone marvels at the sight. As the children dance around the tasty effigy, Hansel and Gretel's father points out the moral: "Heaven has spoken: evil will not last. And when we cannot bear our grief, the good Lord will send relief."

TANNHÄUSER

Opera in Three Acts
by
RICHARD WAGNER
Première: Hofoper, Dresden, October 19, 1845

ACT I

IN THIRTEENTH-CENTURY Thuringia, two mountains face each other across a lovely, green valley. One is Wartburg, where stands the castle of the Landgrave. The other is called the Venusberg, so named because according to legend, the pagan goddess has taken refuge in the underworld beneath it, and from there she preys upon the souls of men. The current object of her passion is Tannhäuser, a knight-minstrel of surpassing musical gifts, whom she has seduced and holds in thrall with the sensual arts and pleasures of which she is so great a mistress.

One day, Venus and Tannhäuser recline in the rosy light of her grotto, watching nymphs, satyrs, and sirens indulge in a wild Bacchanalia. Tannhäuser, perplexed, suddenly turns to Venus. "I had a dream in which I heard bells. It seems forever since I have heard such merry sounds, for here time has ceased to exist, the heavens and the earth are no longer a part of my life. Tell me, Venus, shall I ever experience these earthly things again?"

Venus is astounded at the possibility that he has wearied of the blissful life of a god. "You should be singing praises of this realm of love," she reproves him.

Tannhäuser expresses his gratitude to Venus and the wonderful existence he has known in her kingdom. "But," he adds, "I am still a mortal and I long for the natural beauties of our earth: the forests, the sky, the song of birds, and the merry sound of pealing bells. Queen and goddess, I must leave your land. You must allow me to depart!"

This request enrages Venus, and calling him a traitor, she refuses his request. Then sensing that anger is useless, she changes her tactic and glowingly enumerates the beauties and wonders of Venusberg. "Our union will be a celebration of love and you shall be an equal. My beloved knight, how can you leave me?"

Tannhäuser promises to sing her praises always, but declares he must return to earth.

"Then go, you fool!" she replies. "You will come back one day, begging to return. Having been here, you are cursed and can never gain salvation!"

Tannhäuser does not believe her. "I will find it in the Virgin Mary!"

Magically, the grotto dissolves and Tannhäuser finds himself in the beautiful valley between the mountains. Grass grows under his feet and overhead stretches wondrous blue sky. In the distance can be seen the castle of Wartburg. A shepherd sings a song about the lovely month of May, and a group of pilgrims stop to pray at a small shrine under the trees. "He who is faithful and atones for his sins shall be saved by penance!" The shepherd calls to them wishing them a safe journey to Rome and asking them to pray for his soul too. As the pilgrims disappear in the distance, Tannhäuser, moved by their faith in the Almighty and His mercy, drops to his knees in fervent prayer.

A hunting horn announces the approach of Landgrave Hermann of Thuringia and his retinue of knights. They come upon the praying Tannhäuser and are surprised to find their long absent compatriot. One of them, Wolfram, asks where he has been.

"I journeyed in faraway lands where there was no rest. I am here to make my peace and then travel onward, for I must never look back."

The others, led by the Landgrave, insist he must not go so soon and the good-hearted Wolfram adds, "For Elizabeth's sake."

Tannhäuser is visibly shaken by the mention of her name.

Wolfram continues: "Though you did not win our singing competition when you were here, one glorious prize you did win—your songs captivated the heart of that very special woman. When you left here, she no longer cared to listen to us. Now, good minstrel, you must return so that Elizabeth will once again take part in our festivals." His plea is echoed by the others, who suggest that any former disagreements be put aside.

Tannhäuser embraces his former companions. "Now I feel at home in this world I once left. Take me to Elizabeth."

The Landgrave and his men hail the miraculous return of their prodigal comrade and rejoice that their songs will once again be heard by the woman they revere. To the sounds of their horns, the knights leave for the castle of Wartburg.

ACT II

In the castle, Elizabeth enters the great hall of the minstrels, joyful with the news of Tannhäuser's return. Accompanied by Wolfram, he approaches her and kneels at her feet. At first she is embarrassed and shy, and turns away, but finally recovering her composure, she asks him where he has been.

Once again he replies vaguely that he was in far-off lands. "All I remember is how I longed to see you again. It was a miracle that has returned me to this place!"

Elizabeth thanks heaven for this miracle and confesses to the knight how much his songs had affected her—like none she had ever heard. "I felt things I had never felt, and yearned as I never had before. Then when you left, the peace and pleasures I had known were also gone. The songs the other minstrels sang were dull. With you went all my heart's happiness!"

Tannhäuser says, "If my verses touched your heart, it is the god of love who should be praised." Together they thank the Almighty God for uniting them, and restoring them to happiness.

To Wolfram this loving scene is torment, for it spells the end of his own hope to capture Elizabeth's heart. But noble knight that he is, he graciously accepts his fate.

As the two men leave to prepare for the contest, the Landgrave arrives and congratulates his niece on once more taking her rightful place at the song festival. "The nobles I have invited are responding in great numbers because they have heard that you will be reigning over this great singing contest."

In a magnificent procession the guests, lords, knights, ladies and their retinues are ushered into the great hall. They praise this noble hall of art and hail the prince of the land, the Landgrave Hermann. He and Elizabeth take their seats of honor as the minstrels enter and bow before them.

Graciously, the Landgrave welcomes guests and competitors to the competition, making special note of Tannhäuser's presence. "For this contest, the subject shall be the true nature of love, and the minstrel who sings of it best shall be granted whatever he may desire. Elizabeth shall preside. Now, bold singers, your reward has been named, so step forward and accept our thanks in advance."

The pages place the names of all the contestants into a golden vessel. Elizabeth draws the name of the first contestant and the pages call Wolfram von Eschenbach.

The minstrel steps forward and sings of the sight of a beautiful clear fountain and, by analogy, relates this to the glories of spiritual love. Appreciative murmurs of "Yes" and "How true" ripple through the audience. Only Tannhäuser takes exception. Springing to his feet with a sweep of his harpstrings, he turns the image around, noting that such a fountain is as inexhaustible as his yearnings are insatiable. His song ends, "Wolfram, I know, for I have seen what love truly is."

Walter von der Vogelweide steps forward to take his appointed turn. His song claims chastity, not lust, is the basis of the truest form of love. This song too garners praise from the nobles and derision from Tannhäuser. "To me," he counters, "true love means pleasure!"

This blunt statement shocks the audience, and one knight, Biterolf, jumps up to elaborate on how inspiring purity is. "For woman's virtue I would do battle."

"Then your life has been lacking in love," Tannhäuser retorts.

The knights call for him to be silenced. Some even draw swords, and the Landgrave must calm the hall.

Finally, it is Tannhäuser's turn. "I sing to the goddess of love from whom all miracles come. Only through passion can man know about love, and those who have never experienced this are truly wretched. They should go to Venusberg!"

The hall is scandalized. All the women leave save Elizabeth, who trembles at what she fears is about to happen. The Landgrave declares that this minstrel has experienced the pleasures of Hell in Venusberg and calls for the other knights to kill him. As they all rush to fall upon him, Elizabeth steps in front of Tannhäuser to protect him. In amazement, they ask how she, a spotless maiden, can defend the man who betrayed her. "Cast away your swords. If I, whom he has so sorely hurt, can pray for him, would you

deny this man the chance to earn salvation? Let him repent." The knights
are moved by her plea. Through Elizabeth's voice, his right to seek salvation seems to be heaven's wish.

"Tannhäuser," the Landgrave addresses him, "we have expelled you
from our ranks and you shall seek expiation of your sins. Repentant pilgrims travel in bands seeking atonement. They travel to the Holy City in
Rome and you must join them. In that city you must cleanse yourself of your
heinous guilt. If you do not atone, our swords can still kill you!"

Elizabeth vows to pray for him. "Accept my life as a sacrifice," she
offers.

Tannhäuser, wretched at what he has done to Elizabeth, throws himself
at her feet and swears to atone so that he may eventually be united with her.

In the valley, the pilgrims are setting off on their pilgrimage, and Tannhäuser hurries to join them on their journey to Rome.

ACT III

Summer has passed, and it is autumn in the Wartburg valley. Coming
down through the woods Wolfram finds Elizabeth deep in prayer at a lonely
shrine. It agonizes him to see her praying for another man, but he hopes she
will get her wish and that Tannhäuser will return with a papal pardon.

Suddenly, the silence of the forest is shattered by the approach of the
returning pilgrims chanting praise of the forgiving Lord. As they pass by
her, Elizabeth searches for Tannhäuser, her initial excitement turning to
hopelessness as she does not find him among them. When the last straggler
is gone, she is desolate. Kneeling once again, she renews her prayers to the
Virgin Mary. "Allow me to die here so I may enter the sacred kingdom as a
worthy handmaiden. Only, through your divine grace, please pray for Tannhäuser that he may be redeemed."

Wolfram is so deeply in love that he asks if he may accompany her; to
which she gently but firmly responds that she must go alone. As he watches
her walk slowly back to the castle, Wolfram prays to the evening star to
welcome Elizabeth warmly when she enters heaven as a holy angel.

Night falls, and as Wolfram continues to sit by the shrine, another ragged
pilgrim appears. It is Tannhäuser, looking so drawn and haggard that at
first Wolfram doesn't recognize him. When he does he is astounded that
Tannhäuser would return to Wartburg without a pardon from the Church.

"Fear not, Wolfram," Tannhäuser says wearily, "for I have not returned to your fold, but rather to find again the wonderful path to Venusberg!"

Wolfram is shocked by this blasphemous declaration and asks for an explanation.

Tannhäuser relates the tale of his exhausting pilgrimage to Rome. "Never before has anyone been so fervently penitent as I. I prayed for salvation so that Elizabeth would weep no more. I slept in the cold, sacrificed my blood, and journeyed through Italy blind to its beauty, all as penance. When in Rome I prayed throughout the night and as the sun rose the bells pealed and you could hear great cheers promising salvation for those assembled. Then God's messenger came before us and all the people knelt before him. He pardoned and blessed thousands, commanding each in turn to rise. Finally, I went before him and confessed my evil ways. I pleaded with him to release me from my bonds and free me from my pains. He answered, 'If you have partaken of the pleasures of Venusberg and been near the fires of Hell, you will be damned forever! Or condemned until such time as the staff in my hand sprouts fresh green leaves.' I was so crushed by this condemnation that I fainted and when I awoke all I heard were the other pilgrims singing songs of praise. This sickened me and has driven me back to the bosom I once enjoyed; I shall return to the depths and the enchantments of Lady Venus!"

"Stop," Wolfram cries; "you are a madman." Clouds begin to swirl about them and through the darkness a vision of dancing nymphs approaches. Wolfram is terrified by this "impending arrival of Hell" while Tannhäuser happily calls his mistress from the land of love.

Magically, Venus appears and bids him leave this world that has excommunicated him. "Come away. Be mine forever."

Tannhäuser moves to go with her, but Wolfram holds him back, pleading that salvation is still possible. "There was an angel here on earth who prayed for you. Now in heaven, Elizabeth watches over you. At God's throne she will be heard! You shall be saved!"

"Elizabeth!" Tannhäuser repeats the name, suddenly spellbound.

Venus' cause is lost and with her ghostly retinue, she disappears.

The day begins to dawn and from Wartburg Castle a funeral procession descends into the valley. Headed by the Landgrave, minstrels and nobles carry a coffin containing Elizabeth's body and chant, "The sainted maiden now stands beside the heavenly host." They set the bier down, and Tannhäuser, growing ever weaker, drags himself over and kneels beside it. The pallbearers continue: "Blessed shall be the sinner for whom she has prayed."

With his final breath Tannhäuser begs, "Saint Elizabeth, plead for me!" He collapses and dies.

Suddenly some young pilgrims arrive, bearing the staff of the Pope. It is green with newly sprouted leaves. "Hail this miracle of grace!" they cry. "The Lord has shown Himself, and sinners, though they come from Hell, may be saved. Hallelujah!"

Exalted by the miracle, the mourners pick up the coffin and proceed on their way, gladly acknowledging Tannhäuser's redemption. "He shall enter the sacred peace!"

SALOME

Opera in One Act
by
RICHARD STRAUSS
Première: Königliches Opernhaus, Dresden, December 9, 1905

"HOW BEAUTIFUL the Princess Salome looks tonight!" The words are those of a love-struck captain, Narraboth, in the army of Herod, Tetrarch of Judaea. The time is A.D. 30, when Christ wanders in Nazareth, stirring some of the populace to believe that he is the new Messiah.

On this beautiful moonlit night, Narraboth is gazing into the palace banquet hall from his post outside where he is in charge of the soldiers who guard the prisoner Jokanaan. A disciple of Christ, Jokanaan has been imprisoned by Herod because he publicly denounced the ruler for marrying his brother's divorced wife, Herodias. Jokanaan is being held in an old cistern that stands in the palace courtyard.

Herod, whose passions are matched only by his fears, now lusts after his wife's young daughter, Salome, and both women are attending the dinner party he is giving, a dinner at which he is attempting to conciliate the Jews who are his subjects and to please the Romans who are his protectors.

As Narraboth continues to watch Salome, commenting on her every move, his comrade, a page, warns him that his obsession is dangerous. But Narraboth cannot take his eyes away from her.

From the depths of the cistern rises the voice of Jokanaan, prophesying the coming of Christ, but the soldiers do not understand what he is talking about.

Meanwhile Salome, bored with the dinner conversation, comes out onto the terrace.

Once again Jokanaan cries, "The Son of God is coming."

Intrigued, Salome asks to see the prophet, but the soldiers tell her that Herod has issued strict orders: no one is to speak with him. Undeterred, she takes her request to Narraboth, who tries to refuse but is soon seduced into disobedience. He orders the soldiers to open the well.

Slowly coming up out of the cistern, Jokanaan inveighs against Herod: "Let him come forth that he may hear God's voice!"

"Of whom does he speak?" Salome asks.

"No one knows, Princess," Narraboth tells her.

Jokanaan continues, now denouncing Herodias. Despite the ferocity of his words and wildness of his appearance, Salome is fascinated and insists on taking a closer look at him. As she approaches, Jokanaan recoils. "Daughter of Sodom, don't come near me. Wear a veil, put ashes on your head, and go into the desert and seek out the Son of God!"

Narraboth beseeches her to go back inside.

Salome ignores him. She tells the prophet, "I love you. Let me touch you. Your body is so white. Your skin must be cool as snow."

"Hold your tongue, daughter of Babylon. I listen only to the voice of the Lord, my God!"

Salome now calls his body hideous, but asks to touch his hair. Again she is rebuked. Now his hair is horrible, but she asks to kiss his ruby red lips.

"Never, daughter of Sodom, never!" is his reply.

Salome is now obsessed, and keeps asking for a kiss. Unable to bear it, Narraboth stabs himself and falls dead at her feet. Neither Jokanaan nor Salome takes any note of this. Jokanaan importunes her to seek out the Lord, to bow at His feet, and to ask forgiveness.

Deaf to his words Salome only persists: "Let me kiss your mouth, Jokanaan."

"I will not look at you, Salome. You are accursed. Accursed!" he declares and descends into the cistern.

223

Herod, accompanied by his wife Herodias and the dinner guests, comes out onto the terrace seeking Salome.

"You look at her too much," Herodias complains. She wants to go back inside, but Herod refuses and orders the torches lit so that they may remain outside.

Suddenly he notices Narraboth's corpse. "Take it away," he orders, but he is frightened and feels as if a cold wind has blown up. Once again Herodias counsels that they go back inside, to no avail. Over her objections, Herod invites Salome to drink wine with him, to eat some fruit with him, and finally to sit beside him on her mother's throne. Salome curtly refuses each of his invitations, pleasing Herodias and angering Herod.

From the cistern comes the voice of Jokanaan, prophesying death to sinners. This infuriates Herodias, who urges that the prophet be turned over to the Jews. The Hebrew guests heartily agree with her, but Herod refuses on the grounds that the prophet has been said to have seen God. This provokes a heated intellectual argument among the Jews until it is once again interrupted as Jokanaan calls out, "The day is at hand. His feet are on the mountain. He who is the Savior of the world!" This sets off another argument, the Jews claiming that the Messiah has not yet come, and the Nazarenes insisting that the Messiah has indeed come and performed miracles everywhere, including raising people from the dead. This horrifies Herod, who, in fear of those he has killed, orders that this Messiah be found and prevented from raising any more of the dead.

Once again the voice of Jokanaan pierces the air. "God has cursed this daughter of Babylon! A crowd of men will stone her, and revile her, and crush her with their shields."

Convinced that the prophet speaks of her, Herodias demands that he be silenced.

Herod brushes her off: "I did not hear him mention your name." He turns to Salome and begs her to dance for him.

Herodias orders her not to dance, and at first Salome pleases her mother by refusing. But when Herod swears on his life to give her whatever she wants, she agrees to dance for him.

Herod is again seized by an "icy wind" and declares that he hears in the wind the beating of the wings of a huge black bird hovering over the terrace. Just as suddenly, he becomes very hot and rips the regal wreath from his head. "Now I can breathe again. Dance for me, Salome!"

As Jokanaan cries out again, Herodias begs Herod to go inside. "I will not have my daughter dance while that man cries aloud from the cistern!"

But her wishes are ignored and Salome announces she is ready. As she dances, Salome seductively lures and teases Herod. One by one she removes her seven veils, each time with increasing excitement. Swaying back and forth, undulating, she stops near the cistern, then renews her dance at a feverish pitch, ending erotically and throwing herself on the ground.

"Wonderful! Ah, wonderful!" Herod exclaims. "She has danced for me! Now, Salome, I will give you whatever you desire!"

Slowly and with utmost deliberation, she says, "I want a silver platter."

Herod is amused at the modesty of her request. "And what do you wish upon it?"

Salome rises, laughing. "The head of the prophet Jokanaan!"

Herod's terror is matched only by Herodias's delight in her daughter's wish. Herod tries desperately to bribe Salome with anything else, with valuables, and finally with half his kingdom. But no matter what is offered Salome responds, "I want the head of Jokanaan!"

Herodias reminds Herod that he swore an oath before all these witnesses, but Herod continues to try to dissuade Salome. He reminds her, "Jokanaan is a man who has 'touched God.' If he is killed, who can imagine what disasters may befall?"

"Give me the head of Jokanaan!" is Salome's grizzly response.

Herod sinks into his chair defeated. "Give her what she asks." Herodias removes the ring of death from her husband's nerveless hand and gives it to a soldier who turns it over to the executioner. The executioner descends into the cistern. Seeing his ring gone, Herod cries out, "Some great misfortune will surely befall us!"

Salome waits impatiently near the mouth of the cistern wondering aloud why there is no sound, no cry from the doomed prophet. Almost frantic with anticipation, she imagines that the executioner has failed in his mission and orders the page and the soldiers to descend into the cistern to complete the ghastly job. Just then the arm of the executioner extends from the cistern holding aloft a silver tray bearing the bloody head of Jokanaan. As Salome grabs the tray Herod is sickened, and the Nazarenes kneel to pray.

Savoring her triumph, Salome croons over the head of Jokanaan. "How much wiser it would have been to have let me kiss you. Your eyes, so full of rage, are closed now. Your red viper of a tongue stirs no more. Nothing was as white as your body! Nothing as black as your hair, or as red as your lips. Why didn't you look at me, Jokanaan? Then you would have loved me!"

Herod can stand no more and decides to go inside. As his slaves put out the torches, the stars disappear and a great cloud covers the moon. In the darkness, Herod is about to leave but stops as he hears Salome murmur, "Jokanaan, I have kissed your lips! The taste was bitter. Was it the bitterness of blood or love?"

A ray of moonlight breaks through the clouds, illuminating the young woman as she lies on the ground with Jokanaan's lips pressed against her own.

Herod, terrified and completely revolted, orders, "Kill that woman!"

With lightning speed the soldiers rush forward and crush the ecstatic Salome beneath their shields.

PELLÉAS AND MÉLISANDE

Opera in Five Acts
by
CLAUDE DEBUSSY
Première: Opéra-Comique, Paris, April 30, 1902

ACT I

SCENE 1

IN AN imaginary medieval kingdom called Allemonde, Prince Golaud, grandson of old King Arkel, and heir to the throne, is hunting in the forest and has traveled many miles from the castle in his chase of a wild boar. He is lost, and wanders through the deepening gloom, searching for a path that will take him home. A forest brook leads him to a wellspring, and there, as in a visionary image, sits a beautiful young woman. She is hardly more than a girl, with long blond hair, and she is weeping. When he asks her why, she shrinks away from him, crying, "No, no, don't touch me."

Gently, he questions her but she will tell him no more than that she was born far away and has fled her home due to some dire and obscure danger, and now she is lost. The mystery only deepens when noticing a crown shining at the bottom of the stream, Golaud offers to retrieve it, but she threatens to throw herself into the water if he does.

He reassures her that he will let it be, and introduces himself.

She notices that his hair is beginning to go gray, and that he is very tall, and she murmurs that she is getting cold.

"What is your name?" he asks.

"Mélisande," she says, but will tell him no more, not even how old she is.

Growing even more tender and concerned, Golaud tells her she must not stay alone, and urges her to come with him. When she asks where he is going he answers, "I don't know. I, too, am lost." Timidly, and at a distance, she follows him into the forest.

SCENE 2

The stone walls of the castle of Allemonde enclose the melancholy air of a house that has been visited much by illness, death, and old age. Golaud's father has been dead for many years, and his first wife has died, leaving him with a young son, Yniold. Now the man to whom his mother, Geneviève, is married lies seriously ill. The castle is cold and the windows, tightly shut against the winter, are covered with hangings that dim the light within and mute the few sounds of youth that issue from the child Yniold, and from Pelléas, Golaud's much younger half-brother.

Six months have passed since Golaud met Mélisande, and he has written a letter to Pelléas describing how he met and married her, which Geneviève now reads to Arkel. Golaud still knows nothing about his new wife's past, and why she still weeps, but he would like to bring her home and asks Pelléas to intercede for him. "I know my mother will understand, but I am afraid grandfather will be angry, since he wished me to marry Princess Ursula and end the war between our countries. If all is well," Golaud instructs, "then three days after you receive this letter light a lamp on the castle turret. I will see it from my ship. If it is not there, then I shall sail away and never return."

The kind old king does not wish to tamper with what appears to have been the hand of fate. "Golaud has been unhappy since his wife died. Let him have his wishes!"

Pelléas enters, tears in his eyes, and reveals that he has also had a letter from his friend Marcellus. "He is dying and asks that I come to see him." Arkel says he must wait for his brother to return and harshly reminds Pelléas that his own father is ill, possibly dying in a chamber above. "Can you make the choice between your friend and your father? It would be well to wait a while." Pelléas maintains a tearful silence, as Geneviève reminds him to light the lamp in the castle turret.

SCENE 3

Mélisande and Geneviève walk in the garden below the castle. The forest presses in upon them, its heavy foliage closing out the light. Only the prospect toward the sea is open, and there a cold white light pierces the fog while waves crash strongly against the rocky shore below.

Mélisande says the everpresent darkness depresses her and Geneviève tries to comfort her by saying that one grows accustomed. Ascending the steep path from the sea, Pelléas joins them, somewhat reluctantly, it seems. They talk of the storm that is brewing, hear the distant chants of sailors, and watch a ship moving slowly out to sea. Mélisande sadly notes it is the boat that brought her, leaving now.

As night begins to fall, Geneviève declares that it is time for all to go inside and that she must fetch Golaud's son Yniold. "Pelléas, you take Mélisande back to the castle."

As he takes Mélisande by the arm to lead her up the steep, dark path, Pelléas offhandedly says, "I'll probably be leaving tomorrow."

Mélisande is clearly upset. Childlike, she cries, "Oh, why must you go?"

ACT II

SCENE 1

To escape the noon heat of summer, Pelléas and Mélisande have wandered through the woods to a remote glade in which sits an old and abandoned fountain. "It is called the 'fountain of the blind,'" Pelléas explains, "because it is said to heal the sightless. But it has not helped Arkel, who is almost blind, so no one comes here any more."

Mélisande marvels at the water's bottomless depth and clarity and leans far down trying to put her hands into it, but only her long hair can reach it.

"Was it not by a fountain that you met Golaud?" Pelléas asks.

"Yes," she says shortly, and as she answers his questions about that meeting without warmth or interest, she takes off the ring given her by Golaud, and tosses it into the air, heedless of Pelléas's warnings. Suddenly, the ring falls and they watch helplessly as it sinks deeper and deeper into the clear water. Pelléas tells her they will try to retrieve it another day, but now they must return to the castle for it is getting late. "I heard the clock strike twelve just as your ring fell into the water."

"What do I tell Golaud if he asks for the ring?" Mélisande asks.

"The truth!" Pelléas replies.

Scene 2

The castle is in turmoil when they return; Golaud has been hurt while hunting. As Mélisande sits by his bedside, he describes the accident to her. "Just as the clock struck twelve, my horse bolted right into a tree and fell on top of me. I felt as if my heart was broken, but I am all right." Mélisande offers to spend the night watching him while he sleeps, but he says it is not necessary. Suddenly, she starts to weep and confesses that she does not like living at the castle. Golaud tries to console her and to find out who or what is disturbing her. Is it perhaps his mother? Arkel?

"No. No," she responds.

"Pelléas?"

"Oh he rarely speaks to me, but that is not it. It's that . . . that . . . one never sees blue sky here. The forests make it so gloomy."

He finds her distress childish and tells her that now that summer has come there will be sun everyday. Tenderly taking her hand in his own, he suddenly notices that her ring is gone. His alarm is instant and he questions her closely.

"It must have fallen off when I was picking shells for Yniold near the cave by the sea," she lies.

"Go get it right now," he orders.

"But it is dark," she pleads.

He tells her to get Pelléas to go with her. "You must get that ring. I must have it. Wake Pelléas and take him with you. Get the ring before the sea takes it away!"

Weeping, Mélisande leaves, once again overwhelmed by her unhappiness.

Scene 3

The moon is obscured by clouds, and in the dense darkness not even the white foam on the crashing waves can be seen, as Pelléas and Mélisande grope toward the entrance to the cave. They know full well that the ring is not there, but Pelléas advises her to study the cave well, so that should Golaud question her about their search, she will be able to describe it.

The clouds move and the moonlight illuminates the entrance to the cave. Inside, Mélisande gasps at the sight of three old men sleeping huddled on the ground. Pelléas tells her that there is a great famine in the land and these are the poor.

"Let's leave!" she says. She is petrified.

He tells her to speak more softly so as not to wake the men. But she will not stay, and acquiescing, Pelléas leaves with her.

ACT III

Scene 1

In one of the castle's towers, Mélisande sits by the window, combing her long silken hair and singing a song. Pelléas, walking on the path below, hears her.

"Oh, Mélisande," he calls, "let your beautiful hair fall from the window so I may see it."

As she leans out the window, he asks to touch her hand because he is leaving the next day.

She is petulant and will not give him her hand unless he promises to stay.

"All right then, I shall wait," he agrees.

She leans out as far as she can and her long magnificent hair streams down, enveloping Pelléas. He wraps himself in her tresses, half playfully, half ecstatically vowing never to release her.

Laughing with childlike delight, she cries, "Let me go. I shall fall."

"No, no. You are my prisoner," he teases.

"Pelléas, someone may come."

He burrows even further into her hair until she warns, "Someone is coming; I think it's Golaud!"

He lets go but her hair has become entwined in the branches. As Pelléas tries to free her, Golaud appears.

Gruffly he calls them a pair of children and tells them to stop playing. "It's late. You mustn't lean out the window!" he scolds Mélisande, and then continues along the path, taking Pelléas with him.

Scene 2

Bringing Pelléas into the caverns beneath the castle, Golaud leads him to a stagnant pool, and says, "It smells of death, don't you think? There, lean over the rocks near the edge of the pool so you can get the full impact of the odor. But hold my arm, Pelléas, so you don't slip in."

The air is stifling and Pelléas is frightened by the ominous flicker of the lantern as Golaud's hand trembles. "Let us leave," he begs.

Golaud relents, and silently they creep out.

SCENE 3

Outside the caverns, Pelléas gratefully rejoices in the fresh air. "How sweet is the breeze and the smell of newly watered shrubs. Look, Mélisande and our mother are at a window in the tower."

Apropos Mélisande, Golaud warns Pelléas to stop playing such childish games with her as they had the night before. "She is very delicate and now she is with child. The slightest shock could have ill effects." He hesitates, then continues: "I have seen you together, and it looks as if there could be something between you. Need I say more? You are older than she. Stay away from her—as much as possible."

SCENE 4

Outside the castle Golaud sits with his little son Yniold on his knee. "We don't see each other much any more, my son," Golaud says. "You're always with Mélisande. Tell me, is Pelléas with her often?"

"Always," Yniold answers.

"And do they quarrel?"

Yniold has trouble answering, and as his father grows impatient, he senses his anger and begins to cry. "You hurt my arm."

To calm him, Golaud promises a gift of bow and arrows, and returns to questioning him. Yniold reveals no more than that Pelléas and Mélisande have talked about Yniold and how he resembles his father. "They sit in the dark a lot, and cry, and once they kissed."

Suddenly, a light appears in the tower window and Golaud lifts his son up to his shoulders and orders him to tell what he sees.

"Mélisande is there with Uncle Pelléas," the boy reports. "They're not speaking, just staring at the light."

"Is that all?" In his irritation with his son's childlike replies, Golaud squeezes him again and Yniold is frightened and asks to be put down. Golaud insists that he continue to look and tell him what is happening, until he pushes the boy to the verge of hysteria. Still frustrated, Golaud finally gives in and puts him down. "Let's go," he barks at his terrified son.

ACT IV

Scene 1

Pelléas's ailing father is now recovering. Regarding Pelléas with a strange clairvoyant eye, his father has told him that he has the expression of a man who hasn't long to live. To save himself, he must go away. Reporting this to Mélisande, Pelléas extracts a promise from her to meet him that evening at the fountain of the blind, and he hurries away just as King Arkel comes into the room.

The kindly king assures Mélisande that with the recovery of Pelléas's father some happiness will return to this mournful castle. "It has been so sad for you—so young and beautiful and with the freshness of life—to live under the shadow of death."

Suddenly, Golaud comes in, his forehead bloodied, he says, by a thorn bush. Mélisande offers to wipe it.

His response is unnaturally violent. "Don't touch me, do you hear? Go away. Where is my sword?" He turns to Arkel. "A peasant was found dead of starvation on the shore. You'd think they are all trying to die under our eyes!" Again he demands his sword. Mélisande trembles as she gives it to him. "What are you afraid of?" he snarls. "What is in your eyes?"

Arkel tells Golaud that there is nothing but innocence in her eyes. "Innocence!" Golaud begins to rant wildly, berating Mélisande because he cannot fathom the thoughts that lie behind her eyes. But rather than appeasing him, his sarcasm and anger only work him up into an uncontrollable rage. He tells her to go away, then grabs her hands, pushes her away, and once more seizes her, this time by her long hair, and violently jerks her back and forth, telling her that she will follow him on her knees. "Your hair is good for something," he shouts as he yanks her to and fro. Crazed, he laughs hysterically and says, "You see I laugh like an old fool." A cry from Arkel stops Golaud. He lets go of Mélisande and with forced calm mutters irrationally, "You can do what you choose. I'm too old and I'm not a spy. I'll leave it to chance, simply because it is the custom!" He walks out.

A stunned Arkel asks Mélisande, "Is he drunk?"

"Oh no, he just doesn't love me any longer," she answers. "How unhappy I am!"

"If I were God," declares the old king, "I would take pity on the hearts of men."

SCENE 2

In the moonlight Pelléas waits at the fountain for Mélisande, filled with conflicting emotions. He knows that it would be better to leave right away, but he cannot bear to do so without seeing her once again. He promises himself that he will look at her carefully so that he will not forget anything.

Mélisande arrives, breathless. She is late because she was waiting for Golaud to fall asleep, and then in her hurry, she ripped her dress. She has run all the way.

Pelléas pulls her out of the moonlight. "This is probably the last time I shall see you," he begins. "I must go away tomorrow."

"Why must you?"

"Surely you know."

She insists she does not understand.

"You really don't know that it is because . . . ." He kisses her suddenly. "I love you."

Mélisande whispers, "I love you too."

Overwhelmed by what they have been hiding from themselves and each other all these months, they pour out their feelings now, until they hear the clang of the gates as the castle is locked and bolted for the night.

"We won't be able to get back into the castle tonight!" Pelléas warns.

"Good," says Mélisande.

With total abandon, they throw their arms around each other.

Suddenly Mélisande hears a noise. "It is Golaud!" she whispers. "He saw us kiss and he has his sword!"

Helpless and terror-stricken, they cling to each other. Golaud rushes toward them and strikes at Pelléas, who falls dead. For an instant Mélisande seems to wait for death, but lacking the courage, she runs off into the dark forest.

ACT V

Mélisande has given birth to a daughter, and she now lies close to death. Arkel, the Doctor, and Golaud hover over her bed. Golaud is filled with remorse and although the Doctor assures him that the trifling wound he gave her could not possibly have caused her illness, he is inconsolable and he laments that he killed without reason. "They only embraced like children!" he cries. "I did not mean to kill them."

Mélisande wakes and asks the kind Arkel to open the window. It is evident from her words that she is confused and does not recall what has occurred. Cautiously, Arkel tells her that Golaud is in the room. She is not at all upset, only surprised that her husband isn't beside her. Hearing this, Golaud asks the Doctor and Arkel to leave them for a while. When they are alone, Golaud begs Mélisande to forgive him.

She says, "But what is there to forgive?"

Golaud tells her how sorry he is for all the wrong he has done her, but he cannot restrain himself from asking the question which still tortures him. "Tell me the truth. Did you love Pelléas?"

"Of course I love Pelléas. Where is he?"

Her innocence and simplicity unnerve Golaud. "Mélisande, please tell me, did you love him with a guilty love?"

"No, no. Why do you ask?"

"You must not lie at the moment of death."

"Am I going to die?" she asks. "I didn't know!"

Golaud can bear it no longer and shouts, "Mélisande! Where are you?"

His raised voice agitates Mélisande and brings Arkel and the Doctor back into the room. "It's useless," mutters Golaud. "I shall never know."

To calm Mélisande, Arkel asks, "Do you wish to see your little daughter?"

Too weak to hold her child, Mélisande gazes at the infant in Arkel's arms, and says, "She doesn't laugh, and she is so small. She too will weep."

The serving women of the castle suddenly file into the room and stand along the wall, waiting silently. They do not answer when Golaud frantically demands to know why they have come.

"Don't shout. She's going to sleep. She has closed her eyes!" Arkel counsels. Without a word Mélisande lifts her arms as if reaching out for someone. Desperately sobbing, Golaud tries to tell her again that he did not mean to do what he did, while the women, as one, fall to their knees and the Doctor solemnly nods his head. Mélisande is dead.

Arkel is stunned at how quickly and quietly it has happened. "Don't stay here, Golaud," Arkel pleads. "She was a sad, small, mysterious girl. Lonely, as we all are. Come, we must take the child out of this room so that she may thrive in her mother's place. Poor wee thing, it's her turn now."

SAMSON AND DELILAH

Opera in Three Acts
by
CAMILLE SAINT-SAENS
Première: Hoftheater, Weimar, December 2, 1877

ACT I

IT IS the year 1156 B.C. in Palestine. The Philistines have subjugated the Israelites, enslaving many of them. In the city of Gaza, a group of Hebrew slaves congregate at early dawn in the square outside a temple to the Philistine god, Dagon. They lament their bondage and call upon their own God, Jehovah, to free them. "Aren't you the God of deliverance who brought our tribes from Egypt? Have you forgotten the sacred promises you made to our forefathers?" They grow angry. "Are you no longer with us? Must we plead in vain?"

As their wailing rises in intensity, a young man steps forth and calls to his brethren to bless the name of their God. "The Lord speaks through me, and promises us freedom, but it is we who must first break our bonds. Once again we must establish the altar of the God of Israel." At first, the slaves are unwilling to listen to this arrogant youth, and continue to berate their Lord. Undaunted the young man calls them fools, reminding them that their God is the "God of battle," who will arm them with invincible swords! The young Hebrew, known as Samson, is so passionate in his plea that the slaves are swayed, and they chant loudly, "He is God's messenger. Let us rise up and Jehovah will deliver us!"

Drawn by their shouts, Abimelech, the Satrap of Gaza, comes out of the temple, attended by several Philistine guards. He is angered by the slaves' insolence, and ridicules them for calling on a God so deaf to their pleas. Samson is not intimidated. Facing Abimelech, he calls on the Lord to strike the blasphemer down, and his certainty that God will defend the faithful inspires the slaves to urge each other on. Their cries of defiance grow louder. Ever more incensed, Abimelech draws his sword and attacks Samson, but the Hebrew easily disarms him and strangles the Satrap with his mighty hands. Overwhelmed by the towering figure of Samson holding their dead leader's sword, and by the menacing murmur of the slaves, the Philistine guards retreat in confusion. The Hebrews, buoyed by victory, leave the square, bent upon revolt.

The doors of the great Temple of Dagon swing open, and the High Priest, followed by servants and guards, strides down the steps to stop beside Abimelech's lifeless body. He is outraged, and orders the soldiers to avenge the murder, but they tell him they are powerless before the Hebrews. The High Priest calls them cowards. A messenger rushes in bearing the news that in their continuing rebellion the Hebrew mob, led by Samson, has destroyed the harvest. The terrified Philistines now advocate flight. As they leave, taking Abimelech's body with them, the High Priest curses the God of Israel and vows to crush the rebellion along with its leader.

The sun is now fully risen. A group of old Hebrew men and women assemble in the square to praise God. They are joined by the victorious warriors and their hero, Samson. It is his hour of triumph.

Once again the temple doors open, and some Philistine maidens, bearing garlands, emerge. Leading them is the beautiful Delilah. She congratulates Samson on his triumph, and seductively tells him how passionately she desires him and reminds him of the pleasure he has found before in her arms. Aided by the counsel of an old Hebrew, who warns him that she is dangerous, Samson manages to hold himself aloof. But obviously, it grows more difficult as he is increasingly attracted to the honeyed promises of the seductress. She joins the other maidens in a sinuous dance during which Samson tries unsuccessfully to avoid looking at her. But he is mesmerized by her every move. Their dance ended, the maidens return to the temple. Delilah lingers, murmuring her enticements and ardently bidding him to visit her. Samson watches her longingly as she slowly withdraws up the steps and disappears within the temple doors.

ACT II

In the valley of Sorek, Delilah sits outside her house one evening waiting for Samson and planning how she will avenge her people and satisfy her gods, once she has enslaved him with erotic delights.

Lightning from a distant storm flickers over the mountains. Delilah's musings are interrupted by the High Priest, who has come to seek her help. "Our soldiers are mortally afraid of Samson," he tells her. "You are the only one who has been able to subdue him. At your knees he seemed powerless. You must help us defeat Samson, and you can name your price."

"I am not interested in gold. If I truly loved him, no riches could make me betray him. I have only pretended to enjoy him, but I hate him as much as you do." Delilah then admits that despite Samson's passion for her, he has not revealed the source of his mighty strength. "But I expect him again tonight," she continues, "and this time I have prepared my weapons: Samson cannot resist my tears."

The High Priest blesses her; united in their lust for Samson's destruction, they plot to capture him later that night.

Alone, Delilah waits in the darkening night for Samson to come. When he doesn't arrive she begins to wonder if perhaps his heart is impervious to love. She peers anxiously into the night, but sees nothing.

The distant lightning continues to illuminate the sky. A reluctant Samson slowly approaches Delilah's house, all the while telling himself to flee. Before he can tear himself away, Delilah runs to him and bombards him with professions of her love. Desperately Samson tries to reject her passionate advances. He explains that because the Lord has chosen him to lead the Israelites, he must say farewell.

Delilah, in tears, counters with, "A god greater than yours speaks to you through me. It is the god of love."

Samson weakens. "I surrender. The Lord may strike me down, but I love you, Delilah."

She has won. As they exchange vows of love, the lightning draws closer. A clap of thunder interrupts their embrace, and Delilah pushes him away asking, "How can I trust you? I am jealous of your God, and the compact that binds you to him. What is the secret of your great power?"

He will not reveal it. Growing angrier every moment, she claims that if he cannot trust her, he does not love her. Samson is racked by her persistence, but remains adamant. In frustration, Delilah screams, "Coward! I despise you! Goodbye!" and runs into her house.

The full force of the storm has hit. With the heavens fiercely raging around him, Samson stumbles about and raises his arms imploringly to the sky, seeking God's help. Receiving no answer, he runs into the house and to Delilah's arms, his love for her now stronger than his vow to God.

When, in the throes of love, Samson reveals to her the source of his great strength—his long hair—Delilah cuts it off and calls for the Philistine soldiers, who rush from their hiding places and capture the now helpless man.

ACT III

Shorn of his hair and his power, Samson has been blinded by the Philistines and incarcerated in the prison of Gaza. Chained to a heavy millstone, he pushes it around and around, like a beast of burden. He is a shattered man, and begs God to relieve him of his misery. "My path parted from yours, my God. Take my poor broken soul," he pleads.

Adding salt to his wounds, the other prisoners reproach him for having destroyed their revolt. Repeatedly they ask, "How could you betray us for a woman?"

The accusations make Samson even more wretched and he cries in anguish, "Brothers, your lamentations fill me with guilt. May God take my life to assuage your anger." But the accusations do not cease, nor do Samson's labors at the millstone.

Suddenly Philistine soldiers enter, unchain Samson, and drag him off.

In the Temple of Dagon the Philistines are gathered praising the oncoming dawn. To celebrate their victory they are holding a bacchanal. In every corner, people are carousing—drinking, eating, dancing, making love. The High Priest and Delilah survey the scene, and Delilah proudly accepts the toasts of the crowd.

Led by a child, Samson is brought into the temple. As the High Priest mocks him, the fallen Hebrew leader begs God to let him die.

Goblet in hand, Delilah approaches Samson and gloats, "Remember my caresses and how much you wanted me. But for me love was only a weapon and I stole your secret to avenge my gods and my people!"

The High Priest taunts Samson again, telling him to pray to Jehovah to restore his sight. "I too will serve your God if he answers your prayers."

Thus tormented, Samon calls on God to restore his sight so that the miracle may silence the pagan priest's tongue. But the derogatory laughter of the Philistines is the only response.

Delilah and the High Priest, taking their cups of wine, make a libation over the fire which burns on the altar. While the Philistines file by, joyously singing to celebrate the sacred rite in praise of the victorious Dagon, Samson, head bowed, stands with the child, silently praying. As the ceremony reaches its climax, the High Priest orders the child to lead Samson to a place between the two great pillars so that he too may offer praise to the mighty Dagon.

"Glory to Dagon," cry the Philistines. But their shouts are suddenly silenced by the rising thunder of Samson's voice as he implores the Lord to remember his servant and to restore his strength.

His prayer is answered. Samson rocks the pillars. As the Philistines scream helplessly, the mighty walls crumble and the Temple of Dagon collapses, killing all within.

LOHENGRIN

Opera in Three Acts
by
RICHARD WAGNER
Première: Hoftheater, Weimar, August 28, 1850

ACT I

KING HENRY the Fowler, sovereign of the German States in the tenth century, has come to Antwerp to ask the nobles of Brabant for their help in fighting off an invasion by his Hungarian neighbors to the east. But he has found much dissension in the duchy.

Assembled outside the walled city, on a plain near the Scheldt River, the Brabantians listen, together with the Saxon and Thuringian forces that Henry has brought with him, as Henry outlines Germany's problem and asks why there is turmoil in Brabant.

Count Frederick of Telramund, an old friend of the King whose life he once saved in battle against the Danes, steps forth to explain. Before the old Duke of Brabant died, he assigned Frederick to act as guardian to his children, Elsa and Gottfried. One day the children went for a walk in the woods, from which only Elsa returned. She could not explain her brother's disappearance, and Frederick was convinced that she killed him. He tells the King, "Her father gave me permission to marry Elsa, but horrified, I renounced my betrothal to her and took Ortrud, Princess of Friesland, as

241

my bride. Good King Henry, I accuse Elsa of fratricide, and claim this land as my own. Will you judge the case?"

King Henry, shocked by the gravity of the charge, asks the Count what motive there might be for such a heinous crime. Frederick offers the theory that Elsa, in love with another man, hoped that with her brother out of the way she would take command of the land, and be free to marry her secret lover.

Henry orders that Elsa be brought in to face judgment, and hangs his shield on the great oak tree before which he sits, signaling he will hold court. All the men draw their swords and declare that no sword shall be returned to its scabbard until justice is done.

Elsa arrives, followed by her ladies-in-waiting. She has a withdrawn air about her, as if lost in some other world, but she nods thrice, acknowledging she is indeed Elsa of Brabant, that she accepts King Henry as her judge, and that she knows the charges brought against her. But when the King asks for her defense, she cannot answer.

"Are you guilty, then?"

Her only response is, "My poor brother!"

The assembly buzzes with comments on her bizarre behavior and King Henry gently urges her to tell her story.

"One day, in my anguish I was praying to God. I sighed, and the sound seemed to echo into the heavens. My eyes grew heavy and I fell asleep." The King reminds her that she is here to defend herself against a murder charge, but she continues her tale. "While I slept I dreamt of a knight in shining armor. He approached me, a golden horn at his side. I knew he came from the heavens, and I felt greatly consoled. This knight shall defend me!"

Something in her tale casts doubt about her guilt in King Henry's mind and he calls on Frederick to prove his charges. The Count says, "You heard her speak of a lover. My charge is true." He offers to defend it with his sword.

The King has no choice. Thrusting his sword into the ground, he declares, "Frederick, Count of Telramund, you shall defend your accusation in mortal combat, before God. Elsa of Brabant, whom do you choose as your champion to defend you against the Count?"

Without hesitation she answers, "The knight who appeared to me in my dream shall defend me, and as reward he shall wear the crown of my land, and I shall be his wife!"

The King orders the heralds to summon her champion. The trumpeters stand at the outer edge of the judgment circle, facing the four points of the compass, but two fanfares fail to call forth Elsa's knight. Elsa drops to her knees to pray. Suddenly, a strange and wondrous sight appears upon the river—a beautiful swan draws a small boat, upon which stands a knight, dazzling in his beauty and his bright armor.

Jumping onto the shore, the knight thanks his faithful swan, bids it farewell, and bows to the King. "I have been sent here to defend Elsa of Brabant, if she will accept me."

Kneeling before him she readily agrees to his brave offer.

"Then I shall be your husband and guard your land. But you must promise never to ask where I have come from, what my name is, or who my ancestors were."

Her belief in him is total and she promises that she will never ask.

The knight announces to the astonished crowd that Elsa is innocent of the charges brought against her and that she shall be vindicated by God's judgment.

The nobles urge Frederick to withdraw the charges but sure of his own cause, he refuses, accepting instead the call to arms. At the behest of the King six of the nobles mark out the field of combat.

The two warriors declare their faith in God, all the nobles pray that God will give the righteous man the strength to win, and King Henry strikes his shield with his sword signaling the duel to start. The combatants step inside the circle, surrounded by the awed crowd.

The mysterious knight attacks quickly, and soon he knocks Frederick to the ground. His sword to the fallen man's throat, he declares, "Although victory is mine, I will spare your life so you may dedicate it to penitence!"

As Elsa rushes to him, the soldiers sheathe their swords, the King takes his shield down from the oak, and everyone cries "Hail" to the hero.

The crowd joyfully carries Elsa and the mysterious knight away.

Crushed and shamed, Frederick drags himself to Ortrud and collapses at her feet. Undaunted, Ortrud vows to oppose this man who has destroyed her power.

ACT II

It is night in Antwerp and the fortress is brilliantly lit as the knights and nobles feast in celebration of the marriage which is to take place upon the morrow.

Outside, dressed in poor peasant clothes, Frederick and Ortrud sit watching, still lingering at the scene of their disgrace, though they have been ordered to leave by morning. She is consumed by a desire for revenge; he laments the loss of his rank and honor. He now distrusts his wife and accuses her of having tricked him. "Why did you give me the information that made me accuse Elsa? You lied, promising me I would rule Brabant if I refused Elsa's hand and married you instead! You lied, and God has punished us."

She scoffs at his accusations. "You were not defeated by God, but by your opponent's magic. The way to break his magic strength is to force him to reveal his name. But the only one who can do that is she whom he made vow never to ask. Thus we must trick Elsa into asking the forbidden question. The only other way to conquer his magic power is to make him bleed!"

Frederick is eager to accept, but he is still somewhat mistrustful. "Beware, wife, if you are deceiving me."

"Stay calm," Ortrud snaps back contemptuously, "and I will teach you the joy of vengeance."

Suddenly Elsa appears on a balcony of the palace; thinking she is unobserved, Elsa thanks the gentle breezes for bringing her knight and champion. Quietly Ortrud orders Frederick to hide. "You take care of the knight. I will deal with Elsa!"

"Elsa!" Ortrud calls out.

Startled, Elsa asks what she is doing there.

Humbly, Ortrud complains of her unhappy, undeserved fate, and the remorse that racks her poor, defeated husband. She cleverly contrasts her wretched fate with Elsa's present happiness. This so touches the gentle Elsa that she pardons Ortrud and hurries down to bring her into the palace.

While she waits Ortrud calls on her evil gods. "Bless my treacherous task so I may take revenge!" As Elsa comes out, she throws herself at her feet.

Elsa is stunned by Ortrud's shabby appearance. She tells her to rise, and promises, "I will ask my future husband to forgive your Frederick, too. Dress in splendid garments, for tomorrow you will come with me to my wedding."

Ortrud thanks her profusely, offering Elsa the only thing of value she has left. "Allow me to look into the future, to ensure that no evil lurks before you. Are you certain that the magic that brought your splendid knight to you will not one day carry him away?"

Elsa is confident of her groom's fidelity. "Come in, poor woman, and let me teach you the joy of total trust."

As they enter, Ortrud thinks to herself, "I will make her pride her downfall."

Day breaks and trumpet fanfares sound from the palace. Frederick finds a hiding place near the door of the cathedral, and people begin to gather. The King's herald proclaims the King's command—that Frederick of Telramund is banished and that the stranger sent by God to defend Elsa shall rule as Guardian of Brabant. Today they are invited to help celebrate the wedding. But on the morrow, they must follow their new ruler as he leads them to glory in the King's service. The people hail the new Guardian of Brabant, and most of the men eagerly agree to honor his call to battle.

Four of the nobles, however, grumble against being forced into what they see as a foreign war. "But who can stop him?" one asks.

"I will!" The nobles are shocked to see the banished Frederick emerge from the shadows of a buttress. Boldly, he announces that he himself will accuse the mysterious knight of sorcery. The nobles think he is mad, and as four pages approach to clear a path for Lady Elsa, they quickly push Frederick back into hiding.

The crowd cheers repeatedly as a magnificently dressed Elsa and her ladies-in-waiting make their way from the palace to the cathedral. Just as Elsa is about to enter the church, Ortrud rushes up from the end of the retinue and stands in her way. "I will no longer crawl at your feet. I will take back what is rightly mine! Before my husband was falsely judged and banished, his name was highly honored in this land. But does anyone know even the name of the knight who has supplanted him? Do you know his past, or from whence he came, or even when he may leave? Of course not, for he forbade anyone to ask these questions!" The crowd mutters of blasphemy and Elsa quickly defends her knight's nobility, calling the charges slanderous. But Ortrud continues her assault, challenging Elsa to ask him to reveal the magic lying at the root of his power. "If you do not ask it must be you are afraid that his purity will be disproved!"

Elsa is speechless.

A cheer from the people heralds the approach of the King, the knight, and their retinue of nobles.

"What is the trouble here?" asks the King.

Elsa calls on her knight to protect her from Ortrud. "She accuses me of trusting you!"

Comforting his weeping bride, the knight orders the evil woman to leave.

Suddenly, Frederick steps forward and demands to be heard. "You have all been deceived by sorcery." People cry out to seize him, but undaunted, Frederick continues to accuse the knight of using black magic. "If he is honest, why does he not reveal his name, his rank, and heritage?"

The knight refuses on the grounds that he won his victory fairly. "I don't have to answer to anyone, except Elsa."

Elsa says, "How could I ask when the answer might endanger him?" But secretly, she is shaken. She feels the stirrings of doubt.

While the King and the nobles express their trust in the knight, Frederick whispers to Elsa: "Allow me to draw blood from your hero. That will break his magic and he will never leave you." As Elsa tries to thrust him away, he adds, "I will remain nearby tonight should you change your mind."

Noticing that Frederick is talking to his bride, the knight interrupts abruptly and orders Frederick and Ortrud to be gone and out of his sight forever. Then he asks Elsa if she doubts him.

With sweet loyalty, she says, "My champion, my love for you is far superior to the power of any doubt."

To the joyful cheers of the crowd and the rich sounds of the cathedral organ, the knight and the King lead Elsa to the church. Glancing back, Elsa glimpses Ortrud's hate-filled threatening face, then enters the cathedral for her wedding.

ACT III

SCENE 1

Led by her ladies-in-waiting, the nobles, and the King, Elsa and her husband are ceremoniously ushered into the bridal chamber. After the King joins their hands and the others bestow blessings on their love, they all depart, leaving the newlyweds alone for the first time. They are rapturous with joy. The knight claims their love is extraordinary, citing the fact that they dreamt of each other before their first meeting. When he tenderly calls Elsa by name, she remarks on how sweet it sounds when he says it, and how much she would like to utter his. He tries to sidestep this implicit question, counseling her to accept his mysterious nature as one accepts the fragrant breezes that waft from the garden.

She persists. "But if I alone knew, would it not prove me worthy of your love? For I would protect that knowledge with my life."

Her husband reminds her, "I risked my life believing your vow. Forget your doubts and celebrate our love. Let it suffice that I am of noble birth, and no crown could be greater than what I abandoned when I came here."

His words serve only to distress her more. "Ah, you are already longing for the home and the joys which you have forsaken. I fear you will not stay here. What have I to keep you? You have the powers of magic. But I, soon I will not even have my beauty. Even now I can envision the swan drawing the boat toward us to take you away! Only knowing who you are can possibly put my mind at ease! I must ask you."

"Elsa, don't—"

She cannot stop herself. "Where do you come from? What is your family?"

As the knight bemoans what she has just done Frederick and his four conspirators rush in, swords drawn. Elsa quickly hands her knight his sword and in one crushing blow he strikes Frederick to the ground. Shocked by this turn of events the others sheathe their swords and fall on their knees before the powerful knight.

Sadly, he tells Elsa that their happiness has now been forever lost, and he orders the attackers to take Frederick's corpse to the King. Then he rings the bell for Elsa's ladies-in-waiting. "Dress my bride so we may go before the King. There I will answer her questions."

Scene 2

It is daybreak on the banks of the Scheldt River. Slowly the Brabantine army assembles, and King Henry tells them how proud he is to have such troops defending Germany.

The air of celebration is stilled as Frederick's four conspirators approach and set his covered body down before the King. They say only that the Guardian of Brabant will reveal the corpse's identity. The mood grows even darker when Elsa arrives looking pale as death. Her husband soon follows, looking equally somber, and he hushes the soldiers as they try to cheer him. "My lord," he announces to the King, "I cannot lead these brave soldiers to battle. This man, Frederick of Telramund, attacked me at night. I killed him and now I ask for judgment."

All agree that the killing was justified.

"Now, I must accuse my God-given wife of betrayal. You all heard her vow never to ask my origin. Unhappily, she has broken that vow; I must now answer her questions and reveal my heritage." The hushed crowd listens attentively to the knight's tale. "In a faraway land where mortals have never stepped, there is a castle called Montsalvat which has within its walls a marvelous temple. Inside the temple there is a Holy Grail of such wondrous powers that it is guarded as the holiest of treasures. The angels placed this Grail into the protection of only the purest men, and once a year a dove comes down from heaven to renew its magic powers. To protect them from evil, the men who are entrusted with guarding the Grail are endowed with supernatural powers. When one of these knights is sent somewhere to fight for virtue, he retains his magic powers only if he remains anonymous. Once his identity is known he must leave. I was sent to you by the Grail. My father, Parsifal, is the keeper of the Grail and I am the knight Lohengrin!"

Tenderly, Lohengrin reproaches Elsa. "Why did you have to know my secret? Now, deeply as I love you, I must leave you."

The crowd cries out in protest and Elsa begs him, "Do not leave me. Stay, if only to witness how I will atone."

But despite her pleas and those of the knights to lead them into battle, Lohengrin insists he cannot remain. He predicts, however, that King Henry's forces shall return triumphant.

On the river, the beautiful swan glides to the shore pulling Lohengrin's boat. Sadly he turns toward it. "The Grail calls for me, though I wish it were not so. Elsa, had we succeeded, after but one year of marriage I could have enjoyed your happiness when your brother, who is still alive, would have returned with the Grail's blessings. Now when he returns I will be long gone, but I leave for him this horn to help him in danger, this sword to give him victory, and this ring by which to remember me." He kisses Elsa farewell and steps aboard his boat.

Ortrud suddenly appears and triumphantly she tells Elsa that the swan who will draw her lover away is actually her brother. "It was I who cast the spell upon him. I recognized him by the chain I placed around his neck. Had he stayed, the knight would have freed your brother." Oblivious to the outrage of the crowd, she shouts, "My gods have been avenged."

Lohengrin sinks to his knees in prayer, and as everyone watches, a white dove flies down. Lohengrin removes the chain from the neck of the swan. It submerges, disappearing into the water. In its place appears a handsome young knight. Lohengrin lifts him to land. "Behold Gottfried, the rightful Duke of Brabant!"

Ortrud shrieks and falls to the ground.

As Elsa and Gottfried embrace, Lohengrin boards his vessel and sails away, guided by the white dove. Elsa cries out desperately, "My husband!" Moving ever further away, Lohengrin stands in his boat, looking forlornly back. As he disappears into the horizon, Elsa falls lifeless into her brother's arms.

ORFEO ED EURIDICE

Opera in Three Acts
by
CHRISTOPH WILLIBALD GLUCK
Première: Burgtheater, Vienna, October 5, 1762

ACT I

ORPHEUS, A great musician of antiquity, mourns the death of his beloved wife Euridice. In the lovely secluded grove where she has just been buried, he stands among the shepherds and shepherdesses who are strewing the grave with flowers and lamenting her untimely end. Orpheus is inconsolable and the funeral rites make him feel even more wretched. When he can no longer bear the pain, he orders his servants to finish placing the garlands and leave.

Orpheus calls to his beloved. "Euridice! Euridice! Where are you? The flowing brook drinks my tears and echoes your name, but you do not appear. Oh, gods, give back to me she who made my world enchanted. I would rather die than live without her. I have no fear. For my beloved, I will descend myself into the dreadful realm below."

Suddenly Amor, the Goddess of Love, appears and tells him that the gods have taken pity on him and she has been sent to help him. "You will be permitted to cross into the infernal world. If, with your lyre, you can calm the monsters and the furies of Death who guard the gate, Euridice can return with you to the world of the living." Orpheus is incredulous but listens attentively as Amor lists the rules. "You may not look at Euridice until you are out of the Stygian pit. Further, you must not tell her about this restriction. If you weaken even once you will lose her forever." With these warnings, the Goddess of Love disappears.

"Euridice, mine again!" Orpheus is overcome with wonder and joy, but contemplates the conditions set by the gods with some dismay. "It will be difficult to avoid looking directly at her and not be able to explain, but I am resolved. I will do it! I will retrieve my Euridice. Help me, gods! I accept your challenge!"

ACT II

SCENE 1

Armed only with his lyre, Orpheus approaches the entrance of the under-world through a frightening rocky landscape. Fog swirls around him, pierced by licks of fire. As he comes closer, he is warned off by ghostly shrieks and the eerie roar of Cerberus. Undaunted, Orpheus plays his lyre, and walks unharmed through the gloom and the flames. A crowd of furies surround him and demand, "What mortal are you that dares come to the dreaded underworld, where there is naught but the cries of the damned?" They weave eerily around him, whispering of the terrors that lie in wait.

Orpheus pleads to the phantoms for mercy, explaining his plight, his pain, and his suffering. His musical entreaty calms their fury. The gate is opened and he passes through unharmed.

SCENE 2

Orpheus finds himself in a lovely meadow, surrounded by blue skies, trees, flowers, and flowing brooks. The peaceful chirping of the birds ac-companies the Blessed Spirits as they dance about. Orpheus has reached the Elysian Fields and he is momentarily enchanted. "How sweet and tran-quil is this land where the fortunate heroes have gone. But even shrouded in peace, I am tormented by my grief. Only Euridice can give me heavenly delight!"

He asks the gentle spirits if they can help him find her.

"She is coming!" they answer, and instruct him to turn around. Orpheus obeys and sees his beloved. She is standing across the meadow, draped in veils. Quickly, he averts his eyes.

The happy spirits lead Euridice to Orpheus. They counsel her not to lament leaving the peace of the Elysian Fields, for in exchange she is being reunited with the most loving and faithful of husbands. Hand in hand, Orpheus and Euridice begin the journey home.

ACT III

In a forest somewhere between the world of the spirits and the world of the living, Orpheus leads Euridice toward their destination. She is incredulous, still not certain if she is dreaming or if this is real. Orpheus reassures her that he is real and urges her to continue moving so they may leave this gloomy realm. "My undying love for you has caused the Goddess of Love to reunite us and our love will live again! Come let us not delay!"

Euridice cannot understand why he won't look at her.

"We must press on" is all he will say.

"Have I lost my beauty?"

"Do not doubt," he pleads.

"I can see you no longer love me!" she accuses. "Why should I return to a loveless life?"

Desperate, he begs her to trust him, but she insists on an explanation. "I must remain silent," is Orpheus's only reply.

Euridice decides that his silence conceals some horrible secret. "He is planning to desert me once we have returned. I cannot bear it. I would rather die again. Grant me, my love, one final glance!"

Unable any longer to resist, Orpheus relents and turns to look at her. Suddenly she grows weak and falls to the ground. "Orpheus, I am dying!"

Orpheus knows he has broken his vow and weeps bitterly as Euridice's life ebbs away. "What can I do now? I have lost her once again. Euridice, speak! Answer me. Once again my world is dark and empty!" Having lost all hope Orpheus calls on the gods to let him die. "Beloved, wait for me! I will return to the underworld with you." He pulls out a dagger with which to stab himself.

Just then the Goddess of Love arrives and restrains him. "You have proven your fidelity and I shall make you suffer no more. Euridice will live again. She is your reward!"

Euridice comes to life again. Orpheus is overcome with gratitude and sings praises to the Goddess of Love, sentiments echoed by the spirits.

"Now leave this place," Love suggests, "and return to earth where you may enjoy the delights of your love."

Orpheus, Euridice, and the spirits praise the power of love. The goddess responds, "If love burns in your heart then heaven is at peace; and if heaven is at peace then the pains of love turn to ecstasy."

Orpheus and Euridice, happily reunited, continue on their way to the land of the living as the spirits dance about them, blessing their journey.

DON GIOVANNI

Opera in Two Acts
by
WOLFGANG AMADEUS MOZART
Première: National Theater, Prague, October 29, 1787

ACT I

SCENE 1

LATE ONE night in seventeenth-century Seville, Leporello, manservant to the nobleman Don Giovanni, stands guard outside a grand house while his master is within, attempting to seduce the owner's daughter, Donna Anna. Leporello is growing tired of the Don's late night amorous escapades, but on this occasion his solitary vigil is interrupted by Donna Anna's shouts for help as she and the masked Don rush out of the house. She grabs hold of him trying to prevent his escape and to discover his identity. When, in answer to her cries, her father, the Commendatore, comes out of the house armed with a sword, she runs to get help. Fearlessly, her father confronts the masked intruder and challenges him to a duel. Don Giovanni does not wish to fight the older man, but the Commendatore insists and the Don draws his sword. The duel is brief. The Don mortally wounds the Commendatore and, leaving the body in the street, escapes with the terrified Leporello.

Donna Anna returns, accompanied by her fiancé, Don Ottavio, and some servants. Horrified at the sight of her dead father, she faints. Don Ottavio revives her and tries to console her. But she is beyond consolation. She wants Don Ottavio to avenge the murder.

"By our love, I swear I will," he agrees, and escorts his grieving fiancée into the house.

SCENE 2

Early in the morning, Leporello and Don Giovanni stroll along a deserted street. The servant, after exacting a promise from his master to remain calm, tells him: "You're leading the life of a scoundrel!"

His promise notwithstanding, Don Giovanni is enraged at the man's temerity and browbeats Leporello until the servant promises silence and friendship. Mollified, Don Giovanni suddenly changes the subject. "Hush!! I smell the fragrance of a woman."

Leporello mutters, "What a nose!"

Remaining discreetly hidden, they watch as a woman in traveling clothes appears. They can barely see her, but can hear her as she recounts her shame and anger about a man who has betrayed and deserted her. Intrigued by this damsel in distress, Don Giovanni chivalrously presents himself to her.

Face to face, they recognize each other. He is dismayed, and she flies into a rage. "You villainous snake, I knew I'd find you."

"Calm down, dearest Donna Elvira," he pleads, but she is not to be placated. As she continues to berate him, Don Giovanni orders Leporello to "tell her everything," and with Donna Elvira momentarily distracted, he makes his escape.

Left alone with the angry woman, Leporello "consoles" her with tales of his master's exploits. "Don't be so upset, you are neither the first nor the last woman he has jilted." Sparing her no details, he enumerates Don Giovanni's international conquests: in Italy, 640; in Germany, 231; 100 in France; and here in Spain—1,003! Relentlessly, Leporello continues: "Women of all sorts: peasants, maids, countesses, baronesses, even princesses. And of every description: young and old, large and small, short and tall. He is in service to all women."

Filled with a combination of disgust and awe, Donna Elvira vows she will love him no more. She will take revenge.

SCENE 3

In the countryside near Don Giovanni's castle, a group of peasants joyfully celebrate the impending marriage of a young couple, Zerlina and

Masetto. Don Giovanni and Leporello happen upon the merry scene, and drawn by the pretty young girls, the Don whispers, "Certainly I will find another conquest here." He introduces himself to the betrothed couple and publicly offers them his protection. He then orders Leporello to take the merry-makers to the palace and serve them chocolates, coffee, and wine, adding with meaningful emphasis, "Take special care of my friend Masetto. I will stay with the charming Zerlina." Masetto protests, growing increasingly angry and sarcastic, until Don Giovanni, indicating his sword, advises him to obey. Leporello leads the celebrants, and a very reluctant Masetto, away.

"At last we are alone, sweet Zerlina," Don Giovanni woos. "We have gotten rid of that idiot!"

Zerlina tries to remain loyal to Masetto, but it is difficult to resist the Don's seductive words: "I am a nobleman and cannot allow a girl as beautiful as you to marry him. I'll make you my bride. Give me your hands and whisper 'Yes.'" Halfheartedly, Zerlina protests that he will betray her, but soon promises "to ease the pain of unrequited passion!"

About to run off together, they are intercepted by Donna Elvira, who warns Zerlina of Don Giovanni's treachery and victoriously drags her away.

The Don shakes his head. "What a morning! Even the devil is against me." Before he can depart, Donna Anna and Don Ottavio come by and, believing him to be an influential nobleman, ask his help in their search. The Don says, "Everything I have is at your service."

But Donna Elvira has just returned and heard him. "He is a liar," she shouts; "he betrayed me."

Don Giovanni assures Donna Anna and Don Ottavio that Donna Elvira is crazy, but they clearly don't know whom to believe. Kissing Donna Anna's hand in respectful farewell, Don Giovanni takes Elvira away. Suddenly Donna Anna gasps breathlessly: "Don Giovanni is the murderer of my father! Just now, as he spoke I recognized him. He is the intruder." She tells Don Ottavio the whole story of the attack and, in parting, once again demands vengeance. Alone, Don Ottavio wonders how a nobleman could have committed such a heinous crime, but his happiness is linked to Donna Anna's, and he knows he must avenge her.

Back at the palace, Leporello greets his master on his return and tells him of his valiant efforts to keep the outrageously jealous Masetto calm. Don Giovanni is delighted by his servant's efforts. He takes a glass of champagne and toasts his plans for a wild party filled with feasting, drinking, dancing, and women.

SCENE 4

Into the palace garden come Zerlina and Masetto, she swearing innocence of any wrongdoing, while he remains unrelentingly morose. She pleads, "Beat me then. I'll be meek as a lamb, but I'll love you anyway. Think of the joy and happiness we will have."

He is almost ready to yield when they hear Don Giovanni approaching and Zerlina's sudden fluster makes Masetto once again suspicious. He hides in an arbor to spy on the encounter.

As Don Giovanni orders his servants to bring the guests inside for entertainment, Zerlina tries desperately to make herself invisible, but in vain. The nobleman sees her and says, "Stay with me, dearest. My heart is full of love for you!"

Knowing that her fiancé is watching, she is petrified and her worst fears are realized when Don Giovanni, trying to pull her into the arbor, walks right into Masetto. Recovering his poise quickly, he chastises Masetto for hiding in the trees when his Zerlina needs him. Music can be heard in the distance and the host tells the young couple to join him in some dancing. Arm in arm, they return to the party.

Donna Anna, Donna Elvira, and Don Ottavio, dressed as masked revelers, make their way into the garden, trying to steel themselves for an encounter with the Don. Spotting the three masked figures through a window, Leporello tells his master about them, and the gallant host orders him to invite them to the party. The servant obeys, and Don Ottavio accepts. The three masked avengers then pray to heaven to protect them as they enter the palace.

SCENE 5

In the great hall of the palace, the ball is in full swing. The minuet ends and interrupting his flirtation with some pretty girls, Don Giovanni greets the three masked guests with a toast to "Liberty!"

Dancing is resumed and Don Giovanni deftly swings Zerlina into the twirling couples, while Leporello stands in Masetto's way. As Masetto tries to get to Zerlina, Leporello forces him to dance with him. The three masked guests watch and wait. As the momentum of the dance mounts, the Don maneuvers Zerlina into another room. But the music and laughter are not sufficient to drown out her shouts for help and the dance comes to an abrupt halt. Sensing trouble, Leporello has sneaked unnoticed into the other room. In a frenzy, Masetto and some of his friends try to break down the door.

Suddenly the door opens and Don Giovanni, sword in hand, throws Leporello to the ground accusing him of attacking Zerlina. Playing along, the faithful servant begs for mercy. But the others aren't fooled by this sham and as, one by one, Donna Anna, Donna Elvira and Don Ottavio unmask, they charge Don Giovanni with his crimes.

Unafraid and ever unremorseful, Don Giovanni quickly draws his sword and pulling Leporello with him, he pushes through the crowd and escapes.

ACT II

SCENE 1

Strolling with his master through the streets of Seville the next evening, Leporello tries to resign from the Don's employ. "I'm tired of almost getting killed," he explains.

Don Giovanni refuses to listen and bribes Leporello back into service with four gold pieces.

"At least, stop chasing women," Leporello pleads.

"Impossible. I love beautiful women. They are my life." He describes his newest prospect. "Did you see Donna Elvira's maidservant? There is a beauty, and she will be my next conquest! Give me your cloak."

Leporello obliges and the two men exchange cloaks just as Donna Elvira appears at the window of her room. Seeing an opportunity to get rid of her, Don Giovanni hides behind Leporello and cries "Elvira! My adored one." With Leporello trying valiantly to mime the appropriate gestures, Giovanni continues his verbal wooing. "Joy of my life, come to me or I'll kill myself." Hard as it is to believe, Donna Elvira wants so much to believe that she finally consents to join him.

Leporello is disgusted with both his master's heartlessness and Elvira's credulity, but does not know how to extricate himself when Donna Elvira emerges from the inn and rushes to him.

She berates the disguised Leporello for having deserted her. "Swear to me you will be faithful."

Of course Leporello swears fidelity and when the still hidden Don Giovanni makes a horrifying noise, Donna Elvira and Leporello run off together.

Alone, Don Giovanni turns his attention to his newest exploit. Taking his mandolin in hand he sings a ballad which begs for just a look at her. But just as a figure appears at the window, Don Giovanni's wooing is interrupted by the arrival of Masetto armed with a musket and a pistol, accompanied by some villagers carrying sticks. Disguised in Leporello's cloak, Don Giovanni calls the Don a worthless scoundrel.

Masetto is pleased to have this ally and asks where he and his men might find the Don so that they can kill him. Don Giovanni devises a strategy for them. "He can't be far from here. Send half of your men in this direction and the rest the other way. Be quiet and quick and you'll capture him." As the villagers sneak away, Giovanni detains Masetto and, alone with him, disarms the poor man by pretending to examine his weapons, then gives him a good thrashing. Beaten, Masetto falls to the ground while the Don dashes off.

Searching for her fiancé and drawn by Masetto's cries of pain, Zerlina approaches, lantern in hand. She listens to his story, scolds him for his jealousy, and then consoles him, kissing his wounds and helping him to his feet. Tenderly she tells him that she will heal him with her love, and helps him limp away down the street.

Scene 2

Having wandered through the streets of Seville, Donna Elvira and Leporello find themselves in the courtyard of Donna Anna's house. Still believing Leporello is Don Giovanni, Elvira is more in love than ever, while he is getting desperate to rid himself of her before she finds out. In the darkness he steals toward a door, but his escape is thwarted by the sudden appearance of Donna Anna and Don Ottavio. Leporello hides in one corner of the courtyard and Donna Elvira in another.

While Don Ottavio implores Donna Anna to stop grieving, and she maintains her stance of inconsolable sorrow, Leporello resumes his search for the exit, but when he finally finds a door, he bumps right into Masetto and Zerlina.

"Now I've caught you, you villain!" Masetto shouts, alerting all the others, who quickly surround the cringing man. They accuse him of murder and declare, "You shall die!" Only Donna Elvira, still deluded, pleads for mercy for the man they all believe to be Don Giovanni. The others are astonished, but unmoved. As Don Ottavio moves in for the kill, Leporello throws off his elegant cloak and reveals himself. Robbed of vengeance, Donna Anna storms into the house while the others argue over who shall have the pleasure of beating the impostor. By some very quick doubletalk, the clever servant distracts them while he creeps toward the door and makes an escape.

Turning attention once more to the real villain, Don Giovanni, Don Ottavio tells the others that he will seek retribution for the killer of the Commendatore. In view of their common purpose, he asks them into the house, and vows again to avenge his beloved Donna Anna. Masetto and Zerlina go with Don Ottavio and Donna Elvira follows but not until she has once again cursed the wicked traitor whom, unfortunately, she adores.

SCENE 3

It is after midnight and Don Giovanni has taken temporary haven in a churchyard, while he laughs over his most recent escapade. Leporello arrives and angrily tells him about the perils of being Don Giovanni.

The nobleman is only amused. He tells Leporello, "I, meanwhile, met a pretty young girl and everything went smashingly until she realized I wasn't Leporello!"

Leporello is enraged by Don Giovanni's laughter, but his angry words and the Don's light banter suddenly cease as an ominous voice intones, "Before daybreak your laughter will end."

The two men are stunned. Don Giovanni reaches for his sword, demanding, "Who goes there?"

Again the mysterious voice shatters the night's silence: "Leave the dead in peace."

Leporello is terrified, but the Don concludes it must be someone hiding on the other side of the wall playing a joke on them. Then he notices that nearby stands a statue of the Commendatore, and he orders Leporello to read the inscription. Petrified and protesting, Leporello only does so when the Don prods him with his sword. He reads: "I await heaven's revenge upon a villainous assassin!"

Don Giovanni laughs. "Splendid. Invite the Commendatore to have supper with me." Leporello thinks his master has gone mad, but when Don Giovanni threatens to kill him, he obeys and issues the invitation.

The statue nods its acceptance.

Leporello is beside himself. "Did you see that?"

Airily the Don says, "Don't be such a buffoon." But as the statue nods again, his nonchalance begins to crack a little, and his voice has an edge to it as he shouts, "Speak up, man. Will you come?"

The statue answers, "YES!"

Don Giovanni's smile fades. "Come, Leporello, we must get ready for our guest." They hurry out of the churchyard.

SCENE 4

In Donna Anna's house, Don Ottavio assures her that the villain will soon be captured and asks her once again to marry him. She says she cannot so long as she is still mourning her father. He calls her cruel, but she counsels him to be patient. She does love him and hopes that heaven will once again shine down on her. Mollified, he swears to stay with her to share her sorrows.

SCENE 5

In the great hall of Don Giovanni's palace, the table is laid and the musicians and servants have taken their places for the late supper. The nobleman orders Leporello to serve the supper and the musicians to play. Don Giovanni savors every bite of his meal under the glaring eyes of Leporello, who, his master knows, is faint with hunger. When he orders Leporello to remove one of the dishes, the servant discreetly sneaks some food for himself. Enjoying the game, Don Giovanni waits until Leporello's mouth is full and then asks him a question. The servant barely manages a muffled response. The Don then orders him to whistle along with the music, and unable to do so, Leporello admits his offense. "You've so often said your cook is such a master I just had to sample something!"

The banter is interrupted by Donna Elvira, who bursts into the room begging the Don to change his way of life. He mocks her, telling her either to join him for supper or leave. Frustrated, she goes to the door. As it opens, she lets out a blood-curdling scream. Don Giovanni orders Leporello to investigate the source of her terror. The petrified servant returns to report that the Commendatore is coming.

Don Giovanni is incredulous. There is a knock at the door. "Answer," he orders.

Falling to his knees, Leporello refuses.

"Then I will do it myself."

Leporello hides under the table while the Don opens the door and is forced back into the room by the inexorable advance of the stone figure. Trying to remain collected, Don Giovanni orders Leporello to set a place for their dinner guest.

The Commendatore tells him not to move. "I do not need mortal food." He issues an invitation to the Don: "Come sup with me."

With great bravado, Don Giovanni agrees.

"Then shake my hand as a token of good faith," the statue demands.

Thrusting his hand into that of the statue, Don Giovanni screams, "It's colder than the grave!"

While Don Giovanni struggles in the icy grip, the Commendatore repeatedly demands that he repent.

"No! No! No!" Don Giovanni screams and pulls his hand away.

"Then your time has come," the statue announces. Suddenly a chasm opens in the floor, and flames leap up. Don Giovanni is engulfed. "Agony," he cries, as he sees the undying tortures of Hell that await him. While Leporello looks on in terror and disbelief, Don Giovanni sinks into the earth and the statue disappears.

Into the sudden calm rush the five avengers. "Where is Don Giovanni?" they demand. Leporello tries to tell them what happened, and they conclude that the statue must have been the specter that they saw. Content that the world is now rid of the villainous Don Giovanni, Don Ottavio again asks Donna Anna to marry him. "Give me one year for my heart to heal," she answers. Zerlina and Masetto propose to go home for supper, Donna Elvira decides to enter a convent, and Leporello prepares to find a better master at the local inn. Before they go their separate ways, they all agree that Don Giovanni has finally and fittingly gone to Hell, and that his life and death prove the ancient moral: "All sinners get their just rewards!"

SUOR ANGELICA
(Sister Angelica)

Opera in One Act
by
GIACOMO PUCCINI

Première: Metropolitan Opera, New York, December 14, 1918

THE SCENE of our story is an Italian convent in the latter part of the seventeenth century. A beautiful sunset casts a golden glow across the cemetery, through the olive bushes and the well-kept vegetable garden. A particularly brilliant ray of light strikes the font, which stands in the center of the courtyard. In the church, the holy sisters are singing the Ave Maria. Two lay sisters, late for the service, hurry across the courtyard and enter the chapel. Another sister follows, kneeling at the door to kiss the threshold as an act of penance for being late.

The service ends, and the sisters file out two by two, bowing reverently before the Abbess as they pass. The Monitor reproaches the two tardy lay sisters for failing to do penance as Sister Angelica had done. "As penance," the Monitor instructs, "you must repeat the prayer for the hungry, needy, and oppressed twenty times." The Monitor then instructs Sister Lucilla to work at her spinning wheel in silence as punishment for making the other sisters laugh in chapel. "And you, Sister Osmina," the Monitor continues, "you were hiding roses under your sleeve; go to your cell as punishment.

Hurry, our Blessed Lady is watching!" Sister Osmina follows the orders, angrily closing her cell door. Having administered the necessary punishments, the Monitor rewards the remaining sisters with free time to do as they wish. They scatter gleefully to their favorite activities. Sister Angelica waters her flowers, while Sister Genevieve reflects on how beautifully the sunlight streams through the tree tops. The other sisters note that these golden light rays mean the Blessed Virgin will smile upon them. A novice asks why the sisters expect an act of grace.

The mistress of the novices explains: "Three evenings each year, the rays of sunlight turn our font to gold. On these days, the Lord grants us a blessing."

The sisters, realizing that another year has passed, remember their poor Sister Bianca Rosa, who has been dead a year. "Let's sprinkle some golden water on her tomb," Sister Genevieve suggests.

They begin to talk about their worldly desires, and most declare that they don't have any. Sister Dolcina, a bit rotund, confesses that she desires something juicy and delicious to eat, which makes them tease her. Sister Genevieve asks Angelica, who has said nothing, what she desires most. Angelica says she has no wishes and returns to caring for her flowers. A few of the sisters whisper to each other that Sister Angelica has lied. She has been at the convent for seven years without any news from home. They have heard that she comes from a very wealthy family and was forced to take the veil. She is in exile, and the sisters wonder why.

Suddenly the Nursing Sister rushes in to tell them that Sister Chiara has been stung in the face by wasps. Angelica quickly gathers herbs and flowers to prepare a soothing remedy for the afflicted nun.

Two other sisters return to the courtyard laden with provisions from the town. Sister Dolcina's wish comes true; she receives a branch of fresh berries which she generously shares. One of the returning sisters tells the others that an opulent coach waits outside the convent. Sister Angelica is suddenly nervous and interested. She asks if the coach is upholstered in pale blue silk and if the arms are carved in ivory. The other sisters notice her agitation. The convent bell rings, signaling a visitor. They wonder excitedly whom it will be for, but noticing how intensely Angelica is praying, they sweetly hope it will be for her. Soon the Abbess enters and sends away everyone except Sister Angelica. The Abbess tells Angelica that her aunt, the Princess, has come to visit her. She cautions her to be humble and submissive. "Remember, every word you speak will be heard by Our Lady."

"I pray she hears all I say," Angelica responds.

Left alone, Angelica paces back and forth until the door opens and an aging, aristocratic lady enters walking with the aid of a beautiful cane. Angelica, seeing her aunt, emotionally rushes to embrace her, but the Princess only extends her hand for Angelica to kiss as staring coldly, she averts her head, and begins to speak.

"Twenty years ago, your noble parents died and left their children in my care. Their property and estate was equally divided, but I was granted the power to change this should I see fit. Your little sister, Anna Viola, is to marry a man who is willing to pardon the disgrace you brought upon our family. Therefore, you shall renounce all claims to any inheritance. Here is the document I have prepared. Sign it!"

"How," asks Angelica, "can my mother's sister be so merciless?"

The Princess tells Angelica that the only word that comes to mind is penance!

"I have repented," Angelica says, "but I can never forget my little baby, my tiny son whom I only saw once before we were separated. Tell me what he looks like," she begs.

The Princess hesitates, but when Angelica presses, she says, "Two years ago he was stricken with an illness. We tried, but nothing could save him."

"He is dead?" Angelica asks.

The Princess nods.

Angelica falls to the ground sobbing uncontrollably. It grows dark, the silence broken only by Angelica's heartbroken sobs, until the Abbess, carrying pen and ink, comes back with two sisters. Silently and obediently Angelica slowly rises, drags herself over to them, and signs the parchment. The Princess is ushered out of the garden. Alone, Angelica weeps for her poor child who died without his mother's tender kisses. "When shall I meet you in heaven?" she cries. "Speak to me, beloved one." As she thinks of joining him, she is filled with a strange mystic exaltation.

The other sisters returning from the cemetery come in to comfort her. "Our Lady has heard your prayers and will grant your wish."

Angelica's spirit soars with a newfound ecstasy. "Now," she says, "I know what I must do."

Singing the praises of the Sainted Virgin, the sisters all return to their cells.

Later that night, everything is still. Angelica emerges from her cell carrying a small vessel that she fills with water from the font. Slowly and lovingly she adds various plants—oleander, laurel, nightshade, and hemlock—talking to them as if they were friends. "You shall bring me the peace I seek. I hear my little son calling, 'Mamma, come to Paradise.' Farewell, my sisters. I die for him." With these words, she drains the cup.

The act done, the cup falls from her hand and she plummets back to reality as she realizes that to commit suicide is a mortal sin. "I am damned!" she cries, and in anguish she prays to the Madonna for salvation. In the distance she hears a choir of angels singing, "Regina pacis, Salve, Maria." Angelica begs for a sign of mercy and the angels respond with a prayer to the Virgin interceding on Angelica's behalf. Miraculously, a bright light bathes the church; Angelica, in a rapturous state between two worlds, sees a vision of the Blessed Virgin coming through the church door with her child. Slowly, Angelica reaches for the child, and as the angels intone "Salve Maria" she falls dead.

HISTORY
AND
HUMANITY

DIE MEISTERSINGER VON NÜRNBERG

Opera in Three Acts
by
RICHARD WAGNER
Première: Hoftheater, Munich, June 21, 1868

ACT I

ONE SUMMER evening in sixteenth-century Nuremberg, a congregation is ending the church service with a hymn to Saint John, whose feast day will be celebrated on the morrow. To one side, near a pillar, stands a young knight from Franconia, Walther von Stolzing. He catches the eye of a beautiful young woman, named Eva Pogner, who is sitting in a nearby pew with her chaperone. Though not a word has passed between them and they have never met, she returns the young man's glances with increasing interest.

As the crowd leaves the church, he stops her and says, "Excuse me for presuming, but I must know whether you are betrothed." Eva slyly asks her nurse, Magdalena, to return to their pew to retrieve a kerchief and brooch which she says she may have left behind. But Eva cannot answer Walther's question simply, for although betrothed, she does not know to whom. Magdalena returns and explains that Master Pogner has promised his daughter's hand to the Mastersinger who wins the prize at the contest to be held the following day. Walther is dismayed. The Mastersingers are a group of middle-class tradesmen who have developed a rigorous craft around the art of singing, creating for that purpose a guild that is artistic in ideals but sometimes pedantic in approach. As in the other guilds to which the men belong, it is usual to start as an apprentice and work one's way up before one can become a master. And Walther, as an outsider, cannot possibly know the Guild's exceedingly difficult rules of competition and performance.

Eva rashly says she will accept no winner but Walther.

Magdalena calls to David, her sweetheart, who with other apprentices is carrying in benches for the evening's trial songfest, and asks him to teach Walther the rules so that the couple may have a chance at being united. The two women leave and as they go Walther vows to do everything possible to win Eva's hand. He remains behind with David.

Some of the other apprentices who are setting up the church for the trial singing are annoyed at David for not helping. "How cocky David is!" they taunt. "The perfect apprentice to his Master the cobbler-poet, Hans Sachs!"

Playing a "Mastersinger," David orders Walther to begin. But the distraught knight does not know how. David is amazed that Walther wants to try to become a Mastersinger immediately although he has never attained even the lowest rank. Still, he tries to explain the complex rules and regulations of how to sing a proper song, but he only succeeds in confusing Walther totally. Finally, David counsels Walter: "Give up your dream to become a Master and become a 'Poet' and 'Singer' first, for a Mastersinger is a poet who creates a new melody to go with his rhymes."

Walther insists that he will make the attempt, nevertheless.

David returns to work with the other apprentices, and under his supervision they set up a small stage on which there is also a box for the Marker, who, concealed behind curtains, will note on a slate every error in a song, or deviation from the rules. While they work, David laughingly talks about the naive knight who seeks to become a Mastersinger without proper training.

Walther sits on a bench to wait, the mockery of the boys making him nervous. At last the Masters enter, and the apprentices hurry to their places.

Prominent among the Masters is the town clerk, Sixtus Beckmesser, who has hopes of winning Eva Pogner's hand at the competition the next day. Walther approaches Master Pogner, Eva's father, and asks for admittance to the Guild. Intrigued, Pogner tells the other Masters of the knight's wish and promises to present his name for the competition. Beckmesser is very suspicious. Pogner calls the meeting to order and tells the assembled Masters of his plans for the next day's Midsummer celebration in the meadow. "To prove how much we honor art in Germany," he tells them, "I, Veit Pogner, a friend of art, will give my greatest prize, my daughter Eva, in marriage to the man who is judged the winner of our contest. But she shall sit among the judges and cast the deciding vote!"

After some discussion, the Masters agree to these rules, and Pogner introduces Walther to them. They are surprised by the presence of a knight and suspicious of him, but offer him the chance to present a song to gain admittance to the Guild. Walther chooses the subject of love and the Masters call on Beckmesser to serve as Marker, a task which he always relishes, and particularly in this instance since he suspects Walther is a rival for Eva's hand.

From inside the Marker's box Beckmesser orders, "Begin!" Seated on the singer's chair, Walther bravely embarks on his song of love and nature and tries to ignore the frequent loud scratch of chalk on slate. Suddenly the curtains open and Beckmesser emerges from the box demanding, "Are you finished? There's no room left on the slate!" Angrily he points out the many mistakes that have been made, and all but one of the Masters agree that Walther has violated the rules. Only Hans Sachs, who has found something very fresh and appealing in Walther's freer form, rises to defend him.

Beckmesser, always Sachs's adversary, insists that the knight has spent his chance and has therefore been eliminated. But Sachs asks Walther to continue. Walther resumes his song until unable any longer to bear the noise of Beckmesser's markings, and very offended by the treatment he has received at the hands of these petty tradesmen, he gets up from the singer's chair and storms out of the church.

Beckmesser, sensing victory, enumerates Walther's mistakes and the Masters agree that, contrary to Hans Sachs's opinion, the knight has failed the test. He cannot be admitted to the Guild. Pogner is sorry for he knows that Eva would choose him.

As the meeting breaks up, the apprentices merrily dismantle the stage. Soon the only Master remaining is Hans Sachs, who contemplates the singer's chair, quietly shaking his head.

ACT II

Later that evening, as David is busy closing the shutters outside Hans Sachs's shop, Magdalena comes out of the Pogner home across the way. The two houses face each other across a narrow winding alley that rises between two rows of small, quaint half-timbered buildings. Up and down the street, apprentices shutter the houses and tease each other.

Magdalena is bringing David a basket of food that she has cooked for him, but when he tells her that Walther has failed, she takes the food away and, miffed, goes back into the house. The other apprentices taunt David about Magdalena, starting a scuffle which is quickly halted by Hans Sachs, who hauls David, his own apprentice, into his cobbler shop to work.

Eva and her father come down the street toward their house. He thinks she must be looking forward to the coming day's festivities when she will bestow the prize of herself on a Master of her choice.

"Must it be a Mastersinger?" she asks.

"One of your choice," he reminds her.

Eva notices that Magdalena has come out of the house and is signaling to her. She urges her father to go in, so Magdalena can tell her what happened. When she hears of Walther's failure, she is ready to despair, but together the women decide that perhaps Hans Sachs might know what to do. Grasping at this hope, Eva decides that she will visit the cobbler-poet later that evening.

After sending his apprentice off to sleep, Sachs sets up a workbench in the doorway of his house. He cannot stop thinking about Walther's song. "It seemed to violate all the rules and it was not easy to understand," he muses. "It had an ancient sound, yet at the same time, so fresh and new. It may have made the other Masters uneasy, but it certainly pleased me!" He takes up his work but is soon interrupted by Eva, who makes her way across the street to his door. He engages her in pleasant banter about her impending wedding and she leaves no doubt that she does not want Beckmesser to win. Flirtatiously, she indicates she would prefer a widower like Sachs himself.

"I am too old," he says wistfully. And prodded by Eva, he tells her about the song trial he has witnessed. "A knight sang his chance away. I'm afraid, my child, he shall not become a Mastersinger!"

Eva launches into a tirade about the "nasty, jealous heartless men" in the Mastersingers' Guild. Then, hearing Magdalena call her, she storms out of the cobbler's shop. Sachs now understands Eva's true desire, and, nodding sagely, he thinks, "We must find a way!"

In the street Magdalena tells Eva that Beckmesser is planning to serenade her from beneath her window. "How will we get rid of him so that you can be with Walther?"

"You shall stand there in my place!" Eva decides.

From within the house, Master Pogner calls his daughter, but Eva does not answer, for Walther has arrived, and she rushes into his arms. "I shall award the prize to no one but you!" she declares.

Walther points out that he failed the trial, and Eva says that she will run away with him. At this moment they hear the call of the night watchman coming down the street and they hide behind the lime-tree. When the night watchman has passed, Magdalena stands at the door calling, and Eva goes into the house.

Concealed behind his doorway, Hans Sachs has overheard the lovers' plans and decides he must prevent the elopement. Soon Eva, disguised in Magdalena's dress, comes out again, ready to flee with Walther. But before they can get away Sachs opens his door, illuminating the street. The lovers hide in the shadows but are effectively immobilized.

Sixtus Beckmesser comes along and stands beneath Eva's window, lute in hand, preparing to serenade. Sachs works away on some shoes he is making for Beckmesser, the blows of his hammer resounding through the night air. Knowing the noise will drown him out, the frustrated singer demands that the cobbler stop. Sachs insists he must finish the shoes. While Beckmesser strums ever more loudly on the lute, drawing Magdalena (dressed as Eva) to the window, the argument continues. Finally Sachs proposes, "You sing your song and I shall only hammer when you make a mistake," to which Beckmesser agrees. As the would-be lover sings, Sachs gleefully marks each error with a loud hammer blow. Beckmesser tries desperately to get through the verses, but Sachs is merciless and finally demands to know if the song has ended, because "you have made so many errors I have finished the shoes!"

Awakened by the ruckus, David looks out the window. Recognizing Magdalena, he comes tumbling out of the house, armed for battle with his rival. As the noise wakes the neighborhood, windows begin to open, then doors, and the street soon fills with people eager to settle old grudges. In no time at all, it is an authentic free-for-all. At the peak of the battle, Eva and Walther again try to get away, but they are stopped by Sachs, who pushes Eva into her father's arms, and pulls Walther and David into his own house.

A horn call announcing the return of the night watchman brings the fight to an abrupt halt and sends the combatants scurrying back into their houses.

"Hear ye, hear ye. It's eleven o'clock by the church. Beware of ghosts, and praise God our Lord!" he calls as he makes his way down the now deserted, peaceful moonlit street.

ACT III

The morning sun streams into Hans Sachs's workroom where he is so deeply engrossed in reading that he does not at first even notice that David has returned from delivering Beckmesser's new shoes. David reminds his master that it is Saint John's Day.

"Do you know your song?" Sachs asks.

To please him, David sings a lovely song about a child baptized by Saint John in Jordan, then brought to Nuremberg, where the name John becomes Hans. Suddenly realizing that it is his Master's name day, David begs Sachs to try for the prize. "Many people say you could defeat Beckmesser in the singing competition."

Sachs teases him for wanting a woman in the house and sends the youth off to dress for the day's festivities.

Alone, Sachs muses on the madness of the midsummer night just past, and resolves that on this Midsummer Day he will perform a noble deed to counterbalance the violence and vanity around him. His thoughts are interrupted as Walther comes out of the bedroom and tells him that he had a beautiful dream. Sachs guesses that the dream was about Eva and encourages Walther to pursue his quest. With genuine feeling, he explains the philosophical basis for the Masters' rules and urges Walther to apply them. "Tell me your dream and I shall write it down."

With some hesitation, Walther begins: "On a morning radiant with rosy light, and blossoms scenting the air, a garden bids me stay."

Sachs writes, occasionally interrupting Walther to advise him of the rules he must follow to make the dream a poem and Master-song. Walther learns quickly but when he reaches the end of the second verse, he does not know how to finish the song. Sachs assures him that the final measures will come to him by the time the competition starts, and they leave the room to dress for the festival.

Master Beckmesser, already dressed for the day's festivities, yet bearing wounds from the previous night's brawl, limps into the empty workroom. Snooping around, he sees Walther's song written in Sachs's hand and, much to his chagrin, assumes that the cobbler will enter the competition. He hurriedly pockets the paper just as Sachs, now also dressed in festive clothes, enters. He taunts Beckmesser by reminding him of the previous evening, until the wounded town clerk can bear it no longer and bursts into a tirade, accusing Sachs of trying to win Eva.

"My friend you are mistaken," Sachs tells him.

Beckmesser pulls Walther's song out of his pocket. "Then what is this, you liar?"

Sachs does not undeceive him. Instead he offers the poem to Beckmesser as a gift.

The town clerk is beside himself with joy at the prospect of using a poem by the great Hans Sachs. "Promise that you will not tell anyone that the song is yours." Sachs agrees but warns him that it will not be so easy to find the appropriate music to go with it. Beckmesser says smugly, "You are the poet, but I am the composer." Swearing eternal gratitude, he lavishes praise upon him and hobbles away gleefully.

Eva, dressed in a magnificent white gown, looking pale and nervous, enters Sachs's workroom. She has come on the pretext that her shoe pinches. While Sachs obligingly examines it, Walther walks in, now dressed in the dazzling garb of a knight. He and Eva gaze at each other while Sachs makes a show of repairing the shoe, and asks for someone to entertain him with a song.

Walther suddenly breaks out with the last stanza of his dream-poem.

At the end Sachs says quietly, "Now that is a Master-song." He slips the shoe onto Eva's foot. "Much better now, isn't it?"

Eva throws her arms around the cobbler—this man whom she has loved through childhood and girlhood, who has always petted and protected her and nurtured her soul and her mind. She almost wishes she could thank him with more than her gratitude. "If I did not so much love another, the prize would be yours."

"My child," he answers, "I had to find the right man for you so I would not be tempted to woo you myself." He calls David and tells him that a Master was born today in the person of Walther von Stolzing. Then, in an impromptu ceremony, he promotes the apprentice to journeyman, which means that David can now marry Magdalena. Full of the happy prospects before them, they all leave joyfully for the Pegnitz Meadow.

In a large meadow by the winding Pegnitz River, the people of Nuremberg assemble for the contest. As the crowd watches, the trade guilds march in singing their songs and carrying colorful banners: shoemakers, tailors, bakers, all followed by their apprentices. At last with great pomp and flourish, the Mastersingers arrive. Eva, surrounded by her friends, takes the place of honor on the stage that has been erected. The crowd cheers, especially their beloved Hans Sachs, for whom they sing a hymn.

Sachs humbly thanks them for the tribute, and then carefully explains the rules of the competition, stressing the unusual, very human prize that goes to the winner.

During all this Beckmesser has been hectically studying Walther's song, desperately trying to learn it. The start of the contest is officially announced and Beckmesser, as the oldest of the Masters, is chosen to begin. He takes his place on the stage and nervously strums his lute, playing a short prelude to give himself courage. He sings Walther's words, clumsily trying to fit the beautiful poetry into the melody of his serenade. Occasionally he forgets a word and peeks at the manuscript. His performance is a ludicrous mess. The Masters can hardly believe their ears, and finally burst into uncontrolled laughter. Furious, Beckmesser points to Sachs as the author of this awful song. "I wish," the cobbler says, "that I were the author."

"You are mocking us," they cry.

Sachs insists it is a beautiful song provided it is sung by the author and he calls Walther from the crowd. Confidently the knight ascends to the singer's mound and with impassioned grace proceeds to sing the rapturous song of his dream. As he makes his way through the verses, the Masters whisper among themselves, for while the form is new, it is indeed beautiful. When he has ended, the people and the Masters are unanimous in their acclaim. He is the winner.

Walther is led onto the platform where he sinks to one knee and Eva places the victor's wreath on his head. Veit Pogner, delighted by the outcome, welcomes the knight into his family and into the Master's Guild. But still stung by his rejection, Walther refuses this second honor. The wise Hans Sachs counsels him not to scorn the traditions of the Guild and to honor the Masters of German art.

Walther relents. Eva takes the wreath from his head and with warmth and affection places it on the head of the poet and Master Hans Sachs. He embraces the couple, and while the apprentices dance merrily the crowd shouts, "Hail, Sachs, beloved man of Nuremberg."

ANDREA CHÉNIER

Opera in Four Acts
by
UMBERTO GIORDANO
Première: La Scala, Milan, March 28, 1896

ACT I

IT IS the eve of the French Revolution. In the de Coigny palace, servants
bustle about the ballroom in preparation for the evening's soirée. Under the
direction of the Major-Domo, they rearrange the furniture, then follow him
out, all except one—a young man named Gérard, who fluffs up the pillows
on the sofa while mocking the useless aristocrats who make love on it. His
derisive laughter is interrupted by the sight of his aged father staggering
under the weight of some tools he is bringing in. Gérard rushes to relieve
him of the burden, and the old man leaves. Sickened by his father's life of
servitude and the prospect of his own, Gérard rebelliously denounces the
frivolity and waste in this upper class world of fancy clothes and minuets.
"I, son of a servant, in my livery, I judge you: Your hour has arrived. You
are doomed."

The Countess de Coigny, her daughter Maddalena, and her daughter's
maid Bersi come into the room and Gérard looks longingly at Maddalena,
but only for an instant, as the Countess fires a series of orders at him and he
assures her that everything is ready.

277

She turns to her daughter. "Maddalena, you haven't finished dressing yet and our guests will be here any minute."

Maddalena makes fun of the stifling, uncomfortable corsets and clothing she must wear and, complaining about these ridiculous conventions, runs off to dress.

Some guests arrive. Among them is the writer Fléville, who introduces his companions, including a highly promising poet named Andrea Chénier. But the Countess and Maddalena, who has returned, are more interested in the Abbé, who has just come from Paris with news. He tells them that the monarchy is tottering. The King has lost control, and the mob has defiled the statue of Henri IV.

Fléville recommends that they ignore these problems and instead spend the evening enjoying the party and the Pastorale that is about to be performed.

When the little presentation ends, the Countess, seeking more diversions, asks Chénier to entertain them. He says, "At this moment, my muse prefers silence," which annoys her and she turns away.

Maddalena bets her friends that she can make the reluctant poet speak of love. Confronting him, she requests a verse fit for a bride or a nun. Immediately he refers to love and she embarrasses him by informing the entire room of how she has won her bet.

Angrily, he tells her, "Now, my lady, you will learn the true meaning of the word 'love'!" His voice silences the company as he improvises an impassioned poem in which he couples love of country with criticism of the Church and a plea for the poor, comparing "the splendor and wealth of the Church" with "an old man who begged for a morsel of bread." Then, turning to Maddalena, he tells her that he thought he saw sympathy in her eyes but her scornful words saddened him. "Do not reject love. It is the essence of the world," he concludes.

She is visibly shaken and quietly apologizes. The Abbé and the other guests are scandalized by the tirade; but Gérard, standing on duty, has listened intently.

The Countess, trying to get the party rolling again, invites her guests to dance the gavotte. But the strains of the music are soon interrupted by sounds of an approaching mob which shouts, "We suffer day and night. We are hungry people, dying upon this barren earth!" Suddenly a crowd of ragged beggars, led by Gérard, bursts into the ballroom. The music stops and the Countess orders her servants to throw out the intruders. Gérard tears off his servant's uniform and quits her employ. Taking his father with him and swearing that they shall never suffer again, he storms out.

"Reading has ruined Gérard," says the Countess. "Doesn't he realize that I wear a simple dress when I go to visit the poor?" The Major-Domo tells her that the rabble has been ousted. She orders the musicians to continue and the dance resumes as if nothing had happened.

ACT II

Paris, June 1794.

Revolution has taken over the city and has begun to eat its own. The terror is full-blown. One day at a table in the Café Hottot, Bersi is questioned by a spy for the Revolutionary Tribunal. Desperately she tries to convince him that she is indeed a daughter of the Revolution. She tells him that she loves the free life she lives and to prove it raises her champagne glass in a toast as a cart of condemned prisoners rolls by. Bersi leaves, but the spy, still unconvinced by her protestations because he has seen her with a mysterious blonde woman, writes in his notebook: "Citizen Bersi glanced significantly at Chénier, who was seated at a nearby table, obviously waiting for someone. We must watch him!" He gets up and disappears into the shadows.

Roucher, a friend of Chénier, arrives at the café. "Chénier, . . . I've been searching for you all day!" Discreetly, he hands him a passport and begs him to flee the danger which threatens.

Chénier refuses. "I believe in fate, in a power that makes one man a poet and another a soldier. I must stay now because I am waiting for what I know will be the great love of my life." He tells Roucher that a mysterious woman has been sending him beautiful and enthralling letters. "I don't know where she is but she has asked me to meet her here." He shows Roucher a letter written in a feminine hand on elegant, scented paper and signed: "Hope."

Again Roucher urges Chénier to flee, telling him that the woman must be a courtesan who will certainly send the poet to prison. Chénier is stunned and as they watch a crowd on the bridge cheering the leaders of the Revolution, he accepts the passport and promises to leave in the morning.

Among Robespierre's entourage on the bridge is Gérard, who, as a fiery speaker, has achieved some prominence in the Revolutionary government. He calls over the spy and tells him he must find the woman with blue eyes and blonde hair that he has been looking for. The spy, assuring Gérard that she shall be found, continues to keep a watchful eye on Roucher and Chénier. Mingling in the crowd, Bersi quietly advises Chénier to wait because soon a woman who is in grave danger will come to see him. "Her name is Hope!" The poet transmits the news to Roucher, and deciding to arm themselves, they leave. But Gérard's spy has seen it all, and as darkness falls, he lurks nearby.

Night watchmen patrol the streets and lamplighters dispel some of the darkness.

Maddalena, wrapped in a cloak, cautiously makes her way down the street, frightened because she sees no one waiting. "Andrea Chénier!" she calls.

Out of the shadows he comes to meet his mysterious correspondent and in a few moments he recognizes her.

The spy, realizing that she is "the beautiful blonde," runs off to inform Gérard.

Pouring out her heart to Chénier, Maddalena recounts her fears and sadness while in hiding, how as she watched him through the months, she has felt closer and closer to him, until convinced that he would protect her, despite her rudeness to him the one time they met, she felt impelled to write to him. "I am all alone now," she ends. "Will you help me?"

"Always and forever." Having fallen in love, Chénier is fearless. "With you I can embrace life, or if need be meet death."

Together, they are transported by the sublimity of this moment. They love each other and swear to stay together—in love and in death.

Accompanied by the spy, Gérard bursts upon them and tries to take Maddalena from Chénier, who draws his sword. Roucher arrives armed with pistols and obeys Chénier's order to flee with Maddalena. As Chénier and Gérard duel the spy runs off to get help. A quick thrust by Chénier wounds Gérard, but as he falls, he counsels the poet to flee before he is captured so that he may protect Maddalena. Chénier escapes just as friends and soldiers rush up to help.

"Who did it?" they want to know.

Before he collapses, Gérard manages to whisper, "I don't know . . ."

Carrying off the wounded Revolutionary, the crowd blames the Girondins for the attack, shouting "Death to the Girondins!"

ACT III

The courtroom of the Revolutionary Tribunal is a public meeting place for the faithful. On this morning late in June, a crowd listens perfunctorily as a *sans-culotte* lectures them on the need for contributions. The response is feeble until Gérard, recovered from his wound, enters and takes the podium. His impassioned plea for money and men brings the room to life. "You should give your sons to the cause of France!" he cries. Trinkets and coins pour into the urn that is passed around, and an old blind woman led by a boy approaches Gérard.

"My name is Madelon. My son and one grandson have died for the Revolution. I am old." Then thrusting the boy forward she says, "This is my last grandson. He is strong. He can fight and he can die. Take him!" Gérard accepts the boy, and the crowd, their revolutionary fervor once again ignited, ushers the old woman out, cheering wildly for liberty.

Gérard sits down at a table to prepare the day's business. The spy comes in to report that Andrea Chénier has been arrested. Gérard is more interested in the whereabouts of Maddalena. The spy convinces Gérard to prepare Chénier's indictment in order to draw Maddalena out of hiding. Gérard begins to write, but suddenly, disgusted by the disintegration of his once lofty principles, finds himself unable to go on. He drops his pen. "My path once seemed glorious. I thought I was a giant. But I'm still a servant— obedient only to my own passions." Nevertheless, he signs the indictment of Chénier and hands it to the spy.

Maddelena rushes in and in a trembling voice addresses Gérard. "You may not remember me. I am Maddalena de Coigny. Please listen. I need your help."

Gérard tells her bluntly that he arrested her lover because he loves her and wants her. "Ever since we were children playing in the meadow, I have wanted to hold you and kiss you and run my hands through your blonde hair."

"If my body is the price for Chénier's life, then I am yours!" she declares. Emotionally, she tells Gérard of the horrors she has lived through— her mother killed, her family home burned to the ground, the hunger, the hiding, the loneliness. "I am virtually a corpse which you may have."

Gérard is so moved by her and by her willingness to sacrifice herself for Chénier that he promises to try to save him.

A noisy crowd presses into the courtroom to watch the trials of the day, their excitement mounting as the jurors, the officials, and the accused, Chénier among them, file in. As Dumas, the presiding judge, calls their names, each prisoner stands to face the jeers and catcalls of the mob. When the crowd calls Chénier a traitor, Gérard shouts, "Let him speak in his own defense."

His voice ringing, Chénier reviews his past. "I have been a soldier. My pen has been my sword against hypocrisy and I have always sung in praise of my country. I am no traitor. Though my life may near the white reefs of death, I am proud of what I have done. You may kill me, but my honor will live!"

Gérard, switching his role from prosecutor to witness, speaks on Chénier's behalf, admitting that his indictment was false. This involves him in a shouting match with the chief prosecutor, Fouquier. Fouquier says he is insulting justice and Gérard bursts out, "Our justice has become tyranny." He forces his way over to Chénier to embrace him while the angry crowd calls for his silence.

Pointing out Maddalena, Gérard tells Chénier, "Look. She's here."

"Then I die happy!" Chénier declares.

Gérard says, "Let us still hope."

The judges return quickly from their deliberations and Dumas delivers the verdict: "Death."

"Death," Fouquier repeats, and orders the guards to remove the prisoners.

"Andrea!" Maddalena shouts as Gérard tries desperately to reunite the lovers. But the crowd bars the way and the doors close behind the condemned.

ACT IV

In the courtyard of the prison of St. Lazare, Chénier, a slab of wood across his knees serving as a writing table, pens his final verses, while Roucher sits beside him. The jailer, Schmidt, tells Roucher that it is time to leave, but in return for some coins allows him to remain. Chénier finishes the poem and reads his final elegy—in praise of poetry—to the deeply moved Roucher. The two friends embrace and say goodbye.

Gérard and Maddalena are admitted to the prison by the jailer. Maddalena tells him that she will change places with a condemned female prisoner named Legray, and to secure this fatal exchange she bribes Schmidt with some jewels and money.

Gérard is close to tears. "Maddalena, you make death a fate to be envied." He rushes off to see Robespierre in the hope that he can still save them.

Chénier is thrilled to see Maddalena again, even if only for a moment. "Just to look into your eyes consoles me."

"I have not come to bid you farewell, but to die with you," she says.

They fall into each other's arms, and as they hear the ominous drum roll, they declare that death is the triumph of their love.

Schmidt calls the names of Chénier and Legray.

They step forward. "Here we are." The words are proud, exalted, and they step into the line of people moving inexorably to the guillotine.

TOSCA

Opera in Three Acts
by
GIACOMO PUCCINI
Première Teatro Costanzi, Rome, January 14, 1900

ACT I

THE YEAR is 1800, the day is June 17, the city Rome. The armies of the French republic, led by Napoleon, have been spreading the Revolution through Europe. In Italy, a republic was briefly established, but the French forces have been pushed back and once again the monarchists are in the ascendance. The republic has been overthrown, its leaders jailed, its sympathizers silenced.

Cesare Angelotti, a high official of the short-lived republic, has escaped from prison. He sneaks into the empty church of Sant'Andrea della Valle. He is exhausted and panicky as he searches for the key to the private Attavanti chapel, a key that his sister, the Marchesa Attavanti, has hidden for him. Angelotti finds it in the nick of time and quickly lets himself into the family chapel just before a fussy old Sacristan shuffles into the church to take care of some chores.

The Sacristan's puttering and muttering is soon interrupted by the arrival of the painter Mario Cavaradossi, who is working on a painting of the Madonna. The Sacristan and the artist examine the unfinished painting, and the churchman notices that the Madonna bears a striking resemblance to a young woman who has been visiting the church quite regularly during the past few days.

Cavaradossi admits that he has used this mysterious woman as his model. "She was so involved in her prayers that I could paint her face without being noticed," he confesses. The artist picks up his palette to resume work and muses how through his art he has blended the beauty of this mysterious blonde woman with his love for the singer Floria Tosca, a dark beauty. The Sacristan, annoyed by all this talk of women, leaves.

Alone, Cavaradossi is soon disturbed by a noise from the private chapels and surprises Angelotti as he emerges from the Attavanti chapel. The ex-prisoner's fear of being recaptured quickly turns to joy as he recognizes his fellow Libertarian Cavaradossi. The painter offers to help him but just then Tosca is heard calling "Mario, Mario" from outside the church. Cavaradossi thrusts the food basket at Angelotti and rushes him back into the chapel. With Angelotti safely hidden, Cavaradossi unlocks a side entrance to admit a stunning, dark-haired woman with brilliant black eyes.

The slight delay has filled Floria Tosca with suspicion and jealousy and she accuses her lover of hiding another woman. Cavaradossi denies any infidelity and reaffirms his love, placating Tosca with the promise of a late-night rendezvous. Tosca tells him how wildly she loves him, and they have a moment of tender avowal. But Cavaradossi is anxious to hurry her away, so that he can help Angelotti escape. As she is about to leave, she stops to gaze at the unfinished Madonna. Noting that the features are those of the Marchesa Attavanti, her jealousy is renewed. Again Cavaradossi soothes her and in parting she compliments him on his work, only lightly admonishing him to change the Madonna's eyes to black.

With Tosca gone, Cavaradossi returns to the Attavanti chapel to discuss escape plans with Angelotti. The Marchesa has left some women's clothes in the chapel, but before Angelotti can assume the disguise, the ominous boom of a cannon is heard announcing his escape from the prison—the Castel Sant'Angelo. The two men hurriedly pick up the clothes and, leaving the church, take the winding road to Cavaradossi's villa.

The Sacristan runs into the church looking for Cavaradossi in order to tell him some exciting news. Word has just reached Rome that Napoleon has been defeated at Marengo. He is disappointed to discover him gone, but hard on his heels the choirboys rush in, shouting and laughing at the prospect of a celebration.

The noise is abruptly silenced by the entrance of Baron Scarpia, the feared chief of police, together with his retinue of agents. "Is this a house of worship or a madhouse?" he bellows.

The stammering Sacristan tries to explain but is interrupted by the Baron's orders to prepare a Te Deum in celebration. The choirboys slink out, while Spoletta, Scarpia's assistant, begins to search the church for the escaped Angelotti. Scarpia quizzes the frightened Sacristan about the prisoner's escape and searches the Attavanti chapel. There he finds a woman's fan that Angelotti has left behind. A marking on it attracts Scarpia's attention—the crest of the Marchesa Attavanti. When he also notices that the Madonna in the painting has the features of the Marchesa, he links Cavaradossi to Angelotti's escape. "Ah," he mutters, "the pieces are beginning to fit together." He relishes this connection since he has long desired to steal Tosca away from the painter.

At this moment, Tosca unexpectedly comes back to the church to see Mario, only to find him gone. Scarpia approaches her and shows her the fan of the Marchesa, telling her that it was found on the painter's scaffold and that it belongs to the woman whose portrait is so evident in Cavaradossi's painting. Tosca's jealousy is once more ignited. As the nave of the church begins to fill with celebrants for the Te Deum, Tosca, swearing to surprise the lovers, hurries off to Mario's villa. The sly Baron orders Spoletta to follow her and catch Cavaradossi and Angelotti.

As the church reverberates with the sacred, soaring sound of the Te Deum, Scarpia savors his malicious aims. "I will have them both," he mutters. "One on the gallows, the other in my arms, her black eyes growing faint and languid in the grip of passion."

ACT II

It is evening. Only a few hours have passed. In his apartment on an upper floor of the magnificent Farnese Palace, Baron Scarpia pens a note to Tosca summoning her to see him after she has sung the cantata for the Queen. Spoletta comes in to report on the search for Angelotti. Nervously, he admits they did not find him at Cavaradossi's villa. Scarpia is quick to anger and is only appeased by the information that Cavaradossi has been brought back in custody, as he undoubtedly knows what has happened to the escaped prisoner.

"Bring him in here," Scarpia orders, "and bring in the judge and the executioner as well." A moment later Spoletta pushes Cavaradossi into the room, the judge and the executioner following behind. As the strains of the celebratory cantata float through the open window, Tosca's voice soaring clearly over the chorus, Scarpia begins to interrogate Cavaradossi. Of course the painter denies any knowledge of Angelotti's escape. The fruitlessness of his questioning is beginning to frustrate the Baron when he is interrupted by Tosca, who appears at the door. She has come in response to Scarpia's note, and growing alarmed when she sees Cavaradossi, she rushes to his side.

He whispers to her, "Don't tell them what you saw at my house. Your testimony could convict me."

She understands, and pretends to be calm as Cavaradossi is taken to the torture chamber followed by the judge and the executioner. Alone with Tosca the Baron asks what happened when she followed Mario to the villa. She tells him that when she arrived, Cavaradossi was alone. She remains steadfast. But soon Cavaradossi's cries of pain coming from the torture chamber weaken her.

She falls on the sofa, sobbing. "You are torturing me as well."

Unmoved, Scarpia orders the torturer to tighten the screws still further.

Tosca can bear it no longer. She tells Scarpia that Angelotti is hidden in the garden well outside the villa. Mario is brought back in, and hears Scarpia victoriously order Spoletta to return to the villa to search the well. Though broken and bloodied, Mario is furious with Tosca for having betrayed the secret.

Just then Sciarrone, another of Scarpia's aides, enters with the news that the previous report of an Austrian victory was wrong. It is Napoleon who has won at Marengo.

Exuberantly, Cavaradossi cries out, "Victory! Down with tyranny."

Scarpia only smiles. The painter has given him the excuse he has been waiting for and he sentences him to death for treason.

As Mario is led away to await execution, the distraught Tosca asks the Baron how she can save her lover's life. Scarpia's price is high: her love and passion. Tosca is horrified. She appeals to Scarpia for mercy. She cries out to God. She spits out her loathing and contempt for the Baron.

Scarpia is relentless. "I love your hatred," he says; "it only makes you more desirable."

Spoletta returns to report that Angelotti has killed himself, and that the gallows are being prepared for Cavaradossi.

Scarpia turns to Tosca. "Well . . . ?"

Given no choice, Tosca nods agreement.

Scarpia quietly promises her that Cavaradossi will receive a mock execution at dawn, and orders Spoletta to treat Cavaradossi the same way they dealt with Count Palmieri. The henchman understands and leaves. Scarpia pens a pass of safe-conduct for Tosca and Cavaradossi and then turns to the beautiful singer gloating, "Tosca, now you are mine!"

But, unnoticed, Tosca has taken one of the knives from the dinner table, and as Scarpia moves to embrace her, she stabs him. He crumples to the floor—dead. With a sense of irony Tosca says to herself, "Now he is dead, I can forgive him. And to think that he made all of Rome tremble."

Calmly she removes the safe-conduct from the corpse's hand. With a mixed impulse of religious reverence and theatrical drama, she lifts a crucifix from the wall and puts it on the corpse's chest and places two lit candles near his head. Then she leaves the room, quietly closing the door behind her.

ACT III

Dawn is breaking. The Rome sky is beginning to lighten over the Castel Sant'Angelo. Beyond the walls of the prison the sights of Rome are coming into view—the Vatican, the Basilica of St. Peter's. In the distance the pure voice of a shepherd can be heard singing; the bells of a nearby church ring for matins. At the top of the prison, a roof terrace sits empty and foreboding.

Then the total stillness of the scene is disturbed as a group of soldiers lead Cavaradossi out onto the terrace from his cell. The jailer tells him that he has but one hour to live. Cavaradossi asks for one last favor: to write a letter of farewell. The request granted, Cavaradossi sits down at a small wood table. He writes a few lines to Tosca but as he remembers their moments of tenderness and passion, he is overcome by the thought of the life he is losing, and beaks into sobs. While he sits with his head bowed in tears, Tosca enters.

She shows him the safe-conduct that she has obtained and tells him what she has done and of the mock execution that is planned. "You will be lined up before a firing squad. Only it will be a faked execution. On the first report of gunfire, fall to the ground and play dead. Don't move until the soldiers have all left. Then you and I will flee to safety—and to freedom."

The lovers embrace, trying to conceal their happiness from the troop of soldiers who have marched into position for the execution. The jailer informs the condemned man that it is time. Tosca and Cavaradossi pretend to say goodbye and Cavaradossi takes his position for the execution.

Tosca watches. The time seems interminable. At last the loud crack of gunfire resounds through the Castel Sant'Angelo. Tosca, ever the actress, notes to herself that Cavaradossi's fall was worthy of a great actor. As the soldiers file out she slowly approaches her lover, all the while whispering instructions for him not to move. When the last of the soldiers has left she runs over to him. "They're gone, Mario. Get up." When he does not answer, she calls more urgently. Finally she turns his body over and realizes that the evil Scarpia has double-crossed her. Mario Cavaradossi, painter, lover, and Libertarian, lies dead.

Tosca's sobbing is quickly interrupted by loud cries from the courtyard below. "Scarpia has been stabbed!!! He is dead!! Tosca killed him. Don't let her escape."

Tosca springs to her feet just as Spoletta rushes up to her, yelling, "You will pay dearly for this murder."

With the dramatic flair that she has used throughout her life as an actress, Tosca cries, "I will pay for his life with my own." She shoves Spoletta away and rushes to the parapet. From this height, she screams, "Scarpia, we will meet before God." And on her last words, she hurls herself over the ledge to her death.

UN BALLO IN MASCHERA
(A Masked Ball)

Opera in Three Acts
by
GIUSEPPE VERDI
Première: Teatro Apollo, Rome, February 17, 1859

AS IN Verdi's original version of *Un Ballo in Maschera*, the story that follows is set in Sweden in the eighteenth century during the reign of King Gustav III. In trying to arrange for a production of the opera, Verdi ran into trouble with the political censors of the Bourbon government in Naples. He then moved the production to Rome, but in order to satisfy objections from the Vatican, which did not approve of a Catholic monarch being portrayed in this way, he transferred the locale to colonial Boston, and Gustav became Riccardo, the Governor. Many productions still employ the censored version of the story with its Boston setting, and its mixture of Italian and English names, but the implausibility is so apparent that it would seem to require much too great a suspension of disbelief.

ACT I

SCENE 1

It is a bright, cheerful day in eighteenth-century Stockholm. The usual group of soldiers, courtiers, and petitioners has assembled in a reception room of the Royal Palace for King Gustav's morning audience. Most of them eagerly await their King, who is generally popular with the people. However, two nobles, Count Warting and Count de Horn, secretly hate him for wrongs they feel he has done them—Warting for the death of his brother, and de Horn for the expropriation by the government of his ancestral castle. As they mingle with the crowd, the noblemen conspire to avenge themselves.

"His Majesty!" Oscar the page announces, as Gustav unassumingly enters from his private rooms. Exchanging warm greetings, Gustav accepts petitions and assures each person that he will do what he can. Oscar then hands him the list of people to be invited to a masked ball. Among the names is one, Amelia, that makes Gustav's heart pulse a little faster. He is secretly in love with Amelia, but guilty about it because she is the wife of his most trusted aide, Count Johan Ankerstrom. While Gustav peruses the list, Warting and de Horn decide that this is not the time to murder the King, and they leave with the others as Oscar ushers them out.

Ankerstrom comes to see Gustav privately. Urgently, he tells him, "Your Majesty, there is an evil plot against your life. Nowhere are you safe, not even in your own palace." Gustav dismisses the news, not even wishing to know the names of those who conspire against him, and he assures his faithful secretary that the love of his people and the power of God protect him from danger. "Hate is stronger than love," his aide persists, but his argument is interrupted by a new arrival, the Judge.

"Your Majesty," the Judge begins, "I have papers for you to sign which will banish the evil witch Ulrica, who lures people to her cave and foretells their futures. We suspect her of many crimes and I have ruled that she should be exiled."

Gustav turns to Oscar. "What is your opinion?"

"I wish to defend this witch," the young page protests. "No doubt she has a pact with the devil, because she is able to foretell the future. But it helps all sorts of people who can learn things they need to know from her. You should absolve her!"

Gustav makes a swift decision. He orders Oscar to call the courtiers back into the room and invites them all to join him at Ulrica's cave. "Come disguised!" he bids. "I think this will be great fun for all of us. I myself will come as a fisherman!"

Warting and de Horn decide that this little frolic may provide just the setting in which to carry out their assassination plans. Ankerstrom again pleads with his King to be careful, but Gustav is gleeful as he anticipates the sport of the coming expedition.

SCENE 2

It is dark and dirty in Ulrica's hut. What little light penetrates the room has a dim poisonous glow that reflects the witch's eyes as she tends a large smoking cauldron of evil-smelling brew. A rapt crowd watches in silence as she openly calls on Satan to assist her. Gustav, disguised as a commoner, quietly observes the scene, waiting for his comrades to arrive. Christian, a sailor, steps forward to have her read his palm. "Good news," she tells him. "Very soon you will receive a higher rank!"

Gustav, unable to resist, writes a note and discreetly slips it into Christian's pocket.

The sailor, delighted by Ulrica's favorable prediction, reaches into his pocket to give her a reward and finds the paper Gustav has placed there. He is astounded when he reads the note—from Gustav to his dear *Lieutenant* Christian! "It is true, I have my promotion!" he shouts.

The crowd cheers Ulrica's clairvoyance.

There is a knock at the door and Ulrica admits a servant whom Gustav recognizes as one of Amelia's, and hears her say, "My mistress seeks your advice, Ulrica. She waits outside but must see you privately." Ulrica orders the throng to leave, but as everyone else obediently files out, Gustav hides himself in a dark recess of the hut. From here he hears Amelia ask the fortune teller how she can exorcise the guilty love she feels for their ruler.

In his hiding place, Gustav is thrilled at this proof that Amelia loves him.

Ulrica tells her there is a magic herb that will restore her heart to her husband. "But you must pick the herb yourself at midnight in the cheerless swamps to the west of the city, where the gallows stand!"

In spite of her terror, Amelia resolves to accomplish the mission that very night, and Gustav mutters to himself that he will follow and protect her.

Clamoring voices outside demand admittance. Amelia is ushered out through a secret door, and into Ulrica's den pours the crowd, which now includes officers and gentlemen of the court, all wearing disguises. Gustav leaves his hiding place and casually joins the others, then steps forward to demand that Ulrica read his palm and tell him his future.

"Yours is the hand of a great man," she begins. Suddenly she drops his hands and orders him to ask no more of her. Gustav is insistent and finally, against her will, she pronounces his fate. "You will die very soon, but not on the field of battle. You shall be killed by the hand of a friend! This is what the stars declare!"

A murmur of horror passes through the crowd, but Gustav regards the prophecy as a joke, while the conspirators, Warting and de Horn, are astounded by its accuracy.

"Tell me," Gustav demands, "who is going to kill me?"

Ulrica complies. "Your assassin will be the first man to shake your hand today."

Gustav laughingly extends his hand to each man in the room but each refuses it. At this moment, Ankerstrom enters the room and unknowingly takes his sovereign's proffered hand. Gustav laughs with relief: "You see, the prophecy is already proven false, for the man who has just shaken my hand is my dearest friend. Ulrica, your devil has not been giving you good advice. But anyway, I will not banish you as was requested!" Then he generously throws her a purse of gold.

She thanks him, but still warns, "Among your friends there is at least one traitor!" She is interrupted by the shouts of the townsfolk who, led by Christian, have assembled to praise their great King.

"How can I be suspicious when all these wonderful people adore me?" Gustav asks.

Nearby, Warting and de Horn mutter angrily at the cheers of the crowd, and plan revenge.

ACT II

Late that night, Amelia makes her way carefully across a deserted field on the outskirts of the city. As she nears the gallows she is terrified, but hearing a distant clock strike midnight she steels herself to go on and find the magic herb prescribed by Ulrica. Suddenly she thinks she sees a head rising from the earth and drops to her knees praying to the Lord to give her strength.

It is Gustav who emerges from the shadows. "Why are you afraid!" he asks.

"Take pity on me, my lord. Even though you love me I belong to your dearest friend and ally!"

Gustav protests, telling her of the remorse that consumes his soul but that he cannot help the love he feels for her. Again she begs him to leave her alone, but he insists he must first hear her say that she loves him.

"Yes! I do love you," she confesses, "but it is your duty as a noble to protect me from my own heart!"

Gustav is ecstatic. Carried away by their feelings, they pour out their hearts to each other even though they know they must renounce their love.

Suddenly, Amelia hears someone approaching and drops her veil over her face.

Across the field comes Ankerstrom looking for Gustav to warn him against the conspirators who are waiting in ambush. "Take my cloak and depart on that path. You will be safe."

Amelia, hidden behind her veil, is petrified that her husband will discover her, but nonetheless insists that Gustav flee to safety without her. He, of course, does not want to. "If you don't, I will show my husband who your conquest is!"

Realizing his predicament, Gustav asks Ankerstrom to undertake a delicate assignment: "Promise me you will escort this lady back to town. When you reach the city gates you will leave her and go in the opposite direction. However, you must do this without looking at or speaking to her."

His aide swears to do as he asks, and begs him to flee. "They are coming, each with a dagger meant for you. You must save yourself and your people!"

Gustav is finally persuaded to leave, but does so ridden with guilt toward both his friend and his love.

As Amelia and her husband turn back to the city, they are stopped by Warting and de Horn, who, when they realize they have lost the King, want at least to discover who his mistress might be. Faithful to Gustav, Ankerstrom draws his sword to protect the woman's identity, but he is outnumbered, and Amelia, to defend him, lets her veil fall to the ground.

"Amelia!" Ankerstrom cannot believe his eyes.

The conspirators cruelly ridicule him for his fidelity to a man who has stolen his wife.

As the duplicity of his King and friend is borne in upon Ankerstrom's consciousness, he grows enraged and bids Warting and de Horn meet with him at his home the following morning.

Intrigued by the invitation, the conspirators agree and, still laughing at what they have just witnessed, make their way back across the field.

Alone with his wife, Ankerstrom tells her, "I have pledged to escort you to the gates of the city, and I will keep that promise. Let's go!"

Amelia follows him, filled with foreboding.

ACT III

Scene 1

No sooner have they reached home than Ankerstrom confronts his wife and accuses her of adultery. "Your guilt is obvious and your prayers useless. Only your blood will atone for your betrayal." Desperately Amelia tries to defend herself, protesting that he has convicted her with only one piece of false evidence. "I may have loved him, but only for a brief moment and I certainly never disgraced your name or honor!" Grim and unpersuaded, her husband insists she must die. "Please," she begs, "before you end my all too brief life allow me to embrace our son one last time. Allow him to touch the mother he shall never see again."

Ankerstrom relents and as Amelia leaves the room, he reflects more calmly, "She is not the one I must kill. It is Gustav's blood that should flow to avenge this sin. He was the one who betrayed me, his dearest, most loyal friend. Like myself, Amelia was Gustav's victim." Seeing her in this light, he remembers how sweetly and ardently they once loved, and is filled with sadness at its having been replaced by the hatred he now feels.

De Horn and Warting arrive for their meeting and Ankerstrom stuns them with the news that not only does he know of their plot to kill Gustav, but also has the documents to prove it. Angrily they accuse him of planning to reveal the plot. "On the contrary, gentlemen. I wish to be part of your conspiracy. I swear it, on the life of my only son." The intensity of his emotion convinces the others that he means what he says. "One more thing," Ankerstrom adds. "You must let me be the one to kill the King." On this they cannot agree since each of them wants personal satisfaction. At last, they conclude that the only way to decide is to draw lots.

As they prepare to do so, Amelia comes in to announce that Oscar, the page, has arrived.

Angrily, her husband tells her the page will have to wait. "But since destiny has sent you in here at this moment, you must pick a name from this vase," adding sarcastically, "with your innocent hand."

Trembling, she draws a slip of paper and hands it to de Horn.

As he reads, de Horn's face registers disappointment. "Ankerstrom. The task has fallen to you."

Exultant, Ankerstrom calls heaven just, while Amelia realizes that he and the others are planning to assassinate the King.

Ankerstrom now calls for the page. Oscar has come to present a formal invitation to the masked ball that very evening. "His Majesty particularly requests your presence. It will be a splendid affair!"

Realizing that the scene will be perfect for a murder, Ankerstrom accepts the invitation for himself and Amelia.

Amelia berates herself for her own inadvertent role in the conspiracy and wonders how she may warn Gustav, while the men contemplate what disguises to wear and relish their imminent revenge.

SCENE 2

Alone in his study, Gustav sits at his writing table. He has realized that he must give up Amelia forever, and he pens an official order sending Ankerstrom and Amelia to Finland. "Then we will be separated and my love for her will be silenced." It is agonizing to sign, but finally he does it.

As the music for the ball begins in another part of the palace, Oscar enters Gustav's study to hand him a letter given him by an unknown woman, with instructions to deliver it secretly. Gustav reads the warning that during the ball someone will attempt to kill him. He brushes it aside. Not to go to the ball would be cowardly. And besides, he cannot resist seeing Amelia one more time. Feverishly excited, he leaves to prepare for the masquerade.

SCENE 3

In the richly appointed ballroom, gaiety reigns among the disguised and dancing guests. Dressed as monks, Ankerstrom, de Horn, and Warting huddle in a corner to plot the murder. Ankerstrom is gloomy, convinced that their target will not appear. Realizing that they are becoming conspicuous, they separate.

Ankerstrom soon discovers that Oscar has been watching him. "You came without your King?" he reproves him. But much to his surprise, Oscar informs Ankerstrom that Gustav is indeed at the ball. He is reluctant, however, to reveal His Majesty's disguise. Ankerstrom presses him. "There are crucial matters that I have to discuss with the King. If disaster results, it will be your fault." Oscar finally yields and describes Gustav's costume.

Amelia, in her disguise, has found Gustav and warns him again that he is in mortal danger.

"Who are you?" he asks, but she won't tell him, pleading instead that he leave while he can. Suddenly, he recognizes her. In tears she begs him to flee to safety because she loves him.

"I am not afraid of death, Amelia, because my love for you is stronger. Just being near you makes my heart beat wildly."

"Think of how shameful it all is."

"Tomorrow, it will end. I am sending you and Johan to Finland, even though I love you! This is our last farewell."

Unnoticed, Ankerstrom has crept up to them and as they separate, he steps between them and stabs Gustav, who falls to the floor. Oscar rushes to his side, pointing accusingly. Guards seize the assailant and tear off his mask. The stunned assembly breaks out in cries for his death.

"Let him be," Gustav orders, and indicates that Ankerstrom should approach. "Listen to my words. As I die, I swear to you that your wife is pure. I loved your wife, yet she remained faithful to you." Then he gives Ankerstrom the sealed order. "I promoted you to a new position. You were both to have left. I loved her but could not offend you."

Ankerstrom is filled with remorse for his tragic mistake, Amelia with anguish for the three of them, and the others with misery at the loss of their beloved King.

Strength ebbing, Gustav raises himself a little. "I am still ruler here and given that power, my pardon absolves everyone of guilt." Then, with his final breath, he bids them all farewell.

THE BARBER OF SEVILLE

Opera in Two Acts
by
GIOACCHINO ROSSINI
Première: Teatro Argentina, Rome, February 20, 1816

ACT I

SCENE 1

EARLY ONE morning in a small square in the city of Seville, a band of musicians stands beneath a balcony playing a serenade. With them is a handsome young man whose figure and face are almost entirely covered by a cloak. He is the Count Almaviva, and he is singing to the beautiful object of his affections. When the serenade elicits nothing but silence the Count dejectedly pays the musicians—so generously, in fact, that they thank him profusely and endlessly until Almaviva has to push them away so they will not awaken the entire neighborhood.

Finally, there is quiet, but it is soon shattered by a confident and noisy man who strides down the street, announcing, "Clear the way for the general factotum of the city! It is dawn and I am on my way to my barber shop. Lucky am I, called for here, there, and everywhere. I am Figaro, the Barber of Seville. Bravo, Figaro!"

The Count calls out, "Hey! Figaro!"

The Barber recognizes the disguised Count, having worked for him once in Madrid. The Count explains that he is incognito and that he needs

Figaro's help. He has been trying to meet the beautiful young woman who lives in the house with the balcony. "How lucky that you met me," Figaro responds, "for I am the barber, surgeon, apothecary . . . in fact, general factotum to this very household! The girl you have seen is the ward of the Doctor who lives here."

Suddenly, the balcony door opens and Rosina appears holding a piece of paper. She looks around for her ardent serenader, but too late; her guardian, Doctor Bartolo, is on the balcony with her, demanding to know the contents of the paper. "It's nothing, just the words to an aria from the opera *The Useless Precaution*," she tells him as she casually drops it to the street below. The Count quickly snatches it before returning to his hiding place under the balcony.

Pretending to be very upset at the loss, Rosina asks her guardian to please fetch it. But, of course, when he reaches the street the paper is gone. Realizing that she has tricked him, he returns to the house threatening to have the balcony sealed off, and orders her back to her room.

Figaro and the Count eagerly unfold the paper to read: "I have been intrigued by your constant attentions and would like to know more about you: your name, rank, and intention. My guardian will be leaving the house soon. When he's gone find some way to contact me. You may be confident that I will do almost anything to break my chains!"

The Count is rapturously happy, but his joy is tempered by Figaro's account of the gruff old guardian, who, desiring Rosina's dowry, has decided that the only way to get his hands on it is to marry her himself.

The house door opens as Doctor Bartolo emerges. He announces to the servants, "I am going now to complete the wedding arrangements," and instructs them that the door is to be kept locked and only Don Basilio is to be admitted.

The Count, having overheard all this in his hiding place, is worried, and asks Figaro about Don Basilio. "He is a good-for-nothing matchmaker who is always broke and has recently become a music teacher. Rosina is his pupil. But now we must find a way for you to tell her about yourself." The Count says he wants to keep his rank and wealth a secret until he is certain that Rosina loves him for himself. Figaro understands, and noting that Rosina's shadow can be seen behind the shutters suggests that the Count explain everything in a serenade.

He begins, "My name is Lindoro. I adore you and wish someday to marry you."

To his astonishment, Rosina responds, "My beloved, continue!"

"Your Lindoro," he resumes, "cannot give you wealth, only love from early morning until late at night!"

The voice inside responds, "Rosina, faithful and smitten, gives you her heart . . ." But before she can finish, she is whisked away.

The Count, frustrated and feverish with love, tells Figaro, "You must get me into that house before nightfall! I will reward you with gold if we succeed!"

With a promise like that, Figaro is immediately filled with ideas. "A regiment is expected in Seville today," he muses, "and the soldiers will be lodged in private homes." He snaps his fingers. "You, dear Count, will dress as a soldier and we will have you assigned to Doctor Bartolo's house. Further, you must pretend to be drunk, which will make the Doctor less distrustful." The two men set off to put the plan into action.

SCENE 2

Rosina has been clearly smitten by her serenading suitor. She thinks, "My guardian will never consent, but using my wits I shall succeed and Lindoro shall be mine. Now if I could only get this letter to him. Perhaps the good Figaro can help me."

Just then Figaro comes in and wishes her good day, but before they can discuss the delicate situation, Doctor Bartolo returns home and Figaro is forced to hide.

"I shall kill that scoundrel, Figaro," Bartolo storms. "He has drugged the servants so that Berta can't stop sneezing and Abruzio can't stop yawning!" Rosina coolly states that she finds Figaro adorable, and goes off to her room.

Don Basilio arrives bearing the news that a secret admirer of Rosina's, the Count Almaviva, has arrived in Seville.

"We must do something," Bartolo declares. "I must marry Rosina!"

"Slander is the answer!" Basilio advises. "We must slander the Count, spread a rumor discrediting him. It will grow and grow like a storm, rippling gently at first, but finally exploding in a huge uproar. That will fell our good Count!"

Bartolo is intrigued by this plan and is impatient to set it in motion and, followed by the fawning money-hungry Basilio, goes to his room to hatch a plot.

Figaro emerges from his hiding place, delighted to have overheard the conversation and amused that the old boor believes Rosina would become his wife. "But now I must talk to that girl." Right on cue Rosina emerges from her room, and Figaro greets her with the news of Bartolo's plans to marry her. Dismissing that as lunacy Rosina wants only to hear of the man who earlier had serenaded her. "He's my cousin," Figaro lies, "a fine lad who has come here to seek his fortune. He has one great weakness, however, he is dying of love for a certain girl." When Rosina protests that this man interests her, Figaro feigns surprise: "The girl he loves is vivacious, has black hair, rosy cheeks, bright eyes, and beautiful hands. And her name," he teases, "is Rosina!"

She blushes happily at the news while she coolly claims to have known all along. "But how can I speak with him?" she asks.

"Write him a short note, just a line of two!" She shyly and prudishly refuses while Figaro continues to coax, until to the barber's amazement, she hands him a letter she has already written. Figaro departs with the note, shaking his head at the wiles of women. "I thought I could be her teacher but she can teach me a thing or two!"

Doctor Bartolo returns, demanding to know of Rosina what Figaro wanted, why the pen has been used, and why her finger is tinted with ink. Deftly she sidesteps his inquisition, improvising an answer for each of his queries, but he is not satisfied. "My girl, a doctor of my standing will not be tricked by your lame excuses. You must fabricate better stories. If you're not careful you will be locked in your room, my dear Rosina!"

"Do what you wish," she retorts; "it will only sharpen my wits!" and in a huff she returns to her room.

There is a loud knock on the door and Berta, still sneezing, comes in to open it, admitting the Count, disguised as a drunken soldier.

"What do you want?" the Doctor demands.

Playing the part to the hilt, Almaviva mangles Bartolo's name, calling him Balardo, Bertoldo, Barbara, etc., while Bartolo fumes and tries to correct him. The Count staggers about, hoping to find his beloved Rosina, but she is nowhere to be seen.

Bartolo orders him out, but the Count presents a document which he claims is his billet for lodging, explaining that his regiment is in town and he has been assigned to the Doctor's house. Rosina comes back into the room and inching his way over to her the Count finally whispers to her, "I am Lindoro!"

Seeing his ward beside the interloper, Bartolo gruffly orders her back to her room; the "drunken soldier" giddily begins to follow her but is stopped by Bartolo, who tells him he may not stay because "the Bartolo house is exempt from having to lodge troops," and having announced this, he rummages through his desk looking for the appropriate document. While he is thus occupied, Almaviva tries to slip a note to Rosina, who, despite Bartolo's orders, has remained in the room. Suddenly Bartolo's voice is heard booming the words of his precious document: "Let it be known that Doctor Bartolo is exempt . . . ," but before he can finish, the "drunk" has grabbed it from him and discarded it, declaring: "I will remain here!" The enraged Bartolo attacks him with a walking stick, which the Count deftly knocks to the floor and then drops his letter beside Rosina. She, in turn, coyly drops her handkerchief over it and then retrieves both.

"I saw that!" Bartolo shouts. "Let me see that paper!"

Without missing a beat Rosina substitutes a laundry list and gives it to him. While the befuddled Doctor ponders this, Berta comes in to announce that the barber has arrived, but her words are barely audible over the noise caused by the continued arguing among Bartolo, Rosina, and the Count, and Don Basilio, who has joined the fracas.

"Calm down!" cries Figaro as he enters. But even he cannot put an end to the tumult.

A loud banging at the door brings the shouting to an abrupt halt. "It's the police! Open in the name of the law!" The door bursts open and the police pour in: "No one move! What is the cause of this disturbance?" Everyone at once protests innocence and accuses the others. "Silence," booms the officer, and, turning to the Count, announces: "You are under arrest!"

But the Count wafts his identity papers before their eyes and the officer and police stiffen into a smart salute. Everyone else, except Figaro of course, is bewildered and Bartolo is stunned into total paralysis.

ACT II

SCENE 1

Some time later Doctor Bartolo contemplates what has happened. "That 'soldier,'" he decides, "did not belong to the regiment. He was probably an emissary of the Count Almaviva sent to contact Rosina. One is not even safe in one's own home!" His thoughts are disrupted by a knock at the door.

Standing there is the Count, now disguised as a music teacher. He enters, uttering, "Peace and joy, peace and joy," and tells Bartolo that he is Don Alonso, a pupil of Don Basilio, who is sick and cannot give Rosina her lesson. To allay the Doctor's rising suspicions the impostor quickly tells the following story: "This morning at an inn I met a Count Almaviva and by chance this note written by him to your ward fell into my possession. If I might speak to Rosina I could convince her that it was given to me by a mistress of the Count, thereby proving that he is only toying with Rosina's affections!"

The Doctor is delighted by this slanderous scheme and compliments "Don Alonso" on being such a fine student of Don Basilio.

The Count waits nervously while the Doctor goes to get Rosina: "Come, my dear," he beckons, "Don Alonso will give you your lesson today!"

Rosina recognizes her suitor and willingly joins him at the harpsichord. "I will sing the aria from *The Useless Precaution*," she says, and then while the Doctor dozes in an armchair she cleverly improvises an aria in which she tells "Lindoro" of her love and how she trusts him to free her from her guardian.

He promises to do it.

Doctor Bartolo, rousing himself, compliments her on her beautiful voice but then complains about the music. "In my time music was better," he asserts. He is just illustrating his point with a melody when Figaro enters announcing that he has come to give the Doctor his shave. Bartolo is in no mood for a shave, but Figaro is insistent and the Doctor finally agrees. Giving Figaro a bunch of keys, he instructs him to go down the corridor and get the towels needed for the shave. Figaro is delighted to be in possession of these keys and deftly manages to steal the key to Rosina's balcony door.

Finally all is prepared for Doctor Bartolo's shave, but there is another delay as Don Basilio comes to give the music lesson. "How are you?" Bartolo asks. Basilio is confused. The Count and Rosina are afraid that he will expose the impostor music teacher. Pulling Bartolo aside, and still pretending to be Don Alonso, the Count tells him to say nothing of the letter because Basilio doesn't know about it. This prompts Bartolo to suggest to Basilio that he return home and go to bed. Figaro, coming to the rescue, scrutinizes Don Basilio, feels his head and declares in somber tones, "You might have scarlet fever," at which the others react in horror, ordering him to go home. Basilio is bewildered, but on receipt of a generous purse from the Count is convinced that he is ill. He takes his leave, bidding everyone a lengthy good night. They finally shove him out the door.

The long delayed shave begins with Figaro creating as much commotion as possible to allow the Count and Rosina to talk undisturbed. The Count tells her that he and Figaro will return at midnight to abduct her. "We have the key to the balcony." She is delighted. But Bartolo has grown suspicious and, despite Figaro's distractions, manages to overhear the Count say something about a disguise. Bartolo is enraged and swathed in foam and towels accuses the two men of being villains and threatens to kill them. Angrily he chases the plotters out of his house while Rosina manages to slip into her room.

Bartolo then orders one of his servants to fetch Don Basilio, while he himself goes to stand guard at Rosina's door.

SCENE 2

"So, dear Don Basilio, you do not know a man named Don Alonso?" Bartolo asks. "Then he must have been an emissary of the Count. They are plotting something! Clearly there is no time to delay! I will go fetch the notary at once and have the marriage contract drawn up." On second thought he decides to send Don Basilio instead.

Doctor Bartolo calls for Rosina and when she reluctantly appears, he shows her the letter "Don Alonso" gave him. "You see, Rosina, Don Alonso and Figaro are plotting to deliver you to Count Almaviva!"

Rosina is enraged to learn that her beloved Lindoro has duped her and in a fit of spite offers herself to Doctor Bartolo. "I shall marry you instead!" She then confesses that Lindoro and Figaro are planning to abduct her from the balcony at midnight!

"I'll stop them," he swears. "I'll return soon!" And with that he dashes out of the house.

Left alone, Rosina is torn between her anger at Lindoro for having deceived her and her hope against hope that he will still return and make her happy.

Outside a terrible storm rages with winds and rain, thunder and lightning. When it has subsided Figaro and the Count, wrapped in cloaks, creep quietly down the street, to the Bartolo house, carrying a ladder, with which they climb up to Rosina's balcony and enter the house.

"There is your beloved Rosina," Figaro declares, but instead of a happy bride-to-be, they see a sullen, enraged young woman.

She orders them to stand back. "You ungrateful wretch!" Rosina snarls. "You pretended to love me so that you could deliver me to that lecherous, treacherous Count Almaviva!"

The Count is stunned but delighted and asks, "Then you truly love Lindoro?"

Rosina sadly confirms that this is so.

"Then," says her beloved, "I can keep it a secret no longer. I am not Lindoro. I am the Count Almaviva!"

It is Rosina's turn to be astonished and delighted. Indeed, she is ecstatic to discover that she is to become the Countess Almaviva.

Figaro too is happy, but his immediate concern is to get the lovers, who now wish only to embrace each other, out of the house. As he begins to lead them out he sees two men with a lantern standing at the door, and decides they must leave via the balcony, but a quick investigation reveals that the ladder has been removed. Trapped, they wait nervously as the two men come in. They are none other than Don Basilio and the notary. The clever Figaro quickly intercedes and tells the notary he has been summoned to marry the Count Almaviva and this young woman. "Where is Doctor Bartolo?" Don Basilio demands, but his silence is quickly bought by the Count for a gold ring and the threat of two bullets in the head.

With record speed the papers are signed and Rosina and the Count are married just as Doctor Bartolo bursts in, followed by an officer and his men. "Arrest these thieves!" he demands, pointing at Figaro and the Count.

The Count orders them to stand back. "This woman is my bride, and I am the Count Almaviva." Turning to Bartolo, he says, "Your greed shall not stand in love's way. However, you may keep Rosina's dowry."

These last words produce a stunning transformation in Bartolo, who immediately recovers from his anger and graciously accepts defeat. Everyone blesses Rosina and the Count, and Figaro merrily blows out the flame of his lantern, signaling the end of another job well done by the famed Barber of Seville!

THE MARRIAGE OF FIGARO

Opera in Four Acts
by
WOLFGANG AMADEUS MOZART
Première: Burgtheater, Vienna, May 1, 1786

ACT I

IN A sparsely furnished room in the castle of the Count Almaviva near Seville, Figaro, a servant of the Count, is busily measuring floor space, while Susanna, his wife-to-be, is fussing with her wedding veil. Figaro tells her that he is measuring the area to find the best place to put their bed. To Figaro's amazement, she is appalled at the prospect of this handsome room becoming their bedroom. Susanna explains that the room's proximity to the Count's chambers makes her a fairly easy mark should he send Figaro on some fool errand. "Our dear Count," she explains, "is interested in reinstating the law which grants him the feudal 'Droits du Seigneur,' and he wants to claim those rights with me!"

Figaro is outraged. At the time of his marriage to the Countess, the Count willingly gave up this feudal right to take the groom's place for the wedding night when any of his subjects marry. Now, evidently, he is no longer so enchanted with his wife, and his eye has begun to rove. A tiny bell summons Susanna to wait on the Countess. Left alone, Figaro vents his anger and vows that the Count will dance to his tune. A scheme beginning to form in Figaro's clever mind, he rushes off to set it in motion.

The room does not remain empty for long. In comes the aging spinster Marcellina, housekeeper to the Count, accompanied by the elderly Doctor Bartolo, with whom she is discussing a legal contract she holds in her hand. Figaro once borrowed money from her, promising that he would either pay it back or marry her. Since he has not repaid her, she contends he cannot marry Susanna *and* that he must marry her instead! Doctor Bartolo is delighted. Years ago, when he was guardian of Rosina (the Countess) and wanted to marry her himself, Figaro foiled his plans, helping the Count to win her instead. Now Bartolo sees an opportunity for vengeance and vows he will force Figaro to fulfill his contract and marry Marcellina.

Marcellina is encouraged by Bartolo's involvement. She remains in the room to snoop, and is surprised by Susanna's return. The two women compliment each other sarcastically, but when Susanna mocks the older woman's advanced age, Marcellina storms out.

Returning to her wedding preparations, Susanna is interrupted by the young page, Cherubino.

The impetuous adolescent is distraught. "The Count caught me alone with Barbarina, and for that he has ordered me to leave. I will never see you again."

Susanna is amused. "I thought it was the Countess you loved."

Cherubino admits it but can hardly aspire so high. Then, catching sight of one of the Countess's ribbons, he snatches it away from Susanna, giving in exchange his latest love song.

Susanna is entertained by his youthful ardor, but is alarmed when the Count is heard approaching. Cherubino ducks behind a chair.

The Count is delighted to find Susanna alone and immediately begins to speak of love to her. She is annoyed by his talk, but also nervous that he will find the page. In any event, the Count's advances are soon interrupted by the approach of Don Basilio, a music teacher and accomplice of the Count in his amorous adventures. The Count, not wanting to be caught alone with Susanna, decides to hide behind the chair where Cherubino is hidden. The agile page has anticipated this, and just as the Count slides behind the chair, Cherubino slips onto the seat, where Susanna hastily draws a cover over him, all in a split second, as Don Basilio walks in.

An incurable gossip, Basilio prattles on to Susanna about Cherubino's habit of staring longingly at the Countess until an infuriated Count emerges from behind the chair and orders the delighted Don Basilio to find the scoundrel, Cherubino, and throw him out! Susanna tries to persuade the Count that Basilio is just a vicious gossip and not to be heeded.

The Count demurs. "I've caught Cherubino before. Earlier today, I went to see Antonio, the gardener. His daughter, Barbarina, seemed so nervous, I began to look around, and when I lifted the tablecloth, there was . . ." For emphasis, the Count snatches up the cover on the chair. ". . . Cherubino!"

The poor page looks as if he is trying to disappear. Basilio is beside himself with joy, the Count choleric with rage. But before he can punish Cherubino, Figaro marches in leading a group of servants who have come to sing the praises of their "enlightened" lord. They tell him they are honored to serve a man who has abolished the "Droits du Seigneur." Figaro points out that he and Susanna are the first to be married under the new decree, and asks the Count to place the bridal veil on his "chaste and spotless" bride, thereby signifying permission to marry. The Count stalls the would-be revelers by promising a lavish celebration later that evening. The servants file out, disappointed.

Figaro remains behind with Susanna, Cherubino, the Count, and Don Basilio. He asks why at such a joyous time Cherubino is depressed. Susanna explains that he has been banished by the Count. Cherubino now kneels before the Count and begs forgiveness, subtly reminding him that he overheard his passionate advances to Susanna. The Count forgives him, but to get rid of him orders Cherubino to join a military regiment stationed in Seville. Pleased with his solution, the Count takes Don Basilio with him and leaves the room.

Figaro advises Cherubino to ignore the Count's orders and to wait until after the wedding before departing for the glories and rigors of military life. Cherubino listens enthralled until he realizes that Figaro is making fun of him. He rushes out, more depressed than ever.

Left alone at last, Figaro and Susanna collapse laughingly into each other's arms.

ACT II

Later the same day, the Countess Almaviva is sitting alone in her room, melancholy over the waning of her husband's love. Susanna comes in and tries to console her by pointing out how jealous he still is. The two ladies are suddenly interrupted by Figaro, who is cheerful now that he has devised a plan to thwart the Count's advances to Susanna. To make him more jealous, he will send his lordship an anonymous letter informing him that his wife has a lover. Then Susanna will offer to rendezvous with him in the garden. Instead of Susanna, however, it will be Cherubino dressed as a woman who will keep the appointment. "And when our roving Count least expects it, the Countess will surprise him. Cherubino will be here soon so that you may dress him up for his meeting with the Count!" Figaro assures the women that all is safe because the Count has gone out hunting and is not expected back for a while. Very pleased with himself, Figaro leaves.

Within moments there is a knock on the door, and in marches Cherubino, dashingly dressed in military attire. Susanna coaxes Cherubino to sing his latest love song, a tender testament to his infatuation with love in general and with the Countess in particular. Then the women lock the outside door, and Susanna begins the difficult task of dressing the boy in women's clothes. Cherubino fidgets constantly, always trying to gaze at the Countess, while Susanna strives valiantly to make a convincing job of the disguise. Charming as he is, nothing seems exactly right and Susanna goes to her own room to look for other clothes.

Alone with Cherubino, the Countess teases him about her ribbon which he has wrapped around his arm and he shows her his hastily issued army commission, which she notices has not yet received an official seal. A loud knock at the locked bedroom door and the angry, bellowing voice of the Count throws them both into a panic. The frantic Cherubino gathers up his clothes, looking for a place to hide, and as the Count continues to shout, rushes into the Countess's dressing room, locking the door behind him. Trying to regain her composure, the Countess unlocks the bedroom door to admit her angry husband.

"Since when do you lock your door?" he rages.

Flustered, she explains that she and Susanna have been trying on clothes for the wedding, and that Susanna has just gone to her own room. At this moment a tremendous crash inside the dressing room fuels the Count's suspicions. The Countess changes her story, saying that Susanna has actually gone into the dressing room to try on her wedding gown. The Count doesn't believe a word, but demands, in that case, to see Susanna. Meanwhile, unseen by either one, Susanna has slipped into the room, and observing how the situation has developed, she hides in an alcove. Pretending outrage, the Countess refuses to give her husband the key to the dressing room door. The Count's limited patience runs out, and he decides to get some tools so that he can force his way into the dressing room. He locks the door to Susanna's room and taking the Countess with him, the Count also locks the main bedroom door from the outside.

Susanna now rushes to the locked dressing room and tells Cherubino that he must get away. Coming out of the closet, the page realizes that there is no other way to escape so he jumps out of the window. There is a loud crash beneath. Susanna screams, then runs to the window and is relieved to see that Cherubino is alive and almost out of sight. She takes his place in the dressing room to await the Count's return.

As they walk back in, the Countess tries to defuse the bomb she is sure will explode when the Count forces open the dressing room door. She tells him, "You won't find Susanna in there, but rather a young boy who certainly can give you no cause for jealousy. It's only Cherubino!"

The Count flies into a rage, and accuses her of being unfaithful. Angrier than ever, he swears he will kill the boy inside when, to his surprise, the door opens and Susanna walks out, curtsying to her lord and lady. The Count, totally bewildered, inspects the interior of the dressing room himself. The Countess tries to conceal her own bewilderment and Susanna quietly tells her lady of the page's dramatic escape. The Count, satisfied that the dressing room is indeed empty, returns to the bedroom full of apologies for doubting his wife's fidelity.

The Countess is now righteously incensed, and it takes some begging on his part, but at last she weakens. "Why is it, Susanna, women can never be firm?" She and Susanna explain that the mysterious letter the Count received was part of a trick Figaro was going to play on him. The Count is angered at this hubris on the part of his servant, but agrees to forgive in return for his wife's pardon.

Just as all seems to be settled, Figaro comes in ready to take Susanna off to the wedding. But the Count detains him, telling him that there are a few matters that first need to be resolved.

"What do you know about this letter?" he asks, showing Figaro the anonymous note. Despite the Count's persistent questioning and signals from the women that the truth is known, Figaro steadfastly denies any knowledge of the mysterious missive.

With the situation at a stalemate, Antonio, the gardener, bursts into the room carrying a handful of crushed flowers. Outraged, he tells the Count that many objects have been thrown out of the windows into the garden, but "Today," he yells, "a whole man was thrown from the window, destroying my flowers!!!"

The Count's suspicions are again aroused, and he questions the gardener thoroughly about the incident.

The women whisper to Figaro for help and he claims responsibility for the jump. He explains, "I was waiting here for Susanna when I heard your lordship shouting outside. Remembering my perhaps misguided letter, I got so scared, I jumped."

Antonio approaches Figaro. "Then this paper I found in the garden must be yours."

The Count snatches it. "Do you know what this paper is?" he asks.

While Figaro looks through his pockets pretending to try to figure out what he has lost, the Countess sneaks a look at the paper and recognizes Cherubino's commission. She whispers this information to Susanna, who passes it on to Figaro, who in turn tells the Count that the paper is Cherubino's commission.

"Why did you have it?" demands the Count.

Figaro is stymied. "It needed . . ." The Countess quietly tells Susanna that it needed sealing and she passes it along. Again Figaro has the answer and the Count crumples the commission in anger, realizing that he has been foiled again.

The others are just beginning to sigh in relief when Marcellina, Doctor Bartolo, and Don Basilio come in to present Marcellina's case against Figaro. This is just what the Count has been waiting for. He is delighted, Susanna and the Countess are shaken, and Figaro is enraged. The adversaries shout insults at each other until the Count restores some semblance of order by serenely stating that he will judge the case. Everyone else storms out.

ACT III

That evening, alone in the main hall of his castle, the Count muses on the bizarre happenings of the day, and is somewhat sullen when Susanna comes in and asks to borrow smelling salts for the Countess, who is suffering from a headache. This is only a pretext. In fact, the Countess has urged her to make a tryst with the Count.

"You had better keep them for yourself," the Count tells her. "You will certainly need them after you lose your bridegroom to Marcellina."

Susanna shrugs. "I will free Figaro from his debt with the dowry that you promised to give me if I complied with your desires."

The Count is thrilled by Susanna's sudden submission, but he can hardly believe his good fortune. Repeatedly, he makes her promise to meet him in the garden later that evening. Repeatedly, she promises to do so until at last he lets her go. Running into Figaro on the way out, she tells him that without lawyers he has won his case. Unfortunately, the Count has overheard her remark and once more suspects that his servants are trying to thwart him. Enraged, he vows he will defeat them, and storms out.

The Countess comes in, looking for Susanna. Alone, she reminisces, yearning for the early days of her marriage when she and the Count were so much in love. The memories reinforce her determination to regain her husband, and she leaves in search of Susanna.

The Count returns to render a decision in Marcellina's case against Figaro. The principals assemble along with Don Curzio, legal aide to His Lordship. "The decision is clear," Don Curzio announces. "Figaro must either marry or pay Marcellina."

As Marcellina and Doctor Bartolo gloat over their victory, Figaro stuns them with the news that since he was of noble birth he cannot be married without his parents' consent, and since he was a foundling, he does not know who they are. They demand proof of his alleged noble birth, and he tells them that jewels and fancy embroidered clothes were found with him. "Still more conclusive," he continues, "I have a birthmark branded on my arm."

"A spatula on your right arm?" Marcellina asks.

Figaro is very surprised. "How did you know?"

Bartolo points at Marcellina and tells Figaro, "This is your mother!"

The spinster returns the favor: "And this is your father." She points to Bartolo.

The Count and Don Curzio can't believe their ears and eyes as they watch the reunited family embrace happily. Just as Figaro is kissing his newfound mother, Susanna comes in bringing a purse to pay the debt, but the sight of Figaro wrapped in Marcellina's arms enrages her. Figaro calms her down, explaining that he is the illegitimate offspring of a onetime romance between Marcellina and Doctor Bartolo. When she recovers from the shock, she too rejoices and even manages to embrace Marcellina. Thwarted again, the Count leaves in a huff, taking Don Curzio with him.

At Marcellina's insistence, Bartolo agrees to marry her that very evening in a double ceremony with Susanna and Figaro. Hugging each other, they all go off to get ready.

Susanna re-enters with the Countess and the two women laugh as she tells the incredulous Countess of the most recent events. The Countess decides that they must reinforce the net if she is to trap her wayward husband, and she instructs Susanna to write a note telling the Count to meet her in the pine grove of the garden that evening. They seal the note with a pin, adding the words: "Please return the pin."

A group of peasant girls enters to bring their freshly picked flowers to the Countess. She accepts them graciously. "But who," she asks Barbarina, "is that shy girl hiding behind you?" Barbarina says it is her cousin who has come for the wedding. Susanna and the Countess comment on how much she resembles a certain young page. As the "girl" kneels before the Countess, the Count and Antonio rush in and pull off her bonnet, revealing that "she" is none other than Cherubino. Once again the Count is furious and threatens Cherubino with punishment, but Barbarina reminds him of promises he made her every time they kissed. Embarrassed, the Count gives permission for Barbarina to marry Cherubino.

Figaro arrives and announces that the wedding procession is ready to begin. The Count's loyal subjects file into the hall for the double wedding, and the Count, grouchy about the way everything has gone against him, and still suspicious of his servants and his wife, grudgingly performs the marriages.

As she kneels before him, Susanna secretly slips her note to the Count. It marvelously improves his mood, and he announces that this glorious double wedding will be celebrated with fitting splendor, including fireworks and dancing. The crowd cheers the Count's generosity and, as the Count and Countess leave the main hall, the newly-married couples embrace happily.

ACT IV

Night has fallen, and the darkness which obscures the garden is pierced by the light of a lantern. Barbarina walks through the garden searching for the pin that the Count has given her to return to Susanna and which she has lost. Figaro and Marcellina come by and she blurts out her troubles. Before she knows it, she has told them the Count's exact instructions: "'Return this pin to Susanna, and tell her that it is the key to the pine grove.'"

Taking a pin from Marcellina, Figaro gives it to Barbarina and sends the girl on her way. Then he gives vent to his distress. That his wife could be unfaithful on their wedding night! He tells his mother that he will get revenge on behalf of all cheated husbands and rushes off. Marcellina, who feels it is women who are always the victims, decides that she will warn Susanna.

Figaro leads Basilio and Bartolo into the garden and instructs them to remain hidden until he calls for them, when they are to rush out and surprise the lecherous Count and Susanna. Basilio and Bartolo hide while Figaro lingers to bemoan the suffering caused men by the treachery of women. Then he joins the others in hiding.

Susanna wanders in. Warned by Marcellina, she knows that her jealous husband is spying, and decides to torment him by musing aloud of the joy that awaits her when her lover joins her later that evening. She goes into the pavilion, where she exchanges cloaks with the Countess. The Countess, now disguised as Susanna, enters the pine grove. As she waits for the Count, Cherubino unexpectedly arrives on the scene. He believes her to be Susanna, and decides to have some fun. As Figaro and Susanna watch from their separate hiding places, Cherubino asks the disguised Countess to kiss him. Just as he is growing more and more importunate, the Count arrives for his rendezvous. Both the Count and Figaro rush forward to thwart the page's advances, but in the darkness Cherubino escapes and the Count hits Figaro, who staggers off.

At last the Count is alone with the woman he believes to be Susanna. He presents her with a beautiful jewel. The Countess, imitating Susanna's voice, accepts the gift. Figaro, still convinced that the woman is indeed Susanna, decides that he has seen enough and he makes a great deal of noise, which sends the Count off into the trees and the disguised Countess into the pavilion.

Susanna, disguised as the Countess, now comes out of hiding to meet Figaro, who is livid over what he has just seen. He tells the "Countess" about it. Replying, Susanna forgets to disguise her voice, and Figaro recognizes her. Now he joins the game, but does not tell her. With mock seriousness, he says he wants revenge for what Susanna and the Count have done to him, and he offers his "services" to the "Countess" so that they may both get even.

Now Susanna is beside herself with rage, and explodes: "I'll teach you to behave." She chases him around the garden, hitting him whenever possible, until he surrenders to laughter, confessing that he knew all along she was Susanna. He falls at her feet. "I recognized the voice that I adore." Reconciled, they throw their arms around each other.

Hearing the Count as he stumbles back into the grove looking for Susanna, they decide that the only way to bring this crazy day to an end is to get even with him.

Susanna quickly resumes her disguise as the Countess, and she and Figaro embrace. The Count is enraged when he thinks he sees his wife in Figaro's arms, and he rushes forward, calling to his servants for assistance. Susanna, as the "Countess," manages to escape to the pavilion, but Figaro is caught and begs for mercy, as Basilio, Bartolo, Antonio, and Curzio come running. The Count rushes to the pavilion to get his unfaithful wife, and pulls out Cherubino, Barbarina, Marcellina, and finally Susanna, still disguised as the Countess. In shock, the others watch the "Countess" beg her husband for forgiveness. They too add their pleas to hers. The Count only becomes more adamant in his refusal.

Suddenly, a soft, sweet voice is heard, another voice asking him to forgive. They are all silent as the real Countess emerges from the pine grove. Then, Susanna, still on her knees before the Count, removes the cloak that was her disguise.

Realizing, for the moment at least, the foolishness of his ways, the Count drops to his knees before his wife to ask for her forgiveness and love. Magnanimous in victory, she pardons him. The happy couples embrace, and then rush off into the darkness to celebrate.

RIGOLETTO

Opera in Three Acts
by
GIUSEPPE VERDI
Première: Teatro La Fenice, Venice, March 11, 1851

ACT I

Scene 1

IT IS the Renaissance, and the artistic brilliance of the age is matched only by its pervasive lust and political opportunism. At the Court of Mantua, as in most Italian cities of the time, debauchery reigns and violence is commonplace. Each night the nobles and courtiers gather for the evening's entertainment in the magnificent palace of the Duke, and through the bright and richly furnished halls, the revelers dance and eat and plot a new seduction or form a new cabal. Most licentious of them all is the handsome and charming Duke himself, whose many infidelities are notorious.

Tonight he confides in Borsa, one of his courtiers, that his latest quarry is a beautiful young woman whom he has seen in church every week for three months. "I finally followed her home. She lives in a remote street, and some man, I could not tell who, visits her very night. But she does not yet know me."

A group of ladies and cavaliers passes by and the Duke is disturbed by one very lovely woman, the Countess Ceprano, whose beauty he praises loudly. When Borsa cautions him to be more discreet, so her husband cannot hear, he disdainfully declares that all pretty women are fair prey and that he has nothing but scorn for jealous husbands, and besides he has never lost his heart to any one woman. Under the watchful eye of the Count Ceprano the Duke dances with the Countess and flamboyantly pleads his passion. He ends his declaration by escorting her out of the room.

As they leave, the court jester, a hunchback named Rigoletto, mockingly observes, "What honor for the house of Ceprano."

As the other guests laugh, Count Ceprano angrily follows his wife. Rigoletto strolls away, looking for other objects of his ridicule.

While the dance continues, Marullo, another courtier, brings some astounding gossip to his fellow guests—the ugly hunchback, Rigoletto, has a mistress he visits every night! As the noblemen reflect on this bit of incredible news, the Duke returns with Rigoletto, both followed closely by an enraged Ceprano. The Duke asks Rigoletto for advice on how to get the Countess Ceprano away from her husband and the jester suggests imprisoning the Count.

"No, no," says the Duke.

Growing meaner, Rigoletto advises beheading him. Ceprano angrily draws his sword. Rigoletto continues to taunt him and the Duke must finally tell his jester to be quiet and leads him away in order to restore peace.

But there is no one this lowly jester has not offended with his mockery, and led by Ceprano, the nobles now agree to meet at the home of Rigoletto's "mistress" on the following night to take revenge on him.

The Duke and Rigoletto return to the drinking and dancing guests. Suddenly there is a scuffle at the door and a black garbed figure bursts in.

"Monterone," the guests murmur apprehensively.

This nobleman demands revenge for the Duke's seduction of his young daughter.

The Duke does not even bother to reply. Instead, he allows Rigoletto to deride the grief of the distraught father, and ridicules him for disturbing the party.

With insult added to injury, Monterone's fury escalates. "I shall never leave you alone," he shouts, "even if you kill me."

"Arrest him," the Duke orders.

As he is taken away, Monterone, his face contorted with contempt, turns to Rigoletto. "You may laugh at a father's grief. But I place a curse on you as well. A curse on both your houses."

317

SCENE 2

The next night, as Rigoletto makes his way down the dark street to his home, a small knot of terror builds within him. He cannot rid his thoughts of Monterone's curse. Passing the Ceprano Palace, he nears the gate to the house next door where his daughter, Gilda, lives.

Out of the shadows steps a dark cloaked figure. He points to the sword concealed beneath his coat. "I am a swordsman and for a small fee I will gladly dispatch any rival you may have for the affections of the woman in your house!"

Rigoletto shows some interest and asks how such assassinations are accomplished.

"My sister lures the prey into our house. There I swiftly kill him! My name is Sparafucile, from Bourgogne. If you need my services you can find me here any night!"

Rigoletto watches as the mysterious assassin disappears into the night, and thinks of how alike they are: "He kills with a dagger and I with my tongue. That wretched curse, why won't it leave me? I know I am vile and vicious but nature has already cursed me, and men have corrupted me." How he hates his life and despises himself and envies the Duke for whom he must act the monstrous buffoon. Only in his own home can he stop being a man who enjoys hurting others. Again thoughts of the curse return to plague him, but this time he forces himself to dismiss them, and enters the courtyard of his house.

A beautiful young woman rushes to greet him. His daughter, Gilda, is the only thing in life he treasures, but his joy in seeing her is always overlaid with fear lest she be discovered and become another victim of the Court.

Naturally she is lonely and bored. He wants to know whether she has left the house.

"Only to go to church," she assures him. She asks him to tell her about his life, what he does, who his friends are, where he was born. He does not want her to know about the horrible life he lives and will tell her nothing except that her mother was an angel whose loss he still mourns.

"You are my family, my friends, my life. You are all I have."

Rigoletto calls for Giovanna, the nurse, and instructs her to make sure the doors are always locked and to watch over his daughter carefully. Suddenly, he hears a noise outside and rushes out to investigate.

While he is gone, the Duke, disguised as a student, slips into the garden unseen, except by Giovanna, to whom he tosses a purse. Rigoletto soon returns, still disturbed, and asks if anyone has ever followed Gilda home from church. Reassured by Giovanna's "Never!" Rigoletto embraces his daughter and prepares to leave. Again he cautions Giovanna not to open the door to anyone.

She asks, "Not even for the Duke?"

Rigoletto responds, "Especially not for the Duke!"

Gilda is filled with guilt at having lied to her father, for in fact she has seen a young man follow her from church. He was very handsome and has been in her thoughts all day and in her dreams at night.

The Duke steps from his hiding place and kneels at Gilda's feet, motioning to Giovanna, who discreetly obliges by going into the house.

He ardently declares his love. Gilda at first tries to make him leave, but she soon succumbs to the seductive charms of the poor student who calls himself Gualtier Maldè. She admits she loves him.

Outside on the street Ceprano points out the house of "Rigoletto's mistress" to Borsa. Giovanna has heard the noise and she rushes to the garden to warn Gilda and her lover that someone is coming. Reluctantly, they bid each other farewell.

Alone, Gilda muses rhapsodically on the beloved name of Gualtier Maldè, the first name to make her heart beat with passion. She takes her candle and makes her way up to the balcony that leads to her room. Ceprano and the other courtiers watching from the street see her and, still believing she is Rigoletto's mistress, prepare to abduct her.

They are interrupted by Rigoletto, who, still anxious about Gilda's safety, has returned. Ceprano wants to kill him, but Marullo declares that revenge will be sweeter if they fool the jester.

In the dark, Rigoletto cannot see them. "Who goes there?" he cries out suspiciously.

Marullo tells him that they are going to abduct Ceprano's wife and the jester is so relieved he offers to help. On the pretext of putting a mask on Rigoletto, Marullo blindfolds him, and instructs him to hold the ladder in place. Rigoletto obliges, not even realizing in the intense darkness of night that he cannot see. He stands by as the noblemen climb up the ladder, break into his house, and carry his struggling daughter away. Suddenly, he hears the faint terrified cries of "Father! Father!" He tears the blindfold from his face and rushes into the house. Too late. Savagely, he drags out a stunned Giovanna. Then realizing what has happened, he drops to his knees and piteously moans, "Ah-h-h, the curse!"

319

ACT II

The Duke wanders about his palace, fuming. Having made another visit to Gilda's house, only to find her gone, he is sure she has been abducted and swears vengeance. And now that she seems beyond his grasp, he is sure that she is the one woman in the world who might have inspired in him true and lasting affection.

His moment of sentiment is soon aborted. The courtiers burst in to amuse him with the story of how they have fooled his jester. They of course believe that they have stolen Rigoletto's "mistress," but the Duke realizes it is Gilda, and on being told that she has been brought to the palace, he rushes off to see her.

Rigoletto ambles in, trying to conceal his despair by humming a little tune. All the while he moves about restlessly, trying to find some signs of his daughter. Enjoying his pain, the others taunt and tease him.

A page enters with a message from the Duchess to the Duke. When Rigoletto hears the courtiers tell him that the Duke is unavailable and cannot see anyone, he drops all pretense and declares that they must return the girl they abducted in the night. The noblemen mockingly tell him that if he has lost his mistress he should look for her elsewhere.

With frightening intensity he bellows, "It's my daughter I want!"

The courtiers' taunts have been silenced, but they restrain Rigoletto as he hysterically tries to force his way to the Duke's chambers to rescue Gilda. Wild with anger, he demands that they return her. When his curses elicit no response, he turns to entreaties, pleads forgiveness, and begs them to give him back his beloved daughter.

Suddenly, Gilda emerges from the Duke's bedroom and throws herself into her father's loving arms. Desperately he tries to act as if nothing has happened. But weeping, Gilda tells him that she must speak to him alone. Rigoletto orders the courtiers to leave and now somewhat abashed, they do. Gilda pours out her tale. "Each time I went to church," she tells him, "I saw a handsome youth. Our lips never spoke but our eyes met in love. Last night he came secretly to see me at the house and told me he was a poor student and that he loved me. He was so sweet, so . . . glowing. He awoke my heart to love. After he left, that band abducted me and brought me here!"

As Rigoletto tries to console his daughter, Monterone, in chains, is led by guards through the hall on his way to a prison cell. Seeing a portrait of the Duke he despairingly observes that his curse has apparently been for naught.

Rigoletto shouts after him, "No! You shall have your vengeance!" He shakes his fist at the portrait and vows to take revenge on the lecherous Duke.

Gilda pleads for the Duke. "Though he has wronged me, I love him. For my sake, forgive him."

"No!" Rigoletto declares. "I shall have revenge!"

ACT III

On a bank of the Mincio River toward the outskirts of the city stands the ancient, isolated inn of Sparafucile. Under cover of darkness, Rigoletto has brought Gilda to this deserted spot in the hope of proving to her how base the Duke really is. For in the month that has passed since she was abducted for his pleasure, her love for the Duke has not waned, and even as they approach the inn, she pleads with her father to forgive him.

Roughly, Rigoletto asks, "Would you love him even if he betrayed you?"

"But he adores me," she replies.

He urges her to look through a crack in the ramshackle wall. Inside, the Duke sits at a table and loudly calls for wine.

As Sparafucile fills his glass, the Duke laughingly holds forth on the fickleness of women.

Sparafucile's voluptuous sister comes down the stairs to join the Duke. As Gilda watches, the Duke tells Maddalena that ever since the day he first laid eyes on her he has adored her. Maddalena is too experienced to believe this is the first time he has ever said these words to a woman, and coquettishly she teases him. It only makes him more ardent.

Gilda moans, "My heart is broken," and she turns to her father for comfort. Certain that his daughter is finally convinced of the Duke's duplicity, Rigoletto instructs her to return home, dress in men's clothes, and travel to Verona where he will join her after he has exacted vengeance.

When Gilda has left, Rigoletto finds Sparafucile, to whom he pays the first installment of the assassination fee. "I shall return at midnight after the deed is done to pay you the balance." There is a flash of lightning in the sky. "I myself shall throw the body into the river."

Sparafucile acknowledges the orders with a nod, and says to himself, "A storm is coming."

Meanwhile, the Duke's flirtation with Maddalena has been progressing, and when Sparafucile's return interrupts them, the Duke decides to stay the night. Shown to an attic room by Sparafucile, he promptly falls asleep.

Maddalena tells her brother she is taken by the handsome guest and wants him to live, but the assassin is interested only in the money that the murder will bring and orders her to fetch his sword.

A tremendous storm is brewing. Gilda, disguised in the clothes of a man, stands on the street outside the door to the inn. Spying through the hole in the wall, she sees Maddalena give her brother the sword and hears her say, "Brother, that man looks like Apollo. I love him. We must not kill him!" Sparafucile does not answer. Instead, he pulls out a sack in which to hide the body. Maddalena then suggests that he kill the hunchback himself when he returns.

Sparafucile's professional pride is offended and he declares, "No client of mine has ever been cheated!" Maddalena threatens to warn the Duke and Sparafucile finally promises that should someone else come to the inn before midnight, that person shall die in the Duke's place.

It is small comfort to Maddalena. "In this weather no one will come here."

Hearing this, Gilda decides that life is not worth living without him and she shall die in the Duke's place. As a nearby clock strikes eleven-thirty, she knocks.

Sparafucile is surprised, Maddalena delighted.

"Give a poor beggar shelter for the night!" Gilda calls, and prays to God for mercy.

Maddalena opens the door, the assassin grabs the disguised Gilda and brutally stabs her.

The violence of the storm has abated as Rigoletto approaches the inn and waits for the clock to strike twelve when he may savor the moment of vengeance for which he has been lusting. Exactly at midnight Sparafucile greets him and lays down a sack. "Here is your man! He's dead! Let us toss him into the river."

Rigoletto pays him and says he will throw the corpse into the river by himself.

"Do it further down where the water is deeper," Sparafucile advises, and re-enters the inn.

Rigoletto gloats over the sack and kicks it a little. He debates opening it so he can enjoy the sight of his master's lifeless body, but decides not to take the time. He starts to drag the sack to the river. Just then the voice of the Duke, muted but clear, floats on the night air. Bewildered and terror-stricken, Rigoletto quickly cuts open the sack, asking himself, "But then who is this?" He turns the body to see the face and screams. "Gilda! God! My daughter!" Desperate, he bangs on the door of the inn but there is no answer. Still alive but very weak, Gilda calls to her father. As he cradles her in his arms, she feebly tells him, "I am so sorry to have done this to you, but I loved him so much that I had to die for him! Forgive us, my father. I shall join my mother in heaven and pray for you there."

He begs her not to die. But as she once more asks forgiveness, her voice fades away and he is left with her dead body in his arms.

Bending over her, Rigoletto sobs pathetically and utters two words: "The curse!"

THE CORONATION OF POPPEA

Opera in a Prologue and Two Acts
by
CLAUDIO MONTEVERDI
Première: Teatro di SS. Giovanni e Paolo, Venice, Autumn 1642

PROLOGUE

HIGH IN the heavens above ancient Rome, the Gods of Virtue and Fortune squabble with Love over whose power is the greatest. To settle the dispute, it is clear that they are going to meddle in the affairs of mankind.

ACT I

SCENE 1

Returning from battle, in the ceaseless wars of the Roman Empire, the noble Ottone goes directly to the house of his mistress, Poppea. It is not yet dawn and he is dismayed to find Imperial guards protecting the entrance. He realizes that while he has been at war, the faithless Poppea has taken the Emperor Nero as her lover. He is devastated. "I stand here alone wooing the cold marble of her house, while Nero lies in her warm arms!" His voice awakens one of the guards, and Ottone runs away.

By now both guards are awake and they curse Poppea, Nero, Rome, and the army for making them stay awake during the night, until they decide that it is wiser to keep one's eyes open and one's mouth shut.

Nero and Poppea emerge from her house, she pleading with him to stay, because, she says, she cannot bear to be away from him. He is clearly swayed by her pleas but explains that Rome cannot know of their love until he repudiates the current Empress, Ottavia.

"You will come back?"

He swears he cannot live without her and she lets him leave.

SCENE 2

Excited by her conquest of the Emperor, Poppea gleefully anticipates putting on the royal robes. "Nothing can prevent my ascent," she gloats, "for Love and Fortune are my allies." Poppea's nurse, Arnalta, tries to temper her lady's optimism, cautioning that Fate has a way of twisting the best of events so that they become deadly. Poppea again affirms her faith in her gods. "I have Love and Fortune fighting for me."

The skeptical Arnalta declares, "It is crazy to have faith in a blind little boy with a bow and arrow, and a hairless hag!"

SCENE 3

In the Imperial Palace, Ottavia bemoans her fate. "What am I doing here, a scorned Empress whose husband finds happiness in the arms of Poppea!" She calls on Jove to punish Nero. "If you don't," she tells him, "you are impotent!!" Frightened by the blasphemous nature of what she has said, she retracts, deciding to contain her grief and to suffer her torment and anguish in silence.

The philosopher Seneca enters to confer with the distraught Empress. Seeing her tears he comments on the irony of her plight. "You have risen to the seat of empire but endure the cruelties suffered by slaves. But tears are unworthy of you."

She tells Seneca that Nero wants to repudiate her so he may marry Poppea. "You, Seneca, the Roman Senate, and my people must pray for me. I must even offer prayers for myself!"

With this admission she takes her leave, accompanied by her page, who, in parting, angrily warns Seneca, "If you do not help the Empress, I will burn your books and your beard!"

Alone, Seneca has a vision of the goddess Pallas Athena, who warns him of omens foretelling his downfall and death if he meddles in this affair. No sooner has the vision faded than Nero enters, loudly proclaiming that he has decided to rid himself of Ottavia in order to marry Poppea. As his counselor and long-time mentor, Seneca tries in vain to dissuade him. The Emperor arrogantly declares, "I don't care what the Senate or the people think. I will rip out the tongue of any person who dares to speak against me!!"

Seneca notes that "Silencing men only causes more of them to talk."

Nero fumes: "Ottavia is frigid and barren."

Seneca responds, "He who is unjust needs excuses!"

This drives Nero into a rage, and with the words "Poppea shall be my wife! I don't care about you, the Senate or the people!" he departs.

SCENE 4

That night, in the arms of Poppea, Nero passionately tells her how he wants to share the crown with her. Drunk with love he declares that Rome and even all of Italy are too small to pay proper homage to her beauty. She takes advantage of his amorous state to play politics. "Do you know that Seneca, that wise counselor of yours, tells everyone that he is the ruler of the land?"

Still angry at Seneca's advice earlier in the day, Nero explodes: "That doddering old fool?" Without so much as a second thought, he calls to the Captain of the Guard and orders him to find Seneca and tell him that he must die before the night is out!

Her maneuver successful, the cunning Poppea victoriously takes the Emperor into her arms.

SCENE 5

Outside Poppea's house Ottone bemoans her rejection of his love. Poppea comes out onto the balcony and orders him to leave her alone. "I have abandoned you in order to win a throne."

He is bitter. "So your only emotion is ambition? My devotion means nothing?"

She says, "I belong to Nero!" and goes back into the house.

Ottone consoles himself with the thought that there is nothing really human about Poppea except her beauty. He tries desperately to think of other things but he is still obsessed. The lovely Drusilla appears. She has long been in love with him, and in his efforts to forget Poppea, Ottone tells her he loves her.

"Just like that?" Drusilla asks.

He explains, "Love is volatile, like fire, and can burn quickly!"

326

Drusilla is easily convinced. Her heart filled with joy, she takes her leave to go see the Empress. Alone, Ottone sadly realizes that while he may speak of loving Drusilla, his heart is still filled with Poppea.

SCENE 6

In the royal garden of the Imperial Palace, the page, driven by sudden new urges, pursues a maidservant. "I am always thinking of your white breasts," he confesses.

She is amused by his discovery of love and he, although overcome by its sweetness, wants to know should love turn bitter would she be able to remove its sting. When she answers yes, they declare their love for each other and innocently decide they will be happy together.

SCENE 7

"Solitude," Seneca muses, "is the haven where the intellect may function best. Away from the crises of the Court, alone with my thoughts is where I feel most secure."

His peace is disturbed by the Captain of the Guards. "Seneca, I am saddened to have found you, although it is you whom I seek. I have been sent by Nero . . ."

Before he can finish, the wise Seneca interrupts: "I understand. Go and tell Nero that I have obeyed. By night I shall be dead and buried."

The news has spread and Seneca's faithful students come to bid their master farewell. "My friends, my time has come. Death is but a short, anguished moment, and it precedes a journey to Olympus, which is the true home of happiness."

His students are unconvinced by his philosophical approach, for none of them would wish to die, and they beg him not to do so. But the wise Seneca knows when the end has come and orders his pupils to prepare his bath so that his blood may flow on the road to death just as life flows.

ACT II

SCENE 1

Nero and his companion Lucano drunkenly cavort about the Imperial Palace in celebration of Seneca's death. They sing love songs to the face which inspires glory and ignites love, and to the lips which cause India and Arabia to offer up their finest pearls and perfumes. Their carousing becomes wilder and more foolish until collapsed in laughter, they toast destiny!

SCENE 2

In another part of the palace, Ottavia has summoned Ottone, and reminding him that he owes his rank to her family, she orders him to kill Poppea. At first he is appalled, but soon the desire for vengeance supplants his horror and although still torn, he agrees to carry out the desperate plan. When Drusilla enters, he asks to borrow her cloak to use as a disguise.

She is only too happy to be of help. "I would give you my life as well." Cautioning him to be careful, she offers to disguise him with her own hands.

SCENE 3

Exulting over Seneca's death, Poppea prays to Love to make her consort to the Emperor. The faithful Arnalta calms her lady with a lullaby until her mistress is sound asleep. Quietly, Arnalta leaves.

The God of Love appears and notes how peacefully Poppea sleeps, unaware that a sword is about to destroy her. As Ottone, disguised as Drusilla, stealthily approaches the sleeping form and murmurs, "Farewell, my beloved," the God of Love stays his hand. Poppea awakens and cries out, forcing Ottone to flee and summoning Arnalta, who orders the servants to chase "Drusilla" and capture her.

SCENE 4

The real Drusilla, waiting happily for news of her rival's end, is confronted by the enraged Arnalta. "Take her prisoner," she orders the guards.

Nero happens by and when he hears of the plot to kill Poppea orders that Drusilla be punished by torture before she is executed. But Ottone steps forward and admits that he alone is guilty, and that it is he who should die.

"No!" says Drusilla. "It was I!"

Fed up with both of them, Nero orders that they be banished to the furthest deserts, stripped of their wealth and rank. "Further," the Emperor continues, "Ottavia is repudiated and banished forever from Rome. Put her in an unsturdy craft and cast her in the waters to the mercy of the winds. Thus shall my anger demonstrate its power."

Stripped of her position, Ottavia bids an emotional farewell to Rome, her fatherland, and her friends. Sadly, she accepts her cruel fate and leaves her family and country, a proud woman, her crownless head held high.

Scene 5

Delighted by the happy turn of fortune, Arnalta announces throughout the streets of Rome that today *her* Poppea ascends to the lofty rank of Empress. Now she too will be elevated to a higher position. "Everyone will flatter me and will call me 'your ladyship,' and how I shall enjoy it," she revels. "Though full of lies, I shall drink their flattery to the brim." Yet, wise woman that she is, her euphoria is tempered by the profound observation that "those who die rich die sadly, but those who die after a life of labor find death to be a pleasant release."

Scene 6

The Imperial Palace is aglow with festivities as consuls and tribunes assemble amid great pomp to confer the rank of Empress upon Poppea. "All Rome declares that you shall wear the crown before which Asia, Africa, and Europe do obeisance!" they declare. Seated at Nero's side, Poppea proudly accepts the crown.

As the consuls and tribunes depart, the Emperor and his new Empress gaze longingly at each other. Embracing, they promise there shall be no more strife or death. Their passion re-ignites in the glow of achieved ambition. They vow to remain together forever as they tell each other, "I am yours. You are mine. You are my joy and my idol." As they celebrate the omnipotence of Love, they are oblivious to the defeat of Virtue.

BORIS GODUNOV

Opera in a Prologue and Four Acts
by
MODEST MUSSORGSKY
Première: Maryinsky Theater, St. Petersburg,
February 8, 1874

PROLOGUE

SCENE 1

IT IS the end of the sixteenth century in feudal Russia. Czar Feodor, son of Ivan the Terrible, has just died without any heirs and the country is left without a natural successor to the throne, for Feodor's only brother, Dimitri, was killed in mysterious circumstances some years before.

The country is in turmoil. The peasants are starving and disaffected, and the boyars—the nobles and landed gentry—have long had an uneasy truce with the czarist regime which, they feel, has usurped much of their power. The nobility is riddled with rival factions and ambitious princes. But only one man is the logical successor—Boris Godunov. Son-in-law of Ivan the Terrible and his most trusted councilor, he has been de facto ruler all through the reign of Feodor. In agreement with the Patriarchs of the Russian Orthodox Church, the Duma has elected him Czar of all Russia.

Seemingly reluctant to accept the crown, Boris has retired to Novodievitch Monastery near Moscow. In the square outside, however, a demonstration has been organized. A crowd of Russian peasants is herded by a police officer who orders them to kneel and pray for a new Czar. As soon as he walks away, they stand up to revile him behind his back and complain about their hard lives. When he returns, they fall to their knees again and in response to his prompting, chant loudly: "Oh, Father, do not forsake these poor peasants. Give us a Czar. Make Boris relent and accept the throne."

The police silence the crowd to allow the clerk of the Duma to address them. "People of Russia, Boris *still* hesitates. Pray to the Lord to convince Boris to lead our troubled land." His exhortation completed, he enters the monastery. Silently, the peasants watch.

As the sunset casts its rays across the courtyard, blind pilgrims enter, praising the faithful and denouncing the corruption that plagues Russia. They circulate among the peasants to distribute amulets and icons. Then, resuming their prayers, they slowly file into the monastery. Some of the peasants compare their prizes, but most stand there dubious and perplexed, bantering with each other until the police officer rounds them up again and orders them to assemble at the Kremlin on the next day.

SCENE 2

The bells of the Kremlin peal, announcing the coronation of Czar Boris Feodorovich. The great square is thronged with people. Flags fly and the gold domes of the churches gleam brightly in the sun. To the sound of solemn chimes, a procession of boyars descends the grand staircase of the Imperial Palace, their destination the Cathedral of the Assumption across the square. Borne in their midst stands the majestic figure of Boris. Inspired by the richness of the spectacle, the sonorous ringing of the bells, and the mood of the crowd, the people cheer wildly.

Bearing his crown and scepter, Boris waits on the cathedral porch for the cries of "Glory" to fade. He addresses them: "My soul is sad, obsessed by evil premonitions. Oh, heavenly Father, I implore you to bless my reign and make me just and merciful. We go now to the tombs of Russia's former monarchs to pray for guidance. Then we shall feast. All are welcome, from boyar to serf."

As the procession moves to the Cathedral of the Archangel, the police desperately try to control the exuberant crowd. The bells ring out again. In renewed frenzy, the people of Russia shout, "Glory to the Czar!"

331

ACT I

SCENE 1

In an austere cell in the Chudoff Monastery, Pimen, a very old monk, writes by the dim light of a candle. Nearby sleeps Grigory, a young novice. Pimen contemplates the massive task on which he has been working. "But one more story to finish and my chronicles will be complete. Perhaps some day a monk will open these books and thus learn the truth of the history of our homeland, a history through which I have lived." With prayers of the monks echoing in the distance, Pimen returns to his writing.

Grigory wakes with a start. Troubled by a recurring dream, he finds solace in the peaceful, contemplative figure of Pimen. Hearing Grigory, Pimen blesses him, and the young monk recounts his harrowing dream. "I walked up a long, twisting staircase which led to a tower. From there all of Moscow was visible. The people swarming in the square below pointed at me. They mocked me and I felt shamed and frightened. Suddenly I fell from the tower. And then I woke!"

Pimen counsels him to fast and to pray. "Even this late in life, if I sleep without praying I sleep restlessly, dreaming of the wild indulgences of youth . . ."

"Ah, but your youth was so exciting!" Grigory interjects. "You fought in great battles and saw the glories of Ivan's court. I have been nothing but a monk. I have never fought in great battles nor have I dined at the Czar's table."

Pimen tells his young colleague not to be taken in by the seeming dazzle of the world outside. "Many times our greatest Czars would have traded their thrones for the humble pallet of a monk. Ivan the Terrible sat here, tears in his eyes, and repented. When his son, Czar Feodor, converted his royal apartments into cells for prayer, Russia was a peaceful land." Pimen's voice grows stern as he concludes, "But now God is angry, for we harbor a murderer!"

Grigory is curious. "Is it true that you were in Uglich when Dimitri was murdered?"

"Yes, and I saw the villains who did the deed after they were captured, and heard them confess that it was Boris who planned it." He adds, "Had Dimitri not been killed he would be your age and ruler of all Russia."

In the distance the church bells ring the Matins. Pimen extinguishes his lamp and Grigory helps him to the door of the cell. Remaining behind for a moment, Grigory is swept by sudden ambition. Perhaps no other dares accuse Boris, but he will avenge the heinous murder of that innocent child.

SCENE 2

At a lonely inn somewhere near the Lithuanian border, two mendicant friars, Varlaam and Missail, greet the proprietress with a call for wine. Accompanying them is Grigory, disguised in peasant's clothes. While the hostess gets the wine, Varlaam asks Grigory why he is so anxious to get to Lithuania. "It makes no difference where you are so long as there is plenty of wine." Taking the bottle from the hostess, Varlaam breaks into a fiendishly gleeful ballad about the battle of Kazan where Ivan the Terrible slaughtered the Tartars.

The song concluded, Varlaam and Missail are soon nodding from the effects of the wine. Grigory, who has refused to drink, seizes the opportunity to question his hostess about the route to Lithuania. She tells him it is not far away but the police have set up roadblocks. "They are looking for some criminal who has escaped from Moscow. But the guards will catch nothing because there are other ways to go." Amiably, she describes a route through the countryside.

A loud knock stops the conversation and rouses the two friars from their drunken sleep. Police come into the inn and demand that the three men identify themselves.

Grigory says, "I am from a nearby town and have been showing these fathers the way to the border. I will soon return to my village."

The guards stare suspiciously at Varlaam and one of them takes out a warrant. He explains, "A heretic monk has escaped from Moscow and the Czar has ordered that he be captured and hanged." Unrolling the orders he asks, "Can anyone here read?"

Seeing an opportunity to save himself, Grigory takes the warrant. When Grigory reaches the part in which the accused is described, he cleverly substitutes a description of Varlaam.

Immediately the police seize Varlaam, who pushes them away. "Let me see that myself." With great difficulty he works his way through the warrant. Suddenly he realizes that the description of the culprit fits Grigory perfectly and he points at the young man.

Drawing his knife, Grigory jumps through the window. It takes the guards several seconds to recover from their surprise and give chase.

ACT II

Some six years have passed since Boris ascended the throne. In the privacy of the Czar's sumptuously furnished apartments in the Kremlin, Xenia, his daughter, weeps bitterly over a portrait of her dead fiancé, while Feodor, his son, intently studies a map.

The children's Nurse tries to console Xenia without success. Also wishing to cheer Xenia, Feodor starts to play a joyful game with the Nurse which grows more and more raucous only to come to a sudden halt when Boris enters the room. The Nurse looks terrified and the Czar gently reassures her that he is not angry. He is concerned with Xenia's grief. He puts his arm around her and counsels her to dry her tears and talk to her friends. When Xenia and the Nurse leave, Boris lets the Czarevich tell him about his maps and advises him to learn them well. "The day when the entire Russian kingdom will be yours may not be that far off." As Feodor returns to his studies, Boris glances at some documents, but his mind is elsewhere.

Although his rule has been relatively peaceful and the soothsayers predict a long, illustrious life for him, his soul is in perpetual torment. "Even my family is blighted," he muses. "My beloved daughter's betrothed taken by death. How fearful is the wrath of God toward the guilty. All about me there is nothing but darkness." His gloom spreads to thoughts about his nation and his rule. "Despite my prayers, God sends rebellion, rumors of conspiracy abound, Lithuanian uprisings threaten, and the people of Russia are plagued by hunger, poverty, and disease. The name of Boris is cursed throughout the land." He grows even more wretched as he thinks of his agonizing sleepless nights haunted by the horrible vision of a helpless, bloodstained child begging for mercy.

Boris is roused from his morbid meditation by the news that Prince Shuisky, one of the most powerful men in the country, wishes to speak with him. As they wait for Shuisky to enter, Boris listens to a little story his son relates and says tenderly, "I only wish I could live to see you proclaimed Czar of all Russia. Gladly I would give up my power so you might take my place!"

Boris then greets Shuisky with angry accusations of treachery and of leading the boyars against the crown. Shuisky cunningly ignores the tirade and reports that a pretender to the throne has surfaced in Lithuania. "Further," he adds, "he has the backing of the Polish Court and King!"

"What name does this pretender use?" Boris asks, suddenly anxious.

Shuisky couches his answer carefully. "Believe me, mighty Czar, your kindness and mercy have made you loved by all, but devoted as I am to you, I must tell you the truth. Should this pretender succeed in crossing the border from Lithuania the people of Russia might follow him because the name he uses is Dimitri."

Shaken by this news, the Czar orders Feodor to leave, and turning to Shuisky he angrily orders that all Russian borders be heavily guarded so that no one can enter the country. "It is unheard of—children rising from the dead to question the rights of living Czars who were elected by the people." Laughing wildly, he grasps the Prince by his collar: "Shuisky, tell me, the child who was killed, was it definitely Dimitri? Tell me the truth!"

Half frightened, half sly, Shuisky describes in graphic detail how he watched the mass grave for five days. "The other bodies had already begun to decompose. But despite a large gaping wound, the royal child's corpse remained unchanged; a smile on his lips and his little hands folded together . . . as if he were in his cradle."

Boris can bear no more and dismisses Shuisky. He sinks into a chair, unable to breathe. "One stain upon the soul and damned for all eternity." The room grows dark, and the clock begins to chime. "It is so oppressive, the constant hammering. My head is splitting open." Boris grows delirious and thinks he sees a vision of the dead child. Frantically he cries, "Go away, child. Leave me. It was not I . . . others did it." Petrified, the great Czar hides his face in his hands and drops to his knees praying to God. "Have mercy on my soul! Forgive the guilty Czar!"

ACT III

Scene 1

In the castle of Sandomir, Princess Marina of Poland is having her hair done while some girls try to entertain her with a song about her beauty. She stops them. "You are very flattering," she says, "but I prefer the old ballads, songs about the great Polish victories and our brave warriors."

Dismissing her attendants, Marina contemplates the tedium of her life, with its frivolous pleasures and numberless insipid suitors. There is only one who has caught her interest—Dimitri from Moscow—who has sworn to avenge the murdered Czarevich and unseat the usurper, Boris. She smiles as she thinks of him. "I will capture his heart and he will bring me glory and power. I will dazzle the stupid folk of Moscow and make the boyars kneel at my feet. They will write legends about me." As she preens herself before the mirror, she bursts into laughter, but it strangles in her throat as she realizes that the priest Rangoni has entered the room.

Respectfully, he approaches her. It is her duty, he tells her, to bring the heretic church of Russia back to the true church of Rome. "You have the power to do this. With your beauty you can convert the Pretender and then convince him to further our cause."

She demurs. She says she is too worldly, too sinful, too ignorant, to inspire religious feeling in others. Obviously, she does not like to take orders from others, and the priest grows angry. "Marina, your face is distorted. The devil has taken possession of you!"

Terrified, Marina drops to her knees before Rangoni, begging forgiveness.

"Obey the envoy of God," he orders. "You will do as I bid!"

SCENE 2

Grigory, now the Pretender Dimitri, waits in the castle's garden, anxiously hoping that the beautiful Marina will join him. His thoughts are interrupted by Rangoni, who says, "Marina begged me to tell you, Czarevich, that she loves you."

At first Dimitri is suspicious and disbelieving, but the priest insists that it is true, and that Marina suffers because he holds himself aloof and the Court gossips. Ecstatic, Dimitri promises to take Marina with him all the way to the throne of Moscow and in gratitude promises that Rangoni can remain at his side as an adviser.

Both men hide as a crowd of revelers comes out of the castle. The men boast drunkenly of conquering the Muscovites, and the women make catty remarks about Marina's icy heart. Marina, flirting openly with an old marquis, calls for more wine and as they return to the castle, her guests drink a toast to the time when she will wear the crown of Russia.

Dimitri, still hidden, is shaken. "My adored Marina on the arm of another man! I must forget her! To battle! To my heritage! To the throne of the Czars!"

As he is consoling himself with visions of glory, Marina returns to the garden alone. At the sight of her, he is lovesick once again. Tenderly he tells her of his love and how doubts about her feelings torture him.

She is unsympathetic. "I am so tired of amorous declarations. Tell me, when will you be Czar?"

"Marina!" He is shocked. "Does power mean more to you than love?"

"If all you want is love, then go home to Russia where you can have your pick of women. I desire only a crown."

He falls to his knees, begging her not to taunt him so, pleading for her love.

Mercilessly, she prods him with her foot. "Your love has made you forget your goal. I have nothing but contempt for you. Go away."

This is more than Dimitri can bear. Drawing himself up, he angrily tells her, "I shall lead my warriors into battle and I shall sit on the throne in Moscow, and from that lofty spot, I will look down upon you, mocking you, you silly insolent Polish girl!"

Marina is actually pleased by this outburst. "I only wanted to reawaken your pride." With words of love, she woos him until he is convinced that she adores him. He calls her his queen, and they embrace, Marina dreaming of a throne, Dimitri of the happiness he will find in her arms.

ACT IV

Scene 1

The Granovitaya Palace in the Kremlin is abuzz with a special meeting of the council of boyars, called to discuss the threat posed by the approaching army of the Pretender. The boyars agree that the villain must be caught, tortured, killed, and left to hang in a public place, and that all of his supporters should be executed.

They are soon joined by Shuisky, who brings a distressing tale about the state in which he found the Czar the previous evening. "He was pale and covered with sweat and began to tremble wildly. He muttered incoherently. It sounded very strange, as if he was speaking to the ghost of the Czarevich, ordering the child to leave him!"

The boyars are incredulous. But suddenly Boris enters the hall speaking the very words Shuisky has just uttered. "Go, child! Leave me!" He finally realizes where he is and, regaining his composure, greets the boyars.

Shuisky asks the Czar's permission to bring in a wise old man who feels he has an important tale to disclose. Hoping that somehow he will hear something to quell his constant torment, Boris consents. Shuisky brings in Pimen, who relates the following story:

"A shepherd came to me one evening with an amazing story. He had been blind since childhood, and had tried many cures, all for naught. One night as he slept he heard the soft voice of a child calling 'Grandfather, go to the Cathedral of the Transfiguration in Uglich and pray upon my tomb. I am the Czarevich Dimitri and now I am one of the Lord's angels performing miracles for Russia.' The shepherd heeded these words and went to the tomb and as soon as he got there he began to cry and suddenly his sight was restored!"

Boris, who has listened to the story with growing perturbation, now clutches his heart and cries out in pain. A boyar catches him as he falls. Sensing death is near, Boris calls for his son and his vestments. Some of the boyars help him to his throne while the others fetch the Czarevich. Feodor soon arrives and Boris orders the others to leave. He then tenderly bids his son farewell. "You shall inherit my crown, but never ask how I got it." Haltingly, he tries to give some words of advice: "You will have problems. Never trust the boyars, treat treachery harshly, and be just to the people. Stay pure and innocent. Protect your sister Xenia." His voice growing fainter, Boris prays to the Lord to help his son and to protect the Russian throne.

An ominous funeral bell peals its mournful sounds. A procession of monks enters the hall, mercilessly chanting of Boris's guilt-ridden vision—the dying child. Suddenly Boris's strength seems to return and he stops the mournful dirge, declaring, "Wait! I am still the Czar!" He clutches his heart again. "God have mercy . . . Forgive me!" He points to Feodor and cries, "There is your Czar!" With these words, Boris topples to the floor . . . dead.

SCENE 2

In a forest near the village of Kromy a high-spirited mob of revolutionaries drags a boyar into a clearing, forcing him to sit on a log. With gleeful cruelty, they gag him with rags and, dancing around, mock and taunt his loyalty to Czar Boris. To further humiliate him, they sit an old hag from the crowd next to the captive to serve as his "mistress." Laughing, they bow to the ground to honor the disheveled couple.

The village idiot runs into the clearing chased by a bunch of boys. To stop their teasing, the half-wit shows them a penny he has found and the rowdies snatch it, making him cry.

The two friars, Varlaam and Missail, join the crowd. They denounce Boris for his sins and for the suffering he has caused. Electrified by these words, the people vow to overthrow the Czar and vanquish tyranny. Varlaam and Missail urge them to welcome the true Czar, delivered by

God's hands, the Czar Dimitri. Excited by these words the mob yells, "Death to Boris."

Two Jesuit priests approach, intoning praises for Dimitri in Latin. Angered by the competition, Varlaam and Missail encourage the crowd to seize the Catholic priests, which they start to do. They are just about to hang the poor men when they are distracted by a fanfare and the arrival of horsemen in white capes and, in their midst, the Pretender Dimitri. The mob cheers wildly and the boyar, whom the crowd has forgotten, rushes to Dimitri's side and swears allegiance to him. Dimitri asks all to follow him into battle, "For our sacred country! To Moscow! To the Kremlin!" Joined by the Jesuits, the friars, and the jubilant mob, Dimitri leads his troops onward.

Only the simpleton is left, sitting alone in the forest. The sound of the rabble grows distant, replaced by the roar of a great fire. As if he can see the terrible darkness that will soon cover the land, the simpleton weeps for the poor people of Russia.

THE ABDUCTION FROM THE SERAGLIO

Opera in Three Acts
by
WOLFGANG AMADEUS MOZART
Première: Burgtheater, Vienna, July 16, 1782

ACT I

BELMONTE LOSTADOS, son of a Spanish nobleman, has sailed to Turkey in search of his beloved Constanza, whose ship was captured by pirates. Along with her maid, Blonda, and Belmonte's servant, Pedrillo, she was sold to the Pasha Selim, and Belmonte has traced them to a palace on the seacoast. As he ponders how to enter, Belmonte spies an aging, portly fellow atop a ladder, picking figs and singing a song.

"Excuse me, sir," Belmonte ventures, "is this the house of the Pasha Selim?"

The fig-picker ignores him and continues to sing. Again Belmonte asks and again gets no response. Impatiently, Belmonte shouts, "Enough! Is this where Pasha Selim lives?"

"Yes," the man answers curtly as he gets off the ladder and prepares to leave.

Belmonte holds him until he admits he is the Pasha's servant. "Then tell me, where can I find Pedrillo?"

The mere mention of this name enrages the servant. "I'd like to wring his

340

neck, then have him roasted on a spit over a flame, and finally put his head on a spike!" Defending Pedrillo, Belmonte follows the other man to the palace, but the servant bars the door, declaring, "You're not coming in. You only want to steal the beautiful women."

Belmonte pretends to leave but remains discreetly out of sight. As the fig-picker stands there, Pedrillo appears and teases him, "Hey, Osmin, are those figs for me?"

"I only have poison and daggers for you," Osmin snarls, and threatens to have Pedrillo beheaded, hanged, burned, bound, drowned, and beaten. Having worked himself into a fury, Osmin storms into the palace.

"Pedrillo," Belmonte calls softly.

Pedrillo cannot believe his eyes and is overcome with joy at seeing his master. "Your Constanza is fine," he is quick to report. "The only problem is that she is the object of the Pasha's affections. However, he is waiting for her to love him and so far she has remained faithful to you!"

Belmonte burns with desire to see his beloved once again, but before he and Pedrillo can figure out a way to accomplish this, Pedrillo makes him hide again because the Pasha and Constanza are about to disembark from a brief boat trip.

"Constanza," the Pasha asks, "why are you so sad? I could order you to love me, but I would rather that you came to love me on your own."

"Forgive me, Pasha, but I cannot. I swore fidelity to my own beloved. Our love was all happiness. That is why this separation is so hard for me to bear, and why I can never love you." She walks away leaving the Pasha disturbed at her steadfastness, but with the attraction he feels for her heightened by the faithfulness of her spirit.

Pedrillo approaches the Pasha and introduces Belmonte as an architect who has studied in Italy and traveled to this great land to offer his services. Intrigued by any new interest, the Pasha agrees to see him again on the morrow. "Pedrillo, take care of our visitor's needs!" he orders as he leaves.

Pedrillo is delighted by the initial success of the scheme, but Belmonte can think only of his Constanza. "If I could but speak to her!" Pedrillo promises they will accomplish this as well and leads him toward the palace garden.

Their path is suddenly blocked. "Halt! Where do you two think you're going?" Osmin demands.

"I'm taking this architect the Pasha just hired into the palace!"

Osmin refuses to allow them through. An argument ensues until finally Pedrillo and Belmonte force their way past Osmin into the palace.

341

ACT II

In a garden on the palace grounds Blonda rebukes Osmin for trying to order her about. "The way to attract a woman is with tenderness, kindness, and affection."

Osmin is unconvinced. "Here in Turkey, I am the master and you are the slave; I command you to love me right now!"

This only amuses Blonda. "I am a freeborn Englishwoman. Just you try coming near me."

Osmin begins to lose his temper. "Into the house," he orders.

"I'm not going anywhere. My mistress Constanza is a favorite of the Pasha. Just a word from me and you could be whipped. Now get away from me." Osmin tries to hold his ground, but she darts at him like a striking panther. "I will scratch out your eyes."

"All right, all right," he mutters and leaves.

Constanza comes into the garden still lamenting her separation from Belmonte.

Overhearing her, Pasha Selim warns that the time for decision is approaching. His patience is nearing its end. "By tomorrow you must return my love!"

She is steadfast. "My lord, I will always respect you, but I can never love you. And your great power cannot frighten me because I would welcome death."

Angered, the Pasha threatens her with unspeakable tortures.

"You may torture me in any way you will. It shall only strengthen my resolve to remain faithful to my beloved. Of course, if you could find it within your heart to spare my life, then heaven will bless you. But if you insist on torturing me, then so be it, for in the end I will be freed by death!" She leaves the garden. Stunned by her courage and effrontery, the Pasha stands a moment before following her.

Pedrillo creeps in, quietly calling to Blonda. He tells her of Belmonte's arrival and how he has succeeded in getting him into the palace. "At midnight, Belmonte and I will come with ladders to your windows and free you and Constanza. Don't worry about Osmin because I will give him some wine laced with a sleeping potion. Now go and tell Constanza and bring her here to see Belmonte."

Blonda is ecstatic. She burbles on so about the joy of bringing this great news to her despairing mistress that Pedrillo must finally urge her to go.

While he prepares the wine for Osmin, Pedrillo voices his misgivings about the dangers of carrying out their daring escapade, and screws up his courage. His prey returns to the garden full of his usual imprecations, but Pedrillo returns insults with amiability as he entices Osmin into breaking Moslem law to drink a glass of wine. "Come, Osmin, forget your hatred. Here is some fine wine from Cyprus that you will surely enjoy." As Osmin weakens, Pedrillo offers him a choice between a small bottle or a large bottle.

"Give me the big one!" Osmin demands, and greedily guzzles the spiked wine.

Unused as he is to alcohol, the potion soon takes effect and Osmin grows more and more incoherent. As the muddled drunken Osmin barely drags himself off to bed, Pedrillo bids him good night.

Belmonte arrives. "Where is Constanza?"

"Here she comes now!" Pedrillo answers.

Constanza and Belmonte gaze at each other for a moment, then rush into each other's arms. As Constanza weeps with joy, Belmonte kisses her tears away. Meanwhile, Pedrillo reviews the abduction plans with Blonda. But they are no sooner celebrating their coming freedom than the men are struck by sudden doubts about the fidelity of their women. Belmonte asks Constanza if she and the Pasha . . . , while Pedrillo questions Blonda about Osmin!

Constanza is deeply wounded, but it is Blonda who brings the men back to their senses with a smart slap across Pedrillo's face. Then the women angrily order their unworthy men to leave.

"Forgive us!" the men plead.

Before long both Constanza and Blonda are saying, "If you are truly sorry, we will forgive!"

Happily, the couples embrace, praising the power of love, and abjuring jealousy.

ACT III

At midnight, Pedrillo and Belmonte quietly take their positions beneath the windows of the Seraglio, eager and nervous. To give the signal, Pedrillo breaks into a ballad about a young lady taken captive in a Moorish land.

"Hurry," Belmonte urges, but four verses are sung before a window opens. Pedrillo holds the ladder in position as Belmonte helps Constanza to descend, and the two run off.

"Now I must free my Blonda!" Pedrillo declares, but before he can bring her down the ladder, they are intercepted by a fuming Osmin.

"Now I have caught you in the act," he bellows; "you are done for." As guards bring in Belmonte and Constanza, whom they have captured, Osmin snarls, "And I suppose you were just out for a walk?"

Belmonte tries bribing Osmin, but the servant only wants their heads, and he orders the guards to take the four prisoners to the Pasha.

In the royal suite, Osmin apologizes for disturbing his master's rest. "But our Christian friends were trying to abduct our women. Your architect tried to steal your Constanza, but I had him stopped. Guards bring them here!"

Selim regards Constanza reproachfully. "Is this the thanks I get for allowing you such freedom?"

"My lord," she responds, "I know I am guilty. But my heart belongs to Belmonte. I will gladly die, but please spare his life."

Belmonte kneels before the Pasha and pleads for everyone's freedom: "Ask whatever you will. I am from a wealthy Spanish family and can pay your ransom. My name is Belmonte Lostados!"

At the mention of this name the Pasha grows excited. "Your father, commandant of Oran, is one of my arch-enemies! He robbed me of my property and my honor! But worst of all he deprived me of the one I loved! What a wonderful twist of fate, to hold such power over the son of a foe. I will take my revenge. Come with me Osmin and hear my instructions!"

This sudden disastrous change in their destinies causes Belmonte to bemoan their bad luck. But Constanza encourages him to view death only as a passage to eternal bliss. "Better to be killed together than to live alone." As the two lovers ecstatically bid the world farewell, Pedrillo trembles at the thought of the boiling oil Osmin is only too ready to fry him in, and admires Blonda's blithe fortitude as she airily says she doesn't care how it's done if she has to die.

Pasha Selim returns, accompanied by his retinue. He addresses Belmonte. "Miserable slave, are you ready?"

Belmonte calmy draws himself up. "Revenge yourself."

The Pasha pronounces sentence. "Belmonte Lostados, I despise your father far too much to do as he would do. Therefore, I will free you and your beloved Constanza. Return to your land and tell your father that I have repaid his evil with goodness."

Everyone is astonished by this wonderful gesture. Only Osmin objects. "Not my Blonda too."

The Pasha points out that he is better off without this difficult woman who would undoubtedly be the end of him.

Led by Belmonte each of the four praises the Pasha for his benevolence, acknowledging the debt and gratitude they owe him. When her turn comes, Blonda can't help taking a dig at Osmin as well, and he becomes so enraged that he implores the Pasha to let him torture the foreigners, and grows so furious that he charges out of the room in a frustrated rage.

"Revenge is hateful," they all agree. "But forgiveness takes a noble soul!" As Belmonte and Constanza, Pedrillo and Blonda are ushered from the palace to their boat, the Pasha's subjects sing his praises, wishing him justly deserved fame and honor.

WOZZECK

Opera in Three Acts
by
ALBAN BERG
Première: State Opera, Berlin, December 14, 1925

ACT I

SCENE 1

"NOT SO fast, Wozzeck, not so fast." Relaxing comfortably in a chair in his room, the Captain does not appreciate the speed with which his orderly is giving him a shave. He is a man who craves deliberation in all acts, both his own and others'. "You are making me nervous. What do you think I will do with the minutes you save me?"

Wozzeck, who does this daily chore for the few extra pennies it brings him, says merely, "Yes, sir. All right, sir."

The Captain waxes philosophical about time and the weather, but Wozzeck's monosyllabic responses finally irritate him, and he accuses the man of immorality because he has fathered an illegitimate child.

Wozzeck retorts, "The little brat won't be viewed any differently by the Lord if he is blessed or not. The Lord said, 'Suffer the little children to come unto me!'"

The Captain finds this remark insufferable and leaps from his chair. "You are trying to confuse me."

Wozzeck tries to explain himself. "It's hard to be moral when you have no money. It's easy to be virtuous when you are wealthy. My kind of people are always unfortunate. Even in heaven they'll make us work."

This kind of talk makes the Captain unhappy and he says, "All right, you're a good man. But don't think so much. Now run along because I'm tired. No, don't run. Walk slowly and down the middle of the street."

Obediently, Wozzeck leaves.

SCENE 2

In a wooded area on the outskirts of the village, Wozzeck and Andres, one of his comrades, are busily cutting sticks. Wozzeck says he believes the place to be cursed, but Andres tells him this is nonsense and sings a silly song to amuse himself.

Wozzeck's haunted feeling persists and he thinks he sees a human head rolling around on the ground. Catching his mood, Andres grows uneasy. He tries to get Wozzeck to sing along with him, but in vain. As the sun sets, Wozzeck's visions grow ever more vivid and horrible. "Look! A fire! Rising out of the earth and going toward heaven. And a roar, like trombones, rising from the ground!"

Feigning calm, Andres points out that night has fallen and that drum rolls are being played by their platoon. "It's time for us to return."

Slowly, they head for the village together.

SCENE 3

As she watches from the window of her room, Marie hums the march of the military band coming up the street. "Do you hear the band?" she asks the baby cradled in her arms. Soon the band arrives under Marie's window. Her friend, Margaret, standing just outside, points to the handsome Drum Major, who waves to Marie.

As Marie waves back, Margaret taunts, "Aren't we friendly!"

Angered, Marie slams the window shut and tells her baby, "My son, the child of a whore, you bring such joy to your mother." Rocking the child, she sings him a lullaby.

Just as the baby falls asleep, there is a knock at the window. It is Wozzeck and she invites him in.

"I can't. I must return to the barracks."

"Why are you so upset?"

He tries to explain: "I am haunted by a shape in the skies. It followed me all the way here. Now, everything is dark. Something bad is going to happen."

347

To distract him, she shows him the baby, but he is too disturbed to notice, and hurries away down the street.

Marie shakes her head over her poor lover. "He's so afraid he didn't even look at his son." Suddenly, unable to bear the constant difficulties of her life, she cries, "Lord, it's so awful to be poor!"

SCENE 4

One sunny afternoon Wozzeck visits the Doctor who is using him as a guinea pig for some foolish experiments in nutrition. For subjecting himself to the Doctor's experiments, Wozzeck earns three groschen a day. In return he must do everything the Doctor says. His current regimen includes a diet of beans only, and absolutely no coughing. As he enters, the Doctor upbraids him. "I saw you coughing before. This is very bad. What good is your word? Have you been keeping to your diet of beans?"

Wozzeck nods.

"Good. Next week you can have mutton. But you mustn't cough."

"I couldn't help it."

The Doctor gets angry. "Don't tell me such things. I've proved that the muscles are subject to human will."

"But it was my nature, not my mind."

"Don't give me philosophy."

"But, Doctor," Wozzeck pleads, "in certain people there is a nature . . ." Suddenly he is telling the Doctor about his hallucinations. Wildly, he talks about darkness, toads, Marie, and red glowing lights.

The Doctor crows delightedly, convinced he has himself produced this aberration. "You are a great case," he tells Wozzeck. "Keep it up and I will give you a bonus." He is hardly able to contain himself. "You will make me famous." Snapping back to his professional manner, he orders Wozzeck to show his tongue.

Wozzeck obeys.

SCENE 5

At twilight, the Drum Major struts about in front of Marie's house, while she stands at her door admiring his manly build.

He tells her, "Wait till you see me Sunday when I wear my plumes and white gloves!" She walks over to him and they continue flirting until he grabs her in an embrace. She wrestles with him until she breaks free. "Don't touch me!" she cries, but does not move away.

"A wildcat, hey?" He draws himself up and towers over her, then determinedly embraces her again.

More quickly than he expects, she succumbs. "Oh all right, then," she says, and they disappear into her house together.

ACT II

SCENE 1

One bright, sunny morning, Marie sits in her room alone with her child and admires herself in the mirror, paying special attention to a pair of beautiful gold earrings which adorn her ears. Occasionally, when the boy stirs, she cajoles him back to sleep and returns to admiring her jewelry.

Wozzeck comes in behind her and asks, "What do you have there?"

Caught off guard she blurts out, "I found them."

"Two together?" he asks unbelievingly. But he decides not to create an argument. "My son is always sleeping, and I am always toiling. Here is some more money, Marie. I must leave now."

Marie is consumed with guilt. "I am wicked," she confesses to herself.

SCENE 2

The Captain and the Doctor meet one day on the street.

"What is your hurry?" the Captain asks.

"Where are you going so slowly?" the Doctor counters. "You have grown fat and bloated. You are likely to get apoplexy. You could even become paralyzed." He becomes enthusiastic. "You could become part of my research!"

The Captain begs the Doctor to stop. "You will make me die of fright."

Wozzeck, hurrying by, salutes the two men.

"Hey, Wozzeck!" the Doctor calls. "Come over here!"

Wozzeck obeys and instantly becomes the butt of the other men's insults. Cruelly they taunt him about Marie's infidelity.

"I am a poor soul," Wozzeck pleads. "Marie is all I have; please don't joke about her!" As Wozzeck grows agitated the Doctor takes his pulse and carefully notes and enumerates every reaction.

Increasingly distraught, Wozzeck finally bursts out, "I should hang myself! At least all would be resolved then!" and rushes away without saluting.

SCENE 3

"Good morning!" Marie greets Wozzeck as he comes rushing up to her. He is not in a good mood and now grimly accuses her of being unfaithful.

"Was it here you met him?" He mimics the Drum Major.

"Many people walk by my house. I can't stop them from doing that!" she protests.

Losing control, Wozzeck repeats his accusation.

"And what if I *was* with him?" she challenges. "Don't touch me! I would rather you put a knife in me than put a hand on me!" And she goes into the house.

Left standing in the street, Wozzeck repeats the words "put a knife in me" as if in a trance. "I feel so dizzy!" he mutters. Slowly he moves down the street. "I'm falling."

SCENE 4

Apprentices, soldiers, and servant girls dance around a tavern garden while others look on. A few gather around two drunk apprentices who are holding forth about the dreariness of life unless seen through the rosy light of brandy.

Wozzeck comes in and sees Marie dance by with her Drum Major. Hearing her gleeful voice, Wozzeck, depressed, laments the power of lust. As she whizzes by again, his sadness turns to fury and he is just about to storm onto the floor, when the music ends and the dancers return to their seats. Wozzeck retreats into the shadows and listens to the others carrying on drunkenly. Andres comes by and asks why he is sitting all alone.

"I'm comfortable, and I'll be even more comfortable in the grave."

"Are you drunk?"

Wozzeck replies, "I can't afford it!" Tired of this conversation, Andres turns his attention to the dance floor.

Nearby, a drunk apprentice delivers a nonsensical sermon, until his jeering, cheering friends carry him off.

Wozzeck still sits alone. The village idiot creeps up to him and whispers, "I smell it! It reeks of blood!"

Wozzeck is shaken. As the dancers, including Marie and the Drum Major, return to the floor, Wozzeck sees a red mist and twisting bodies. Eerily he repeats, "Blood! Blood! Everything is going to be red. They are all in it . . . ."

Scene 5

Later that night Wozzeck lies awake in his barracks while his comrades sleep. He is obsessed by visions of Marie and the Drum Major as he saw them dancing together. He wakes Andres to tell him that he has visions of a knife blade.

Andres is tired. "Go to sleep!"

Wozzeck lapses into prayer.

The Drum Major stumbles into the barracks, obviously intoxicated and bragging about "his woman" with her beautiful breasts and firm thighs. Andres asks who she is.

"Ask Wozzeck!" the Drum Major laughs. He then provokes Wozzeck to fight and quickly gets the better of him. Drinking more brandy, and continuing to taunt the defeated Wozzeck, the Drum Major finally stumbles out the door. Wozzeck slumps back on his bed and Andres notices that he is bleeding. The other soldiers settle back to sleep.

"They follow one after the other," Wozzeck mumbles. His eyes open and haunted, he stares straight ahead.

ACT III

Scene 1

Her room lit only by a candle, Marie sits beside her child, reading in the Bible about an adulterous woman. Drawing her son closer, she turns the pages, preoccupied with thoughts of Wozzeck. Because she feels guilty, she worries about why he has not stopped by for two days. As she absently leafs through the Bible, her eye is caught by a passage about Mary Magdalene. "Oh, Lord," she burst out, "have mercy on me too!"

Scene 2

Wozzeck and Marie come down a wooded path toward the pond. It is evening and she wants to return to town, but he insists they rest a bit and reluctantly agreeing, she sits down with him. He reminisces about their meeting, his manner gentle but strange. Growing nervous, Marie jumps up to go. He pulls her back down and kisses her.

"Look at how red the moon is," she says, for the sake of saying something.

351

Wozzeck surreptitiously draws a knife. "It is red like the color of blood-stained metal."

She jumps up again demanding to know what he wants.

"I want nothing and no one else will have anything either!" With these words Wozzeck grabs Marie and plunges his knife into her throat. She falls to the ground. He leans over her body and utters one hollow word: "Dead!" Then he runs away.

SCENE 3

At a tavern later that night Wozzeck watches the dancers, encouraging them to leap about. Between glasses of wine he sings at a shout and then, suddenly jumping to his feet, he grabs Margaret and dances a few steps with her. Stopping as abruptly as he started, he bids her sit with him. They flirt a little until he says, "I feel like a fight tonight!" and she notices there is blood on his hand. Her cries attract a crowd and Wozzeck tries to explain that he cut himself.

Margaret points out that the blood is on his elbow too. As everyone continues to comment on the smell of human blood, Wozzeck grows more agitated and, shouting about the devil, rushes out of the tavern into the night.

SCENE 4

Wozzeck has returned to the pond in the woods and by the light of the moon searches frantically for the murder weapon. He is terrified by the rustle of every leaf. Staggering around, he trips over Marie's corpse and finds the knife. "It will betray me. I must get rid of it." He takes it and throws it into the pond where it sinks like a stone. The moon, still blood red, emerges from behind a cloud and aggravates Wozzeck's fears. "I didn't throw it deep enough." He wades into the water and his search for the knife turns into a need to wash himself clean of blood. He walks in deeper and deeper until he is over his head. And drowns.

The Doctor and the Captain, walking on a path to the pond, hear an eerie sound. The Captain exclaims, "The water is calling, like someone drowning." The Doctor is fascinated and wants to investigate, but the Captain is frightened and drags the Doctor away.

SCENE 5

It is a bright, sunny morning, and the children play noisily in the street in front of Marie's house. Her son rides his hobby horse. Other children run over with the news of Marie's murder. "Your mother's been killed!" one child shouts to him.

As the others run off to see the corpse, he continues to ride on his hobby horse: "Hop! Hop! Hop!" Then suddenly noticing that he is alone, he skips after the other children.

LOUISE

Opera in Four Acts
by
GUSTAVE CHARPENTIER
Première: Opéra-Comique, Paris, February 2, 1900

ACT I

IN AN attic dwelling in a working-class district of Paris near the end of the nineteenth century, Louise, a young seamstress, stands at the window, raptly listening to Julien, a poet who lives across the way. From the balcony of his studio he woos her with the promise of undying love. She blows him a kiss, then turns nervously to see if her mother is returning. Julien presses her. Her parents have refused to let them marry. If the second letter he has just sent asking for her hand does not elicit a favorable reply, she must elope with him. "All you do is tell me to be patient," he complains.

Torn between filial devotion and her passion for Julien, Louise cannot decide what to do. To change the subject she asks how he fell in love with her, and they begin to recall for each other the silent glances and secret whispers, the sights and scents of the lively Paris streets, the tableaux of spring against which their romance has blossomed. So caught up are they in each other that Louise does not notice that her mother has returned and is standing at the door.

Listening to their passionate words and the evidence that they have been meeting behind her back, Louise's mother grows furious. She angrily pulls her daughter away from the window, orders Julien to be still, and slams the window shut.

Silently, Louise helps her mother prepare dinner, trying to hide her distress. Her mother, however, will not leave the matter alone and proceeds to ridicule the exchange she has overheard. She caricatures Julien's words of love and grabs her daughter's arm. "What if your father knew of this? Your father who thinks you are so good and innocent. It would kill him."

Louise pleads with her mother. "Why don't you let us marry?"

"That ne'er-do-well! That pillar of the tavern!" When Louise tries to defend Julien her mother says, "Instead of boasting, you ought to be ashamed to have a lover."

"He is not my lover, but the way you behave, you will push me into it!"

At a loss for words, her mother tries to cuff Louise, until footsteps on the stairway bring the fracas to an abrupt halt.

Louise's father comes in, holding a letter. He wearily hangs up his cap, and father and daughter embrace. The mother scurries to the kitchen to prepare the soup for dinner while Louise sets the table under the loving gaze of her father. The soup arrives and is ladled out by the man of the house. For a while no one speaks, each one seemingly engrossed in private thoughts.

"What a long day," the father sighs. "I'm not as young as I once was." They lament the misfortune of having to work so hard for so little while others don't have to work at all. It is clear that Louise's parents perceive their artist neighbors as loafers. The meal over, the father sits down to smoke his pipe while his wife and daughter clear the table. Knowing it is from Julien, Louise puts the letter into her father's hands. He opens and reads it carefully.

The mother's rage boils up once more. Her husband points out that the letter is polite. "He does indeed love Louise." But his wife will not hear of giving Louise's suitor even a moment's consideration and accuses him of every vice she can think of.

"It's not true," Louise shouts and her mother slaps her. Finally, her father separates the two women, leading the mother away as Louise bursts into tears.

As the mother sullenly begins to iron in the kitchen, the father consoles his daughter. "We love you so much that we feel we must be cautious in these matters." The mother mumbles caustically that these matters are impossible to argue, but her father listens to Louise sympathetically. As she tells him how much she loves the young poet, he puts his arm around her. "My child," he says, "love is blind, and you do not have the experience to be a judge of character. Promise me that whatever we decide, you will obey. Because if you were to betray my love, I would be unable to go on living!"

"I shall love you always," she answers, and bursts into tears.

He tries to distract her. "Come, read me the paper. It will make you forget and save my poor eyes."

Louise picks up the paper and begins to read: "Spring is our most beautiful season. Paris sparkles like a continuous party." She cannot go on. Paris lies so close, but she feels as if its romance and glamor will never be hers. As the clock chimes, she longingly whispers, "Ah, Paris."

ACT II

SCENE 1

The early morning mist of an April day drifts through the steep, crooked streets of Montmartre. In a small square, life begins to stir: a milkwoman and a paper girl sleepily open their stalls; ragpickers and scavengers sift through the rubbish that has been put out the night before. Everyone grumbles a little in envy over the rich who can afford to stay in bed. A pimp, strutting around in his evening cloak, tries to seduce the paper girl and boasts, "I am the Pleasure of Paris." The milkwoman chases him away with her broom, and as he rushes around the corner he knocks down a ragpicker. The ragpicker wearily picks up his scattered scraps and mumbles, "That is the wretch who stole my daughter." He continues to sniffle as he goes about his work, and the others cluck sympathetically.

More people fill the square as the mist lifts: policemen, a young urchin, a street sweeper. Julien and some of his Bohemian friends peer around the corner of a building and cautiously approach. They look surreptitious, as if they are plotting. And indeed, Julien is hoping to intercept Louise on her way to work. "If her parents have again refused my proposal, we'll take Louise away with us."

Julien's bold scheme is greeted by "Bravos" from his friends, who decide that they will make Louise their Muse. Their loud banter brings several young women to the windows of the houses facing the square, which inspires the young men to clown for them and blow kisses. Pretending his cane is a guitar, their aspirant songwriter sings a song, bringing a flurry of cheers and coins from the windows.

It is almost time for Louise to arrive and Julien orders his pals to leave. He is very nervous and not at all sure that he will prevail. As the seamstresses begin to arrive at work, Julien hides behind a kiosk.

Finally, Louise and her mother enter the square, the older woman grumbling, certain that Julien has followed them. "I'm going to tell your father that you should work at home."

Louise has caught sight of Julien and makes him a sign, but when her mother kisses her goodbye she obediently enters the workshop. Her mother lingers, suspiciously glancing about, but eventually she walks slowly away. Julien emerges from his hiding place. He is hesitant at first. Then in a burst of courage he rushes into the shop and drags out a reluctant Louise. He demands to know her parents' decision. When she tells him that they have refused he tries to convince her that her parents have no right to ruin her life. Louise is utterly torn and pleads with him to understand that her father would die if she ran away. Julien is not to be placated. As people in the street brush by them and the street vendors shout their wares, he begs her to flee with him. He points to the top of Montmartre. "Up there, lovers can be free." Putting his arm around her, he tries to pull her with him. "If you love me, Louise, you will come with me now."

She struggles out of his arms and promises that one day she will be his wife. Then, tenderly blowing him a kiss, she disappears into the atelier. Julien slumps, alone and dejected.

SCENE 2

In the shop the young women busily ply needles and scissors, some humming cheerfully over their work, others gossiping about the operas they have seen and the Duchess whose dress they are making. Louise, however, does not join in. Noticing her silence the others begin to speculate that she has troubles at home. One of them disagrees. "I believe Louise is in love!" This possibility elicits loud exclamations.

Louise remains oblivious to the chatter and when she is confronted she answers simply, "I'm not having an affair."

The discussion now turns exclusively to affairs of the heart. The forewoman tries desperately to get the seamstresses to pay attention to work, but they go on animatedly until the sound of a band playing in the distance distracts them. A few girls go to the window to investigate. They report, "There's a band and a handsome singer who is going to serenade us!"

At the first strains of his song, Louise realizes that it is Julien. The other women cheer him on, but Louise hears the desperation in his wooing, and thinks, "Poor Julien."

The dressmakers throw coins and blow kisses, but Julien sounds more and more anguished. As he pleads with Louise to respond, the girls make fun of him and tell him to call it a day. Finally one of them reports that he is going away.

Louise jumps up. "I'm not feeling well, I'm afraid I have to go." She picks up her hat, calls "Goodbye!" and rushes out the door. The others look at each other in astonishment, then run to the windows just in time to see Julien and Louise walking away hand in hand.

ACT III

It is early in the evening in a small garden at the top of Montmartre. Beyond the neighboring roofs lies the whole city of Paris, a few lights already twinkling in the dark. Julien leans on the balustrade and regards the scene, lost in blissful thought. Louise comes out of the house and, putting her arms around him, lovingly tells him that ever since the day she became his, life has been a fairy tale.

"Are you happy?" he asks.

"Too happy."

"No regrets?"

"What is there to regret? My mother's continual abuse? My poor father, he loved me but he believed everything she said."

"They had no right to tyrannize you. Parental love is just egoism."

"Even my father?"

"He was just blinder than the rest." Julien takes her in his arms and points toward the city. By now all of Paris is aglow with flickering lights, and echoes of excitement drift up to them from the streets. "The sounds of Paris at a party," he murmurs. "Oh, Louise, it is all for you. Away from Paris, Louise would not be Louise, and without Louise, Paris would not be Paris. You are my symbol of Paris. I love you!"

In love with the throbbing city which leaves them free to love and to live, their words and embraces grow more passionate, and as the sky over Paris lights up with fireworks Julien and Louise ardently draw each other into the house.

One of Julien's Bohemian friends comes stealthily into the garden followed shortly by others, carrying a large package. They unpack lanterns and bunting and quietly set about decorating the garden. The activity attracts the people of the neighborhood: vagrants, street urchins, artists, some of their working-class neighbors and girls from the shops. When Louise and Julien appear at their door, they are cheered and applauded and the crowd calls for the crowning of the Muse. Dressed as the Pope of Fools, one of Julien's friends comes forward to set in motion an elaborate pageant. Dancers weave among the crowd, then move away to reveal one lone dancer. The "Pope" instructs the Dancer to indicate who shall be crowned. The Dancer gathers flowers from the hands of children and takes them to Louise.

"Oh beautiful Chosen Sister," the "Pope" declares with mock heroics, "you are a poem of light; accept the homage of your knights!"

The artists and the shopgirls surround Louise and ask if she will be Queen of Bohemia. She agrees, setting off another round of cheers and another declaration of love from Julien. It is a merry crowd. The party continues, old and young alike dancing and joking, and enjoying the happy clamor.

Suddenly, there is a commotion at the far end of the garden, and the crowd moves aside as if to make way for a specter. It is Louise's mother in such evident suffering that her passage silences the gaiety, and group by group, the now hushed revelers disperse. The Pope of Fools delivers a barking ominous laugh. Julien rushes to Louise's side to protect her.

The crowd gone, a terrified Louise runs toward the house while Julien blocks her mother's path. Her mother pleads with him: "I do not come as your enemy. We have given up trying to regain our daughter, but Louise's father is very ill and I come only to beg that you let her return home. Perhaps her love can save him." Louise is profoundly disturbed, and seeing the effect her words have had, her mother tells her, "One night I heard your father sobbing. I found him lying in the doorway of your old room crying, 'Louise! My dear child! Louise!'" She turns back to Julien. "Please let her come with me. Only she can save him."

"Promise that she will return," he demands. When her mother agrees, Julien consents. "Go, you messenger of joy, and remember I shall count every moment!"

Troubled and ambivalent, Louise follows her mother, blowing Julien a kiss as she disappears down the path toward the twinkling lights of Paris. The lament of the ragpicker for his lost daughter is heard in the night air as Julien, left alone, calls out, "Pretty one."

ACT IV

It is a summer evening. Louise's father has recovered but appears old and crotchety. Despite his somewhat improved health her parents have kept Louise with them. As night falls, Louise sits staring out the window. Seeing her daughter thus, her mother cannot resist the opportunity to comment on how much brighter the street is since the building where Julien lived has been torn down. Louise's father complains bitterly about his failing strength and how the young push their elders out of the way. Then, turning to Louise, he complains about the selfishness of children: "All your life you cover her with love, and the moment some stranger comes along he poisons her mind and turns a once happy home into one filled with acrimony and hatred."

"Come help me clean," her mother calls. Wiping her tears, Louise obediently goes to the kitchen where she reminds her mother of her promise.

"You didn't think we would let you return to that sordid life!" her mother retorts.

While her father listens intently Louise boldly cries out in favor of free love, echoing Julien's words. The argument between mother and daughter grows heated as each tries to have the last word. The mother ends it. "It's time to go to sleep. Say good night to your father!"

Louise goes to her father and presents her cheek. He tries to hug her but she pulls away. "Louise, Louise, aren't you my child any longer?" he pleads. "Remember how happy we once were." Then in a pathetic effort to recapture the past, he pulls her down on his lap like a child and begins to sing the lullaby he had sung to her when she was a little girl.

She begs him to consider *her* happiness: "At my age, life with no freedom is worse than death! We would have no quarrel if you would only keep your promise."

Angrily her father retorts, "The freedom you seek is the right to bring shame to your family, the right to walk the streets!" Their heated argument continues, neither parent nor child willing to bend. Finally, utterly frustrated, Louise's father says bitterly, "You are a stranger. It is not *my* daughter who speaks this way!"

Through the open window waft the alluring sounds of the Paris streets at night. As if hypnotized, Louise draws closer to the window. "Paris! Paris!" she cries. "Take me back to my lover! Bring me my poet knight whose love

360

made me a Muse!" Her father is infuriated by her brazen outburst and her mother orders her to be still. But Louise has by now lost control and continues to taunt her parents. "Oh, he will come back to me, and I will get drunk again on his kisses. Come to me, Julien. Take me forever."

"You wretched girl!" her father shouts. "The streets of Paris are lighting up. The ladies of pleasure are out there! Go! Go! Join them!" Now the mother tries desperately to restrain him but her husband relentlessly attacks his daughter with a torrent of pent-up venom, finally frightening her. When he lifts a chair as if to throw it, Louise, terrified, runs out the door.

Remorse sets in immediately. He drops the chair, and runs to the door. Imploringly, he calls "Louise! Louise!" Hearing the outside door slam shut, he rushes to the balcony, but the sound of her fast retreating steps echoing on the deserted pavement defeats him. Shaking his clenched fist in the direction of those twinkling lights he names his true enemy in a final sob: "A-a-ah . . . Paris!"

FIDELIO

Opera in Two Acts
by
LUDWIG VAN BEETHOVEN
Première: Theater an der Wien, Vienna, November 20, 1805

ACT I

IN A prison near Seville languishes an innocent victim of injustice, Don Florestan. This eighteenth-century nobleman has incurred the enmity of the Governor of the prison, Don Pizarro, an evil man who uses his position to imprison anyone he deems a threat to his own power. Because Florestan was trying to expose the Governor's crimes, he has been seized and thrown into the most subterranean cell of the prison, where he remains unknown to all but Pizarro. Not even the jailkeeper, Rocco, knows his name. He only knows that the poor man is alone and dying of starvation as Pizarro has ordered. Outside the prison, rumor has it that Florestan is dead.

On a sunny day, in the empty courtyard of the prison, Rocco's daughter, Marzellina, irons some clothes, while she tries to fend off the attentions of Jacquino, the gatekeeper, who is in love with her. Although she has previously given Jacquino some encouragement, Marzellina is grateful now when his wooing is periodically interrupted by people knocking at the gate, because she has fallen in love with her father's new employee, a young errand boy, Fidelio. Jacquino's attempts to have a tête-à-tête are finally ended when Rocco returns and gives him some tools to take into the house.

While Jacquino is gone, Fidelio arrives, carrying a heavy load of new chains. Marzellina gazes longingly at him unable to conceal her love for the young man. Rocco indicates that the possibility of Fidelio becoming his son-in-law is pleasing to him and he takes Fidelio's embarrassment to mean that the boy returns his daughter's affection.

But this talk of marriage has made Fidelio uneasy for another reason—in fact, he is not a boy, but a brave and determined young woman—Leonore, the wife of Don Florestan. Convinced that her husband is still alive, Leonore has been searching for him and has taken on the disguise of Fidelio in order to investigate her suspicion that he is being held in this prison. So now, to change the subject, as well as to further her purpose, "Fidelio" asks Rocco to let him help with the care of the prisoners.

While tempted by the offer, the old man demurs on the grounds that there is one prisoner no one but he is allowed to see. "He must have great enemies, for he has languished in this solitary cell for two years. But he won't survive much longer. For the last month I have been instructed by Don Pizarro to reduce his rations."

Hearing this, Fidelio presses harder to help the jailer perform his chores and finally Rocco consents to ask the Govenor's permission. Encouraged, Fidelio goes with Marzellina into the house.

Rocco remains in the courtyard. The sounds of a military march are heard from outside the prison. The imposing prison gate is lifted, and Don Pizarro enters with his entourage. "Where are the dispatches?" Pizarro demands.

Rocco hands them over. Among them Pizarro finds a letter warning him that the Minister of State has been told about Pizarro's transgressions and is planning to visit the prison. Pizarro realizes he must get rid of Florestan immediately. He orders one of his captains to climb to the watchtower accompanied by a trumpeter, and to signal as soon as they sight the Minister's carriage. Pizarro then offers Rocco money to murder the secret prisoner, but horrified at the thought, the jailkeeper refuses. "If you are unable to do it, Rocco, then I will do it myself," Pizarro thunders. "Go down to his cell and dig his grave in the cistern. I will join you shortly, and with one swift stab of my dagger end his life."

As Pizarro and Rocco leave the courtyard, Fidelio emerges from the shadows, having overheard all. Alone, the anguish of Leonore—the ardently loving wife—pours forth from Fidelio. Repelled by Pizarro's cruelty, she is nonetheless hopeful that this secret prisoner is her own beloved Florestan. But whoever he is, she resolves to thwart Pizarro and save the poor soul.

Leonore reassumes the character of Fidelio, as Marzellina and Jacquino come out of the house, and Rocco enters from the garden. Repeating a request he has made before, Fidelio begs Rocco to allow the prisoners to go out into the garden. "It's such a fine day," Fidelio reasons, "and the Governor won't come at this hour."

Rocco is hesitant at first, but finally decides to risk it. "I'll go talk to Pizarro in order to detain him."

As Rocco leaves, Fidelio and Jacquino unlock the cells. The prisoners slowly make their way into the courtyard, their steps hesitant, their sight blinded by the unfamiliar glare of the bright sun. They file out into the garden relishing this moment of freedom and fresh air.

Rocco returns to speak with Fidelio. "I spoke to Pizarro, and he gave me permission to take you into the prison with me today!" Fidelio is overjoyed, but Rocco tempers the youth's enthusiasm by telling him that their task is a grim one. "We must descend to the deepest cell. There we are to dig a grave for the prisoner, because the Governor is going to kill him." Noting Fidelio's horror, Rocco offers to go alone.

But Fidelio persists. "I will go though I die myself."

Jacquino and Marzellina rush in breathless. "Father!" Marzellina yells. "Hurry!!! Pizarro has heard that we have let the prisoners out into the garden, and he's in a rage!"

"Get the prisoners inside—quickly," Rocco orders, but Pizarro has already arrived in the courtyard and demands an explanation. Searching for an excuse, the old jailkeeper coaxes Pizarro to concentrate his anger on the prisoner in the secret cell.

"Then hurry and dig the man's grave, and I'll be satisfied," Pizarro mutters.

While the two men talk, Jacquino and Fidelio usher the prisoners back to their cells. They move slowly, with many a backward longing glance at the cheery sunlight.

ACT II

The scant light of a single lantern barely pierces the gloom of Florestan's subterranean cell. A cistern, strewn with rubble and rocks, looms dimly in the shadows. Shackled to the wall, the only sound the prisoner hears is the dismal clank of his chains every time he moves. Suddenly he cries into the silence, "God! How dark it is in here!" Despairingly, he muses on his fate—how unjust to be struck down in the very spring of his life, when his only crime has been to fight against villainy. Slowly growing more hallucinatory, he imagines that an angel in the person of his beloved wife, Leonore, will come to lead him to freedom, until exhausted, he sinks to the floor.

A flight of stairs is suddenly lit by a lantern as Fidelio and Rocco descend to dig the prisoner's grave. They begin the difficult task of removing the stones from the cistern. On the cold ground, Florestan lies motionless and they fear the man is already dead, until he stirs in his sleep. Then they set to work, feverishly trying to finish the job before Pizarro arrives. As they dig, Fidelio tries desperately to look at the prisoner, but cannot see through the darkness. They notice that he has awakened, and Rocco goes to speak with him, leaving Fidelio to continue the digging. Still, Fidelio cannot see the man's face. Then suddenly Florestan turns toward the cistern.

"My husband," Fidelio whispers, overwhelmed by the recognition.

Engaged in what he believes to be their final conversation, Rocco admits to Florestan that Don Pizarro is the Governor of the prison.

"The man whose crimes I tried to expose!!" Florestan rages. He begs Rocco to send word to his wife, Leonore, in Seville.

Rocco refuses the request, but moved by the man's misery allows him to drink from the jug of wine which they have brought. The kindly jailkeeper also allows Fidelio to give the starving man a piece of bread.

As Rocco signals to Pizarro that all is ready, Fidelio reassures Florestan that God is watching over them, and moves closer to the cistern.

Pizarro descends the stairs. He draws his dagger, throwing off his cloak, and confronts Florestan. "Because you sought my ruin, I've come to take my vengeance."

Florestan faces his tormentor calmly. "You are a murderer."

As Pizarro lunges at his victim, Fidelio rushes out from the shadows and throws herself between the two men. "To kill Florestan you must first stab me," Fidelio shouts, "for I am Leonore, his wife!"

Pizarro is momentarily stunned, but undeterred. "Then you may share his death," he tells her.

Leonore draws a pistol. "If you move one step, I will shoot."

Suddenly, the prison resounds with a trumpet call. The Minister has been sighted from the watchtower. Pizarro realizes that he has been thwarted while the others thank God for their deliverance. From the top of the stairs, Jacquino shouts, "Master Rocco, the Minister and his men have arrived. They are in the courtyard."

Reluctantly, still swearing vengeance, Pizarro leaves the cell, followed closely by Rocco. Filled with joy, Florestan and Leonore fall into each other's arms. Then the brave woman helps her husband up the stairs to the courtyard—and to freedom.

In the courtyard joy abounds as the released prisoners mingle with townspeople. The Minister, Don Fernando, followed by Pizarro and some officers, march in to the cheers of praise from the crowd. When the noise abates, Don Fernando tells them that he has come to redress tyranny. The King has ordered all political prisoners freed. This is greeted by more cheers and rejoicing.

Rocco pushes through the crowd, leading Florestan and Leonore. "Don Fernando," Rocco pleads, "in the name of pity reunite this couple here today. He is the victim of injustice and torture, and she is the brave wife who saved him."

Having thought Florestan dead, Don Fernando is both astounded and delighted to see his old friend. And when Rocco explains how Pizarro was about to murder Florestan, the Minister orders that the evil man be taken away to face justice himself. Then he turns to Leonore. "You, most noble and brave woman, it is you who shall set your husband free. Take the key and unlock his chains."

Leonore unlocks Florestan's shackles and the couple embrace. Amid shouts of joy from the crowd, Florestan and Leonore reaffirm their love for each other, a love which has penetrated the dark secret of a prison and led to justice and freedom.

FALSTAFF

Opera in Three Acts
by
GIUSEPPE VERDI
Première: La Scala, Milan, February 9, 1893

ACT I

SCENE 1

AS HE grows older, Sir John Falstaff, King Henry V's famous knight and boon companion, becomes still more famous for his girth, his unquenchable high spirits, and his often sleazy exploits. A dining room of the Garter Inn serves as his headquarters, and on one particular day he can be found sealing two letters with great satisfaction, after which he sits back in his very large comfortable chair to quaff a huge mug of ale.

His cronies, Bardolph and Pistol, are waiting to hear about Falstaff's newest scheme, but before Falstaff can even burp, they are interrupted by Dr. Caius, a physician who joined their revels the night before. Today he is furious. He accuses Falstaff of having beaten his servants and robbed him. Falstaff laughingly admits it, and orders more to drink. Enraged at this callous indifference, Caius turns to Bardolph. "You and Pistol made me drunk last night and robbed me!"

The two thugs deny and mock and threaten, until the angry man realizes he will get no satisfaction and leaves in disgust.

Falstaff laughs hugely, and tells his friends, "There is an art to thievery.

367

You should learn how to do it properly." Then, realizing he does not have enough money to pay his dinner bill, Falstaff turns to the subject which most interests him at this moment—his letters. "Do you know a rich gentleman named Ford?" he asks. They do, and he continues, "His beautiful wife, Alice, has cast a glance at me. The look in her eyes said, 'I am yours.'"

"Indeed?" says Bardolph.

Falstaff is oblivious to his skepticism. "And then there is another woman, Meg by name. She too is very rich, and she too wants me. These women will prove my salvation. So"—he hands the letters, one to Bardolph, one to Pistol—"deliver these missives to the poor love-stricken ladies."

But the two rogues refuse. It is against their honor to deliver love letters to married women.

Calling them every name in the book, Falstaff denounces both the men and "honor," and orders a page to deliver the letters for him. Then to vent his rage at the two hypocrites, he chases them around the room with a deftly wielded broom, until they flee through the door.

SCENE 2

Hurrying through the garden outside the Ford house, Meg Page and Mistress Quickly run into Alice Ford and her daughter, Anne.

Alice is surprised. "I was just coming to see you, Meg. Something extraordinary has happened."

Meg interrupts. "To me too."

They take out their letters and exchange them. As they read, they soon realize that the fatuous Falstaff has sent them exactly the same love note, changing only the names. The women are more amused than hurt, but cannot resist the temptation to puncture the fat knight's brazen ego, and with Anne and Mistress Quickly, they go off to plot their revenge.

Dr. Caius, Bardolph, and Pistol come into the garden, all telling Ford about the iniquities Falstaff is about to visit upon him. They are joined by Fenton, a young man in love with Anne, who is hoping to get a glimpse of her.

"What are you trying to tell me?" Ford asks.

Having turned against their ringleader, Bardolph and Pistol issue a warning: "To put it simply, Master Ford, Sir Fat Falstaff desires to enter your house, seduce your wife, and dishonor your bed!"

While the outraged Ford swears to guard his wife, the four women return to the garden. Anne and Fenton eye each other longingly, while the others, embarrassed by their suspicions and secrets, pretend not to notice each other, and leave.

Alone in the garden, Anne and Fenton are able to spend a few moments together. Fenton steals a few kisses, ignoring Anne's words of caution. Gently pushing him away, she tells him someone's coming, and he hides behind some bushes just as the other women return.

Still shaking their heads over Falstaff's insolence, they agree he should be punished. Alice has a plan and tells Mistress Quickly, "Go to that portly knight and lure him with the promise of an intimate rendezvous with me! Be convincing!"

Mistress Quickly notices a movement in the bushes, and fearing a spy, the women once again move away, leaving Anne alone with Fenton. He resumes his ardent pleading, but again the young couple is interrupted as the men return, discussing their plans for taking revenge on Falstaff.

"You will introduce me to him at the Garter Inn," Ford instructs Pistol and Bardolph, "but I will use a false name. Then I will skillfully question him so as to discover and thwart his designs."

Not far off, the women can be seen as they hatch their separate scheme. Fenton makes the astute observation that there is mystery in the air. He would rather pursue his Anne, but when the men leave he feels impelled to go with them.

Left alone, the women contemplate the sweet revenge they will take on the fat knight and bid each other good day.

ACT II

Scene 1

Some time later, back at the Garter Inn, Falstaff is again ensconced in his chair with Bardolph and Pistol at his feet, simulating penitence and swearing fidelity to their corpulent master.

Falstaff accepts them with jaded cool. After all, he knows how attractive vice is to the majority of men.

Mistress Quickly arrives and curtsies before Sir John. "Your servant, your grace. I bring you a message from Mistress Alice Ford."

Excited, Falstaff orders Bardolph and Pistol to leave.

Mistress Quickly cleverly compliments Falstaff for his great reputation as a skillful seducer. "Mistress Alice is in turmoil over her great love for you.

She thanks you for the letter and informs you that her husband always goes out between the hours of two and three. He is a fiercely jealous man, but during the hour he is away your grace can safely go to see her!"

Immensely pleased with himself, Falstaff instructs the messenger to inform Mistress Alice that he will be there at the appointed time.

Mistress Quickly has yet another message for the portly knight: "Mistress Page conveys her regrets, for while she too longs to greet you, alas, her husband seldom leaves her side."

Falstaff expresses some concern that the two women may compare notes, but Mistress Quickly assures him that women are born deceivers. A satisfied Falstaff nods knowingly at this explanation, and sends Mistress Quickly on her way, bidding her convey his love to his two conquests and grandly handing her a small coin. She seethes now not only at his conceit but at his tight-fisted reward.

Falstaff has but a moment to savor his triumph before Bardolph returns with the news that a certain Master Brook waits outside with a jug of wine, and wishes to meet the great Sir John Falstaff. "Tell this brook flowing with liquor he is welcome!" Sir John booms happily and Bardolph escorts the disguised Master Ford into the room.

"Sir, excuse the informality of my visit," Ford begins. "I am a man of wealth, who spends his money freely!"

"I should like to know you better!" responds Falstaff.

Ford continues: "I need to talk to you in confidence! There is a certain lovely woman who lives in Windsor; her name is Alice and her husband is a man named Ford. Many times I have written to her of my love, but she does not answer. I have spent fortunes lavishing gifts on her, but alas, I have received no satisfaction. You, sir, are a man of the world, suave and alluring. I come to you with this bag of money and a plan. If you would but seduce this woman, then, once having deceived her husband, she may be willing to turn to me."

Though somewhat taken aback by this hare-brained scheme, Falstaff finds the money impossible to resist. "Dear Master Brook, I will take your money and you have my word as a knight that you shall soon enjoy her favors. Indeed," he goes on, "I have an assignation with your Alice this very afternoon. Between the hours of two and three, while her stupid husband is out, I shall horn the fool. Wait for me here while I go make myself handsome."

Ford is barely able to contain his wrath until the pompous knight is out of the room. That his wife should cuckold him with Falstaff is a nightmare. He curses all women and swears revenge, then calms himself to reassume the persona of Master Brook just as Falstaff, sporting a new outfit, returns. Exchanging cordial compliments, the two men leave the Garter Inn arm in arm.

SCENE 2

In the main room of the Ford house, Alice and Meg listen with great amusement as Mistress Quickly relates how Sir John Falstaff has taken the bait and fallen into their trap. "He will be arriving any minute." Excitedly, Alice issues orders to prepare for his coming until she notices that Anne is standing off to one side, sullen and remote.

"Good Lord," she asks, "what troubles you?"

"My father wants me to marry old Dr. Caius. I'd rather die!" Anne sulks.

The women are consolingly appalled and her mother tells her not to worry, that she will not have to marry old Dr. Caius. This resolved, Alice resumes ordering everyone about so that "the stage will be properly set for the fat suitor!" Merrily, these wives of Windsor put the finishing touches on the plan to trap Sir John.

"He's coming!" Mistress Quickly warns and immediately the women scramble to their hiding posts. Alice picks up her lute and softly plays a melody to which Falstaff, prancing into the room, sings the lyrics, cooing of the passion they will share in the next hour. She tells him he is charming, but when he tries to kiss her, she turns coy, and moving about swiftly she is able to evade his embraces. He tells her he loves her and she accuses him of being in love with Meg Page.

"That ugly old thing?" he protests.

Suddenly Mistress Quickly bursts in, warning Alice that Mistress Meg is just outside, creating a scene and demanding to see her. "Hide," Alice orders, and she pushes Falstaff behind the screen. She motions Meg to come in.

"Alice, be careful. Your husband is storming down the street swearing that he is going to kill the man that you have taken as a lover!" Meg can barely restrain her laughter.

But Mistress Quickly also bursts in with a warning. "Save yourself! Master Ford is coming and he is in a fury!"

Seeing the expression on her friend's face, Alice quietly asks if she is serious or jesting. Mistress Quickly asserts that this is not part of their plan just as Ford rushes through the door followed by Dr. Caius, Fenton, Bardolph, Pistol, and most of their neighbors.

Alice closes the screen around Falstaff while Ford orders his friends to search the house thoroughly for the fat scoundrel. Noticing a large laundry basket in the room, he rummages through it, tossing the dirty linens about in a desperate effort to find Falstaff. When he is convinced that the knight is not hiding in the basket, he rages through the house to search the other rooms, which gives Alice the opportunity to transfer the terrified Falstaff into the laundry basket.

Amid all the confusion the young lovers, Fenton and Anne, huddle behind the screen to snatch a tender moment alone. Ford, who failing to find his prey has now returned to the room, hears a kiss from behind the screen. With the help of his cohorts, he overturns it, revealing Fenton and his daughter Anne with their arms around each other. All are astonished. More furious than ever, Ford orders Fenton out of the house.

Bardolph suddenly shouts, "There he goes!" and all the men charge out of the house in what they believe to be hot pursuit of their portly prey.

Alice acts quickly. She orders her servants to dump the dirty laundry out the window into the Thames River below and tells a page to fetch her husband. The servants oblige, struggling painfully with the extraordinary weight of the basket. Staggering under their burden, they somehow manage to dump its contents, laundry and Falstaff, out the window. Gleefully, Alice brings Ford to the window so that he may see the errant knight floundering about in the water below!

ACT III

SCENE 1

Outside the Garter Inn a shaken and subdued Falstaff meditates on the villainy of the world. "That I, a gallant knight, should be so treated! Virtue is dead. Had my paunch not kept me afloat, I certainly would have drowned!" He calls to the innkeeper to bring him a beaker of wine and drinking it much improves his mood.

Mistress Quickly joins him. "I have a message from Mistress Alice."

"I have had enough of your Mistress Alice!" Falstaff retorts disgustedly.

Quickly tells him he is mistaken. "It was the fault of those terrible servants. If you could see how she suffers. Look, she has sent you this tender letter."

Falstaff cannot resist. As he reads the letter, Alice, Ford, Meg, Anne, Fenton, and Dr. Caius peak from around the corner of the building to see if their new plan to humiliate the knight is working. "He's taking the bait again!" Ford exults.

Falstaff re-reads the missive aloud. "I will meet you at midnight in the royal park, near Herne's Oak. Disguise yourself as the Black Huntsman."

"Love works in mysterious ways!" Mistress Quickly counsels.

Taking this fount of wisdom by the arm Falstaff escorts her into the Garter Inn so she may better explain the nefarious midnight caper.

The plotters are thrilled that the fat fool has bitten once again. As they huddle together, Alice relates the legend of the Black Huntsman and issues instructions: "Anne, you shall be the Fairy Queen, dressed all in white with a veil and crowned with roses. Meg, you will be the green wood nymph, and Mistress Quickly a witch. The children shall dress as elves, spirits, imps, and goblins. Then we will all rush forward and surprise Falstaff in his black mantle and horns. We will taunt him until he has confessed to his lecherous behavior. Agreed? All right then, at midnight, we meet at Herne's Oak!"

Fenton, Anne, Alice, and Meg go off to make their preparations. Ford stays behind to assure Dr. Caius that he will be married to Anne this very night while they are all disguised. Their scheme is overheard by Mistress Quickly, who has emerged from the inn and listens quietly. As the two men leave in cordial agreement, she scampers after Anne to warn her of the marriage plot.

Scene 2

Late that night in Windsor Park, with only the rays of the moon to light their way, the plotters assemble. Fenton embraces Anne, now dressed as the Fairy Queen, and they vow eternal love. Mistress Quickly and Alice soon join them and give Fenton a mask and cloak. Anne notes that he looks exactly like a friar.

Meg arrives, reporting that the imps are hidden in the ditch and all is ready for the evening's follies.

"Silence," Alice cautions. "Here comes the evening's star performer."

They dash off just as Falstaff, dressed in a great cloak and wearing enormous antlers on his head, makes his way into the grove. He muses on how love can turn a man into a beast, but his thoughts are interrupted and his passion once again ignited when Alice approaches. While she deftly evades his embraces, he begs her to yield to his love.

She cautions him, "Meg has followed me. She is here in these woods." This only inflames him the more and he cries, "Let her come too! You can both tear my body to shreds. I love you!"

A cry of "Help!" from Meg brings the seduction to an abrupt end. Alice pretends to be frightened, and when in the distance Meg cries, "Witches!" Alice runs off. Anne appears dressed in white as the Fairy Queen and calls for the nymphs, elves, dryads, and sirens to arise for "the witching star has risen." Terrified, Falstaff flattens himself on the ground in the roots of the great oak. Urged on by Alice and following the Fairy Queen, the spirits advance upon Falstaff's corpulent body as he lies inadequately concealed beneath the oak.

Suddenly the woods are full of people. Only Ford appears unmasked. Bardolph and Pistol wear cloaks, with hoods obscuring their faces. The band of "witches" surround the prone Falstaff and order him to stand. Bardolph pronounces him corrupt. "Let's exorcise him!"

Several elves rush forward making inhuman noises and pounce on Falstaff. In disguise, Alice, Meg, and Mistress Quickly circle around him. "Pinch him," they order, "til he yelps!"

Poor Sir John cries out in pain, but the punishment is relentless as the men pepper him with names. "Rogue! Thief! Pig! Knave!" "On your knees, fatso!" Bardolph beats him with Mistress Quickly's broomstick. They then call for Falstaff to repent.

"I repent! I repent! But please spare my stomach!" he pleads.

In his enthusiasm, Bardolph loses his hood, and Falstaff recognizes him. He stands up. "Why, you . . . viper, mongrel, you rat, you scum . . ." His invective is truly heroic and when he stops, they all applaud.

"Thank you. But let me rest a moment. I'm tired."

Dr. Caius, meanwhile, has been searching everywhere for his intended bride. Mistress Quickly takes Bardolph behind one of the trees to disguise *him* in white gown and veil.

Alice now introduces her portly suitor to her husband, and Mistress Quickly asks, "Did you think two women would give themselves to a fat old man?"

Falstaff admits that they have made an ass of him. Gallantly he adds, "All sorts of clowns jeer at me and revel in it; yet without me, what would they have? It is my gay spirit that gives wit to other men!"

"If I weren't so amused," Ford agrees, "I would certainly kill you. But now we must crown this night's festivities with the marriage of our Fairy Queen. Here come the betrothed now."

Dr. Caius enters, escorting the "Fairy Queen," and they are soon surrounded by the nymphs.

Alice interrupts to introduce another pair of lovers who wish to be married, both dressed in dark cloaks, the man wearing a mask and the woman a heavy veil.

In good humor, Ford declares, "It shall be a double ceremony! Heaven has united you. Off with your masks and veils and be transformed!"

At Ford's command, Dr. Caius removes his mask and Mistress Quickly unveils his betrothed, who, of course, turns out to be none other than Bardolph. And the other couple reveal themselves to be Anne and Fenton. Everyone is amused save Dr. Caius and Ford. The women revel in their victory, and Falstaff asks, "My dear Master Ford, who has been made an ass of now?"

"Dr. Caius and I have!" Ford admits.

Alice corrects him: "All three of you have fallen to the wiles of we Merry Wives of Windsor."

When Anne asks Ford's forgiveness, he graciously relents, declaring, "The man who cannot sidestep his problems must accept them with grace. We consent to this marriage! Now let us all go feast with Falstaff!"

Having now fully recovered his élan, Sir John gaily proclaims, "The whole world is a jest and man is born a jester. We must laugh at each other! But remember, the man who laughs best is the man who laughs last!"

GIANNI SCHICCHI

Opera in One Act
by
GIACOMO PUCCINI
Première: Metropolitan Opera, New York, December 14, 1918

BUOSO DONATI, one of the wealthier men of Florence in the year 1299, has just died. Gathered at his house, his relatives kneel beside the bed, sobbing noisily. For some minutes, hypocritical laments of "Poor Buoso" resound through the room, until one poor old cousin mentions that he has heard a rumor that Buoso's will leaves his most valuable possessions to the monks of Signa. The cries of mourning subside as the worried whisper passes from one ear to another, and in short order they are all searching frantically through the chests and coffers that furnish the room. After several false alarms Rinuccio, Buoso's twenty-four-year-old nephew, discovers the will. But before he will allow anyone to see the document, he bargains with his Aunt Zita for the right to marry his beloved Lauretta. She is the daughter of Gianni Schicchi, a self-made man who is despised by the Donati family because he was born a peasant. Finally, impelled by her own cupidity, and everyone else's impatience, Zita consents to Rinuccio's request. As the other relatives press around her to read the will, Rinuccio sends his seven-year-old cousin, Gherardino, to fetch Schicchi and Lauretta.

The relatives jostle for position, a couple of them climbing on chairs the better to see the handwritten parchment. They read silently, mouthing the words, and slowly their faces cloud until they burst once again into laments—this time, heartfelt. The rumor is true. Buoso Donati has left his most valuable possessions, the house, his mule, and his mills, to the monastery. As they envision the worldly pleasures that the monks will enjoy, their tears turn to anger. There must be some way to get around the will's dictates. When no solution is forthcoming, Rinuccio makes a suggestion. There is one man who may be able to help them and he is none other than the cunning Gianni Schicchi. The relatives hoot in derision and Zita tells her nephew she doesn't want to hear another word about the peasant and his daughter.

At this moment little Gherardino rushes in. "He's coming."

Zita is furious and the others annoyed, but Rinuccio is quick to sing the praises of men like Gianni Schicchi. "They are shrewd and clever and entertaining. Besides, it is deeds that count today and not your family name. So forget your snobbery. It's men like this, merchants, builders, scientists and artists, who are making Florence richer and more splendid." As Rinuccio finishes his impassioned plea, Gianni Schicchi walks in the door, followed by his daughter, Lauretta.

Schicchi at first believes the gloom that he sees before him must mean that Buoso's health has improved, but when he learns that Buoso is in fact dead he turns to Zita with a comprehending nod. "You're disinherited."

She snaps back. "Get out. And take your daughter with you. I will never allow my nephew to marry a girl who has no dowry."

Zita and Schicchi continue to exchange insults until Rinuccio, trying to reconcile them, asks Schicchi if he will help them figure out a way to break the will.

"Help people like this?" Schicchi yells. "Never!"

Lauretta throws herself at her father's feet and begs him to help so that she may marry her beloved Rinuccio. Unable to withstand his daughter's tears, Schicchi asks to see the will. He is depressed by what he reads, but at last his eyes light up triumphantly. Sending Lauretta out of the room, he turns to the relatives and asks whether anyone else knows that Donati is dead. They assure him that only they know. He then orders the corpse removed from the bed and taken into the next room. Just as the women begin to remake the bed there is a knock at the door. It is the doctor, who has come to check on his patient. The relatives are thrown into panic. At Schicchi's bidding they stall him at the door, telling the good doctor that his patient is resting comfortably. But the doctor persists in his efforts to speak with Buoso. Suddenly a voice sounding just like that of the dead Buoso comes from the curtained bed, startling the relatives. Schicchi, in a perfect imitation of Buoso's voice, tells the doctor that he is feeling much better but is sleepy and would like to continue to rest. The doctor is very pleased with the results of his therapy and agrees to return later that evening.

With the doctor successfully deceived and out of the way, Schicchi outlines his plans: "Go to the notary and tell him that Buoso Donati's condition has worsened and that he wants to dictate a new will. When you return with the notary and witnesses, I, disguised as Buoso Donati, will dictate the new will."

Thrilled with the scheme, Zita orders Rinuccio to run and get the notary. All the relatives hail Gianni Schicchi as their savior and help him assume his disguise.

While they all outwardly agree that they will rely on Schicchi's wisdom in dividing up the most valuable part of Buoso's legacy, each privately offers him a bribe if he will only leave the good stuff to them. To each he says, "It's yours," but before he climbs into bed he issues a somber warning: "Remember the laws of Florence regarding the forging of a will: the penalty is the amputation of a hand and exile from our beloved city. So we must be certain to keep this secret among ourselves." They all agree just as Rinuccio returns with the notary and witnesses.

From deep within the curtained bed, Schicchi greets the newcomers in the voice of Buoso, and begins to dictate the new testament in the usual fashion, revoking all previous wills. He modestly requests a very cheap funeral for himself, and leaves a very small sum of money to the church. Quickly he disposes of Donati's small parcels of property, dividing them among the relatives. With mounting anxiety the relatives wait for him to get to the crux of the estate. At last he does and they hear him leave the mule, house, and the mills each in turn to "my dear, dear, devoted friend . . . Gianni Schicchi!!!!!!"

They are wild, but can do nothing until the notary and the witnesses leave for fear of the punishment that would confront them as forgers. No sooner are they out the door than the relatives turn on Schicchi, calling him every name in the book.

Schicchi taunts back, "You miserly lot, now there will be a dowry," and wielding a stick he throws the greedy family out of *his* house. As they scramble out they steal whatever they can.

On the balcony, Rinuccio and Lauretta embrace joyfully and gaze out over the city of Florence, glinting softly in the afternoon sun. Gianni Schicchi watches them with a happy smile and asks simply, "Could Buoso's money have found any better use than this?"

INDEX OF TITLES

INDEX OF COMPOSERS

ABOUT THE AUTHOR

Anthony Jason Rudel, a native New Yorker, grew up in a musical family and spent many hours in and around opera houses all over the world. He studied violin from the age of five with William Kroll. He began his career in professional, classical radio while still at Columbia College in New York.

When Rudel graduated from Columbia with honors in 1979, he was named Program Coordinator at WQXR classical radio station in New York. In 1981 he became Associate Program Director and in June 1985 became Vice-President of Programming. Rudel has written and produced many long-running WQXR series.

Mr. Rudel does public speaking and gave a multimedia presentation on Mozart's childhood, at the convention of the American Association of Child Psychiatrists, in 1982.

Rudel is the son of the late Dr. Rita G. Rudel, who was Clinical Professor of Neuropsychology at Columbia Presbyterian Medical Center, and Julius Rudel, the internationally known conductor.